The
End of
World Order

*Written under the auspices of
the Center of International Studies, Princeton University.
A list of other books written under Center auspices
appears at the back of this book.*

The
End of
World Order

Essays on Normative International Relations

Richard Falk

Holmes & Meier
New York   London

First published in the United States of America 1983 by
Holmes & Meier Publishers, Inc.
30 Irving Place
New York, N.Y. 10003

Great Britain:
Holmes & Meier Publishers, Ltd.
131 Trafalgar Road
Greenwich, London SE10 9TX

Book design by Rose Jacobowitz

Library of Congress Cataloging in Publication Data

Falk, Richard A.
  The end of world order.

  Includes bibliographical references and index.
  1. International relations—Addresses, essays;
lectures.   I. Title.
JX1395.F28   1982   327.1'1   82-15409
ISBN 0-8419-0739-0 (cl.)
ISBN 0-8419-0894-X (pa.)

Manufactured in the United States of America

For
Myres S. McDougal
Inspiring Teacher, Scholar,
Devoted Friend

Contents

Prefatory Note

An accelerated nuclear arms race, military modernization on a global scale, and a high incidence of costly warfare are awakening increasing numbers of people everywhere to the deficiencies of a world order system constituted by sovereign states. At the same time, the persistence of this system seems assured this side of catastrophe. So entrapped, the overwhelming question becomes, "What to do?"

Responding to such an imperative, this book makes no pretense to academic neutrality and disengagement. Indeed, its orientation is shaped as much by participation in struggles against militarism and imperial geopolitics as it is by visits to libraries. Together these essays express an outlook on politics and transformation on a global scale.

As earlier, I have benefited from collaborative work and activities with scholars around the world. I would mention here, particularly, my associations with the Institute for World Order, The Lindisfarne Association, the World Future Studies Federation, "The Reconstruction of Knowledge Project" of the Institute for Policy Studies, the International Peace Research Association, and the Permanent Peoples' Tribunal of the Basso Foundation.

Of course, my best colleagues in intellectual inquiry remain my most serious students, and I am grateful for their challenge as well as their inspiration. I am, in addition, fortunate that Jack Sanderson, Eric Villepontoux, and Cindy Halpern, dedicated and efficient research associates, have helped in many ways with the preparation of this volume for publication. It is my particular pleasure once again to acknowledge June Garson, who oversaw the effort with her usual graciousness, wit, and skill. Once again, also, I thank warmly the Center of International Studies for providing auspices, atmosphere, and a thousand logistical supports; its director, Cyril E. Black, for his continuing warm-spirited encouragement; and Gladys Starkey, the Center's vigorous chief of staff, for her uncanny capacity to accommodate needs, however unreasonable.

I also wish to acknowledge the prior publication of material used here, although in each instance revisions have been made: Chapter 2—Preface from *Hugo Grotius: The Miracle of Holland* by Charles S. Edwards (Chicago: Nelson-Hall, 1981), pp. xiii–xxi; Chapter 3—"Contending Approaches to World Order," *Journal of International Affairs* 31, no. 2 (fall/winter 1977): 171–198; Chapter 4—"The World Order Models Project and Its Critics: A Reply," *International Organization* 32, no. 2 (spring 1978): 531–545; Chapter 5—"The Shaping of World Order Studies: A Response," *The Review of Politics* 42, no. 1 (January 1980): 18–30; Chapter 6—"Beyond Internationalism," reprinted with permission from *Foreign Policy* 24 (fall 1976), © 1976 by the Carnegie Endowment for International Peace; Chapter 7—"What's Wrong with Henry Kissinger's Foreign Policy," *Alternatives* 1 (1975): 79–100; Chapter 8—"The Decline of International Order: Normative Regression and Geopolitical Maelstrom" in *The Year Book of World Affairs 1982* (London: Stevens and Sons, 1982), pp. 10–24; Chapter 9—"Nuclear Policy and World Order: Why Denuclearization," WOMP Working Paper No. 2 (1978); Chapter 10—"Arms Control, Foreign Policy, and Global Reform," *Daedalus* 104, no. 3 (summer 1975): 35–52; Chapter 11—"Satisfying Human Needs in a World of Sovereign States," from *World Faiths and the New Order*, edited by Joseph Gremillion and William Ryan, published and © by the Interreligious Peace Colloquium (now re-named Muslim Jewish Christian Conference), 1979, pp. 109–140; Chapter 12—"Anarchism and World Order" from *Anarchism*, ed. J. Roland Pennock and John W. Chapman (New York: New York University Press, 1978), pp. 63–87; Chapter 13—"An Inquiry into World Order Values," distributed by Planetary Citizens, New York; Chapter 14—"Political Prospects, Cultural Choices, Anthropological Horizons," *Journal of the New Alchemists* 4 (1977): 138–148.

Richard Falk
Princeton, New Jersey

PART ONE

Overview

CHAPTER 1

Normative International Relations: A General Introduction

REALISM AND NEOREALISM

The study of international relations has long been preoccupied with scientific inquiry into the workings of the state system. In this context, scientific implies little more than the search for objectivity. It does not necessarily mean an insistence on either behavioral methods of confirmation or tightly interlinked sets of logical propositions. This latter, stricter image of "scientific" tends to be limited in its relevance to an influential faction of academic specialists in international relations located in North America, although it pertains, as well, to much of the work done under the rubric of "peace research" in Western Europe and Japan.

The former, looser sense of scientific as objective is characteristic of those dominant accounts of the workings of the state system that shape the popular image of what international relations is about. The work of E. H. Carr, Hans Morgenthau, George Kennan, Raymond Aron, Henry Kissinger, Hedley Bull, and Robert Gilpin exemplifies this tradition of inquiry. It builds on the more philosophical underpinnings and outlooks of Machiavelli and Hobbes, but finds non-Western cultural parallels in the work of Kautilya and Musashi. Sometimes, the scientific intention is expressed by describing the approach as "realist." The essence of the realists' claim is to give a faithful account of politics at the level of interstate relations that avoids wishful thinking. This account emphasizes the absence of any shared sense of community or any regularly available and effective system of global governance. In this respect, the emphasis on objectivity is intended to be in marked contrast to the subjectivity of lawyers and moralists or of outright utopians who often blur, it is alleged, the distinction between what is and what ought to be in international affairs.

The realists' view of international relations concentrates its attention upon the role of power in achieving stability and change, especially in relation to the security of sovereign territory. Power, for the realists, is defined ultimately in military terms as recourse to force in war. In this kind of international setting, the general interest of most governments in peace, territorial integrity, and political independence requires reliance on alliances and defense capabilities. Peace, then, depends on the prudent construction and preservation of power balances. The essence of enlightened statecraft by a leader who seeks peace is the establishment of a balance of power, as well as a generalized adherence to a diplomacy of noninterference with the sovereign rights of others. Nuclear weaponry has not altered this realist interpretation of international relations in any essential respect. Indeed, the more generalized desire to avoid nuclear war places an even greater than traditional stress on balance—balance, in the context of national security planning, recently given the more concrete name of "deterrence," and associated in a more explicit way with regional as well as global settings of potential conflict.

Those adventurers of the mind who stress disarmament or demilitarization are viewed by realists as romantics and often styled as idealists or utopians. The mainstream realists are skeptical about any approach to peace that does not acknowledge that sovereign states will retain the capability and insist on the discretion to use force as needed, often unscrupulously, to obtain their ends, which may be expansionist rather than defensive. For this central reason, it will always be necessary to neutralize this capability and inhibit this sovereign discretion by security schemes that make recourse to force costly, and if possible, so costly as to be "irrational."

Another crucial tenet of the realists' creed is reliance, often unexamined, on the generalized rationality of the state system. To establish normative order where there is a general prospect of peace and stability, it is important that the main states, at least, are governed by leaders who read accurately the relation of forces in the world and do not act heedlessly or on the basis of high-risk foreign policies. For this reason, as international relations specialists of mainstream persuasion readily admit, the ordering capability of the system is vulnerable to revolutionary (or counterrevolutionary) actors, who do not heed the rules of the game regardless of consequences. If the revolutionary actor is a minor state, then its impact is usually local and its leadership can generally be toppled from power before too much damage is done. If, however, the revolutionary actor is a major state or group of states, then the system is unstable and vulnerable to war; if conditions of rationality do not pertain, moderate statecraft is imperiled.

It is not always evident to expert observers whether a revolutionary tendency is present in international relations. There continues, for instance, to be uncertainty about the identity of the Soviet Union in this regard. Almost from the onset of the Russian Revolution there has been confusion and controversy about whether or not the Soviet Union was a dangerously disruptive presence in the world. The attitude of the West toward Soviet diplomacy has ebbed and flowed, shifting its tone and character from periods of tension and confrontation to periods of relative calm and cooperation. The advent of nuclear weaponry and the revolutionary turbulence of the Third World have both placed limits on conflict and created numerous occasions for confrontation, the uneasy circumstances wavering in general between cold war and détente, with occasional lurches toward the nuclear brink being described as international crises. Whether the Soviet Union has been in the past or is currently (or has become again) the source of disruption by way of revolutionary challenge, as compared to the states arrayed against it in varying counterrevolutionary stances, is a moot, yet much controverted, question, but one with enormous foreign policy consequences.

Often, too, domestic developments can threaten an existing balance. The current historical phenomenon of revolutionary nationalism, commencing with the movement of decolonialization but continuing beyond it, threatens to undermine the economic and cultural foundations of Western power, especially in the Middle East. There is no assurance that the two nuclear superpowers will stand aside and let the Middle East's nationalistic tendencies unfold as autonomous developments. Yet the effort to control these tendencies is likely to pose an unprecedented threat of general war, partly because the accepted conception of "reasonableness" is drawn into doubt in a critical geopolitical situation where vital interests are perceived as imperiled.

Peace-through-reasonableness is a slender rod in the nuclear age. Governing elites in greatly varying national circumstances, with distinct geopolitical priorities and diverse cultural traditions and historical experiences, will often have discrepant views of what is reasonable. Even with the effort of nuclear planners to extend the concept of reasonableness by making any provocative challenge appear not just unreasonable, but also highly irrational given the consequences of nuclear retaliation, there is no assurance that major actors will conform under pressure to mutually acceptable images of reasonable behavior.

Realists have no answers here, except to warn by historical example that wars occur in situations of geopolitical ambiguity, where each side supposes that its demands are reasonable and those of its adversary are unreasonable.[1] These precedents have encouraged international relations specialists, such as Robert Jervis[2], to emphasize perception and misperception of international reality. In part, the intention here is merely to explain more fully how the state system works. Underlying this intention is the conviction that the system works best if "irrationalities" of perception can be reduced, or guarded against in a rational way.

This stress on rationality is an unacknowledged prescriptive element in the realists' worldview. It functions almost as an equivalent of morality and is occasionally associated with the virtue of "prudence" in the analysis of international relations.

As is evident, mainstream international relations emphasizes the predominance and durability of the territorial, sovereign state. Other nonstate actors are either ignored, or are regarded as marginal or derivative presences on the world scene, whose main role is to promote the goals of states and whose very existence is supported, or at least tolerated, by the intergovernmental network of states. As such, the United Nations is scornfully discounted by realists as "a talking society" or, at most, as a relatively minor way of adapting to the greater complexity of the present world system.

The quality of complexity is stressed in more recent realists' accounts as, for instance, in Stanley Hoffmann's *Primacy or World Order* (New York: McGraw-Hill, 1978). Somewhat greater weight is given to international institutions and regimes, especially relating to trade, money, and oceans policy, as elements that move international relations in a different direction than is stressed by those analysts who focus almost exclusively on the competitive and security aspects of relations among states. The idea of interdependence is taken as the central organizing concept of this neorealist account of international relations. In its most sophisticated formulation so far, that of Robert Keohane and Joseph Nye, the idea of "complex interdependence" is put forward as a second, alternate line of explanation of international relations, one that supplements rather than displaces the traditional realists' line of explanation. The applicability of the one, rather than the other, depends on context: "Our purpose in developing an alternative to the realist description of world politics is to encourage a differentiated approach that distinguishes among dimensions and areas of world politics—not (as modernist observers do) to replace one oversimplification with another."[3]

The "modernist observers" are those who argue that interdependence is so central to relations among states in the nuclear age (war is unthinkable) that the traditional stress on force and war, and hence, on alliance systems and military matters, is obsolete, or at least subordinate. As Keohane and Nye remark, "Our task is to provide a means of blending the wisdom on both positions by developing a coherent theoretical framework for the political analysis of interdependence."[4] And they are appropriately "cautious about the prospect that rising interdependence is creating a brave new world of cooperation to replace the bad old world of international conflicts."[5] Even these disclaimers do not save the neorealists from the counterattacks of the traditional realists who dismiss their claims as "trendy" or, at the very least, exaggerated. Such traditionalists as Hedley Bull, Robert Gilpin, or Kenneth Waltz contend that the continuities of state predominance hold firm and that domains of apparent cooperation administered by nongovernmental actors are always subordinate and contingent, dependent for their autonomy upon tolerance by governments whose principal concern remains security and independence, sustained when necessary by force and threats of force.

There is, finally, in the realists' paradigm a certain ambivalence toward the political realm of power-wielders. One academic expression of this ambivalence is the contention that the boundary between the study of international relations and foreign policy is inherently blurred. There is a methodological confusion deeply embedded in the whole tradition of inquiry. Machiavelli as the main founder or precursor of modern international relations is praised for his objectivity and practicality, for having no illusions about the ways in which sovereign units interact in their pursuit of selfish ends. At the same time, Machiavelli formulated his early-sixteenth-century analysis in the form of advice to his prince, although there has been an ongoing scholarly debate in the history of ideas as to whether Machiavelli intended his precepts to be read literally or ironically. Nevertheless, it seems correct to conclude that Machiavelli's ideas have been *received* as if they were meant to be taken seriously as guidance and orientation by political leaders.

Of course, this cynical stance associated with Machiavellianism is not endorsed explicitly by statesmen. Especially in this century of democratic accountability there has been some attempt, especially by United States leaders, to reconcile foreign policy on the national level with Western moral traditions. Even leading ultrarealists disguise their undertakings by claiming to walk a righteous path. The minimum resistance to the Machiavelli stance expresses itself by way of diplomatic apologetics; anything further generates controversy. The difference on this score between, say, Richard Nixon and Jimmy Carter relates mainly to whether one takes others as they are or tries to portray "friends" as similarly righteous or, at least, reformable. Carter's emphasis on human rights, in the early, idealistic phase of his presidency, was an active principle of moral advocacy as an ingredient of foreign policy, influencing, for example, some decisions to give military and economic assistance. Even though selectively applied, such a moralistic tenet is inconsistent with the realists' principal position. As such, it is criticized by realists as producing either a muddled or hypocritical foreign policy. Even its advocates generally tend to retreat under pressure, as was certainly the case with Carter's tepid forays on behalf of a moral foreign policy for the United States.

An aspect of moralizing diplomacy is realist in motivation, reflecting the liberal insistence that repressive governments make poor, undependable allies. The American experience in Vietnam helped to give this kind of moral realism a temporary influence in the making of foreign policy by way of affixing, for instance, eligibility criteria for the receipt of military credits or economic assistance. Already at the outset of the 1980s this liberal view is losing out to more conventional conceptions of realism that pass no moral judgments on the governing process of allied or friendly states. Moral language is reserved for use in settings that are obviously propagandistic in character, as when the socialist countries are described as being behind "the iron curtain" and the West as constituting "the free world."

But the realist analyst has not worked out a consistent view of the proper relationship between power-wielders and policymakers. For instance, of Kissinger, fellow realist Stanley Hoffmann writes: "His was the loneliness of the short-distance runner,"[6] adept at holding operations, but without any guiding vision of how to establish stability given the various pressures of the present age. Kissinger lends his services to the prince, putting in jeopardy claims of objectivity. Hoffmann tells us that "academic writers" should refrain from either "detailed policy prescriptions" or "grand designs." For the former, "the advantage lies with the policy makers," whereas the latter produces "terrible oversimplification. . . . The world has become too complicated for such schemes." On this basis, Hoffmann proposes some middle ground:

The proper role of scholars—one which is both faithful to the values that ought to inspire academic research and potentially useful to policy makers—is to examine critically the premises of official policy, to compare intentions and results. In other words, a scholar is to judge the performance of the official vehicle and of its drivers, and also to provide as searching a survey as possible of the terrain ahead in order to bring to light alternative itineraries, their costs, and their benefits.[7]

There is in Hoffmann a preoccupation with adaptive understandings of the state system along the neorealist's lines of complex interdependence as essential for avoiding the "peril of politics-as-usual," but there is also a complementary insistence on not carrying the interpretation of current challenges and realities to the point of proposing grand designs.[8] In this realist mode of discourse, the "grand design" is a code phrase for blueprints for the future of international society that anticipate a new world order in which the state is subordinate and the danger of war has been eliminated, or nearly so.

Hence, neorealism is reformist as a matter of necessity. There *are* new realities that complicate our image of what is going on, but the essential focus on balance and security has not been superceded by either nuclear weaponry or complex interdependence. Neorealism seeks to be flexible, yet antiutopian, as well as nonutopian. It is sensitive to charges from traditionalists and, therefore, disavows idealistic inclinations. The neorealists' reformulation is a defensive intellectual posture that seeks to uphold its interpretation of the state system by reference to realist logic.

THE ACHIEVEMENTS OF THE REALIST TRADITION

Any evaluation of this dominant tradition of inquiry must begin with certain acknowledgments. One is struck initially by the persuasiveness of the apparent similarity between realist descriptions and the actualities of statecraft. Power, as ultimately tested on the battlefield, has been the arbiter of international conflict. International law attests to this observation with rules that give validity to peace treaties, even if their consequence is to make legal the depredations of an aggressor state. Statecraft continues to be preoccupied with defense systems and alliances, although the prospect of nuclear devastation places unprecedented stress on the deterrent function of military power, at least in strategic relations. The more esoteric subject matter of interdependence does seem to be producing some structural modifications of international relations, but not as yet, of a fundamental character. The durability of the state system seems confirmed. Patterns of warfare have so far adjusted to the nuclear age without producing irreversible catastrophe. The United Nations has changed few, if any, of the ways in which conflict is waged or resolved. Normative concerns about peace, human rights, or basic human needs seem largely rhetorical. Even coordination of outlook on the part of like-minded governments or elites—the managerial impulse of periodic summit meetings of heads-of-state in the leading noncommunist, advanced industrial countries or evident in the formation of the Trilateral Commission—has not added up to much. Indeed, fears abound of a new era of economic nationalism among states aligned for security purposes in a firm alliance. Territorial statism, whether among socialist or capitalist countries, continues to dominate political consciousness, perhaps more intensely than ever, given the emergence of so many recently independent statelike entities and considering the seaward extension of land-based territoriality in the form of 200-mile-or-more exclusive economic zones at the expense of the earlier nonterritorial notion of "freedom of the high seas." Considerations of ideological identity or class solidarity have not invalidated the realists' assertions about the dominance of the quest for maximum state power, wealth, and prestige. In this respect, nationalism at the state level, although often an ethnic fiction, continues to provide the main organizing focus for political loyalty, especially in states where national identity has persisted for a long time.

The adherence to realist canons of statecraft by leaders in the main communist countries of the Soviet Union and China is further confirmation of the abiding strength of statist logic. Marxism-Leninism, in theory at least, looks beyond the state to class as the fundamental actor on the world stage, yet the reorientation of statecraft in governments of Marxist-Leninist persuasion has been nominal, at least until the present. The intense statist conflict between the Soviet Union and China, the imperial relationship between the Soviet Union and Eastern Europe, the pattern of expediency of Chinese alignments and positions, and the generally nationalistic priorities of Marxist-Leninist governments and various national communist parties suggest the continuing adequacy of the realists' framework of explanation.

Such an assessment of these Marxist-Leninist governments does not imply the historical irrelevance of ideology. The importance of ideology relates to identity and orientation toward foreign conflict. Ideological affinities help create a coherent and legitimate framework of choice that has exerted, for example, some degree of influence on Soviet planners. However, as the Chinese foreign policy since the Sino-Soviet split illustrates, ideological considerations may be subordinated almost completely if a particular geopolitical tendency (here, anti-Soviet goals) holds sway; even in this instance, the Chinese seek ideological coherence and legitimacy by characterizing the Soviet Union as a dangerous social imperialist power that needs to be resisted in the name of antiimperialism.

The geopolitical situation of the Soviet Union and the hostile Western reaction to the Russian Revolution have created an international context in recent decades in which Soviet support for the revolutionary and anti-Western propensities of the Third World has been a natural outcome of a *realist* foreign policy which also appeared consistent with Marxist-Leninist ideology. On deeper levels of planning, Soviet international relations experts seem at least as concerned with the mapping of balances of power, spheres of influence, alliance relations, and traditional geopolitics as their American counterparts. The Soviet intervention in Afghanistan from late 1979 onward has placed a severe strain on the claim that the Soviet Union is a progressive force in the Third World as a consequence of its Marxist-Leninist heritage; ideological affinities are not as persuasive, in terms of international role and identity, as the movement of troops and the commitment to warfare.

Because it provides an alternative image of international relations, the antisentimental feature of the realists' thinking is also salutary, and preferrable to the essentially misleading claims of moralists and legalists. War, injustice, opportunism, and even inconvenience cannot be overcome by appealing to the enlightened self-interest, much less to the altruistic impulses, of statist leaders. Such "rationality" has little persuasive power and is no match for the short-term rationality of protecting vested interests of various kinds. Power systems at every level of social organization tend to be ultrastable in the critical sense of maintaining their basic identity in the face of challenge. The state system, internally and internationally, illustrates this ultrastability. In effect, it is naive to make proposals for drastic change that violate statist logic dependent on voluntary adoption by entrenched elites. Such far-reaching proposals actually have a reactionary political effect, tending to confirm the conservative contention that nothing much by way of change is feasible. As a result, a utopian attempt to overcome realism induces either light-hearted condescension (if only this were possible, of course we would favor it!) or despair (if this is the best we can do, then we have really had it!).

In this central regard, then, the cautionary stance of the neorealists is appropriate. They are alert to the changing character of international relations, but they do not contend that the essential features of statism have been rendered obsolete or are being superseded. At the same time, they reject the relevance of apocalyptic forebodings on the same grounds as they reject utopian schemes—namely, that such forebodings are large enough to overwhelm the only problem-solving capabilities that exist or can be brought into being in the foreseeable future. Politics, as the art of the possible, must work with what exists, which is the limit of what can be done. To insist that more needs to be done is, according to realist or neorealist, to interfere with what can be done without adding anything constructive.

THE INSUFFICIENCY OF REALISM AND NEOREALISM

Despite these genuine achievements, the realist tradition, even as modified by the neo-realist emphasis, seems insufficient in decisive respects. First, its perception and depiction of reality seems to evade critical questions. And if realism isn't realistic, then what is it?

The rationalism of realism makes it almost impossible to take seriously challenges that exceed the problem-solving capacities of the state system. Therefore, the impact of nuclear weapons, and more generally of nuclear technology, is only partially comprehended. As has been often noted, deterrence theory is an extreme application of rational analysis to a circumstance of basic irrationality.[9] That circumstance of basic irrationality is ignored in realist theory, despite its dramatic implications for the future. As nuclear weapons spread to additional states, either directly or indirectly by way of "peaceful" technology, the irrationality of territorial systems of nuclear defense becomes manifest, and the failure of governments to adjust reveals the rigidity, rather than the resilience, of the state system. For realists and neorealists to ignore this erosion of the security system and the consequences of its potential collapse is to neglect the most consequential question in international relations at this time.

Even more evident is the realists' refusal to take seriously the ecological challenge. The viability of the state system was based on the general acceptability of entrusting territorial administration to the governments of states and leaving the oceans as a commons to be administered in a *laissez-faire* manner. With the crowding and modernizing of the planet, the strains on biospheric quality and resource base seem absolutely central to the future well-being and collective destiny of all peoples on earth. A fragmented political order of states cannot adopt the kind of overall regime of stewardship required to meet this multidimensional ecological challenge. Well-documented studies anticipate, for instance, a further increase in world population from 4 billion to 6.35 billion by the year 2000, with as much as ninety percent of this increase concentrated in the poorest countries of the Third World; a widening income gap between rich and poor countries; a decline in per capita food production and consumption in large parts of Africa, the Middle East, and South Asia; and a worsening of environmental degradation in almost every respect—desertification, water and air pollution, atmospheric carbon dioxide, acid rain, ozone depletion, and spills of ultrahazardous materials.[10] How can the mechanisms of the state system be expected to cope with this ecological agenda? Such a question assumes full force when adequate consideration is given to the wide array of strains upon various governments, including those of a shaky monetary indebtedness system and of increasing resource "insecurity," especially in the area of energy supplies. It is small wonder that there has been a global surge of terrorism, a spread of authoritarian rule, and even in the liberal North, talk in high places about "a crisis of democracy."[11]

In the face of all this evidence of disarray, the realists turn away, occasionally pausing long enough to condemn those who take such issues seriously as "alarmists," "salvationists," or "prophets of doom." One searches the writings of realists and neorealists in vain for any considered assessment of how these challenges could support a conclusion of statist sustenance. The realists, even in neorealist trappings, reveal themselves to be true believers who would rather perish with their sinking statist paradigm than cast themselves adrift.

Even such an adept connoisseur of complexity as Stanley Hoffmann has neither time nor patience to assess the merits of radical critiques. He reacts, for instance, against "the gloomy themes" of the Club of Rome's critique of growth-oriented economics with sheer emotionalism: "Scarcity, or zero growth, would generate even worse social frustrations than the fast growth of the period before 1973. In world affairs, zero growth would turn every economic contest into a zero-sum game and promptly bring the scourge of wars of conquest and 'resource interventions' back into the economic arena. . . ."[12] The issue of "reality" is cleverly finessed by the shift to social consequence. Of course, the strains of the state system will intensify as inhibitors of growth emerge, but to dismiss the challenge because it cannot be conveniently or equitably accommodated is to bury one's head in quicksand.

Mainstream international relations is defective, above all else, because it has lost the capacity to raise the right questions. The traditional framework is being undermined by the dynamics of population growth, industrial development, and the technology of violence. Such an interpretation is not tantamount to proposing a grand design, but it does imply a drastic revisioning of the realists' conception of international relations.

In essence, realism is a failure because it has shown an

insufficient capacity to acknowledge emergencies. We are living through a period in which the politics of the double-bind prevails: If one moves to satisfy the pressures of stagflation and unemployment, then the problems of ecological decay are made more severe, whereas if these ecological problems are taken more seriously, then economic fallout occurs. This pattern prevails in all crucial policy arenas, including the critical spheres of energy and security policy.

Realism is also defective from a normative point of view. Human nature is reduced to the aggregate pursuit of selfish goals by secular entities called governments. An egoistic and materialistic anthropology forecloses human possibility on a planetary level. The global, unifying impacts of modern technology are set aside. Patterns of loyalty associated with nonstate configurations ranging from family to species are simply not assessed or even comprehended, nor is the uneven character of nationalistic sentiment around the world taken into account. The realists' framework cannot help generate, or even acknowledge, a vision of the future based on human potentiality. It has even forgotten that long ago it threw away the prison key by adopting a set of assumptions about statist supremacy and egoistic psychology that preclude alternatives. As such, realist thought is unable to acknowledge what genuine foundations for hope exist.

The realists' framework, however, continues to enjoy command over political discourse.[13] Even dissenters must address issues in terms of the state system, alleging that the state is too big or too small or both at once. As such, postrealist thought tends to be derivative and to depict prospects in light of the postulates of the state system. For this reason it is hardly surprising that early and crude antirealist approaches to international relations tended to propose world government or empire as "a solution," that is, a macrostatist solution to the dilemmas of statism. And even the substantial efforts of Immanuel Kant to build "perpetual peace" on the basis of the spread of liberal constitutionalism evolved in relation to the state. Lenin, too, was convinced that a mixture of socialist domestic orders and international working class solidarity would usher in an era of world peace and justice. These outlooks that base world order solutions on either the inward or outward reconstruction of the state were, in the most fundamental sense, caught up by statist logic and were derivative.

Postrealist thought is groping toward the creation of autonomous modes of discourse that are neither oblivious to the actualities of state power, nor so entrapped by these actualities as to be incapable of setting forth a nonstatist array of planetary futures. At this juncture of study and reflection, some of the most important work consists of exposing the epistemological and metaphysical roots of statism in order to explain the constraints arising therefrom.[14] This prepares the intellectual foundation, so to speak, for new patterns of thought. Without such preparations, allegedly bold new ventures of conjecture seem oddly tame.

We find ourselves, then, in a fragile condition. The old realist lines of explanation are too limited to encompass emergent, crucial actualities. The neorealist adjustment is similarly grounded in modes of perception that are unable to take account of the larger challenges and opportunities. At the same time, postrealist gropings, alive to these larger challenges and opportunities, have not yet evolved either the epistemological foundations for a genuinely global mode of discourse, nor a convincing base for a conception of transition from the world that is to the world that might be, and needs to be, if current challenges are to be met. As R. B. J. Walker well concludes, "The trick is to conceive a universe of discourse which allows for both universalism and pluralism, for we are presumably both one and many. But this would be to work within a language as yet unborn, a language even in danger of merely reproducing the contradictions which we seek to escape."[15] Of course, taken literally such an assessment would counsel a mood of alert passivity, waiting for the tablet with the new language inscribed thereon. More figuratively, such an outlook induces a self-critical attitude toward our gropings to forge a new, encompassing language for political discourse on a planetary scale.

NORMATIVE INTERNATIONAL RELATIONS

The realist and neorealist understandings of international relations are essential starting-points, if for no other reason than that they continue to describe the outlook of the main political leaders in the world. As such, these traditional approaches to international relations give us insight into why it is so difficult to acknowledge fundamental challenges or contemplate drastic types of response and reform. The essays that comprise this book explore a treacherous intellectual terrain in which the old is insufficient and the new is not yet adequately available. These explorations are inevitably tentative. Criticisms are ventured with confidence, large questions are posed with urgency, but only the most preliminary contours of response are depicted.

The search for a postrealist orientation is often carried on within the framework of world order studies.[16] Again, the language used is itself an issue. The domain of "world order" has not yet been clearly delimited. The rhetoric of world order is often appropriated by such influential figures as Henry Kissinger or Zbigniew Brzezinski to mobilize public support for what amounts to a new realist fix—a geopolitical perspective that seeks stability, managerial capabilities, and popular uplift, without undermining the hierarchy of states that exist in the world.

Such a conservative conception of world order contrasts with my conviction that stability and hierarchy are no longer reconcilable in politics no matter what the scale of inquiry.[17] Hence, values are critical elements of *analysis,* as well as of advocacy. To make international relations work reasonably well, in other words, requires the significant realization of a series of values: peace in the sense of minimum direct violence and warfare; economic well-being in the sense of satisfying the basic needs of all peoples; social and political justice in the sense of satisfying the basic claims of human rights; ecological balance in the sense of achieving environmental quality consistent with health and safety and of conserving the necessary stock of renewable and non-renewable resources; and governance in the sense of achieving effective and humane structures of authority at all levels of social organization. Normative international relations aspires to promote disciplined inquiry into the ways in which such values can be realized, as well as to expose the value failures of the present and past arrangements of authority and the adverse consequences of "muddling through."[18]

Normative international relations seeks to be as sophisticated about state power as the realists' approach and to avoid both the facile projections of world order utopians and the awkward evasions of Marxists.[19] Its ambitions include diagnosis of the present, projection of the future, and discovery of the creative space by which the predicted future can be brought into closer alignment with a preferred future. Accordingly, it is preoccupied with matters of method and substance, as well as with the translation of thought into action through the mediation of world order values.

Part One of this volume depicts various aspects of this orientation. This chapter, "Normative International Relations: A General Introduction," relates the outlook taken here to other principal ways of understanding international relations. Chapter 2, "The Grotian Quest," argues that the inquirer of today is situated in a context of transition and that what is needed is a synthesis of what has been with what is, in fact, emergent. Normative international relations seeks to provide, in this crucial respect, a better map of reality than the neorealists, not by insisting on its preferences, but by noting the mag-'

nitude of actual emergent tendencies. Grotius did this for his time, and we await a Grotian depiction for our epoch.

Part Two carries forward the emphasis on orientation and outlook but more concretely in relation to the emergence of world order studies as a normative variant on either mainstream international relations or on the projection of utopian blueprints for a harmonious world society. In Chapter 3, the emphasis is put upon the academic styles of inquiry. In the context of international relations, approaches are classified by whether they are system-maintaining (realist), system-reforming (neo-realist), or system-transforming (post-realist). An argument is advanced in favor of the system-transforming perspective as that most closely aligned with the historical forces and as most normatively attractive for all peoples. Chapters 4 and 5 are responses to critics of one particular system-transforming approach, namely the World Order Models Project. The weight of statist thinking is such that it is hard to depict an alternative mode of thinking and acting without being dismissed as naive. The first objective of a postrealist analysis is to achieve credibility as a serious interpretation of what is becoming and what could be. This historical rootedness is the only legitimate line of defense against accusations of utopianism, including the contention that system-transformers divert energy from system-reformers, and thereby are tacit allies of the system-maintainers, who are alleged to be, in their effect, system-destroyers. Postrealist thought, to validate itself, must begin to convince serious students of international affairs that it is in closer touch with the actualities of politics on a global scale than either the realists or neorealists. In the end, scholarship is only a more systematic and reflective form of journalism, to be assessed by its faithfulness to "the actual," including the possible and probable.

Part Three examines these general issues in relation to the participation of the United States in world society as it is now constituted. Chapter 6 deals directly with the relationship of values to state practice and power. It examines the fit between the pursuit of national interests, the avowed purpose of foreign policymakers, and the discernment and realization of a human interest transcending boundaries of state, class, race, and culture. At the core of this inquiry is the structural problem of safeguarding human interest in a setting where the pluralist priorities of states overwhelmingly shape international behavior. Implicit, also, is the historical point that a *laissez-faire* international order, regarding war as a matter of sovereign discretion, has been developed to such a point that now the technology of violence and the ecological agenda pose unprecedented challenges. Until recently, it was not globally essential to draw the distinction sharply between national and human perspectives. It is, of course, important to realize that there are diverse ideas of "the human interest" that reflect concrete experiences of time and place. Such diversity should not be confused, however, with the promotion of the national interest which involves role-playing on behalf of a collectivity—territorially bounded, although politically structured in terms of class and race. The issue is further confounded by the propagandistic side of diplomacy that has led major governments to invoke their devotion to the human interest as a cloak to hide their more selfish pursuits. A key objective of normative international relations, then, is to draw the distinction between national interest and human interest as *objectively* as possible. In the future, as a matter of ideal, the human interest may converge with the national interest. As matters now stand, the divergence is wide and various. Even the national interest is rarely promoted in terms of all the people in a given state; its definition usually expresses the preferences of a given elite who dominate the state internally. For another, the hierarchical relations of states in terms of wealth, power, and prestige give respective state leaders a very different sense of their roles in the world. Some of the elite of subordinate states articulate their national interests to reflect largely the preferences of the dominant state upon which their own private bureaucratic orbits of power are seen to depend.

Chapter 7 considers the analysis in the setting of American foreign policy. More concretely, it considers the principal tensions in the American political identity as playing themselves out in alternative kinds of foreign policy throughout the course of national history. In effect, the Jeffersonian side of the American political tradition supports the shift to a postrealist conception of national interest. This counter-tradition, given the dominant orientation, would help close the gap between national interest and human interest and would, as well, help the United States perceive and respond to the distinctive world order challenges of our time.

This general problem is examined in Chapter 8 in relation to the statecraft of a single exemplary figure, Henry Kissinger. While attempting to present Kissinger as positively as possible and to overlook his flaws of character, this chapter argues that Kissinger's conception of the national interest was inconsistent with the well-being and security of the American people, much less with the interests of humanity considered as a whole. Thus, the dangers of statism require a reformulation of national interest in light of global community to avoid self-destructive effects. Of course, satisfying this imperative is exceedingly difficult, given the short cycles of accountability to which virtually all national leaders are subject. As it happens, individuals with a larger vision are rarely given access to power even if their perspectives are viewed as valid in the long run. Kissinger, besides being a master manipulator of the levers of state power, possessed a consistent, coherent view of international relations that embodied the central tenets of realist thought. Hence, a critical account of Kissinger's worldview is one way to mount criticism of realism itself.

Part Four attempts to apply the orientation set forth in the first eight chapters. In each chapter an attempt is made to criticize the realists' understanding of how to deal with an important world order problem. Chapter 9 argues the case for a comprehensive program of denuclearization that embraces both weaponry and energy facilities. As such, it dissents sharply from the mainstream reliance on preventing the horizontal spread of nuclear weaponry as the heart of a world order approach to nuclear policy. Chapter 10 criticizes arms control theory as an approach to war prevention, arguing that the most dangerous tendencies of the war system are completely untouched by the arms control approach. Also, as with the focus on nonproliferation, the emphasis on arms control plays an ideological role in support of the status quo by seeming to make world order problems soluble without transforming either the hierarchial or fragmented structures of international relations. Chapter 11 expresses a similarly skeptical view of approaches to world poverty carried on within the framework of the state system. Whether foreign aid or the mutual benefits of growth are considered, the prospects of poor peoples seem bleak. Satisfying basic needs requires structural changes, at least at the state level; so long as international and domestic hierarchies shape the world economic process, the domain of international policy will remain, at best, marginal to the solution of problems of mass poverty.

The unity of Part Four rests in its skepticism about current problem-solving approaches not because of bad faith alone, but because the principal structures of governance at the state and global level do not allow appropriate international policy to be established and implemented. Part Five considers law and legal reform as a partial way out, arriving at skeptical conclusions. Given the postrealist point of departure, it seems obvious that law is generally a captive of the existing order, assigned a predominantly conservative role of stabilizing expectations by fixing and protecting rights.

Chapter 12 suggests the futility of regarding law as the principal path for the fulfillment of just claims, considering the unjust structures of national and international society that exist. Law as an instrument of the powerful can rarely serve as an agency of transformation. At the same time, the myths of sovereign equality embedded in international law give the weak states arenas within which to advance claims of justice and to dramatize some of the current tensions between law and justice. Chapter 13 reviews the Grotian quest of Chapter 2, but in more detail. It argues that we are now moving dialectically toward a kind of localist/globalist fracturing of political identity, especially in the West, that is intriguingly comparable to the displacement by statist identity of the localist/globalist split of late medieval Europe. That is, Grotius responded to a realignment of political identity as a consequence of the play of social forces. Today we are experiencing a similar realignment, and legal studies would benefit from a neo-Grotian reorientation. Chapter 14 argues the case more modestly, suggesting that the ecological/world peace agenda cannot be accommodated by a legal order that is limited in its capabilities to adjusting relations among state actors on the basis of mutual agreement.

Part Six is the most exploratory part of the volume. It seeks to identify new frontiers in which either the activity of the mind or the pressure of events embodies the postrealist conception of international relations. Chapter 15 is overtly normative because it specifies values that seem appropriate for a planetary orientation, that is, it addresses the human interest. These values do not create a new dogma. On the contrary, the objective is to establish a framework for dialogue among those who feel the need for a planetary politics, but still experience reality in concrete terms of a particular time, place, and class/race identity. Such a framework has long facilitated dialogue within the state. Realist approaches have permitted dialogue among states. What is now emerging is the search for a way to carry on dialogue if the world as a whole is taken as the basic social unit. At a later stage, movements and political action can and will take shape, but the immediate priority is for conversation and modes of appropriate discourse.

The case for a decentralizing approach to the realization of world order values is considered in Chapter 16. The tradition of philosophical anarchism has long believed that the problematique of states (within and without) is the coercive character of the state itself. Such a perspective is, of course, anathema to mainstream realists who have, since the time of Hobbes, drawn a central contrast between the anarchical order among states and the existence of organized civil authority within states. Industrial civilization, also, has introduced a bias toward bigness, economies of scale, and the inevitability of increasingly complex organizations to manage various aspects of life. Therefore, the *next* stage in political evolution is thought to be a world state, or at least regional-scale states. Any other image of a next stage is almost inconceivable. Taking anarchist thought seriously in the context of world order studies is one way to break out of such a confining image of what is possible. It corresponds also to a more generalized critique of bigness, popularly associated with the work of E. F. Schumacher and pioneered in political realms by Leopold Kohr.

Chapter 17 makes an effort to interpret the ecological challenge in world order terms, that is, as creating part of the case for a post-realist approach to international relations. Chapter 18 considers the question of supranational institutional growth in a spirit that takes seriously the various possible ways to coordinate policy on a global level to satisfy the human interest. At the same time, it is eager to show that some image of "world government" is premature in both an ethical and political sense. The consideration of *global governance* is intended as an improvement upon the discussion of whether world government is desirable, let alone feasible. Governance does not necessarily involve centralization of institutional authority, but it is associated with the quest for structures that best serve and realize values.

This book ends with a foray in Chapter 19 into the difficult subject matter of the cultural and anthropological underpinnings of international relations. These underpinnings are obviously vital for any inquiry into transformative politics, and hence, for the postrealist conception of international relations. The belief systems and prevailing myths that shape a culture set boundaries of civilizational identity on the forms and directions of acceptable change that pertain to social units larger than most, but not all, states. The essence of the person, what is called "human nature," sets more general limits. Realist and neorealist thought, despite disavowing any concern with these matters, presuppose the provincial cultural identity of Western civilization and the material rationalism of the Hobbesian "man." Chapter 19 considers some of the indications that the prevailing cultural imagery of the West is under stress, creating a potential for both breakdown and transformation.

The postrealist attempt to construct an account of normative international relations is centrally animated by this prospect of simultaneous breakdown and transformation. It seeks to direct intellectual attention at this prospect as a necessary prelude to mobilizing political energy. In addition, the form of postrealist thought favored in this volume is broadly populist in spirit. As such, it is skeptical about

entrenched elites being receptive to any message that is transformative in tone and substance. In the end, transformation will depend on social forces that are unconscious bearers of new values
attaining influence *and* a worldview. Hence, world order inquiry, the
essence of normative international relations, needs to become attuned
and receptive to the voices of the oppressed, as well as to those who
speak for those too weak or too poor to have a voice.

Finally, the idea of the oppressed as the potential catalytic force is
not a disguised resurrection of Marxist thinking. Class is only one
dimension of contemporary oppression. Indeed, the newly emergent,
gradually self-conscious members of the invisibly oppressed—those
who live primarily in the affluent countries—perceive themselves as
victims of polluting and hazardous technology, especially in relation
to matters of energy, security, even food. The grassroots antinuclear
movement embracing all of the advanced industrial, democratic
countries of the North is one example. This movement pits the "oppressed" against the entrenched elites, in and out of government, who
continue to affirm, however reluctantly, a nuclear future. It is a matter of prediction, not prophecy, to contend that this struggle will
intensify in the future and link antinuclear concerns with these wider
antimilitary and ecological quality issues. Whether this impending
clash will produce a reoriented political leadership in the West or an
era of authoritarian politics is a critical question. Also in doubt is
whether the invisibly oppressed of the North will join ranks with the
visibly oppressed in the South, those whose revolutionary energy is
largely directed toward the satisfaction of materialist and antiim-
perialist goals. Finally, there is the question of whether, beneath the
negotiations, a new, globally oriented religiosity will emerge to generate new myths, creeds, and symbols. This remains a major, perhaps
decisive, uncertainty.

NOTES

1. See in general, Miles Kahler, "Rumors of War: The 1914 Analogy," *Foreign
Affairs* 58 (1979/80): 374–396.

2. See, for example, Robert Jervis, *The Logic of Images in International Relations*
(Princeton, N.J.: Princeton University Press, 1970); Robert Jervis, *Perception and Misperception in International Politics* (Princeton: Princeton University Press, 1976).

3. Robert Keohane and Joseph Nye, *Power and Interdependence: World Politics in
Transition* (Boston: Little Brown, 1977), p. 29.

4. Ibid., p. 4.

5. Ibid., p. 10.

6. Stanley Hoffmann, *Primacy or World Order: American Foreign Policy since the Cold War* (New York: McGraw-Hill, 1978), p. 80.

7. All quotations after note 6, Ibid., p. 14.

8. Ibid., p. 312.

9. For overview and analysis see Alexander L. George and Richard Smoke, *Deterrence in American Foreign Policy* (New York: Columbia University Press, 1974).

10. See, for example, the conclusions of the 1980 Report on the global future jointly prepared by the Council on Environmental Quality and the Department of State; for an excellent popular treatment along the same lines, see Richard J. Barnet, *The Lean Years: Politics in the Age of Scarcity* (New York: Simon and Schuster, 1980).

11. See Michael J. Crozier, Samuel P. Huntington, and Joji Watanuki, *The Crisis of Democracy: Report on the Governability of Democracies to the Trilateral Commission* (New York: New York University Press, 1975).

12. Hoffmann, *Primacy or World Order*, p. 209.

13. For a suggestive inquiry along these lines see paper by Mark Blasius, "Political Theory and the Discourse of World Order Studies" (Princeton, 1980).

14. In these connections see R.B.J. Walker, "Political Theory and the Transformation of World Politics, " Center of International Studies, Princeton University, Occasional Paper, 8 (January 1980): 1-54; R. B. J. Walker, "Universalism, Pluralism, Hegemony: The Colonization of Discourse and the Contradictions of Global Culture," paper prepared for meeting of World Order Models Project on Culture, Power and Transformation, Lisbon, Portugal, July 1980.

15. R.B.J. Walker, "World Politics and Western Reason: Universalism, Pluralism, Hegemony," Working Paper No. 19, World Order Models Project (New York: Institute for World Order, 1982).

16. The work of the World Order Models Project provides much of the stimulus for this particular mode of normative international relations. See Saul H. Mendlovitz, ed., *On the Creation of a Just World Order: Preferred Worlds for the 1990s* (New York: Free Press, 1975); Johan Galtung, *The True Worlds* (New York: Free Press, 1980); Rajni Kothari, *Footsteps into the Future: Diagnosis of the Present World and a Design for an Alternative* (New York: Free Press, 1974); Gustavo Lagos and Horacio H. Godoy, *Revolution of Being: A Latin American View of the Future* (New York: Free Press, 1977); Ali A. Mazrui, *A World Federation of Cultures: An African Perspective* (New York: Free Press, 1976).

17. For further discussion of this view, see Rajni Kothari, "Towards a Just World," Working Paper No. 11, World Order Models Project (New York: Institute for World Order, 1980), pp. 1–42.

18. Highly suggestive along these lines is Robert Johansen, *The National Interest and the Human Interest: An Analysis of U.S. Foreign Policy* (Princeton, N.J.: Princeton University Press, 1980).

19. On the other hand, certain neo-Marxist inquiries into the world system are most congenial to the approach taken here to normative international relations. See, for example, Immanuel Wallerstein, *The Capitalist World Economy* (Cambridge, England: Cambridge University Press, 1979).

CHAPTER 2

The Grotian Quest

Especially in dark times like ours, decent men and women are often drawn toward the light, only to perish like so many moths. Rousseau perceives his utopian contemporary, Abbé Saint-Pierre, as such a victim: "This rare man, an ornament to his age and to his kind—the only man, perhaps, in all the history of the human race whose only passion was the passion for reason—nevertheless only advanced from error to error in all his sytems, because he wished to make all men like himself instead of taking them as they are and as they will continue to be."[1]

While he opposed endowing illusions with solemn pretentions, Rousseau celebrated the enlivening effects of fantasy: "I created for myself societies of perfect creatures celestial in their virtue and their beauty, and of reliable, tender, and fruitful friends such I had never found here below."[2]

If, however, the purpose of our endeavors is to create a better world, then fantasy, whether self-deceived or self-aware, is of little help. We require instead a special sort of creativity that blends thought and imagination without neglecting to understand obstacles to change. We require, in effect, an understanding of those elements of structure that resist change, as well as a feel for the possibilities of innovation that lie within the shadowland cast by emergent, potential structures of power. Only within this shadowland, if at all, is it possible to discern "openings" that contain significant potential for reform, including the possibility of exerting an impact on the character of emergent political realities.

This shadowland lies necessarily at the outer edge of the realm of politics, although its special emphasis is upon those political possibilities not yet evident to politicians. As such, it is dangerous intellectual work that often engenders rejection, and may even stimulate repression. Power-wielders tend to be scornful of the apparent challenge to their competence, while purists are likely to be alienated by the failure to extend the conception of reform to include structural changes. The more impressive the discernment of possibilities for change in the shadowland, the more likely it will be that those with vested interests will either co-opt the vision, or at least its rhetoric, to conform to their wishes and interests, or reject those who explore the shadowland of structural reform through some form of distortion. The relevance of the shadowland is especially great when an emergent new structure has not yet fully superseded an old structure, in times of transition when the need for bridges between the past and future is the greatest.

In many respects Hugo Grotius was an exemplary visionary of the shadowland, whose life in the late sixteenth, early seventeenth century coincided with the culminating phase of the long transition from the old feudal order to the new order of sovereign states. It is probably not accidental, then, that he led such a difficult personal life, despite the triumphs of his precocious early years. Grotius became a political prisoner in his own country, escaped from jail with a daring plot, lived his remaining years in exile, became a diplomat on behalf of foreign royal leaders, produced his greatest work abroad, and was honored in death by burial close to the very Dutch princes who tormented him while alive. In essence, Grotius was a person of deep conscience who was neither radical nor acquiescent, yet who was deeply committed to leaving the world a better place than he found it. It is also not accidental that Grotius's thought has been misconstrued by detracters and admirers alike over the years, which is one of the fates of those who explore the shadowland.

Grotius came to maturity during a time of religious and political strife, of ripening claims of absolute state sovereignty by the leading monarchs of Europe, and of steadily declining prestige and capacity of the Church of Rome to assert even symbolic authority over the whole of Christendom. It was the time, also, when feudal traditions were being displaced by statist tendencies and administrative capabilities that emphasized territoriality and the domestic centralization of both legitimate authority and military power. Accompanying this process, as with any profound transition in the way collective life is organized, were bloody struggles between those who represented the new order and those who held fast to the old.

Grotius approved of this historical process, yet was appalled by its apparent tendency to generate brutality and unrestrained behavior which resulted in an apparent lapse in the moral quality of relations among separate human collectivities. What Grotius attempted, whether wittingly or not, was to provide the foundation for a new normative order in international society that acknowledged the realities of an emergent state system and yet remained faithful to the shared heritage of spiritual, moral, and legal ideas that any Christian society could still be presumed to affirm as valid. Out of this heritage, Grotius fashioned a grand intellectual synthesis that culminated in the publication of *De Jure Belli-ac Pacis* in 1625, more than twenty years before the rulers of Europe assembled at the end of the Thirty Years War to produce the Peace of Westphalia, the occasion most often selected to mark the formal beginning of the modern state system.

The shadowland that Grotius explored emanated from the idea that restraint and decency could be grounded in law despite the realities of the new age of statist diplomacy. Grotius's system of mutual legal restraint was premised on the reality of an overarching Christian conscience, which he reasonably assumed still mattered to the rulers of the day. Their Christianity persisted despite the increase in their secular autonomy and sovereign stature. In effect, Grotius believed that by activating the Christian conscience of rulers, peaceful methods short of war could be promoted to resolve disputes between royal sovereigns, and that where, in those exceptional circumstances, war did occur, its character could be sufficiently regulated to moderate its cruel character and effects. In retrospect, what Grotius proposed seemed like the only way to acknowledge sovereign prerogatives without endorsing their most nihilistic implications. By drawing on rationality and natural law, Grotius encouraged the European rulers of his day to reconcile their practical pursuits as statesmen with their spiritual and intellectual heritage and thereby to fill, in an acceptable form, the moral vacuum created by the weakening, if not the total collapse, of the Roman Church as a source of international unity and authority. In what respects, if any, the Grotian approach did, in fact, moderate interstate diplomacy is a matter of controversial interpretation, although it has assuredly shaped subsequent efforts to introduce normative elements into the practice of statecraft. The sufficiency of the Grotian approach also needs to be considered in light of the evolving technology of war; whereas *moderation* might have been a sufficient seventeenth-century solution, *abolition*, or at least substantial abridgment, of the war system might alone suffice in the era of nuclear weaponry. That is, from our perspective in history, a shadowland approach only promises a sufficient result if we correctly discern emergent structures of a new, globally oriented system of world order. It is a question of great historical moment whether those who discern emergent structures are wishful thinkers like Abbé Saint-Pierre or are shadowland explorers like Grotius. Given the dangers that confront us, it seems prudent to suspend critical judgment and to remain as receptive as possible to approaches that depict and develop shadowland claims.

Perhaps Grotius is vulnerable to the charge of accommodating statism to an excessive and unnecessary degree. Perhaps the degree of his acknowledgment of statist legitimacy against the claims of popular sovereignty did contribute to the persistent neglect of human rights in international legal theory and practice. Until recently, only states were subjects of international law, while individuals were objects whose rights were derived from the state and dependent upon its government for their protection. Even now, despite an upsurge of interest in human rights, practical and formal realities make individuals almost totally dependent upon the benevolence of their national governments. And Grotius, so attentive to the shadowland, may also have been motivated, as Rousseau charges, by the logic of his personal situation to solicit royal patronage at the expense of individual or personal rights. In effect, Grotius's peculiar sensitivity to the implications of state sovereignty as the new ordering principle of world affairs seems to have been coupled with some insensitivity, from a normative standpoint, to the fate of individuals and groups confronted by repressive patterns of governance.

Charles Edwards has produced a magnificent new interpretation of Grotius's achievement that clarifies its peculiar relevance to our contemporary torments.[3] Edwards is scrupulous and precise in his appreciation of Grotius, neither exaggerating nor underestimating his contributions. We are gently guided by Edwards through complex thickets of academic controversy and thereby permitted a more accurate apprehension of Grotius's thought. In particular, Edwards clarifies the extent to which Grotius combined religious with secular concerns, the degree to which he adapted the natural law tradition to new international circumstances, and the sense in which it seems appropriate to regard him as "the father of international law." Edwards provides a persuasive, well-documented account of these controversies. He also gives us an appreciation of the heroic scale of the Grotian quest to blend disparate moral, legal, and political perspectives into a coherent conception of world order that challenged the secular imagination without abandoning it for either backward-looking religious or forward-looking secular utopian solutions.

What is more, Edwards speculates about what Grotius might do if confronted with the current international situation. This exercise sharpens the distinction between the specific temporal setting of the Grotian solution to the pre-Westphalian puzzle with its limited relevance for our situation and the timelessness of the Grotian quest for openings to the future through shadowland exploration. The particular applicability of the Grotian quest at this moment of history depends upon whether the prevailing structure of world order can be sufficiently synthesized with that structure which is not yet apparent to provide help in this period of transition and whether, in effect, the future order is sufficiently crystallized to cast its shadow backwards into the present.

Grotius makes clear that the sort of normative identity he attributed to human society did not then imply any belief in the necessity or desirability of institutionalization beyond the state, much less beyond world government. On the contrary, any insistence on supranationalism would have run against the powerful current of territorial sovereignty that was so dominant in the seventeenth century. As such, it would have been a species of forward-looking utopianism, allowing wishes rather than the rigorous observation of possibilities to supply the identity of the emergent structure. In our period, in contrast, it is the state system that is being challenged by a variety of novel forms of supranationalism (regional, functional, and global in scope and orientation), although in an ambiguous, and perhaps only preliminary, fashion.

Another important development in the 350 years that have elapsed since Grotius did his work is the changed character of the sovereign state. The government of such a state can no longer be associated with a series of European Christian princes. In the contemporary world, the state is more typically dominated by a faceless bureaucracy that is governed by leaders who are selected and rejected at short intervals or are kept in power for longer periods by sheer brute force, and whose religious and cultural backgrounds embrace the diversities of the main global traditions. The Grotian solution presupposed the personal character of royal rulership in Europe and is not fully transferable to global bureaucracies and the secularization of power that has evolved into the modern post-seventeenth-century state and that has steadily diffused the responsibility and eroded the spirituality of political leadership. It is a mistake to suppose, as do such diverse contemporary commentators on Grotius as Hersch Lauterpacht and Hedley Bull, that the Grotian solution proposes substantive answers that are directly applicable to the transitional torments of the twentieth-century state system.[4] Such a mistake flows, it seems to me, from confusing the Grotian solution with the Grotian quest.

Given the peculiar burdens posed by nuclear weaponry, ecological decay, population pressures, and expectations of equity, the renewal of the Grotian quest in our time cannot rely credibly on a shared heritage of normative traditions as reinforced by the conscience of contemporary leaders. What makes our situation seem so desperate is the vagueness, and even dubiousness, of the normative heritage (especially for non-Western societies) and the uncertain contours of the emergent structure. We seem caught in a historical movement where the burdens on the old order are too great to bear, and yet the new alternative order that hopefully lies beyond the presently perceived horizon of attainability casts no shadow backwards from the future that can be reliably and persuasively discerned. As a consequence, the advocacy of global normative approaches is often understood to be a neo-Machiavellian maneuver by those governments of large states that harbor imperial ambitions, which, in recent decades, has meant mainly the United States and secondarily the Soviet Union. At the same time, within these imperial centers such global speculations are dismissed as the naive and sterile wanderings of alienated minds drawn like moths into the flame of utopian illusion.

Perhaps we should regard the faddish prominence temporarily accorded human rights diplomacy as a pathetic reenactment of the Grotian quest. The normative claim embodied in human rights is, quite simply, that leaders of governments can continue to pursue nationalistic economic, social, and political goals, only if in governing peoples within their territory, they will abide by the most minimal decencies required by international law. No further accusation is mounted by most human rights advocates against the state system as such. Admittedly, the humanizing potential of adhering to human rights is considerable and should not be belittled even in relation to global concerns about peace, justice, and ecological balance. Whether contemporary global and national structures of power actually will allow this potential to be tapped is doubtful. Repression seems integral to the structure, rather than to an aspect of the shadowland, although it may be seen in both. And it is as revealing as it is disquieting to note that the international concern of governments for human rights, realized after it became a goal of American foreign policy at the outset of the Carter presidency, has receded as quickly as it was initiated here and elsewhere.

Compared to the ferment of the seventeenth century with the new logic of the state system taking over from the feudal logic, our transitional challenge is more dangerous and bewildering. The statist logic has not yet been seriously challenged by an alternative logic that conceives the *whole* as necessarily prior to the *part* in matters of ecological stability and military security. The shadowland cast backward onto the present situation of world order does not yet seem to exist. Perhaps we await a Grotius who can teach us to "see" the shadowland

and, without losing persuasiveness, to accord sufficient status to international developments that depart from the premises of the state system.

Grotius came from an independent state in the Protestant north of Europe that was the preparing for revolt against holistic domination of all Europe by the Catholic south. One would similarly expect that our Grotius, if he or she emerges, will come from the Third World rather than from the advanced industrial countries. The shadowland is more accessible to those who are victims of the old order and apostles of the new order but who yet see that the hopes for a benign transition depend on the success of an ideological synthesis.

Our prospects as a civilization, even as a species, continue to seem poor. We cannot manage the technology at our disposal and at the same time sustain present patterns of life. Our social and political relations are distorted by pervasive inequalities that make the powerful and weak alike dependent on violence and even terror. To submit to such a reality is tantamount to renouncing hope for the future. To project mere images of a viable future is to fiddle while Rome burns. To embark upon a revolutionary voyage, given all we now know about the tendency of revolutions to devour their children, is probably to opt for a violent course of terror that does not even contain much promise of genuine transformation.

Without indulging illusions, I believe that the Grotian quest remains our best hope. It offers no easy solace or spectacular outcomes. Yet the Grotian quest remains constructive in our situation, because it is normatively grounded and future-oriented, synthesizes old and new, and cherishes continuities while welcoming discontinuities. Our political life is now so bureaucratized that it is doubtful whether anyone who listens to the voice of conscience could long remain influential. The Grotian quest should probably concentrate on mobilizing the conscience of the people more than on activating the conscience of their rulers.

No venture into the future will succeed without anchors in our past. At this time, we could learn about the present by reexamining Grotius's remarkable achievement of more than three and a half centuries ago.

NOTES

    1. Jean-Jacques Rousseau, *The Confessions* (New York: Penguin, 1953), Book IX, p. 393.

    2. Ibid., p. 398.

3. Charles S. Edwards, *Hugo Grotius: The Miracle of Holland* (Chicago: Nelson Hall, 1981).

4. See Hersch Lauterpacht, "The Grotian Tradition in International Law," *The British Journal of International Law*, 23 (1946): 1–53 and Hedley Bull, "The Grotian Concept of International Society," in Herbert Butterfield and Martin Wight, eds., *Diplomatic Investigations* (London: Allen and Unwin, 1966), pp. 51–73.

PART TWO

General Perspectives

CHAPTER 3

Contending Approaches to World Order

The world order approach to the study of global politics has had its principal intellectual development, to date, in North America. Its perspectives and goals, although not its methodology or rhetorical style, is closely aligned to work done under rubrics of peace research, conflict resolution, and alternative political futures.[1] The United States, of course, is a global presence whose intellectual fashions, for better or worse, exert great influence even as they arouse antagonism elsewhere. Therefore, the global spread of the world order studies and the suspicions engendered by its point of origin are inseparable.

Founded on dissatisfaction with the professional judgment that a statist framework of world politics is here to stay, the world order approach critically examines the durability and adequacy of statism, proposes alternative political frameworks, and considers strategies and scenarios that might facilitate the transition to a post-statist type of world order. Furthermore, it takes the realization of values (peacefulness, economic well-being, social and political justice, ecological balance, and humane governance), rather than materialistic and technological gains, as the decisive criterion of progress in human affairs.

LEGITIMATING "WORLD ORDER"

It has been only a decade since "world order studies" has begun to be taken seriously as an academic focus for teaching and research, and throughout this period, its acceptance has been fitful and controversial. As is often the case, this resistance is expressive of a variety of concerns, some acknowledged, some not.

One characteristic ground of opposition maintains that a world order focus invariably politicizes the learning process, substituting advocacy for analysis. In an uphill battle, now largely won, academics promoting a world order outlook have sought to display analytic credentials within a framework of explicit values. Those who propose a world order outlook essentially argue that an element of study appropriate to higher education involves understanding the place of values in the political process. They conclude that anyone who insists that objectivity exclude normative considerations endorses, wittingly or not, the status quo. In other words, an academic inquiry can never be value neutral.

Another major criticism of the world order approach questions its concentration upon an alleged commitment to world government as a solution for the problems of international life.[2] In this context, critics consistently underscore "the utopian" and sterile character of the position, arguing that its very unattainability makes the serious assessment of such a political solution a waste of time. This sort of criticism implicitly restricts "valuable" inquiry to those possibilities for political development that seem relevant to the conventional wisdom on what it is plausible to expect. At times these critics combine their dismissal of world order as something fanciful with the opposite allegation that its very outlook is pernicious, as it exchanges the diverse character of relatively autonomous, sovereign states for the brave new world of global tyranny. This particular argument against world order studies is explicitly ideological, but as most current world order specialists point out, the target is largely misconceived. Even among those world order specialists who favor "system-change," most are wary by now of centralizing solutions of the sort implied by world government and increasingly favor designs for political futures that stress the potential for decentralizing shifts in the arrangements of power. It is probably a greater mistake these days to associate world order studies with world federalism than with libertarian anarchism, or more aptly, both of these opposed political traditions should be treated as part of the ideological heritage of the world order focus. The world order approach, in fact, does not simply imply a specific configuration of political power and authority at the global level, but moves toward a comparative systems approach on such matters. Alternative political systems discernible at earlier stages in international history are, in effect, compared both with the present world order system built around sovereign states and with a variety of possible future systems, which range from highly centralized images of a world state, to federal and nonfederal conceptions of planetary governance, as well as to various regional conceptions. This comparison extends, also, to a variety of decentralizing images drawn from utopian writings and, in addition, to feudalist forms of organization, anarchist writing, communitarian socialism, and ethnic separatist movements.[3]

There is also a strong cultural criticism which, from a different perspective, rejects world order approaches for their naive rationalism, including their conviction that solutions can be found by intellectuals for the dangers and tragedies of the world through a combination of analysis and good will.[4] The contention of these critics is that world order approaches are largely irrelevant because they generally proceed from an inadequate conception of human nature. Specifically, world order analysts are accused of overlooking the role of unconscious motivation in human behavior. This deficiency, in turn, is connected with the widespread failure in world order literature to appreciate the role of evil and irrationality in all spheres of human affairs, including politics. An adequate appreciation of human nature would either clarify the notion that "peace and justice" are unattainable because of the follies of human nature or induce one to base transformative hopes on the expectation that the deepest levels of human motivation can be influenced. In either event, the political/economic preoccupations of world order studies are scorned as virtually irrelevant. Such a foreshortened sense of human character can yield either a pessimistic or an optimistic judgment about the future. While the pessimistic view tends to reinforce standard approaches to international relations based on "balance of power," "deterrence," and "prudence," the optimistic view is hopeful about the long-range religious and cultural potentialities of human society.[5]

World order studies have been vulnerable to this antirationalist line of criticism. Though the rest of the other social sciences share this vulnerability, such criticism is more telling in this global context, where analysis often emphasizes the necessity for drastic change. It is impossible to fashion a convincing account of change unless coupled with an adequate conception of human nature. It is for this reason that world order theorizing has, in my view, been unsuccessful in its attempts to explain how to proceed from here to there or, to employ more recent terminology, in its attempts to solve "the transition problem." In their defense, it is true that system-changing world order approaches are becoming more aware of the relevance that culture, myth, religion, and value-change have for their central political preoccupation with alternative political futures.[6]

A different threat to world order perspectives than that posed by critics, but by no means a trivial one, arose from their superficial and very short-lived adoption as a mainstream prescription for foreign policy analysis by political leaders in the United States. At the time of his inauguration, President Jimmy Carter addressed these words to foreign nations: "I want to assure you that the relations of the United States with the other countries and peoples of the world will be guided during my own Administration by our desire to shape a world order that is more responsive to human aspirations. The United States will meet its obligation to help create a stable, just, and peaceful world order."[7] On the one hand, the espousal of "world order politics" by the President of the United States was certainly an acknowledgment of the need to carry out some fundamental international adjustments within a normative framework of widely shared values.[8] At the same time, however, the espousal, unaccompanied by modifications of traditional statecraft, reinforced the view that world order thinking is mere verbiage and, even worse, an expression of the ideological insistence of the status quo that "orderly" procedures of adjustment can satisfy claims for change in international life. For this reason, some of those who believe change will occur only as a consequence of a militant social movement from below now regard the rhetoric of world order studies as a contemporary opiate of the people, functioning virtually as an imperial ideology designed to quiet down emergent discontent. The extent to which world order studies has been generated from the United States should also be noted, since it is perceived elsewhere as a managerial "fix" for global issues that merely represents a new geopolitical strategy for perpetuating global economic, political and cultural hegemony. Such an attempt by those at a geopolitical pinnacle to define the terms of conflict and resolution is correctly regarded with suspicion by those in more dependent positions.

Along related lines is the concern that world order advocacy by statesmen and their intellectual cadre falsely reassures the public about the capacity of elites and official institutions to meet the new agenda of international challenges. It is up to the world order studies movement to distance itself from official rhetoric in order to avoid getting swallowed up by it. Such avoidance is not easy, and it is always tempting to assuage ivory tower insecurities by invoking supportive statements by "hard-headed," practical men and women of affairs to demonstrate the acceptance and acceptability of world order concerns. In the last analysis, I think, we must acknowledge a definite split within the ranks of world order studies between system-maintainers, who seek to appropriate world order rhetoric for marginal reforms instituted by official elites, and system-transformers, who seek a populist style involving militant challenge to carry forward their demands for fundamental reform.

A related objection to the world order approach is associated with its apparent emphasis upon order as the missing ingredient in an acceptable world system. The word *order* has repressive connotations, which are evident in the phrase *law and order,* and it implies that strict enforcement of legal rules is the essence of world order. Such a static image is especially inappropriate for those whose perspective advocates a process of transformation to realize minimum goals. Furthermore, the emphasis on "order" is deceptive. In theory, "world order" could be treated as being satisfied by any stable arrangement of parts, including tyrannical and exploitative arrangements. Some academics, therefore, are abandoning the earlier label "world order" in favor of more *dynamic* and *value-laden* terminology such as "a movement for a just world," "just world order," or "human world order." In contrast, however, those who are primarily concerned with stability and managerial efficiency view the central imagery of "order" as an asset, which partly accounts for its acceptability to some political leaders. As is always the case, then, the battle over definitions hides a deeper battle over substance.

A final question concerning perspective reflects the division between idealists and realists on the agenda of global reform. Critics of world order studies mount both lines of attack, accusing world order thinking of being simultaneously "idealistic" in its conception of human potentiality, even as it is "morbid" in its prophetic insistence on mounting dangers of planetary catastrophe. Two responses in the world order literature can be noted. System-maintaining world order approaches deny the charge, rejecting apocalyptic diagnosis and making clear their commitment to gradually improving the quality of order in world affairs over time, without undermining current modes of stability. System transformers tend to accept the charge with the proviso of claiming for their position the imprimatur of "realism," arguing that unless positive potentialities for global reform are quickly realized, international trends and risks will produce the decline and, eventually, the collapse of civilization. Their faith in positive potentialities may not be very strong, but their perceptions do lead them to the conclusion that it is necessary to try by all available means to act as though a peaceful and just world is, indeed, a possibility and that without it we will face the virtual inevitability of gruesome apocalypse.

It is possible, of course, to downplay this upsurge of concern with the future of the world. Perhaps, as some claim, this concern is nothing more durable than an elaborate psychic preparation for the advent of the year 2000. After all, as the year 1000 approached, there was, we know, much speculation about the end of the world, as well as about its imminent salvation. It is probably beneficial to condition world order inquiry by such realizations, to encourage greater modesty of tone and humility of expectation. Part of what has given "world order" a bad name in some circles is undoubtedly its tendency to cry "wolf" about the immediate future in order to get a hearing by the shrill insistence that the human race has only a decade or so to set things straight. Such literal warnings, even if credible, tend to dull our capacities for response. I think this lesson is being slowly learned and that world order projects and studies, as a consequence, are increasingly aware that transformation of the world system presupposes a long, ambiguous struggle dependent on the emergence of a robust global social movement.[9] There is no "quick fix" in the offing, only the slim hope that there will be enough time for a global learning process among elites and masses to evolve in such a way as to encourage a series of political adjustments in the world that are predominantly humane and ecologically sensitive.

TOWARD A DEFINITION OF WORLD ORDER

Reporting on a widely publicized symposium held at Bellagio, Italy, in 1965 and devoted to "Conditions of World Order," Stanley Hoffmann notes that discussion was muddled by conference participants who tended to use *world order* in distinct, inconsistent ways. Hoffmann praises the conference chairman, Raymond Aron, for providing "the composers with a key for their symphony" first by discerning five possible meanings for the term "world order" and then by selecting one of these as the basis for further discussion. According to Hoffmann, these five meanings were distinguished as follows:

Two of the meanings were purely descriptive: order as any arrangement of reality, order as the relations between the parts. Two were analytical—partly descriptive, partly normative: order as the minimum conditions for existence, order as the minimum conditions for coexistence. The fifth conception was purely normative: order as the conditions for the good life.[10]

Aron then proposed that the conferees adopt the fourth variant and concentrate their discussion ". . . under what conditions would men (divided in so many ways) be able not merely to avoid destruction, but to live together relatively well in one planet."[11]

A procedure along these lines also means that the frame of reality is the political experience of the planet as a whole (i.e., the world), constituted by states as principal actors, and shaped both by the character and diversity of domestic structures of authority, as well as by a variety of transnational actors and forces.

More recently, Hedley Bull has articulated, with greater precision and elegance, a similar conception of world order: "By world order I mean those patterns or dispositions of human activity that sustain the elementary or primary goals of social life among mankind as a whole."[12] Such a position acknowledges the fact that a range of ordering options exists to determine how world order might be achieved, but supports the primacy of the state in relation to individuals and the state system in relation to collectivities. Bull draws a sharp distinction between the role of governments as the principal source of domestic order and the more primitive forms of order operative in what he regards as the anarchical setting of international society, "anarchical" being conceived in the technical sense as the absence of government.

Bull maintains that the achievement of order can be assessed only by reference to the realization of "elementary goals of social life," identified as common interests of all peoples:

Thus the facts of human vulnerability to violence and proneness to resort to it lead men to the sense of common interests in restricting violence. The fact of human interdependence for material needs leads them to perceive a common interest in ensuring respect for agreements. The facts of limited abundance and limited human altruism lead them to recognize common interests in stabilizing possession.[13]

Rules as incorporated in international law are generally regarded as beneficial for the clarification and preservation of these common interests, but are not effective in relation to fundamental security for the state. For international society, which lacks governmental capacities and is composed of members with a weak perception of common interests, order is obtained principally by such mechanisms as "balance of power" and "deterrence," encouraging mutual restraint in a manner compatible with the perceived separate interests of governments: "Within international society, however, as in other societies, order is the consequence not merely of contingent facts such as this (i.e., balance of power), but of a sense of common interests in the elementary goals of social life; rules prescribing behavior that sustain these goals; and institutions that help to make these rules effective."[14]

Bull regards "order" of this character as valuable in itself and as "the condition of the realization of other values," including the pursuit of justice.[15] At the same time, however, Bull regards the demand for justice as relating, in a profound way, to the search for acceptable forms of order. If the parties can agree on just results, or if a consensus on an international level can be achieved, then order and justice can be reconciled. It is when there is disagreement among states about the character of just results that the more fundamental ordering goals of international society on which agreement can be presumed suggest, to Bull, the need to accord priority to considerations of order as against the claims of justice.

Finally, Bull considers alternatives to the present reliance on the state system for the achievement of order and justice on a global scale. He concludes that the state system is durable, despite its defects and vulnerabilities, and superior to any alternative conception of world order that can be presented plausibly at this stage of human experience.[16]

A feature of this Aron-Bull approach to world order, the dominant orientation in academic and governmental circles, is its hostility toward "normative" conceptions of world order that stress the pursuit of valued goals as the object of inquiry. Aron calls for the abandonment of such an emphasis because it only leads "to platitudes and to an acrimonious reproduction of the conflicts of values that exist in the world."[17] Bull acknowledges the appropriateness of studying the pursuit of justice as seriously as the pursuit of order, but he believes it is a "corrupting" trait to introduce policy recommendations into the study of world political activity: "The search for conclusions that can be presented as 'solutions' or 'practical advice' is a corrupting element in the contemporary study of world politics, which properly understood is an intellectual activity and not a practical one. Such conclusions are advanced less because there is any solid basis for them than because there is a demand for them which it is profitable to satisfy."[18] Bull closes his book and concludes his argument with this admonition: "The fact is that while there is a great desire to know what the future of world politics will bring, and also to know how we should behave in it, we have to grope about in the dark with respect to the one as much as with respect to the other. It is better to recognize that we are in darkness than to pretend that we can see the light."[19]

The Bellagio meeting also affirmed Hedley Bull's muddling-through-with-the-state-system view of the future both as a prediction and prescription. This approach is aptly treated as a world order approach because it is concerned with the conditions for a satisfactory persistence of the present state system, as well as with comprehending its operating dynamics. Its normative contribution is to make these conditions explicit so that policy-makers and power-wielders will be more likely to perform in an intelligent manner. At the core of this approach is a neo-Machiavellian type of advice to the prince—in effect a counsel of prudence given a spirit of urgency in an era of global politics beset by the pervasive menace of nuclear warfare.

Another quite different approach to world order is a curious blend of ideology and behavioral methodology. The ideology associates world order with degrees of centralizing political authority, while the behavioral methodology measures this tendency by quantifiable elements of international politics. Martin Rochester structures his inquiry by taking note of what he calls "[a] favorite pastime of observers of international relations . . . to speculate on how much progress has been made toward 'world order' and how much progress can be expected in the future." Rochester contends that this speculation has concentrated on "the evolving role of international institutions" and has tended to be flawed by being "normative, impressionistic, and unstructured."[20] His conception of world order might be reduced to the question of how much measurable institutionalization of behavior occurs in international life. This focus leads Rochester to undertake such empirical exercises as the comparison of the roles of the Permanent Court of International Justice, operative between World War I and World War II, and the International Court of Justice, operative since World War II in order to assess whether recourse to international judicial settlement procedures is rising or falling.[21] The central tenet of Rochester's view is that if states are using these judicial facilities more frequently and regularly to resolve their disputes with one another, then it is proper to conclude that a growth of world order has taken place. Political context is ignored. Only the criteria of institutional roles, which include salience and resources, are discussed; there is no mention of the intervening experiences of ideological rivalry between East and West, of decolonialization, or of technological innovation that may affect whether or not institutional facilities will be used and for what.

Such a conception of world order is, of course, absurdly restricted. It implicitly endorses governmental solutions of a supranational character and identifies the growth of world order, presumably something beneficial, with the elaboration of international institutional capabilities. This approach is an empirically oriented extension of world government thinking about world order, as it confines alternatives for the state system to a single model of political development on the global level. Such an emphasis also takes into account the rise of functional pressures, which tend to foster increased international cooperation. It implicitly rejects the earlier view regarding a constitutional convention by government actors as a necessary step in the process of building a consummated system of world order. Another implication of Rochester's viewpoint is that the state system *per se*, however well it keeps order in Bull's sense, is nevertheless inherently incapable of qualifying as a world order system because it is insufficiently centralized. As far as Rochester is concerned, world order is dynamic in a structural and not in a normative sense since it exclusively involves the movement toward institutional centralization. Except by implication, we have no perception that a centralized system will be more efficient in realizing a set of world order values than the current system.

A more sophisticated extension of this perspective, but one that avoids creating normative misimpressions that might derive from the explicit adoption of world order terminology, is the currently fashionable tendency of international relations specialists to study "interdependence." "Measurable interdependence," indeed, makes an effort to combine the objectivity of analysis with behavioral criteria of assessment (that which can be quantified), while not remaining oblivious to changes in behavioral features of international life, which include the rise of transnational phenomena of many kinds.[22] Such an emphasis is transactional and does not view politics from the outlook of "the world," nor does it assess performance of global political systems from the standpoint of normative criteria, or values.

Admittedly, normative approaches to world order usually proceed from specific agendas of concerns and on the basis of a definite program of goals. Saul Mendlovitz and Thomas Weiss define world order as "the study of international relations and world affairs that focuses on the manner in which mankind can significantly reduce the likelihood of international violence and create minimally acceptable conditions of worldwide economic well-being, social justice, ecological stability, and participation in decision-making processes. In short, a student of world order seeks to achieve and maintain a warless and more just world to improve the quality of human life." Implicit in such a view of world order is the quest for a new system of power/ authority. It is not surprising, therefore, that Mendlovitz and Weiss assert that "[a] world order inquiry involves the use of relevant utopias culminating in the statement of the investigator's preferred world."[23] From this conviction that a new system of world order is necessary, there follows the generalized depreciation of the state as an instrument of order or justice. Nonstate actors, ranging from international institutions to multinational corporations, consequently, are looked upon with varying degrees of favor and a concerted effort is made to depict a plausible, minimally violent path of transition to the model or utopia. In the words of Mendlovitz and Weiss, "a concrete behavioral statement of transformation from the present system and to the projected model is necessary."[24]

Gerald and Patricia Mische believe that two kinds of world order must be distinguished on normative grounds. The first, which they reject, "is the order that presently exists on the planet, an order of dependent relationships between allegedly independent sovereignties that are dominated by raw economic, monetary and military power rather than by law." The second, which they endorse, "envisions an order of relationships determined by law and based on universal social justice for all persons; an order whose operative principles embrace the centrality and sovereignty of the human person." In contrast to Bull, the Misches do not regard the state as a minimally adequate agent for the realization of human dignity, and world order in their normative sense means a diminished role for the state and an end of the state system. Their vision of the future is specified in ideological terms as involving a mix of functional centralization ("e.g. peace-keeping, transnational ecological protection, regulation of world trade and of an integrated monetary system, regulation of the uses of the seas, and some global taxation")[25] and political decentralization through the dismantling of the national security apparatus at the state level. Here again the idea of world order is associated with a relevant utopia whose attainability by education and struggle is affirmed as the sole alternative to catastrophic global destiny.

Unlike the analytical approaches, a normative approach necessarily includes tendering practical advice for activists. It seeks to shape and inspire a world movement for systemic change and is not content with solely understanding how the present system operates. At the same time, however, the search for an integrated vision of a preferred future specified in terms that suggest attainability within a reasonable time period (combining considerations of utopian quest and political feasibility) does not necessarily prejudge the character of a solution. So long as the values posited can be realized, any structure will do, although the implications seem to call for some buildup of international institutions in a deliberate fashion to handle certain activities now administered at the state level.

My approach to world order combines analytic, empirical, ideological, and normative concerns in its definition. Such a conception of world order involves studying the extent to which a given past, present, or future arrangement of power and authority is able to realize a set of human values that are affirmed as beneficial for all people and apply to the whole world and that have some objectivity by their connection with a conception of basic human needs, as required for the healthy development of the human person. World order values can be specified in a variety of testable and semitestable ways. Past and future systems can be compared with the present system to the extent that relative value realization can be determined in measurable terms. The role of the state and other international actors is left open, as are the contours of a satisfactory future world order system.

This definition of world order does not assume an ideological stance, as such, because in this sense it is an instance of an analytic definition. Underlying this assessment of the historical situation, however, is also the conviction that the state system is not capable of a satisfactory performance in relation to the values set forth, and that statism under current world conditions poses excessive risks of thermonuclear, ecological, economic, and cultural deterioration, and even of collapse. For these reasons, my approach to world order does entail the construction of relevant utopias, as well as the depiction of transitional paths. However, the role of the state, as distinct from the state system, is uncertain in a transformed system. This conception is also a normative one to the extent that it advocates reliance on "central guidance" mechanisms in response to the functional imperatives of interdependence and decentralization in response to ethical imperatives of humane patterns of governance. My relevant utopia, as such, is similar in its broad conception to the one outlined by Gerald and Patricia Mische, although it considers the domestic arenas of states as the most critical context for world order transformation and is correspondingly skeptical of direct approaches to global reform by way of strengthening the United Nations and the like.

WORLD ORDER STRATEGIES

There are various strategies for achieving world order. These strategies can be most easily understood and appraised if classified in relation to the existing system of world order based on the interaction of sovereign states of unequal capabilities. The scheme of classification adopted here uses the existing system as a point of reference, identifying deviations by degrees of value-realization. Four main strategies can be discerned at the present time:

  —system-maintaining strategies,
  —system-diminishing strategies,
  —system-enhancing strategies, and
  —system-transforming strategies.

Reality, of course, does not divide as neatly as our analytic categories suggest, and a given undertaking may partake of more than one of these outlooks on global reform. What is emphasized here, however, is that attitudes toward change, with respect to the depth and extent of global reform, are the essence of the world order endeavor. And furthermore, world order regression is possible; that is, the classically conceived state system is not, even in the nuclear age, the worst of all possible systems.

System-Maintaining Strategies

Those who control the dominant institutions of government and business generally seek above all else to discover the means to sustain the system. Their search is for stability under constantly changing conditions. The intellectual outlook of system-maintaining strategies to world order is closely asociated with sustaining particular positions and privileges in the status quo. The Trilateral Commission, founded in 1973, at the initiative of David Rockefeller, epitomized a system-maintaining perspective on world order.[26] The Trilateral Commission was formed as a private initiative designed to link elites in North America, Western Europe, and Japan, especially to encourage forming a consensus on issues of international economic policy. A surprising number of its American members and consultants moved into positions of policy-making prominence in the Carter Administration.[27] That is, there is an easy flow between playing official roles in policy formation within the existing system and the kind of image of global reform associated with Trilateral thinking. Zbigniew Brzezinski's shift from intellectual mentor of the Trilateral Commission to President Carter's National Security Advisor is an illustrative instance. The essence of Brzezinski's outlook was that world economic arrangements shaped after World War II served well until recently, but now require recasting through cooperative action on the part of the governments of the advanced industrial countries, i.e., the Trilateral sector of the world economy. With postwar European reconstruction having been completed, with colonialism fully destroyed, and with the rise in prominence of OPEC, a new, more pluralistic situation requires more pluralistic economic arrangements to encourage a healthy economic dynamic. This interpretation of world requirements led to a Trilateral emphasis on trade, money, international financial institutions, and energy policy.[28] For the conceptual frame of world order analysis, two characteristics of this perspective are noteworthy:

    —first, the system-maintaining propensities of principal governments and elites;

—second, the priority attached to coordination of economic policy as the basis for an improved world order.

A system-maintaining perspective tends to emphasize the strengthening and further creation of specialized international institutions that handle economic issues. Daniel Bell, in a statement typical of this outlook, writes the following: "The problem, then, is to design effective international instruments—in the monetary, commodity, trade, and technology areas—to effect the necessary transitions to a new international division of labor that can provide for economic and, perhaps, political stability."[29] An interesting feature of system-maintaining strategies to world order is the stress placed upon *technical* solutions and the corresponding disregard of the political or the normative. One searches virtually in vain through the writings of the Trilateral Commission and kindred perspectives for positive proposals on the United Nations or analyses of the dangers of warfare and ecological decay.

The dominant preoccupation of Trilateralists and their allies is to keep the world economy growing in the face of three sets of threats: rivalry with communist powers, the challenge from the Third World, and the deepening competition among the Trilateral countries themselves. On the level of prescription this assessment of the world scene leads to military preparedness in relation to Communism and to superficial concessions and accommodationism in relation to the Third World.[30] Internal conflict within the Trilateral sector is most difficult to handle, partly because it creates tension between the parties due to the competitive pressures that are escalating in a period of economic stagnation, inflation, and unemployment, and partly because such tension imperils a presumed geopolitical partnership on matters of security, a partnership reinforced by a shared outlook on cultural and many other global policy issues.[31] The Trilateralists seek to avoid a repetition of trade wars by reconciling nationalistic insistence on protectionism with internationalistic pressure for openness. This appreciation of danger induces an intense desire to tinker with the world order system to avoid further deteriorations. Among the elements of the situation that provoke concern are the heavy debt burden being borne by a variety of Third World and European countries, an intensifying struggle for export outlets as productive capacity seems to grow beyond domestic demand in a whole series of product areas, an awareness that OPEC leverage on oil prices and supply makes industrial countries vulnerable, and a related awareness that new sources of energy are both necessary and problematic. The cumulative effect is to create a fear that the world economic system could unravel, producing grave domestic crises and heightening international tensions in alarming respects. In this regard, the Trilateral Commission in the early phases of its operations sought to moderate these dire prospects by divising mutually acceptable arrangements that can "manage interdependence." It should be noted that economic nationalism eroded, from the outset, the capacity of the Carter presidency to implement the trilateral approach and that post-Carter trilateralism has accommodated the rightward swing in American political leadership.

Another quite different dimension of trilateral thinking explores the conviction that international tensions reflect excesses of democratic patterns of governance that produce behavior inconsistent with elite interests; for instance, protectionist demands by certain labor and business interests to safeguard jobs and profits in noncompetitive sectors of domestic industry. It is not surprising, therefore, to discover trilateral sponsorship of studies lamenting the "excesses" of democracy and affirming the importance of inculcating public respect for structures of authority.[32] Among these excesses in democratic societies is the alleged tendency of intellectuals to withdraw their commitment to the legitimacy of the present order.[33]

System-maintaining strategies to world order can be associated with governing groups and their supporting elites in the most powerful states. The organizing objective is to assure efficient economic performance, as measured by economic growth and calculated by GNP increases. Whatever means facilitate such growth are positive and should be encouraged; whatever means interfere, even if it is the exercise of democratic rights themselves, are negative and should be curtailed. The international distribution of power, wealth, and prestige is relevant only to the extent that it poses managerial challenges. The state system, with its reliance on war as the ultimate arbiter of conflict, is accepted as inevitable, and the ecological dangers engendered by industrial technology are downplayed.

System-Diminishing Strategies

It is also possible to regress from system-maintenance. In my judgment, the Reagan presidency demonstrates that such a possibility is more than theoretical. Let it be observed, in passing, that governmental leadership other than that of the United States can play system-diminishing roles in world political affairs—more particularly, the Soviet Union. In fact, in the last several years the United States and the Soviet Union have been reinforcing each other's regressive potential with a net deterioration in the quality of world order as a consequence.

Conceptually, system-diminishing strategies are identified by their failure to maintain current values. Increased arms spending, uses of military force, avoidance of international negotiations, deprecation of international institutions, and reduction of support for assistance to the Third World are indicative of system-diminishing strategies.

Such strategies have been evident in Reagan's foreign policy. The net result has been increased international tensions, including rising fears of nuclear war, and a total repudiation of any serious effort to promote world order values within the existing framework of sovereign states.

Of course, no political leadership associates its policies with a deliberate project of "system diminishing." This label is derived from a judgment about the connection between prescribed policies and world order values. The justification for system-diminishing strategies has to do with the perceived failure of system maintenance and the ideological unacceptability of system reform or system transformation. In essence, system-diminishing strategies derive their inspiration and appeal from the past, together with the claim that the successes of the past can be repeated in the present if we recover our older ways of acting. Reagan's geopolitics, in this sense, is an expression of nostalgia for an earlier, simpler period of international relations.

The substance of system-diminishing strategies has to do with placing confidence in the ordering effects of nationalistic competition in arms. Hence, danger is associated with the strength and motives of potential enemies. A new confidence is bestowed upon military prowess and the political will to fight on behalf of national economic and ideological interests.

System-diminishing strategies reject internationalistic perspectives and techniques. In this regard, even alliances are placed under strain. The will of the strong state is the primary basis of order (or disorder) in the world. Such an orientation seems unlikely to succeed even in the short run. The world is too complexly integrated and even the most powerful states are too vulnerable to developments elsewhere to forgo supranational management. Security cannot be achieved by arms racing, nor can economic and political stability be long sustained in such a context.

Because the pressures for system transformation are growing

great, system-diminishing strategies are to be expected. Drastic global reforms threaten entrenched interests and are unsettling to contemplate. Modest adjustments proposed by system maintenance and system reform seem unconvincing, given the magnitude of the world order challenge. Only system-diminishing strategies seem both sufficiently coherent and consistent with entrenched interests to be responsive to the deepening world order crisis. However, such responsiveness is deceptive, achieved at the cost of acknowledging the integrative effects of modern trends in technological innovation, world economic life, ecological hazard, and political consciousness. For these reasons, despite their imagined attractiveness, I expect that system-diminishing strategies will be discredited by the end of the decade, although they may retain their influence, even in currently democratic societies, through the machinations of increasingly imperiled elites. That is, if system-diminishing strategies manage to avoid provoking catastrophe, then they are likely to be repudiated by public opinion, unless democratic sentiments are themselves overruled.

System-Reforming Strategies

A wider range of initiatives can be associated with a system-reform focus. The critical feature, in this instance, is the realization that structural modifications in a wide series of subject matters will be required to satisfy both interests and values, but that these modifications are not so fundamental as to call into question the basic ordering of international relations around the predominant role of the sovereign state. The 1980's Project of the Council on Foreign Relations is a good example of a system-reforming perspective. Richard Ullman, the director of the undertaking, writes: "The 1980's Project is based upon the belief that serious effort and integrated forethought can contribute—indeed, are indispensable—to progress in the next decade toward a more humane, peaceful, productive, and just world."[34] The pretension of the 1980's Project, despite its sponsorship by the elite Council on Foreign Relations, is to study the future in a universalistic spirit of ideological neutrality and policy pluralism; in Ullman's words: "It is not the Project's purpose to arrive at a single or exclusive set of goals. Nor does it focus upon the foreign policy or national interests of the United States alone. Instead, it seeks to identify the goals that are compatible with the perceived interests of most states, despite differences in ideology and in level of economic development."[35]

Another feature of reformist thinking is a concentration of speculative analysis on a period long enough to be independent of current contexts of choice, but short enough to engage the concerns of policy-makers. Thus, the 1980's Project starts from the premise "that many of the assumptions, policies, and constitutions that have characterized international relations during the past 30 years are inadequate to the demands of today and foreseeable demands of the period between now and 1990 or so."[36] It is interesting to note that the treatment of time, the historical as well as the futuristic aspect, is balanced in such a way as to encompass the span of past experience (thirty years) as the basis for thinking ahead.

The 1980's Project has definitely broken new ground in its attempt to construct an integrated picture of policy choices for the years ahead. It also has opted for a global, as distinct from a nationalistic, perspective, although the American identity of the Council on Foreign Relations, as well as of the main body of participants and their early proposals make it plain that the American auspices and orientation are limiting characteristics. The globalistic aspiration, nevertheless, is significant in itself and expresses some awareness that the expanding planetary agenda must be handled in as cooperative a manner as possible. Furthermore, the 1980's Project is normative in a system-reforming manner, acknowledging the need for normative adjustments in international relations, but failing to question the basic structure of a state-centric system. The ambitious scale and august sponsorship of the 1980's Project is, in any event, a revealing acknowledgment that world order approaches in the basic sense of normative, futurist, and structural studies of the global situation are relevant even for those whose orientation is primarily managerial.

System-Transforming Strategies

The distinguishing characteristic of system-transforming strategies to world order is the acceptance of the need to transform the structure of international relations by diminishing the role of sovereign states in some decisive respects. Even more so than with advocates of system reform, those who propose system transformation seek an integrated strategy of change guided by certain values and aiming toward the construction of a coherent new system of world order.

The World Order Models Project (WOMP) of the Institute for World Order provides an example of a system-transforming perspective. WOMP, initiated in 1968, is constituted by groups of scholars associated with the principal regions and/or actors of the world (Latin

America, Africa, Japan, Europe, Soviet Union, India, United States, with indirect representation for China and for the network of transnational actors). The WOMP group, through periodic interaction, evolved a framework of world order values that were general enough to command consensus within its membership and yet distinctive enough to establish an identity. The values agreed upon as suitable criteria for world order appraisal were minimization of collective violence; maximization of economic well-being; maximization of social and political justice; and maximization of ecological quality.[37] There was discussion at WOMP meetings as to whether the goal of democratizing participation in authority structures within states and in the world system should be emphasized by adopting a fifth value of participation or by incorporating it in the interpretation of the first four values. In essence, the issue was left unresolved with each author free to proceed as he or she wished. It was also understood that the affirmation of a series of values could not be fully reconciled with the concrete realities of social choice where value tradeoffs must generally be made. The varying ways of ranking priorities brought great diversity to the substance of WOMP manuscripts despite agreement on a common framework of inquiry. This diversity is most evident in the proposals made for global reform, especially the contours of a transformed world order system that could be projected as attainable by the end of the century.

In the first phase of WOMP, each distinct group, usually represented by one or two of its members, evolved its own version of "a relevant utopia." This took the form of a comprehensive schema for a positive rearrangement of power, wealth, and prestige on a world scale, together with a transition plan for reaching the promised land. WOMP has published a series of books that explore and analyze these diverse perspectives on forms of drastic global reform that seem desirable and attainable by the 1990's.[38]

Despite its largely American auspices, WOMP has achieved a transnational context for its work. Having engendered diverse conceptions of world order solutions attainable, though not assured, by the 1900's, WOMP is now embarking on a series of continuation studies. First of all, an attempt is being made to link the present to the future through a group of studies of global policy issues that are currently engaging the attention of governmental leaders and public opinion. These studies, essentially, are centered around nonproliferation and nuclear power; human rights; satisfying basic needs; and the new international economic order. The objective of these studies is to demonstrate, in the realistic terms of policy discourse, the distinctiveness of an approach developed from the WOMP set of world order values. An additional goal is to clarify these values in ways specific and controversial enough to avoid the danger of allowing world order advocacy to degenerate into a series of pious platitudes, endorsed by all because of their apolitical character and respected by no one struggling for change because of their failure to be defined in relation to ongoing struggles. To help inspire a movement for global reform WOMP must find ways to mobilize a variety of groups working in widely disparate arenas for peace and justice, often in opposition to official state policy.

The second line of WOMP's current work is concentrated on building a more ambitious transnational consensus on the direction and shape of an acceptable world order solution among those who endorse its values and accept the need for system change as a prerequisite to their realization. The early work of WOMP restricted itself to the agreed values framework and the conceptual commitment to consider system change, to depict a relevant utopia, and to devise a transition strategy. To proceed from this agreed methodology to an agreement on substance may prove difficult, even impossible, given the diversity of outlooks represesnted in WOMP, but even a partial failure will be illuminating to the extent that it discloses the limits of consensual approaches to consciousness-raising on a transnational basis at this time.

WOMP as a system-changing perspective also takes a political stance that is more populist than is characteristic of system maintainers or system reformers. It seeks to inspire, or to take part in, a movement for a just world order, and it regards most political elites, especially those with a stake in the existing system, as likely to resist shifts in values, behavior, and structures. This transnational group of scholars, therefore, is committed to the search for peace with equity and seeks to evolve a globalist ideology that draws on liberalism to check abuses of state power in the relations between governments and people, on socialism to depict a humane set of economic relationships based on societal well-being, on ecological humanism to reorient the relations between human activity and nature, and on global modeling to put complex interactions of societal processes at various levels of organization into a dynamic, disciplined framework. It may be too early in the difficult work of constructing a world order ideology to give a single, overarching label to this enterprise.

The real test of the WOMP perspective will be whether or not it can take roots in the imaginings, cravings, and activities of peoples diversely situated in various parts of the world. The quasi-determinist claim that makes WOMP more predictive than prescriptive is its assurance that a global integrative process is proceeding in any event. Only the normative content of this integrative destiny can be influenced by human action. We can ask over what time span, with what structure, for whose sake, and by reference to what values, norms, and guidelines this global integrative process is likely to follow under a series of alternative patterns of development. WOMP seeks to shift these historical developments away from what appears to be their technetronic and political destiny—a mixture of tyrannical structures and catastrophic occurrence on the plane of conflict and ecological decay. Instead, WOMP seeks to promote an ethical and ecological flourishing in a political setting that joins solidarity of sentiment to diffusion of structure, power, wealth, and authority.

AT THE FRONTIERS

Posing "The Political Question"

The rhetoric and inquiry associated with world order are evolving in response to new perceptions of what is needed to make the world work; that is, to evolve, as a dynamic political system, in a manner consistent with a general attitude of hope about the future. System-maintaining and system-diminishing modes tend to be traditional in their inquiries, as their major goal is to provide policy guidance for exceedingly short time intervals. These modes either identify bargaining space capable of damping down intergovernmental conflicts, especially those conflicts that bear on global economic issues, or call for renewed efforts to prevail over rivals.

System-reforming modes, which are somewhat bolder in scale and ambitious in scope, seek major adjustments to reflect shifts in value/power configurations, adjustments that may require decades for actualization. The distinguishing substantive feature of these approaches is their assumption that the political framework of world order is durable. In more concrete terms this means that a vision of reform that is expected to unfold in conformity with a distribution of power and authority to territorially sovereign governments. Any changes in relative circumstances within or between these governments would have to evolve without benefit of a new pattern of relations among nonstate actors. Most normative modeling initiatives fall into the system-reforming category of world order approaches. Sometimes these models can be used to persuade elites that they could attain their proclaimed goals (for instance, full employment and better distribution of income) by altering their priorities (for instance, investment patterns and tax structure). At other times these models can be useful to expose the failure of the political leadership to carry out the policies it purports to favor (for example, alleviation of poverty at home and abroad).[39] Most model-building exercises seek to increase their influence by proceeding as rigorously as possible with empirical data, computerized modes of analysis, and policy goals reinforced by numerical results. There is little doubt that such an approach may maximize its impact on prevailing political sensibilities and may even entrust a powerful weapon of persuasion to more progressively inclined individuals and groups in positions of control. The limits of this kind of approach to knowledge in the world order field are twofold: first, a foreshortening of inquiry through the acceptance of a framework that seems outmoded and, second, a related failure to pose "the political question" of how to get a hearing for a position, no matter how persuasive its rationale, antithetical to the perceived interests of dominant elites.

System-transforming approaches may also suffer, as mentioned earlier, by a touchingly irrelevant belief that rational argument suffices because global reform is, essentially, a series of adjustments prompted by calculations of self-interest. The world federalist tradition, with its abiding faith in the inevitability of world government, is the most glaring case of a program of action that would become plausible only after decades of struggle, or possibly only after the breakdown of the existing structures of world order in a terrible, traumatic manner. The avoidance of "the political question" involves, even if unknowingly, accepting the legitimacy of the status quo. It also involves attributing to existing political leaders a potential willingness to make those changes necessary to protect the public interest. Such an expectation seems woefully naive. So long as the key elite clusters of the world are diversely situated in its hierarchy and are primarily responsive to particularized interests within their own society, rather than to the society as a whole, there is no chance that voluntary adjustment patterns can initiate and sustain a transition process on such a grand scale.

In the past, successful responses to "the political question" have presupposed an integrated vision of global reform. One modern instance is associated with the Marxist tradition, especially as developed by Lenin and Trotsky. Concrete acts of nonviolent militancy of the sort associated with the imaginative efforts of Martin Luther King, Jr. and Mahatma Gandhi can have a virtually unlimited mobilizing significance. These responses to the political question, adapted to concrete realities, inspired by charismatic leadership, and achieved by perseverance at the tactical level, only sought to accomplish change at the state level. More global projects, such as those espoused by Trotsky, Hitler, or Tanaka, failed at the enactment stage because antiglobal forces of resistance were too strong. It was unclear for sometime whether or not the Chinese Revolution was attempting a system-changing role; as of now, at least in this early post-Mao phase, it seems apparent that the vision of global liberation has been superseded by the drive for the full fruits of national autonomy and a quest for status within the existing framework of international society. Dreams of world conquest and unification have haunted Chinese and other political leaders over the centuries. To date no strategy has succeeded beyond that of ephemeral empire building; cycles of imperial growth and decay have been recurrent features of world historical processes, as depicted by such leading macrohistorians as Toynbee and Spengler.

In world order studies the political question is being posed in terms of "transition" to a new system. To date, however, the attempts have been unconvincing. There is little insight into a credible process of guided change, especially since nonviolence as an orientation is stressed, rationalist approaches are scorned, and a general appreciation prevails that politically entrenched elites will remain unreceptive. How does one encourage a positive transition process (i.e., toward preferred world order values) without merely sitting back and waiting (hoping?!) for the apocalypse?

Some flickers of a credible response to such questions are emergent at the frontier. The global interdependence phenomenon is gradually having an impact on political consciousness in a way that may have a real world order potential. Even those who endorse the system-reform track acknowledge this development as a "social fact" and attribute significance to it. In a recent article published in *Foreign Affairs*, for instance, its editor, William Bundy, noted the following: ". . . something beyond nationalism is slowly taking root in the world . . . the signs of a developing sense of common human destiny *are* present. Such a sense cannot substitute for a careful focus on the present and pressing problems that can only be met through nations. But world affairs will have a very dim future if this universal sentiment fails to show a steady increase from now on."[40] Along the same lines, Ervin Laszlo's major study for the Club of Rome on the goals of mankind gives a central place to "a solidarity revolution," as the basis for hope about the future.[41]

The translation of this latent possibility into politically effective form is, of course, an enormous challenge. At the same time, however, ideas about leverage in the transition process are beginning to take shape. The rise of ethnic nationalism, which poses serious challenges to the authority and legitimacy of sovereign states, is an example of militant politics with a global reform potential as yet unexplored. In addition, more systematic and longer range economic planning at the global level is beginning to occur, spurred on by fears of a slide into economic warfare and by the various vulnerabilities associated with the interdependence problematique. The functional issues of control and management, whether they are in relation to nuclear capabilities, energy supplies, ocean resources, or environmental protection are also building an awareness that "central guidance" of some structured kind is the only alternative to chaos, as is the realization that functional bargains (for example, law of the oceans and trade and monetary reform) cannot be reached or sustained unless they have an equity dimension built into them.

Technological innovations have made us all more aware of developments elsewhere. This awareness includes, at present, concern about the spread of authoritarian politics and repressive methods. Emphasis on human rights is a multifaceted response to this concern. Among its other motives and effects is its contribution to the formation of a global constituency of persons who complement their national citizenship with identities as planetary citizens. Such an expansion of identity and loyalty is critical for transition to a humane system of world order. In fact, acquisition of a planetary outlook and its embodiment in thought, feeling, and action help us grasp what system-transforming kinds of world order are about at this stage of international history. Multiple identity patterns are quite consistent with this imperative. Thus, one can add a planetary identity to national, class, ethnic, religious, local, and family identity; each can be vivid and intense. More and more nongovernmental transnational actors (Amnesty International, International Commission of Jurists, and International League of Human Rights) are becoming primary actors in this human rights sphere, manifesting their primary allegiance to world order values with no territorial constraints.

These factors establish a context where, at long last, a system-transforming movement and an ideology may become realistic possibilities. Such possibilities never existed earlier and almost inevitably made earlier system-transforming visions utopian. And the occasional claim that the utopia could be realized by good faith argumentation only made such positions seem ridiculous, compromising even their role as enchantments for the imagination. In recent years, however, I believe these new possibilities have offered system-transforming approaches a rich opportunity to take steps to found a movement, formulate an ideology, and build bridges between thought and action in the realm of global reform.

Enriching the Inquiry

The drift of scholarly inquiry has been in accord with the wider pattern of the division of labor. As a consequence, technical mastery and specialization have become increasingly valued. In intellectual terms, analysis has grown sharper, with the focus being placed on ever-smaller segments of reality, but at the cost of the progressive detachment of what is known and knowable from a sense of the whole. A unified feature of all kinds of world order thinking is to work against this tendency and to seek a holistic understanding of the world political system. Such an understanding is not yet assisted very much by modern social science. Oddly enough, it is from engineering approaches to complex decision-making and the modeling of whole systems that ways are being found to reconcile the scientific temper of the times with the widely acknowledged importance of comprehending planetary politics as a whole, or to study some national or regional segment to discern how the national or regional part fits into the whole; it would also be helpful to specify the impact which the whole has on the part.

In addition, some efforts are being made in system-transforming approaches to world order to examine the role of culture in generating a range of alternative political futures. Many students of world order look more to the humanities and to religious thought than to the social sciences for intellectual help. Macrohistory, the story of the rise and fall of religious movements, and cultural criticism, along with works of the literary imagination are valued resources of the world order scholar. In this regard, novels such as Ursula Le Guin's *The Dispossessed* and Doris Lessing's *Briefing for a Descent into Hell* and *The Memoirs of a Survivor* are world order "texts" in the quite literal sense of being used in courses. Such works appear to transmit a better overall interpretation of what is happening to erode earlier systems of order and what kinds of future alternatives there are than is derived from studying facts, trends, and proposals of a more traditional reforming intellectual variety. In effect, world order studies needs the synthetic discipline of the novelist more than the analytic discipline of the social scientist.

To overcome the dualisms of the rational/scientific tradition so dominant in the West, it is necessary to create a more unified sense of the inner/outer sensibilities that are sometimes differentiated in Freudian terms. This calls for the separation of the conscious intellect of the ego from the subconscious and unconscious realms of superego and id. Whatever the metaphor, the point remains that behavior cannot be understood in any purely rational reductionist interpretation that limits its observations to external planes of existence. Marxist and liberal interpretations of human endeavor, with their exclusive reference to external relationships, are both flawed in their attempts to explain the failure of societal arrangements. Marxists base their explanation of failure on exploitative relations arising out of the productive process that converts any social order into classes of rulers and victims;[42] liberals refer to the insufficiency of productive output and scarcity that can be overcome, in time, by technological innovation. Marxists await revolution as the dynamic in which victims seize the means of production in order to reorganize society along nonexploitative lines. Liberals, on the other hand, seek only to institutionalize moderation in the state so that abundance can serve as the dynamic providing everyone with the sufficiency needed for life, liberty, and happiness. Both outlooks are overly optimistic, secular, materialistic, and rationalistic, awaiting societal fulfillment in historical time without inner transformation or divine intervention. Both underestimate the religious or spiritual dimension of human personality.

The effort to sustain these hopeful but automatic outlooks on societal liberation in the face of all the evidence exerts an immense strain on the polity, draining it of authentic confidence and making hope depend on the banal bravado of think tank specialists.[43] The more careful and impressive interpretations of prospects for civilization and the planet are filled with foreboding and despair, not necessarily because the apocalypse is around the next corner, but because various forms of Stalinism have discredited socialists' claims, while a variety of ecological constraints have drawn into question liberal expectations based on a modernizing world.[44]

These realizations underscore the need in world order studies for a *deeper* and *wider* conception of knowledge than is customary according to rationalist canons of higher education. Spiritual traditions and insights become relevant, especially as they shape cultural potentials that draw on neglected aspects of national and civilizational heritage. These form a sound basis for forms of cultural renewal supportive of economic and political reforms that correspond to ethical and functional imperatives of organizing life humanely on a

TABLE 1

Scope of World Order Inquiry

Level	Perspective	Unit of Analysis	Explanatory Focus
I	Religion Culture	Civilization	Beliefs, Symbols Myths, Values Consciousness
II	History	Nation-state Region World	Events Patterns, "laws" Narrative line
III	Politics	Polity-State State System	Power, Authority Influence Legitimacy Leadership
IV	Economics	Society Market Class	Wealth, trade Ownership Productive Process Capital Accumulation Process
V	Psychology	Person Group Species	"inner man" motivation behavioral patterns
VI	Biology	Species	Evolutionary patterns
VII	Anthropology	Tribe Species	Alternative societal forms
VIII	Ecology	Ecosystem biosphere	Nature, ecological principles
IX	Astrophysics	Stars, planets, Solar System Galaxies Universe	Physical laws and relations

crowded planet running out of some critical resources.[45] The evolutionary studies of biological time also suggest, in a contrasting way, adaptive possibilities, like mutations, but on a time scale that exceeds the horizons of secular, action-oriented sensibilities. It is these subjects, rather than the world order heartland of politics and economics, that provide for hope despite the currently dismal course of secular trends and prospects.

Some indication of what an enriched inquiry would encompass is suggested by Table 1. This table is designed to identify some boundaries and to suggest the kind of coverage needed. What is left out of such an image is the integrating sensibility that gives coherence to insights drawn from a variety of sources. Without such an integrative effort, the extended inquiry will not lead anywhere. Whether anyone has the capacity to carry out such an ambitious program of study is also to be considered. Perhaps it will require decades of "preparation" until a genius of integration can unfold a generally acceptable conception of world order studies. Afterall, it took centuries to produce St. Thomas Aquinas who gave satisfying coherence to the doctrine and teaching of the Catholic Church.

World order studies of the most traditional variety have confined their inquiry to politics (level III), giving some superficial attention to history and economics (levels II and IV). A sophisticated integration of history, politics, and economics (levels II, III, and IV) would be an important contribution to the orientation of world order values in the related postulates of either system reform or system transformation. What I have argued in this section is the need to bring religion and culture and anthropology (levels I and VII) into play in an explicit way so as to develop a richer sense of tradition and to grasp the potentialities for various kinds of development.[46] To get beneath the rationalistic, bureaucratic superstructure it is, of course, necessary to consider psychology and anthropology (levels V and VII). Longer run potentials for change can be understood by reference to biology, ecology, and astrophysics (levels VI, VIII, and IX), as well as to constraining elements on what is possible. Looking into the distant past creates a context for a more searching, less timebound inquiry into the future, because it liberates, even as it conditions, the imagination.

State, War, and Revolution

System-maintaining, system-diminishing, and system-reforming strategies have, for the most part, taken the state for granted as the principal structural ingredient of international political life. System-transforming strategies have tended to build their image of a future world on a substantially weakened state. What does seem evident is the evolving character of the state and its uneven relationship, as measured in time and space (taking specific history and geography into account) to the realization of world order values. A more sophisticated and differentiated conception of the state as actor is required for all varieties of world order studies, especially to clarify the position of system transformers.

This need for clarification is reinforced by the inadequacy associated with the main ideological perspectives on the modern state. Both liberal and Marxist theories underestimate the autonomous role of the state as an actor with its own set of interests distinct from those of the general population or from those of separate classes, ethnic identities, regions, or religions. Bureaucratic expansion in its modern embodiments alters both the role of and expectations regarding the state. Furthermore, notions of the minimal or weak state, as well as those of the neutral state, seem to underestimate, in decisive respects, the social services and economic interventionary role that a modern citizenry expects from the leadership of a modern state. Circumstances of expanding population accentuate this tendency to assign more and more functions to the state, which in turn generates expanding fiscal requirements. These functions include a need to sustain economic growth and aspire to full employment without fostering inflation, a need that encourages ever-expanding regulatory undertakings. These tendencies toward bureaucratic expansion are further heightened by the complex, hazardous, and vulnerable character of modern technology in which the state simultaneously becomes entrepreneur (by supplying capital), promoter, and custodian. These roles are difficult to reconcile, as is evident in the balance between promotional and protective governmental roles in the context of nuclear technology; this balance is further complicated by countervailing pressure groups of unequal capabilities, such as those of the nuclear industry versus those generated by the general public. Pressures on the state arising from the spread of terrorism also encourage the expansion of bureaucratic claims interfering with a wide range of activities previously regarded as falling within a protected private sphere.

In the international context the role of the state has often been conceived in simplistic terms as the *bête noire* of world order. Such a view concludes that the only obstacle to a just and peaceful world is the demonic preoccupation of states with their military prowess. The state also functions to achieve autonomy for territorial units, and a strong state mechanism, especially in Latin America, Africa, and Asia where countries have endured various degrees of hegemony for centuries, seems closely associated with the successful prosecution of the struggle against imperialism, assuring a given society the fruits of political independence after its liberation has been formally achieved. The postcolonial state, therefore, has emerged in the southern hemisphere both as guardian of independence and as an agency of drastic repression in a growing number of situations where a governing coalition in a particular country is unable or unwilling to satisfy the expectations of important components of the society. The outlook of the state is shaped by the perceived domestic interests and affinities of its governing coalition, although the international rhetoric of Third World solidarity may coexist with a set of official policies designed to perpetuate the social, economic, and cultural norms associated with colonial or even precolonial patterns of relations.

What is required for world order studies is a definite appreciation of these various facets of statism and an appraisal of their normative consequences. On the basis of such an appraisal, it will then be possible to formulate some valid generalizations about the state system, including its links with all forms of violence and warfare in human experience. There is no doubt that status, wealth, and power seem closely correlated with military prowess, and that this correlation pervades international relations. It is also apparent that technological innovation applied to war is quickly spreading the capacity to inflict mass destruction all around the planet, that the waste of talent and resources on military activities is on the rise, and that the strategic arms race between the superpowers continues above and beyond thresholds of stability and restraint in the direction of "first strike" postures.

Does the state, as a political institution, lead to this kind of militarized approach to security as a matter of necessity, or is it possible to envision a set of conditions that would induce a demilitarization? Is the state an entity that is conditioned by the reality of other states competing for ill-defined shares of the fixed stock of planetary patrimony and, therefore, dependent on a "structure of peace" that rests on abiding, mutual exchanges of mortal, genocidal threats, all wrapped in the antiseptic doctrinal language of "deterrence"? These kinds of questions go to the essence of state power and foreshadow the extent to which the ruling coalitions of states themselves can play a positive role in promoting world order values in consistent fashion. In other words, the fundamental issues posed by the inadequacies of the state system to cope with the intertwined trends of violence, crowding, scarcities, misery, and environmental decay can be stated succinctly: Is global revolution necessary? If necessary, is it possible? If possible, then what form will it take? And over what time period? What are the connections between revolutionary politics on the national and the global level?

World order approaches need to confront their relationship to revolutionary tactics, strategies, and thinking. The revolution we consider here, of course, has to do with reconstituting the basis of governance and with creating a context for humane governance throughout the planet. Such a revolutionary goal may involve drastic changes in cultural outlook, or prevailing values, and it may require prolonged struggle, sacrifice, and anguish. Certainly, the character of revolution contemplated here is not centered on the seizure of state power by means of armed struggle, although it may include this meaning in particular national circumstances of persistent repression. The underlying challenge is to transform the exercise of state power in such a way that it will initiate a wider process of transformation that enhances the quality of life throughout the world. It is essential, and seems appropriate, therefore, for system-transforming world order approaches to explore the various facets of this revolutionary possibility.

Planetary Citizenship

Changing patterns of individual and group loyalty and identity play a critical role during periods of political transition. System-transforming approaches to world order emphasize the importance of treating the planet as a whole, which in turn implies recognizing the wholeness of the human race. Such recognition goes against the tradition of making absolute those loyalties (to self, family, tribe, class, nation, region, race, religion, or language group) that have dominated political life on the planet. Now, a growing number of exemplary individuals and associated spiritual groups, while affirming the positive content of their various particular identities, are proclaiming a commitment to an emergent conception and reality of planetary citizenship. Feeling, thinking, and acting from a planetary perspective is what world order politics is increasingly about. The substance of such a perspective centers on the task of establishing humane patterns of governance at all levels of social interaction, from the self to the world.

Initially, at least, one can expect the energy for such a shift in political consciousness to take hold among individuals and non-governmental organizations, especially those with religious and humanitarian missions. It is to be understood that the preponderance of power and wealth will remain concentrated in governments, corporations, and banks. Such entities retain a vested interest in primary loyalty to the part rather than to the whole, whether the part be defined in terms of state, class, or region. A multinational corporation or a world bank may have a planetary outlook in a territorial sense, but its operating logic is based on maximizing profits for its shareholders rather than on increasing benefits for the global community.

As such, its planetary identification is deficient and should not be confused with that of a citizen or group dedicated to the well-being of the whole.

The genuine planetary citizen will not tend to look to official institutions or dominant economic actors for support, at least not at first. If the global situation further decays, then public opinion may achieve access to power for those who by temperament and commitment are dedicated to the realization of political community on a global scale. We have no reason to expect such a development in the near future, unless a major catastrophe generates mass support for the case for drastic global reform. Short of this, populist critiques of official institutions and oppositional politics rather than advocacy of mere reorientations of governing style should become the main political activity of planetary citizens.

NOTES

1. The broad terrain of this intellectual endeavor is usefully surveyed in Juergen Dedring, *Recent Advances in Peace and Conflict Research* (Beverly Hills, Ca.: Sage Library of Social Research, Vol. 27, 1976); also helpful is L. Gunnar Johnson, *Conflicting Concepts of Peace in Contemporary Peace Studies, Sage Professional Papers,* International Studies Series Vol. 4, No. 02-046 (Beverly Hills, Ca.: Sage Publications, 1976).

2. See, for example, Tom Farer, "The Greening of the Globe: A Preliminary Appraisal of the World Order Models Project," *International Organization,* Vol. 31 (1977): 129–147.

3. For a presentation of this range of plausible alternative systems of world order see Richard Falk, *A Study of Future Worlds* (New York: Free Press, 1975), especially pp. 174–220.

4. William Irwin Thompson, *Evil and World Order* (New York: Harper and Row, 1976).

5. In effect, either the flaws of human character are integral to potentials for politics, or these flaws can in time be removed to establish far brighter potentials for political behavior than now seem plausible.

6. For a major attempt to project an alternative future based upon cultural factors, see Ali A. Mazrui, *A World Federation of Cultures* (New York: Free Press, 1976); see also an important earlier work by F. S. C. Northrop, *The Meeting of East and West* (New York: Macmillan, 1946).

7. "Address by President Carter to People of Other Nations," *Department of State Bulletin,* Vol. 76, (February 14, 1977): 123.

8. For a mainstream discussion of these possibilities, alive to the contradictory pulls of domestic and international forces, see Stanley Hoffmann, "No Choices, No Illusions," *Foreign Policy* 25: (Winter 1976–77) 97–140.

9. Saul Mendlovitz in his role as general director of the World Order Models

Project and president of the Institute for World Order has been seeking to initiate such a movement in recent years.

10. Stanley Hoffmann, "Report of the Conference on Conditions of World Order—June 12–19, 1965, Villa Serbelloni, Bellagio, Italy," *Daedalus*, spring 1966, 456.

11. Ibid.

12. Hedley Bull, *The Anarchical Society: A Study of Order in World Politics*, (New York: Columbia University Press, 1977), p. 20.

13. Ibid., pp. 53–54.

14. Ibid., p. 65.

15. Ibid., pp. 96–97.

16. Ibid., pp. 233–256.

17. This is attributed to Aron in Hoffmann, "Report of the Conference on Conditions of World Order," p. 456.

18. Bull, *The Anarchial Society*, pp. 319–320.

19. Ibid., p. 320.

20. J. Martin Rochester, "International Institutions and World Order: The International System as a Prismatic Polity," *Sage Professional Papers in International Relations* Vol. 3, no. 02-025, (Beverly Hills, Ca., 1974), p. 5.

21. William Coplin and Rochester, "The PCIJ, ICJ, League and UN: A Comparative Empirical Survey," *American Political Science Review* 62, pp. 529–550.

22. Robert O. Keohane and Joseph Nye, *Power and Interdependence: World Politics in Transition* (Boston: Little, Brown, 1977). See also Miriam Camps, "The Management of Interdependence: A Preliminary View," Council on Foreign Relations, (New York, 1974); Richard Rosecrance et. al., "Whither Interdependence?" *International Organization*, Vol. 31 (summer 1977): 425–472.

23. Saul Mendlovitz and Thomas Weiss, "The Study of Peace and Justice: Toward a Framework for Global Discussion," in Louis René Beres and Harry Targ, eds., *Planning Alternative Future* (New York: Praeger, 1975), 157.

24. Ibid., p. 158.

25. Gerald and Patricia Mische, *Toward a Human World Order: Beyond the National Security Straightjacket* (New York: Paulist Press, 1977), p. 64.

26. For a description of Trilateral Commission, see the pamphlet entitled "The Trilateral Commission" issued at its inception and seasonal accounts of activities in a newsletter issued quarterly under the title "Trialogue." See also *Trilateral Commission Task Force Reports 1–7* (New York: New York University Press, 1977). For a critical evaluation, see Holly Sklar, ed., *Trilateralism* (Boston: South End Press, 1980).

27. For a full account of the impact on Carter's presidency, see Craig S. Karpel, "Cartergate: The Death of Democracy," *Penthouse* (Nov. 1977): 69–74, 90, 104–106, 130.

28. For Brzezinski's views on these issues, see Zbigniew Brzezinski, "Recognizing the Crisis," *Foreign Policy* Vol. 17 (winter 1974–75): 63–74.

29. Daniel Bell, "The Future of World Disorder," *Foreign Policy* Vol. 27, (summer 1977): 134.

30. See, for example, Tom J. Farer, "The United States and the Third World: A Basis for Accommodation," *Foreign Affairs* Vol. 54 (October 1975): 79–95.

31. See Zbigniew Brzezinski, "U.S. Foreign Policy: The Search for Focus," *Foreign Affairs*, Vol. 57 (July 1973): 708–727; see also the gentle critique by Richard H. Ullman, "Trilateralism: 'Partnership' for What?" *Foreign Affairs*, Vol. 55 (October 1976): 1–19.

32. Michael Crozier, Samuel P. Huntington, and Joji Watanuki, *The Crisis of Democracy: Report on the Governability of Democracies to the Trilateral Commission*, (New York: New York University Press, 1975).

33. Ibid., p. 6–7

34. For a representative statement by Richard Ullman, see his "Foreword: The 1980's Project" in F. Hirsch and M. Doyle and Edward L. Morse, *Alternatives to Monetary Disorder*, (New York: McGraw-Hill, 1977), p. xi.

35. Ibid., p. x.

36. Ibid., p. ix.

37. For the background and rationale of WOMP, see Saul Mendlovitz and Thomas Weiss, "Toward Consensus: The World Order Models Project of the Institute for World Order," in *Introduction to World Peace Through Law*, (Chicago: World Without War Publications, 1973), pp. 74–97; see also Mendlovitz's Introduction to Saul Mendlovitz, ed., *On the Creation of a Just World Order*, (New York: Free Press, 1975, pp. vii–xvii); on the specification on the values see Falk, *A Study of Future Worlds*, pp. 11–39. See also Fouad Ajami, "'World Order': The Question of Ideology" (mimeographed WOMP II paper, 1977).

38. Mendlovitz, *On the Creation of a Just World Order;* Mazrui, *A World Federation of Orders;* Falk, *A Study of Future Worlds;* Rajni Kothari, *Footsteps into the Future: Diagnosis of the Present World and a Design for an Alternative* (New York: Free Press, 1974); Gustavo Lagos and Horacio H. Godoy, *Revolution of Being: A Latin American View of the Future* (New York: Free Press, 1977); Johan Galtung, *The True Worlds: A Transnational Perspective* (New York: Free Press, 1980).

39. For different methodological and normative treatments of this theme see Wassily Leontief et al., *The Future of the World Economy* (New York: Oxford University Press, 1977); Jan Tinbergen, coordinator, *Reshaping the International Order* (New York: E. P. Dutton, 1976); Roger Hansen, "Major U.S. Options on North-South Relations: A Letter to President Carter," in James Sewall et. al., *The United States and World Development: Agenda 1977*, Overseas Development Council, (New York: Praeger, 1977); see also A. Herrera et al., *Catastrophe or New Society?* (Ottawa, Canada: International Development Research Center, 1976); Graciela Chichilnisky, "Development Patterns and International Order," *Journal of International Affairs* 31 (1977): 275–304.

40. William P. Bundy, "On Power: Elements of Power," *Foreign Affairs*, Vol. 56 (October 1977): 26.

41. See Ervin Laszlo et al., *Goals for Mankind: A Report to the Club of Rome on the New Horizons of Global Community* (New York: E. P. Dutton, 1977), especially pp. 415–424. On page 415 he says, "The achievement of world solidarity is the great imperative of our era."

42. For a stimulating account of exploitative preindustrial relations and their link to present societal distortions see Stanley Diamond, *In Search of the Primitive* (New Brunswick, N.J.: Transaction Books, 1974), especially pp. 1–48.

43. For instance, Herman Kahn et al., *The Next 200 Years: A Scenario for America and the World* (New York: Morrow, 1976).

44. See, for examples, Robert Heilbroner, *The Human Prospect* (New York: Norton, 1974); Donella Meadows et al., *The Limits to Growth, A Report for the Club of Rome's*

Project on the Predicament of Mankind (New York: Universe, 1972); Barry Commoner, *The Closing Circle* (New York: Knopf, 1971); Edward Goldsmith et al., *A Blueprint for Survival* (Boston: Houghton, Mifflin, 1972). For my views on these issues, see Richard Falk, *This Endangered Planet: Prospects and Proposals for Human Survival* (New York: Random House, 1972).

On the more specific theme of the various developmental paths' consequences for values, see Peter Berger, *Pyramids of Sacrifice: Political Ethics and Social Change* (New York: Basic Books, 1974); Barrington Moore, Jr., *Reflections on the Causes of Human Misery* (Boston: Beacon, 1972); Victor Ferkiss, *The Future of Technological Civilization* (New York: Braziller, 1974); Richard Falk, "Militarization and Human Rights in the Third World," *Bulletin of Peace Proposals* 3 (1977): 220–232.

45. See Theodore Roszak, *Unfinished Animal: The Aquarian Frontier and the Evolution of Consciousness* (New York: Harper and Row, 1975); also Richard Falk, "Political Prospects, Cultural Choices, Anthropological Horizons," *The Journal of the New Alchemists* 4 (1977): 138–148.

46. For examples of authors who approach global issues with these perspectives, see William Irwin Thompson, *Evil and World Order;* his *At the Edge of History* (New York: Harper and Row, 1971); and his *Passage About Earth* (New York: Harper and Row, 1974); see also Diamond, *In Search of the Primitive* and Northrop, *The Meeting of East and West.*

CHAPTER 4

The First Phase of the World Order Models Project and Its Critics*

This analysis of the World Order Models Projects (WOMP) is divided into two parts: first, a short discussion of the evolution of the WOMP perspective and its links to the traditionalists who emphasize power in a military sense, to modernists who emphasize the multifaceted interdependence of contemporary global politics, and to utopians who propose drastically new arrangements of power and value; and second, a consideration of the more salient lines of criticism developed in Farer's essay (especially, on the distinctiveness of the WOMP approach, on the attractiveness of the WOMP vision of the future, and on the adequacy of the WOMP conception of transition).

THE WOMP PERSPECTIVE

International relations as disciplined inquiry, following Machiavelli and Hobbes, has been preoccupied with the global dynamics of interaction among principal political actors. Since the seventeenth century, states have been the predominant political actors, and a few of these have played especially prominent roles at various stages of international history. As a result, international relations has been, above all else, a study of the state system and its fundamental features at different stages of evolution, with special attention, until recently, being given to the role of the great powers in Europe.

This tradition of inquiry sought to establish an intellectual iden-

*This chapter originated as a response to Tom J. Farer's review essay "The Greening of the Globe: a Preliminary Appraisal of the World Order Models Project (WOMP)," *International Organization* Vol. 31 (1977): 129–147. In preparing this reply I was assisted by my colleagues in WOMP, by a set of astute comments by Professor Samuel Kim of Monmouth College, and by an evaluation of WOMP in a senior thesis by Michael Borrus, who completed his undergraduate studies at Princeton University in June 1977.

tity separate from that of lawyers and moralists, who tended, it was alleged, to confuse the "is" with the "ought," and thereby impair perception of actual patterns of practice, as well as blur requirements for reform. Besides, theorists of state behavior have consistently maintained that normative pressures are virtually negligible in international society, because no governmental institutions of enforcement exist and no global community sentiment of any strength exists. Essentially, state power is subject only to the restraints imposed by other states (sometimes alleging a higher purpose) and to self-restraint. In the nuclear age, this basis of order is more exposed and controversial than ever before. This mainstream international relations tradition has also tended to view drastic modifications in the state system as unrealistic or utopian, expressions of desire rather than of assessed probability. Hence, disarmament, world government, and the like are cursorily dismissed from consideration by most serious students of international relations. Even statist experiments in international cooperation, such as the League of Nations and the United Nations, have been regarded as marginal innovations in the world system, a kind of ornamental extension of the old order, not a challenge to it. Henry Kissinger's spectacular success as a statesman was attributable, in part, I believe, to his clarity about the centrality of state power in international relations, especially welcome in American statecraft which has so often fooled itself and others by masking self-interested policies with an elaborate pretension of moral exceptionalism.

The Machiavellianism of this dominant tradition has always had its opponents who questioned both the descriptive and prescriptive aspects of such an image of international relations. This questioning has grown in intensity and scope in recent decades, originally as a response to the terrible costs of war and more recently in relation to the capacity of the world as a whole to accommodate the interplay between demographic and industrial trends. The interactive complexity of international relations, especially along transnational axes of interaction, has encouraged others to emphasize the need for a more sophisticated view of the dynamics of international behavior than derives from the state-centric view of the world.[1]

Against this background, a subtradition of inquiry has emerged in recent years that devotes attention to the possibilities for "system change." Usually such an outlook is premised on the conviction (for which there is no proof or disproof) that present trends and tendencies are likely to eventuate in catastrophic results some time in the next half century or so. Sometimes the present order is also repudiated on moral grounds—because too many people live unnecessarily in misery, because the present structures rest on violence and threats of violence, or because human potential, both individual and societal, could be more fully and happily realized in an alternative framework. These convictions, whether prudential or moral, can be proved plausible.[2] Novelists have depicted with greater power than social scientists the disintegrative implications of present realities.[3] The task of depicting "a promised land," that is, an alternative to the presently dangerous and unacceptable arrangement of global power, is a challenging one. The most prosaic response is to envision a world state governing all of humanity safely and equitably. Again, creative writers rather than futurologists engage our being more successfully when they imagine utopian societies in which human relations are established in an imaginative, but not simplistic, fashion.[4] But such utopian aspirations, whether literary or not, offer no serious answers to the question of transition—how to get from here to there. The writing of utopias assumes that the envisioned state has been achieved, thereby eliminating political constraints on its attainment.[5]

The transition question is central to WOMP's inquiry. It also acknowledges the difficulty of the question at every level of discourse—political, intellectual, and psychological.[6] That is, WOMP shares with the utopian tradition both a rejection of incremental approaches and a search for existent, appealing images of alternatives to the present system of world order. What distinguishes WOMP, to date, is its emphasis on linking diagnosis of the present to prescription for the future through an inquiry into transition processes. Such an inquiry is beset by difficulty as we do not know enough to establish a persuasive causal model of the future. So far WOMP has managed to produce a series of first-generation efforts to depict preferred worlds and associated transition strategies. These efforts intentionally reflect some of the diversity of perspective—ideological, cultural, regional, epistemological (or methodological)—that exist in the world. At this stage, studying transition more closely approximates taking an inventory of representative attitudes than it does the formulation of testable hypotheses as to the nature of global transformation. There is no coherent body of theory to draw upon. What coherence WOMP possesses comes from a shared commitment by its participants to evolve longer-range strategies to promote humane politics than is common for governments and academic specialists. For Professor Tom Farer, a leading international lawyer in the liberal realist tradition, to label the self-styled skepticism in Carl Friedrich von Weizsäcker's essay as "the most penetrating contribution" in the volume is self-serving in the extreme; it is the one contribution that rejects the enterprise and was included to show that WOMP did not exclude distinguished critics from its work process.

Since 1968, by means of meetings, exchanges of papers and criticisms, and a series of books, WOMP has been seeking to evolve a new orientation toward the subject matter of international relations. This orientation is normative (intent on making goals explicit), futuristic (concerned with trends and counter-trends), systemic (focused on the interrelations of the overall system in a planetary scale of inquiry), constitutive (concerned with design of alternative institutions and procedures), and transdisciplinary (including politics, economics, sociology, philosophy, religion, and cultural anthropology). It is also an academic exercise that has aspirations as yet mainly unrealized.

WOMP is addressing a clear message to the world: the present system does not work; it cannot be incrementally repaired; it can be replaced by one that does work, but not quickly or easily; the prospects for replacement are not encouraging, but are themselves a function of the seriousness and representativeness of the search.[7]

More to the point, however, is the controversy over agents of change. In truth, WOMP as a whole is ambivalent, some authors placing their bets on official elites and their moderate competitors, some being more convinced that the energy for change will come, if at all, from counter-elites who challenge established centers of political and economic power. I believe that WOMP suffers from this ambivalence both pragmatically (failure to create a clear constituency) and intellectually (failure to develop a theory of global change). Although favorable to the diversity of time and place appropriate for a normative discipline of global scope, I believe WOMP would benefit from an increase in ideological coherence vis-à-vis agents of change. My own convictions, here, lead me to favor resolving the ambivalence in the direction of counter-elite strategies, except in those few instances in which progressive social forces hold official power.[8] Otherwise (and here I agree with the purport of Farer's criticism) WOMP's values are invocations of motherhood and susceptible to endorsement by wildly contradictory political movements. It is essential, in my view, that WOMP specify the values it affirms with sufficient concreteness to clarify what it is for and what it is against on the plane of choice and struggle.[9] This is partly a matter of "operationalizing" values (i.e., providing yardsticks by which to measure goals—for example, a minimum annual income of $500 for every person on the globe by 1990). It is mainly a matter of taking sides in on-going political conflicts about whether the existing establishments can be persuaded to reform or whether they must be replaced by struggle from below.

WOMP's indistinct identity is especially serious at this time when the rhetoric of "world order" has been adopted by the official elites in the United States (from Kissinger through Carter). One of the things that Farer argues is that WOMP is futile and foolish because it appears to challenge the legitimacy and efficacy of the new breed of "the best and the brightest." For instance, Farer writes, "The power to effect system reform, if it rests anywhere rests in the hands of Western elites and their middle class constituencies.[10] In my view, a line of controversy should be drawn on this issue; I would rewrite this assertion as follows: "If there is one thing we can be sure about it is that the power to effect system reform does not rest in the hands of Western elites and their middle class constituencies." Power presupposes will, the will is shaped by short-term interests, and these interests are overwhelmingly associated with system maintenance.

In sum, WOMP, in the course of evolving its framework of inquiry, has moved away from the ideological rigidity of its antecedents (for example, the Clark-Sohn plan) without yet achieving sufficient ideological coherence to take on Farer-minded critics in a convincing fashion on matters of allegiance.

PRINCIPAL CRITICISMS

Perhaps because of the "complex interdependence" of my long association with Tom Farer, his review essay devoted to the World Order Models Project (WOMP) was a deep disappointment for me on several scores. Two quotations are expressive of my reaction. The first was uttered by a Republican businessman stunned by Nixon's visit to China in 1971: "When Dick Nixon sells out his friends, he really moves the goods." Farer's elaborate mixture of snipes, barbs, innuendo, and genuine criticism represents this sort of accomplishment; it really moves the goods and has been received with thinly disguised glee by all those disposed to regard WOMP with antipathy.

The second quotation is from *The Futurological Congress,* a novel by the Polish science-fiction writer Stanislaw Lem: "Oh Professor—I felt like shouting—here you sit, and out there the world is coming to an end.[11] What I mean to suggest, of course, is that the perils of the world situation are so severe that we need to gather our energies for constructive efforts. Farer's review, whatever else, is so condescending and acerbic that I doubt that anyone could claim for it a constructive intent or effect.

This said, I would like to concentrate this reply on issues of substance, indulging my vengeful impulses only to the extent of a single long footnote designed to show that Farer has been both unfair and nasty in his treatment of WOMP.[12] In actuality, I (and my associates in WOMP) particularly welcome serious criticism of the WOMP enterprise at this stage, as it is a time for us to wonder how best to proceed. We wonder both about how to encourage a social movement dedicated to the establishment of more humane politics throughout the world and a more viable political framework for the planet as a whole, as well as how to stimulate ways of thinking about the future of world politics that are both more in keeping with unfolding realities and more responsive to human needs and aspirations than prevailing academic and diplomatic modes. Unlike so many earlier quests for a new world order, WOMP does not purport to have the answers, much less *the answer* to the shape of world government. At most, WOMP is insisting on an agenda for world politics that puts system-change at the top. To this end, WOMP is working to create a more adequate framework of inquiry for individuals and groups situated in different parts of the world to consider prospects and proposals for drastic (as distinguished from marginal) adjustments to alarming conditions (e.g., poverty, arms spread) and trends (e.g., population, pollution, terms of trade).

There is one issue of perspective that requires clarification. Farer repeatedly implies that I am trying to obscure my adherence to world federalist thinking so as to gain "mainstream credibility." Such is not the case. My approach is based on genuine opposition to statist solutions to world order problems at all levels of social interaction, especially at the global level. Indeed, I would go so far as to prefer mudding through with the state system than its displacement at this historical juncture by any plausible form of world government. One anxiety I have is that the poverty of political imagination now prevalent will regard world government as the only way out of the statist *cul de sac*, making such a prospect the natural sequel to the state system when and if catastrophe eventuates. Farer's unwillingness to acknowledge my dialectical position on global reform (building downward from the state with respect to economic and political concentrations of functions *and* building outward from the state to encompass the functional dimensions of interdependence) helps convey this false impression. One way of putting the role of institutional development in my writing up through *A Study of Future Worlds* is to view it as neofunctionalism proceeding from the line that goes from Mitrany through Haas, or more descriptively, perhaps as "dialectical functionalism."

But again, as a process and vector for change, WOMP depends

on criticism for growth. And even Farer's determined effort to repudiate WOMP on every count is not without its consoling virtues in this regard. It does touch upon issues that warrant debate, discussion, and clarification.

Values and Assumptions

I think that the main goals of WOMP—to provide a framework for drastic change in the structure of international relations and to participate in a transnational social movement dedicated to global reform—have been misunderstood by Farer. As a consequence, he critically examines the distinctive identity of WOMP on two secondary grounds—its stress on shared values to undergird the direction of global reform and its assumptions about the peril confronting the international political system as now constituted. Farer is correct in his judgment that the four values (peace, economic well-being, social and political justice, and ecological balance) are pieties that can unblushingly be affirmed by spokespeople on all points of the political compass. And, indeed, the selection of these values reflects a diagnosis of what needs to be achieved more than a specific set of positions.

As Farer suggests, the key questions involve trade-offs among values, and even more pertinently, strategic implications of alternative policies. For instance, do deterrence strategies or disarmament proposals have greater prospects of contributing to the avoidance of major war? Or, is it possible to reconcile the pursuit of social and political justice with a continued stress on industrial growth? WOMP, as such, does not propose answers to questions of this sort, although the individual authors representing regional and national perspectives often do. Contrary to what Farer suggests, WOMP, at least at the present stage of its work, does not claim "internal harmony" for its efforts. On the contrary, the diversity of outlook and unevenness of national situation makes it likely that different WOMP perspectives would exist on many issues even if a common left-of-center politics could be attributed to WOMP as a whole. It makes sense for poor countries to orient transitional strategies around developmental issues, to relate values associated with justice to the fulfillment of human needs, and to subordinate or neglect strategic considerations of war and peace. Especially in the present context of Third World assertiveness, such a rewriting of the world order agenda seems appropriate, and this is actually what has been done by such WOMP participants as Rajni Kothari, Ali Mazrui, Paul Lin, and more recently, Fouad Ajami.

At the same time, it remains appropriate for those living in the superpowers (or in their shadows) to be concerned, as is for instance WOMP's Japanese author, Yoshikazu Sakamoto, with the implications of nuclear devastation, ecological decay, and various forms of alienation. For these societies, as Johan Galtung has argued in a WOMP context, certain forms of de-modernization are desirable[13] and certainly a stress on demilitarization appropriate.

A final comment on values relates to the core of shared normative substance embodied in a WOMP perspective. Admittedly, this core is difficult to specify in a way that distinguishes WOMP from other perspectives. It has to do with specifying WOMP's "left-of-center" orientation in relation to global policy issues, which is something that WOMP has not yet done in any systematic fashion.[14] It also has to do with concern about comprehensive policy, as opposed to policy on a given issue. Thus, a WOMP perspective would be consistent with a variety of substantive positions on population policy for a given country or region, but it would insist that analysis and policy recommendations embrace the subject matter of the four values and deal with the expected impact on prospects for drastic global reform of a progressive variety. Hence, one challenge confronting WOMP at the present, as I see it, is to formulate more clearly, if possible, the content of a progressive world order ideology and to distinguish those contexts in which the WOMP framework implies a substantive position from those in which a variety of inconsistent positions could each be convincingly attributed to WOMP.

When we turn to assumptions, we see that Farer serves WOMP with the dual indictment of upholding growth-based economics and state-centered politics. Such assumptions can be properly attributed to Saul Mendlovitz and myself, but not to the other main WOMP participants.[15] Admittedly, Mendlovitz as overall director of WOMP speaks for the project as a whole, and yet as he points out, the WOMP authors did not share his outlook in all respects.[16] WOMP is a confederal intellectual, political enterprise in which the parts are purposely larger than the whole.[17] On the role of the state, there is considerable diversity of view. Most WOMP directors believe that the evolution of strong states in the Third World is a positive world order development, necessary to resist neoimperial patterns of intrusion and domination, a concern given high priority in several WOMP perspectives. Therefore, generalizations about the role of the state as doomed should not be associated with WOMP as a whole. Indeed, I have been influenced by my WOMP colleagues to the extent of separating a long-term critique of the state in relation to a peaceful and just world from a short-term defense of the state in the struggle against imperial tendencies. Indeed, the willingness to acknowledge and oppose these imperial tendencies is part of the progressive content that needs to be specified by the WOMP group.

On growth, too, the WOMP position does not yield an easy generalization. All WOMP directors reject the liberal internationalists' claim, implicit in Farer's essay, that the continued growth of rich countries is crucially beneficial to the development of poor countries. WOMP also seems to have a consensus favorable to the self-reliant and appropriate technological orientations of Third World countries (to the extent feasible). And finally, there is a WOMP consensus that criticizes the over-development of the affluent countries (in terms of waste, resource use, and environmental contamination).

When it comes to apocalyptic content, WOMP has no genuine consensus. By and large, non-American participants are preoccupied with present problems and are less worried about future cataclysm, whether of a nuclear or an ecological kind, than their counterparts in the trilateral countries. In this regard, the commitment to global reform within WOMP is centered on creating a humane politics for the peoples of the world rather than on the doomsday imperative to embark upon desperate actions to save a dying planet. I happen to believe that my WOMP colleagues are underestimating these cataclysmic dangers and their relevance, but it would be a mistake to attribute my belief to WOMP as a whole.

An underlying WOMP commitment that is widely shared has to do with hopefulness about the future. In this sense, it seems reasonable to question whether the position taken by von Weizsäcker can be considered to fall within the WOMP framework, not because it takes a deviant substantive position, but because it is so pessimistic about prospects for change. WOMP does stand for an affirmation of human potential, individually and collectively. This does not imply optimism about the future. It does imply a belief that positive outcomes can be achieved and that human intervention matters. Farer scornfully dismisses this positive orientation as a typical self-delusion of "the modern mind" (p. 131). In my judgment, the theme of human transcendence as a source of insight and energy has always been an ingredient of movements for change (whether in the personal or public realm). I would argue, then, that a certain attitude of hopefulness (encompassing, at least, antifatalist, antideterminist viewpoints) about humanity is a shared, but by no means distinctive, characteristic of the WOMP outlook.[18] Such a characteristic is present in Rousseau, as well as in Marx, and is an essential attribute of any advocacy of drastic change. WOMP is not necessarily revolutionary in its tactics, but its basic premise—that a sequence of small, gradual adjustments is not sufficient—does imply a revolutionary strategy.

But such a strategy need not necessarily be a violent one. Indeed, my own stress on shifts in consciousness, on cultural innovation, and on the emergence of new belief systems is based on an assessment of the revolutionary potential of a nonviolent movement. But the WOMP perspective does not imply a renunciation of violence in all specific contexts. Most, if not all, WOMP participants support their African colleague, Nathan Shamuyarira, in his conviction that armed struggle was legitimate and necessary for the liberation of Zimbabwe (and other repressed countries in Southern Africa) from racist rule.

On WOMP's vision Farer again makes the nominalist error of mistaking the part for the whole. Although purporting to address himself to the defects of WOMP, he confines his systematic criticism to "the preferred world" sketched in my contribution to the Mendlovitz volume. This reservation aside, Farer raises some tough questions.

He alleges that there is a disjunction between the Faustian quest for knowledge that can be used for positive ends and a post-Faustian mentality that is disabled from the quest (being off in a utopian hideout somewhere). There is something to this argument, but not much. The mind is limited in the extreme in its capacity to envision what is possible and to organize its pursuit. To the extent that WOMP relies on an argument, it is bound to be sterile. But the future of world order is not comparable to a debate. The quest for knowledge is to interpret prospects for change as presented by social forces of the real world. And it is wrong to confine these prospects to the materialistic lure of affluence, as Farer does (p. 140). Again, such a view betrays extreme cynicism about human motivation, a view contradicted by the history of religious and political movements of renewal, which have been generally dominated by intangible goals and animated by charismatic personalities. WOMP, as an exercise in normative social science, seeks to interact with those who enter into active struggle for change. Although oriented around the academic question, what to think?, it is motivated by and responsive to the political question, what to do? My experience suggests that world order studies, even if carried on within an academic setting, build a bridge between thought and action that is generally absent in conventional social science, including mainstream international relations.

I agree with Farer that the utopian, post-Faustian, *Greening of America* attitude is not itself potent as an agent of change—at present, it is a countercultural growth flourishing in the interstices of the culture and is derivative and dependent so long as it does not challenge antagonistic structures of power. I would not quibble with Farer's rejection of my uncritical affirmation of counter-cultural tendencies (p. 139). In the American context, I believe more than ever in the importance of counter-cultural phenomena (far more so than in the shifts in elite configurations that result from quadrennial elections) as indicative of receptivity to more life-affirming belief systems and societal choices. At this point, I would discriminate more than I have in the past between countercultural tendencies with genuine transformative potentials and those that are parasitic.[19] Jonah House, Philadelphia and Pacific Life Centers, The New Alchemy Institute, Lindisfarne Association, and the Zen Center are positive illustrations of counter-cultural initiatives that reach out beyond their own boundaries because of a central commitment to transformation. Of course, there is a temptation to exaggerate the significance of such developments, thereby overlooking what Marxists like to call "the relation of forces." Of course, let's be realistic about the role of power and admit the adverse array of entrenched social and political forces. At the same time, let's not be simplistic. The tensions within postindustrial civilization are growing—witness violence-drenched "entertainment," patterns of drug use, and dependence on petrochemical diet—suggesting the end of an era and an impending life-and-death struggle between apostles of repression and forces of liberation.

To suggest, as Farer does, that the only possible way to mobilize mass support for transformation and global reform is by a promise of universal affluence (p. 140) is to prepare for the next war by fighting the last. Farer exhibits a Maginot Line mentality when he premises the prospects for change on the materialistic capacity to deliver middle-class life styles. We do not yet know the shape and form of the next great revolutionary surge, but it seems likely to be post-Marxian as well as postcapitalist in character. The impact of ecological considerations is to reorder in a radical fashion, I believe, the notion of "progress," moving it away from unattainable and dangerous materialistic imagery and toward more qualitative life-sustaining imagery of simplicity and harmony. Of course, the Third World, by and large, must pass through this material transition, at least to the extent of satisfying basic human needs, before it is ready to join in postmaterialistic transformative movements. The unevenness of the struggle for global reform—what is right for most Latin American, Asian, and African countries is not what is right for the trilateral countries of Japan, Western Europe, North America, or for the Soviet Bloc countries—makes it impossible to provide global generalizations. Such a situation again stresses the importance, I believe, of the WOMP effort to encourage a variety of world order perspectives and programs oriented in the perceived priorities of a given region of the planet.

Let me acknowledge here that WOMP has not, as yet, been successful in developing an overall conception of the global prospects for drastic reform. There has been an impulse to promise too much, too soon and, therefore, to bypass the hard work of building the intellectual and ideological foundations of a world social movement. There has been a disinclination to appreciate the full significance of unevenness in developmental terms for global reform prospects. These concerns should be central to the work of WOMP II[20]

When it comes to transitional scenarios, Farer is so entrapped by the materialistic ethos that he cannot countenance the end of growth-based solutions to global economic issues. At the same time, he gives no basis for his confidence in the capacity of the planet to absorb the pressures generated by continuous growth projected indefinitely into the future. His vision of a solution to global inequality and North-South confrontation is the standard liberal recipe of redistributing the growth dividend while leaving the basic structure of inequity untouched (pp. 142–44).[21] Such an internationalistic "New Deal" is itself very unrealistic about the much deeper threat of confrontation that now exists, and it overlooks the growing pressure on the trilateral economies to solve the problems of growth in a context of chronic inflation, unemployment, and rising production costs. There is a crisis for developed-country capitalism that is independent of the ecological constraints, except to the extent that rising energy costs reflect dwindling resource stocks, that environmental requirements are a rising production cost, and that developments like the antinuclear movement complicate the task of growth for advanced industrial economies. It is precisely these considerations that lead arch-elitists to question whether democracies remain governable,[22] when they might more appropriately question whether capitalism remains viable. The pressure to rely on nuclear power, despite its uncertainties and risks, is an ominous indication that the pressure to grow overwhelms the intensifying constraints on growth. These constraints may not be as mechanical or as systemic as the original Club of Rome study implied, but they are nevertheless very real for the advanced industrial world, which in turn is the engine of growth for an integrated world economy.

Here again, WOMP has not yet met the challenge of providing an alternative vision of economic development. Certain elements are present—self-reliance, decoupling from the world economy, the Chinese model, appropriate technology, decentralized socialism, checks on the abuse of state power—but they are presented in largely impressionistic forms, and without economic sophistication.

Closely related to Farer's support for growth-based economics and intersocietal adjustment is his espousal of incremental approaches to social change. For a pessimist about human nature and an optimist on elite capabilities, the limits on positive change are so severe that it is best to appeal to the self-interest of entrenched elites. These appeals must promise that system maintenance is credible, and hence, that viable adjustments are necessarily marginal. WOMP rejects this pessimism about human potential and regards system-maintaining therapies as opiates, although occasionally positive in specific short-run situations if they extend the time available for system transformation. The interplay between incrementalists and structuralists should not be antagonistic, but their beneficial interaction depends on mutual appreciation rather than on claims of exclusive prerogative to specify political priorities.

Farer suggests, rather obscurely, I think, that my conception of a poststatist utopia "may inadvertently lead us . . . to Huxley's Brave New World, which, though a good deal more agreeable for those outside the elite, nevertheless promises its own saccharine way to eviscerate Judeo-Christian man"(p. 142).[23] Judeo-Christian man, I am afraid, must be held largely accountable for the shape of the present world, and although "evisceration" is not called for, fundamental questioning is. And as for Huxley's dysutopia, I find it irrelevant to my vision of a sequel to the state system, which rests so heavily on destructuring bureaucratic networks of domination and revivifying local and individual creativity and resourcefulness. Besides, the WOMP outlook proposes a process, a direction of change, that does not terminate even with substantial realization of WOMP values.[24] For this reason it is misleading to attach utopian labels to WOMP, as WOMP stresses a continuous audit and revision of its envisioned solutions as the future unfolds. Utopian reasoning, as Karl Popper and others have argued, is essentially the depiction of "closed systems," whereas WOMP is concerned with the design of "process" and "open systems."

A CONCLUDING NOTE

WOMP welcomes criticism, engages in extensive self-criticism, and seeks contact with its critics. At the same time, WOMP also takes positions that have adversary implications. Put differently, WOMP has "enemies" as well as "critics." Its enemies are convinced that the road to reform runs through the White House and the Kremlin, that populist politics is wishful thinking or nihilistic, and that dominant social, political, and economic structures on both national and international levels are essentially stable and viable, as well as legitimate. Farer concludes his essay by insisting that the struggle to achieve the WOMP vision(s) "seems likely only to distract from the effort to contain by slow degrees the self-destructive currents of our age." (p. 147) What effort? What distraction? By what reading of cumulative developments can we conclude that "the self-destructive currents of our age" are being contained "by slow degrees?" Or for that matter, being distracted? A closer approximation of the contemporary situation is the failure to contain the self-destructive currents. What then? We can hire deck chairs for the doomed voyage, or we can challenge the crazed skipper who steers us toward collision. Those who hire deck chairs (or worse, request to eat at the captain's table) are the enemies of those who struggle.

Whether WOMP has correctly perceived these critical choices only the future can show. In the meantime, it seems useful for WOMP to solicit support and to do what it is doing in more convincing and effective fashion.

To be more direct, I believe we are living at one of those axial points in human history, vulnerable to chaotic destruction while receptive to transformative vision. Henry Miller, writing more than twenty years ago on the poet Rimbaud, noted the radical possibility that is latent in the long night of accumulating danger:

Only now, at the edge of the precipice, is it possible to realize that 'everything we are taught is false.' The proof of this devastating utterance is demonstrable every day in the realm: on the battlefield, in the laboratory, in the factory, in the press, in the school, in the church. We live entirely in the past, nourished by dead thoughts, dead creeds, dead sciences. And it is the past which is engulfing us, not the future.[25]

NOTES

1. See, especially, Robert O. Keohane and Joseph S. Nye, *Power and Interdependence: World Politics in Transition* (Boston: Little, Brown, 1977).

2. Among the efforts to do this, the following are notable: Barry Commoner, *The Closing Circle* (New York: Knopf, 1971); Edward Goldsmith et al., *Blueprint for Survival* (Boston: Houghton, Mifflin, 1974); Robert Heilbroner, *An Inquiry into the Human Prospect* (New York: Norton, 1974); and Donella Meadows et al., *The Limits to Growth* (Washington, D.C.: Potomac Association, 1972). My argument along these lines is contained

in *This Endangered Planet: Prospects and Proposals for Human Survival* (New York: Random House, 1971).

3. See, especially, several novels by Doris Lessing: *The Golden Notebook* (New York: Simon and Schuster, 1962), *Briefing for a Descent into Hell* (New York: Knopf, 1971), *The Memoirs of a Survivor* (New York: Bantam, 1975), and *Shikasta* (New York: Knopf, 1980).

4. For example, Ursula Le Guin, *The Dispossessed: An Ambiguous Utopia* (New York: Avon, 1974).

5. Farer tends to treat WOMP as a utopian venture, ignoring without analysis the attempt to react against utopianism that is at the core of WOMP motivation (for example, pp. 139–42 and 146–47). Indeed, WOMP writings are often so preoccupied with instituting a process of beneficial change that they devote only mechanical or marginal attention to preferred outcomes. For instance, the essay on Chinese development strategy by Paul Lin that troubles Farer by its presence in the volume has such a character. Of course, Farer could argue (but doesn't) that WOMP's proposals for change in the transition period are so naive or irrelevant as to be tantamount to neglect of the transition process.

6. Hence, when Farer proposes that WOMP authors "out of respect for their own ends . . . have a responsibility to present a coherent, carefully elaborated vision of the possible, one constructed out of demonstrable fact and plausible extrapolation," (p. 130), he is misconstruing both the state of the art and the nature of the enterprise. It is a demand for specification beyond the limits of the mind to know political reality. Further, it is a "reactionary" demand to the extent that it is selectively directed at advocates of change. Mainstream policy makers and analysts, those with the awesome power of decision in the White House or the Kremlin, do not and could not live up to such demands. It is true that there are ways to present arguments—based on numbers, graphs, jargon, computer printout, and formulae—that disguise the openness of history, but the predictive and explanatory content of such "social science" is much less evident than its ideological value in securing acquiescence from a bewildered public. Let me acknowledge at the same time that the work of WOMP could be improved, that not all relevant knowledge is used or effectively presented, and that some techniques of modern social science (such as modeling statistical assessments, systems analysis) could be used to advantage. However, such an acknowledgment needs to be sharply distinguished from Farer's insistence that the future must be known to sustain an argument that the present should be abandoned. (This note reflects the influence of my friend and colleague, Fouad Ajami, now at Johns Hopkins University.)

7. In effect, the perception of world order priorities is a function of time and place. Place is understood as context, including geographical site, cultural tradition, ideological setting, and historical experience. There is no "truth" to be confirmed, except with regard to data (population, arms trends, trading patterns); "appeals," "preferences," and "proposals" are relevant. World order studies can, in this sense, be disciplined, but not scientific; it is an emergent "normative discipline."

8. It is difficult without detailed discussion to consider whether specific elites warrant the designation "progressive" as used here. Do the ruling elites in China? in Sweden? in Jamaica? From what I have said, my criteria for endorsement would involve an orientation associated with humanistic and democratic forms of socialism. Such an orientation might also characterize the elites of international institutions and non-governmental transnational organizations, such as Amnesty International, the General Assembly of the United Nations, and the World Health Organization. Also some

governmental or institutional elites are progressive on a single issue, but lack any general orientation toward change.

9. Such clarity obviously need not (and should not) extend to issues where the focus of a progressive position is obscure or controversial. But it must seek clear positions on such critical issues of substance as those bearing on national security, global energy, new international economic order, and human rights.

10. In this passage on page 143, Farer uses "system reform" to refer to the scale of change that WOMP envisions. He is pessimistic about the capacity of the elites to undertake change on this scale, but he is more optimistic about their receptivity and capability than he is about any alternative coalition of social forces. As I read Farer, then, he is arguing that to look elsewhere than to the elites for the realization of WOMP values is to neglect the one realistic possibility (although even here he is not hopeful about the outcome).

11. Stanislaw Lem, *The Futurological Congress*, trans. Michael Kandel (New York: Avon, 1976), p. 11.

12. Farer's essay includes gratuitous slurs that are somewhat surprising to find in the pages of a scholarly journal. Farer's introductory fantasy suggesting that WOMP is a typical product of sumptuous conference settings is not only mean-spirited, it is untrue. In fact, WOMP meetings have been relatively austere and exceedingly hard-working by comparison with my sampling of international conference fare. If I were to retaliate, in a similar vein, I might begin as follows: "Imagine, a paunchy scholar clad in pinstriped pyjamas, yawning over his second Bloody Mary, sleepless one more night because the phone call from Washington has still not come. Imagine such an aspiring advisor to the prince relishing the prospect of exhibiting his qualifications to serve by heaping scorn on those who would question the credentials of the present political leadership . . ." As I have said, such a line of speculation, whether off the mark or not, is no way to discuss issues of scholarly substance, but it does illustrate the force of *ad hominem* attempts to control mood and render an audience receptive.

I am mildly puzzled by Farer's decision to concentrate almost all his fire on Saul Mendlovitz, ed. *On The Creation of Just World Order*, (New York: Free Press, 1975) a collection of essays deliberately designed to convey the range and variety of WOMP work, but not at all calculated to achieve coherence or depth. It is especially puzzling that Farer should so proceed after acknowledging, as he does on page 131, that reading my essay rather than my book *A Study of Future Worlds* (New York: Free Press, 1975) is comparable to assessing a human torso in "a fun-house mirror."

13. Note here the issue of linkage. Does de-development of the rich societies facilitate or inhibit development by the poor? This complicated, controversial issue needs to be considered in specific contexts—what kinds of de-development are sought? With what effects?

14. See the last section of this chapter, "A Concluding Note," for further discussion of this.

15. Even this degree of generalization is not accurate. Mendlovitz has not emphasized an antigrowth position, and I have significantly modified my indictment of the state and my prediction that it is being rapidly superseded by other political forms.

16. Such is the case with respect to the treatment of authority structures, to what Mendlovitz calls "the formal constitutive order of the world community." As Mendlovitz explains, although he remains "convinced of the value" of the kind of approach taken by Grenville Clark and Louis B. Sohn in *World Peace Through World Law*, 3rd rev. ed. (Cambridge, Mass.: Harvard University Press, 1966), such a view "has been resisted, revised, and ignored by the WOMP groups." The same observation would pertain to

Mendlovitz's oft-quoted (including by Farer, p. 133) and as often misunderstood pre-diction that world government of some form will come into being by the year 2000. See the introduction to Mendlovitz, ed., *On the Creation of a Just World Order,* pp. xv–xvi. Farer fails to distinguish adequately between Mendlovitz's direction of the project and the product produced, but more serious in some ways, he misinterprets Mendlovitz's own views, depicting him as a naive utopian who is waiting around for world govern-ment. On the contrary, Mendlovitz believes, as the passage on the emergence of world government makes plain, when world government comes, its form will most probably be as a dysutopia, as a kind of totalitarian extension of the state system. Hence, Mend-lovitz's view of the future is a much more complicated one than that attributed to him by Farer. All this is significant because WOMP is seeking to evolve a perspective on the future that is neither utopian nor dysutopian, one that assesses trends and possibilities and then offers policy recommendations. For this reason, it is particularly discouraging to be characterized as "utopian" so as to be dismissed as "irrelevant." If we are indeed irrelevant, then it seems reasonable to expect a critic to repudiate *our* claim of rele-vance.

17. At the same time, I think all WOMP directors would join me in hailing Saul Mendlovitz's intellectual and organizational leadership. Without his energy and com-mitment, WOMP would never have been conceived, initiated, and sustained. It is a measure of Mendlovitz's strength that he has gathered in WOMP a group of strong-willed intellectuals, who take a variety of positions on the major issues of world order analysis. From the outset, scholarly creativity and rigor has counted for more in WOMP than ideological allegiance.

18. This attitude also extends to a repudiation of Hobbesian, Lorenzian prespec-tives on the inevitability of human aggressiveness and of war as a social institution. WOMP adopts a more agnostic view of human behavior that can be reconciled with evolutionary positions of human development, including that of Teilhard de Chardin. (I am indebted to Professor Samuel Kim of Monmouth College for this point.)

19. For one notable effort to discriminate in this spirit see Theodore Roszak, *The Unfinished Animal* (New York: Harper and Row, 1974).

20. I use WOMP II to refer to future work by WOMP.

21. Farer's argument on this is spelled out more fully in the provocative article "The United States and the Third World: A Basis for Accommodation," *Foreign Affairs,* 54 (1975): 79–97. This article is an unusually candid appeal to Western elites, suggest-ing that they can hold on to their privileged position without much sacrifice if they handle Third World demands in a shrewd, accommodating fashion. It is a cynical appeal, advocating the admission of principal Third World states (for instance, Iran, Saudi Arabia, and Brazil) to the dominant structure, thereby shattering Third World solidarity and largely nullifying its threat.

22. See the Trilateral Commission study with its unsigned Preface written in the manner of Zbigniew Brzezinski. Michael Crozier, Samuel P. Huntington, and Joji Watanuki, *The Crisis of Democracy* (New York: New York University Press, 1975).

23. Elsewhere Farer has written, "What must be defended in the large is an economic system which rewards the capitalist virtues in investment, innovation, hard work, and sensitivity to the shifting needs and preferences of consumers." See Farer's article "The United States and the Third World," p. 93.

24. I have emphasized this point repeatedly in *A Study of Future Worlds,* pp. 156–57.

25. Henry Miller, Preface to *The Time of the Assassins* (New York: New Directions, 1956), p. x.

CHAPTER 5

The Shaping of World Order Studies

The highest function of criticism is to stimulate an author to think harder, to go further, to reconsider, and, possibly, to try again. At times, often unwittingly, author and critic join in a species of tacit collaboration. I regard Stanley Michalak's generally helpful critique of my book, *A Study of Future Worlds,* in this spirit.[1]

The overall ambition of world order studies has been to work out an intellectual framework useful for understanding and acting upon the great global challenges of our time—the menace of large-scale warfare, the scandal of large-scale poverty, the outrage of acute injustice, the dangers of environmental decay, and the burden of inhumane and/or ineffectual governance at all levels of social organization (from family to planet).[2]

The World Order Models Project (WOMP) sponsored by the Institute for World Order is one of several independent transnational efforts in world order studies that are working toward a comprehensive solutions for these global problems. Other comparable efforts include those sponsored by the Club of Rome, Reshaping the International Order (RIO), and the United Nations.[3] These separate efforts share an emphasis on the *dynamics* of global problem-solving. The *statics* of an alternative structure for the world political system is no longer the essence of world order studies. Such a shift of emphasis is significant, as earlier work had been solution-oriented, generally consisting of a model solution, in effect a blueprint, for a new system of world order that generally amounted to a more or less disguised plea for world government. Such modeling efforts continue, but they have become increasingly subordinated to a consideration of first steps and of transition process.

Beyond this, WOMP as a particular initiative has several distinguishing features: a systemic and nondisciplinary orientation toward politics; a commitment to "soft" modeling techniques, with minimum reliance on quantitative or mathematical methods; a conviction that the global problematique cannot be dissolved by incremental adjustments or as a problem set; a serious interest in imagining alternative global arrangements of power and authority; a related interest in presenting transition scenarios that move from the present to the preferred future; an emphasis which is, in effect, on a politics of transition; and, increasingly, a conviction that the interconnections between personal, societal, regional, and global levels of human organization are an essential focus for study and reflection.

Despite this shared orientation the work of WOMP encompasses a wide spectrum of attitudes, arising from an array of cultural identities and ideological perspectives of its principal participants. WOMP does not have a blueprint for a preferred world, nor does it even yet rest its claim on establishing a definitive framework for inquiry and policy recommendation. Rather, WOMP has stimulated a series of related and somewhat convergent frameworks.[4] More currently, in WOMP II there is a major work-in-progress that considers the struggles of oppressed peoples (including the "invisibly" oppressed of the First and Second Worlds) as the political key to restructuring the world.[5] Such a bottom-up approach to world order is a major departure, I feel, from the top-down, rational humanism of the utopian variety that has been the habitat and heritage of world order studies.[6]

I turn now to *A Study of Future Worlds.* It definitely represents a stage-one WOMP product, reacting against the world federalist and legalistic tradition epitomized by the Clark-Sohn proposals in *World Peace Through World Law,* yet remaining well within the confines of rational humanism.[7] My intention was to write as "an enlightened American" about the kind of preferred world order system that could conceivably be attained by approximately the end of this century. The book was produced in conjunction with comparable proposals drafted by a series of scholars drawn from other parts of the world. As is the case with such an enterprise, not all the planned volumes materialized in practice. Yet it is important, I think, to perceive *Future Worlds* as part of a series comprised of Rajni Kothari's *Footsteps into the Future: Diagnosis of the Present World and a Design for an Alternative,* Johan Galtung's *True Worlds: A Transnational Perspective,* Gustavo Lagos's and Horacio Godoy's *Revolution of Being: A Latin American Perspective,* and Ali Mazrui's *A World Federation of Cultures: An African Perspective,* and complemented by the series edited by the WOMP general director, Saul Mendlovitz, under the title *On the Creation of a Just World Order: Preferred Worlds for the 1990's,* a volume that includes contributions by Yoshikazu Sakamoto on a Japanese perspective and Paul Lin on a Chinese (Maoist) perspective.[8] Against this background, I turn now to Michalak's critique with special reference to his remarks on Marxism, states and the state system, and central guidance.

MARXISM

Michalak is quite correct to suggest that the framework and analysis of my book proceeded from a non-Marxist outlook and thus lacked positive appeal for the most currently influential orientation toward drastic change active in the world.[9] Since writing *A Study of Future Worlds*, I have embraced some elements of a neo-Marxist outlook, principally related to the dynamics of revolution and oppression and the belief that global prospects for reform must be assessed by reference to macrohistorical structures and tendencies. In my judgment, visions of global reform are silly and utopian unless they also qualify as superior journalism, that is, as accounts of evolving societal formations more attuned to reality than either abstract wishes for a different world or *ad hoc* presuppositions that the present world system is more or less inevitable. My subsequent work will reflect this shift in my own political consciousness. And interestingly, this shift of emphasis and outlook has occurred for most, if not all of us, who were associated with WOMP since its beginnings in 1968. Part of this shift has involved the de-Americanization of WOMP in this period, and part has resulted from the rigidity of the dominant structures of power and authority throughout the world. Third World participants were successful in pushing issues of global hierarchy to the forefront. As soon as global hierarchy becomes central, then to a certain extent neo-Marxist concerns and outlooks necessarily become relevant, at least as compared to liberal or non-Marxist perspectives. At the same time, because of WOMP's concern about nonclass forms of oppression, personal and cultural liberty, maximum decentralization of state power, geopolitical nonalignment, and ecological liberation, it is unlikely that this reorientation of world order studies of the WOMP group will make it attractive to mainstream Marxists.

STATES AND THE STATE SYSTEM

Michalak argues that the best way by far to promote WOMP values is to persuade or influence present leaders. Furthermore, he contends that my insistence on politics from below at the state level is generally ill-conceived, that it is a wasteful diversion of energy, and, besides, that such politics are not even possible in repressive and authoritarian political systems, including the Soviet Union. Michalak further contends that I place too much emphasis in *Future Worlds* on changing the external environment of the state (that is, the focus on central guidance) and argue unrealistically about the prospects of working against the kind of mainstream politics that dominates the governing process of principal states. He also thinks I am either naive or ill-informed about the normative potential of Third World revolutionary leaders. Michalak does not regard these leaders as necessarily advancing the cause of WOMP values any further than their predecessors in power.

First of all, Michalak is correct to underscore the possibilities of working for WOMP values by influencing established elites at the state level. However, I contend that these regular channels will be effective only if coupled with pressures generated by the prior success of more radical styles and programs, the configurations of which will vary from state to state. Existing elites in the industrial countries of the North seem entrapped and stalemated by a mixture of cultural traditions and special interest groups. As a consequence, government policy in these leading states continues its quest for a growth-sustaining economic policy complemented by a political process that restricts the discretion of leaders to a managerial inquiry into the domains of incremental adjustment. I argue, in opposition, that the global problematique can only be overcome if the political process provides leadership with a mandate for radical change and adjustment. This mandate can only arise if a new political climate takes shape, one supportive of a new style of leadership at the state level. Such an altered climate would be a consequence of a significant shift in values within a particular society, adapted to varying national circumstances and having the effect of reshaping the priorities and expectations of a substantial portion of the citizenry.[10] Such remolding of the climate might pose "a crisis for democracy," since profits-guided, growth-dependent capitalism would come under increasing attack as the organizational and normative foundation for individual, society, and world, and this attack would undoubtedly stimulate a counterattack by those social forces that would view the emergent anticapitalist outlook as a dangerous challenge.[11]

Michalak argues that it is "utopian" to wait for workers to prefer bicycles to cars. He is skeptical about the prospects for an early transformation of civilization. In essence, the controversy here is partly empirical, partly interpretative. I believe the old models and related paraphernalia of myths, beliefs, and values are being undermined, although it is difficult to assess to what extent and with what effects. These old models have not yet been displaced, or even seriously opposed, by the competing holistic, spiritual, and anarchistic outlooks that are gaining an increasing following at all levels of advanced industrial societies.

There is also a question of whether and in what form it is possible to work against "the established order" in the Soviet Union or, for that matter, any authoritarian society. How can it be done? And how does it relate to undermining the established order in the West? The interaction between the two superpowers would be closely watched in the context of value changes, especially in relation to "security." For the process in the West to go very far, it would have to include the inception of some kind of reciprocal disarming arrangement, and for this to happen, some changes in the Soviet conception of "security" and "world order" would have to occur. Would these reciprocal prospects be encouraged by a less threatening United States posture in the world? Would the Soviet leadership risk relaxing its grip on its own people or would the Soviet people challenge the government more openly and on a larger scale? These questions cannot be answered confidently in advance, but the uncertainty about answers is no excuse at all for not taking steps that seem likely on their own to give more open or liberal societies a better chance for survival and dignity.

In essence, then, I share Michalak's view that there needs to be a greater effort to promote WOMP-oriented change within states, but this effort cannot accomplish much unless reinforced by a more radical movement for political reconstruction. Such a movement is actually forming "in the wings" of the nonsocialist West and will become increasingly visible over the course of the next decade. Whether it will remain marginal or make a mainstream impact remains a question. This movement will be catalyzed by such developments as the struggle against nuclear power, the stagnancy of the world economy, one or another eco-catastrophe, a World War III scare, or a combative use of nuclear weaponry, as well as by a whole series of positive images that arise from a rebirth of religious consciousness and a redefinition of "the good life." Such altered outlooks encourage acceptance of "voluntary simplicity," "nonviolence," "soft energy paths," vegetarian diet, organic farming, appropriate technology. What most of us mean by "security" and "well-being" is under attack and in the process of reformulation, at least in western civilization.[12]

In more theoretical terms, the Hobbesian consensus about self and society is breaking down under the pressures of the nuclear age. It is not only the practical (Humean) appreciation that order comes from habit and mutual convenience, as well as from apprehensions about violence.[13] More than this is happening. A religious reawakening is occurring in the West. It is connected with affirming the sacred as an essential aspect of what makes life worth living and that finds its characteristic expression in symbols and attitudes of unity, in visions of the whole that encompass the natural surroundings of human society. It is too early even to name this cluster of related developments, but it seems likely to alter dramatically in the next several decades our image of what people want and need by way of material goods and services.

It is correct that many of the material deprivations associated with the global structure could be mitigated, and possibly eliminated, by a series of social and political revolutions at the state level in the Third World societies. Such a broad process of national self-determination is, in fact, continuing in the postcolonial period. The revolutionary victories in Iran and Nicaragua during 1979 are indictive of this trend. Relatively small reallocations of investment capital in developing countries could stimulate the production of necessities and, thereby, help to overcome absolute poverty, as well as close the gaps between rich and poor, city and country, favored regions and neglected regions. But these prospects for reform depend on more than the drift of domestic politics. Intervention does occur, neocolonial structures of dependency do exist, ruling elites receive arms and aid from foreign governments, and the world economic structure, especially by way of the International Monetary Fund, constrains the political options of poor countries in a generally regressive manner.

Revolutionary nationalism, with all of its imperfections, seems like the most progressive cure, although assuredly, WOMP values *per se* may not be embraced by the new leadership. On this Michalak's "realism" is well warranted. However, my contention, admittedly not spelled out in *Future Worlds,* is that revolutionary nationalism is a positive stage in the evolution of Third World politics that almost automatically broadens the popular base of the governing process. The new leadership is also globally progressive in the sense of generally adopting the line and outlook of the nonaligned movement, including its emphasis on global demilitarization and call for a new international economic order.

At this stage it is certainly true that value realization for almost every national society depends mainly on internal political dynamics. And yet, such a view is not entirely convincing. The global political and economic structure characterized by hierarchy and fragmentation interferes with and distorts political life at the national level. Central guidance capabilities could not, by themselves of course, guarantee autonomous development at the state level. However, if a transformed global system was itself a product of value shifts in the North, then this new normative orientation would help produce a global setting more conducive to the dynamics of national self-determination. The governments of the North, among other things, would initiate a process of demilitarization (including disarmament), which implies a virtual renunciation of hegemonial and intervention-ary diplomacy. In actuality, WOMP-oriented reforms would allow the state system to flourish for the first time ever in accord with its primary dimension of facilitating autonomous politics at national levels of political integration.

Michalak is very critical about my ideas on leadership. He contends that my call for genuine leadership is unrealistic in the extreme, and that if my idea of a genuine leader could ever be realized, it would obviate the need for drastic global reform. I agree that *A Study of Future Worlds* does not adequately develop a theory of politics and is vulnerable to the line of criticism offered by Michalak. Nevertheless, the central claim made there about political leadership seems to hold up, namely that politics-as-usual is beholden to models of problem-solving that cannot succeed under present circumstances. The adoption of more appropriate models of problem-solving will depend on new configurations of values and interests, giving rise to leaders committed to work for a postcapitalist, humanistic transformation. These leaders will be necessary to build hope and to reduce the prospects of militarist reactions at home and abroad. To call them "genuine" is admittedly circular, as Michalak argues, but it is also a shorthand way of suggesting that ours is a period of transition in a rather specific sense. It is a period in which the old ways are dying, however stubbornly this central reality is resisted by dominant social groupings, and new ways are struggling at the margins to be born. Politics always becomes polarized during times of crisis and transition. In this situation we should expect that the old leadership will advocate a mainstream defensive posture toward the past and future to resist the pressures of a transformative posture that is not yet organized into an official politics.[14]

The overall situation is complex, partly because political struggle is being waged in different forms in the various main regions of the world. What is a genuine leader for the United States may not be suitable for Nigeria or even Mexico. To conceive of the future globally, however, is to acknowledge the unevenness of this struggle. My image of a "genuine" leader is one who carries forward that struggle given the possibilities of a particular arena of power. This unevenness can be indicated schematically. In the North-West (i.e., the noncommunist North), a genuine leader is one with a vision of security, energy, and well-being that is grounded on a nonmaterialist view of individual and collective fulfillment. In the North-East (i.e., the Soviet bloc), a genuine leader is one with a demilitarized vision of state, society, and world system.[15] In the South, a genuine leader is committed to revolutionary nationalism, anti-imperalism (antihierarchy), and some form of socialist development strategy.

In essence, then, I share Michalak's view that it is necessary to promote world order values largely within the confines of the state system. The domestic arenas of national politics are the primary ones for advancing the cause of WOMP-oriented world order at this stage; the external arenas (for instance, the United Nations) are decidedly secondary and derivative. However, to the extent that Michalak also believes that global reform depends principally on persuading existing elites to act more sensibly and more humanely, then we are in disagreement. Part of the disagreement may be semantic. It all depends on what Michalak means by "putting pressure on non genuine leaders" (p. 9). I find his position ambiguous. If it means mainstream persuasion, liberal style, I reject it. If "pressure" includes unconventional politics (adapted to circumstances of time and place), including demonstrations, general strikes, and civil disobedience, then it is similar to what I have in mind.

CENTRAL GUIDANCE SYSTEM

Michalak is critical of my treatment of central guidance on several grounds. Perhaps the most essential is this: if the acceptance of WOMP values precedes the structure, then the structure is gratuitous; whereas if there is no advance acceptance, which Michalak regards as the likely case, then the system is unworkable. Of course, from the vantage point of the present, any alternative order for world society seems implausible, which is to say, we are convinced of the inevitability and durability of present arrangements. It is this outlook that allows Hobbesian images of human nature and society to occupy the terrain of "realism" in international society and that, consequently, makes non-Hobbesian views of the future easy to dismiss as "idealist." I regard this metaphysical entrapment to be a dangerous form of dogmatism that is itself one of the pillars of the present system—that is, reinforcing the perception of its necessity. One role of world order studies is to challenge this false perception of inevitability by positing plausible alternative images of human nature and society.

A *Study of Future Worlds* centers its inquiry upon the global structure appropriate for a world system that would be capable of sustaining WOMP values. Its stress on central guidance is at the expense of emphasizing collective transformation at lower levels of social organization. The idea of a demilitarizing world—central to a positive vision of the future—presupposes shifts in attitudes toward consumption and security, especially in the most affluent portions of the world. There are an increasing number of individuals who are bearers of this positive vision, yet they remain powerless at the level of state power. I depict this upsurge as a trend at the level of individual consciousness that suggests the early phases of the birth of world order. Of course, such an interpretation cannot be demonstrated by facts and figures, much less by official patterns of state behavior.

In any event, the vision of *Future Worlds* presupposes substantial normative underpinnings as a precondition for a demilitarizing process, which is likely to include the relative growth of central guidance capabilities. Without these underpinnings, central guidance would be either futile or tyrannical. It would be premature in a sociological sense, as the requisite sense of community and wholeness would not be present, and therefore, any structure would likely be captured and turned in repressive, exploitative directions.

But substantial underpinnings do not imply a conflict-free world. The degree of normative preparation would vary according to the level of development, culture, and ideology in different societies. The world as a whole would remain diverse. Different priorities would persist, and these might be accentuated by the exposure of mass misery and inequality in a demilitarizing setting. As such, one could expect pockets of resistance within countries, including movements of remilitarization. Regressive governments at the state level would certainly exist in the early decades of a new world order. The outcome of these fundamental conflicts might depend upon the conditions that led to the original force of demilitarization. Did it proceed gradually and peacefully in response to the pressures of accommodating the world population within existing resource constraints? Did this new consciousness "take off" in the form of a religious awakening that spread its beliefs around the world? Did it emerge as part of a process of "picking up the pieces" after some sort of traumatic breakdown—amounting to a super-United Nations as a postcatastrophe response? Regardless of the way a scheme of central guidance came about, however, it would require a constitutional framework that tried to balance efficiency against constraint. This framework would be articulated in the atmosphere of transformation, sensitive to the actual contours of the future. My depiction of such a constitutional arrangement is purely *illustrative* of the type of institutional complexity that might be devised to sustain a political order oriented around the WOMP values.

Of course, such a framework might not work successfully in crisis situations. And, indeed, many of us are fearful about the future because we believe the existing framework of governance does not seem likely to stave off either decay or catastrophe. Michalak would have it that such modeling of constitutional futures entails an "*apolitical* if not antipolitical tone" (p. 13). In part, this characterization is an apt criticism of my inability to give political verisimilitude to a preferred world order system. In this sense, my depiction of politics in a preferred world is marred by a failure of political imagination. In part, however, I believe such criticism stems from Hobbesian dogmatism that refuses to consider as plausible the kind of politics appropriate for a social movement built on premises of human solidarity and cooperative potential.[16] I take my stand on the reality of this possibility.

At the same time, I readily admit that *Future Worlds* overdoes the depiction of global structure. In this respect, its orientation is tied too closely to the political, legal heritage of world order studies. I now believe that the domestic destructuring of state power has to be given far greater prominence. Attention also must be given to the formation of a theory of politics in which constitutional minimalism on all levels of political integration is a striking feature, and further, to the sustainability of the new order that will depend on its capacity to engender allegiance and loyalty without threat or use of force. Demilitarization as a broad tendency and process is unlikely to happen unless accomanied by a religious (not ecclesiastical) reawakening that confirms human unity, the sacredness of nature, and the spiritual worth of the good life. Without this religious dimension, the transition process will reproduce the power struggle of the past and give rise to new cycles of violence and militarization.

Even granting these reformulations, is Michalak correct that the politics of a preferred world will be, at best, technocratic, a dreary variant of social engineering at a global level? He is correct to point out these dangers. I unwittingly contributed to these anxieties by relying upon rational forms of exposition to describe the structure and organization of a central guidance capability. In fact, political consciousness will not mechanically invoke and apply abstractions about world order values. A new political consciousness animated by these values will try to reach decisions, make choices; conflict will occur, but in a political atmosphere dominated by popular deference, even reverence. My optimistic assumption is that the peoples of the world generally will come to trust such governing processes, partly as a consequence of their own participation in them. If power in the sense we now understand it, as conjoined to force and threats, remains the only foundation for stability, then we are truly stuck as a species. Indeed, the rational humanist with this kind of outlook cannot avoid an attitude of despair or cynicism. On such a basis, there is no use hoping or caring. If such an atmosphere develops, we can anticipate that leaders will feel caught in a whirlwind and will embark more actively upon destructive paths. The 1980's will be exceedingly dangerous, a time when the politics of self-destruction are likely to become popular because they foster the illusion of doing something to stem the tide of decay and decline.

CONCLUSION

It is impossible to make bright promises about the future. At the same time, some positive potentialities and glimmers of light exist. We can act on this reality for the sake of our self-esteem, out of a spirit of love for others, out of an experience of the sacred. The darkness is real also. Entering the future will be hazardous, at best. Yet it can also be an exciting, extraordinary time if it includes the anguishing birth of civilizations that produce the economics, politics, culture, and spirituality we require to survive and develop as a species. On the deepest level, I believe, the grounds and justifications of world order studies lie in strengthening these hopes, not by mere preaching or wishing, but by clarifying analysis and by rooting itself in actual historical possibilities.

The most fundamental effort of the world order approach cannot be understood in the same manner as knowledge is generally conceived in the social sciences. The enterprise of world order is dedicated to realizing the potential for reconstructing international relations, rather than in amassing information about present arrangements among sovereign states. I am reminded of the response made by Robert Wilson, a leading contemporary playwright, to an interviewer's question:

Q: Do you feel your work presents a lot of information, a little information, or no information?

A: It's a different kind of experience. I don't think information is very interesting. I'm only interested in architecture.[17]

Architecture is concerned with design and building, as well as structure.

NOTES

1. Stanley Michalak, "Richard Falk's Future World: A Critique of WOMP-USA," *The Review of Politics* 43 (1980): 3–17.

2. An analysis along these lines can be found in Richard Falk, *This Endangered Planet: Prospects and Proposals for Human Survival* (New York: Free Press, 1972), pp. 93–213; compare this with the more restricted conceptions of the world order challenge in Stanley Hoffmann, *Primacy or World Order: America's Foreign Policy since the Cold War* (New York: McGraw-Hill, 1978) and Zbigniew Brzezinski, "Recognizing the Crisis," *Foreign Policy* 17 (1974–1975): 63–74.

3. For some important instances, mainly with an economic slant, see Donella Meadows et al., *The Limits to Growth* (New York: Potomac Association, 1972); Mihajlo Mesarovic and Eduard Pestel, *Mankind at the Turning Point* (New York: E.P. Dutton, 1974); Jan Tinbergen, coordinator, *RIO: Reshaping the International Order* (New York: E. P. Dutton, 1976); Amilcar O. Herrera et al., *Catastrophe of New Society? A Latin American World Model* (Ottawa, Canada: International Development Research Centre, 1976); Wassily Leontief et al., *The Future of the World Economy* (New York: Oxford University Press, 1977). Also relevant, yet less comprehensive in its assessment, is the work of the 1980's Project of the Council on Foreign Relations.

4. This range is conveyed by a series of essays in Saul H. Mendlovitz, ed., *On the Creation of a Just World Order* (New York: Free Press, 1975).

5. "Invisible oppression" refers to exploitative structures of economic, social, political, and cultural relations that are not generally perceived as such. The conception is similar to what Marx had in mind by reference to "alienation." Examples of invisible oppression include security relying on the development and deployment of nuclear weapons and doctrines of mass destruction—industrial operations that cause atmospheric contamination, storage of nerve gas close to urban populations, and emission of low-level radiation by nuclear reactors.

6. Utopian studies have been principally literary and philosophical, concerned with the portrayal of a perfect human community in the manner of Plato's *Republic*. The utopian antecedent of world order studies is a legal, political conception of the world as community, a tradition of speculation that goes back to Dante's *De Monarchia* with its argument on behalf of political unification under the aegis of the Roman Empire.

7. Grenville Clark and Louis B. Sohn, *World Peace through World Law,* 3rd rev. ed. (Cambridge, Mass.: Harvard University Press, 1966).

8. See reference cited in note 4.

9. WOMP has, in fact, made a serious effort to engage scholars from the socialist orbit in its work, that is, Marxist scholars from both socialist and nonsocialist countries. As yet, the published fruits of these efforts are meager. At the same time, the oral interaction has been intense and has made an impact on the outlook of WOMP, especially with regard to strategies of transformation. Principal world order works as of 1982 are listed in Richard Falk and Samuel Kim, "An Approach to World Order Studies and the World System," Working Paper #22 (New York: World Order Models Project, 1982), p. 30.

10. For perceptive inquiry along these lines see Theodore Roszak, *Unfinished Animal: The Aquarian Frontier and the Evolution of Consciousness* (New York: Harper and Row, 1975) and his *Person/Planet* (Garden City, N.Y.: Doubleday, 1978).

11. Such forebodings are sketched by the authors of a much-publicized study of the Trilateral Commission, Michael J. Crozier, Samuel P. Huntington, and Joji Watanuki, *The Crisis of Democracy* (New York: New York University Press, 1975).

12. Western civilization is important even beyond the West. Its perspectives and fundamental outlook have become a shared ideology for ruling elites throughout the world, including the communist countries. There are, to be sure, anti-Western elements among some governing groups, but the essential conviction that science-based technology contains the best promise of societal progress is almost universally endorsed. The Westernization of world political consciousness is almost complete and has, if anything, increased its influence during the era of decolonialization.

13. For a creative inquiry into non-Hobbesian dimensions of order operative in the state system, see Fritz Kratochwil, *Foreign Policy and International Order* (Boulder, Colorado: Westview, 1978).

14. The high rate of abstention from electoral politics in the United States is one expression of this loss of confidence in mainstream channels. Another expression is the increasing perception that the main political parties provide insufficient choice on the questions that matter. The formation in 1979 of a Citizens' party represents a third-party initiative with the definite idea of widening citizen choice and control over public policy.

15. For expressions of what this might entail in the Soviet context, see Andrei Sakharov, *Progress, Coexistence and Intellectual Freedom,* (New York: Norton, 1970); Andrei Sakharov, *My Country and the World* (New York: Knopf, 1975), and Roy A. Medvedev, *On Socialist Democracy* (New York: Norton, 1975).

16. This is also my response to a similar line of criticism in a stimulating and original article by Miriam Steiner, "Conceptions of the Individual in the World Order Models Project (WOMP) Literature," *International Interactions* 6 (1979): 27–41.

17. "Interview with Robert Wilson," *New York Arts Journal,* spring 1977, p. 17.

PART THREE

The United States and World Order

CHAPTER 6

Beyond Internationalism*

There is, at present, a widely shared sense that we are entering a new phase of international history that will condition future American foreign policy. But to condition is not, of course, to determine. There exists a range of responses from which to choose, and it is unlikely that any fully coherent response will emerge during the next several formative years, if at all.

In any case, this seems an unusually propitious moment for the United States to reconsider the basic goals and premises of its foreign policy. A presidential election is in the offing, American society is still experiencing reverberations from the Vietnam defeat, new weapons systems and strategic developments rekindle fears of nuclear warfare, attitudes diverge widely regarding the Soviet threat to American security, and even wider divergencies of opinion exist as to the consequences and character of Third World militancy.

In addition, the symbolic occasion of the bicentennial stimulates a re-examination of the background of American foreign policy. Looking back 200 years involves the use of far longer time frames than is customary for foreign policy analysis. Such an historical perspective shifts attention to the sweep of America's experience as an independent country and thereby helps liberate analysis from preoccupations of the moment. But more than this, reconsidering the past establishes a context for speculating about the future. Another advantage of looking backward is to establish the distinctive political culture that has made America what it has become and is becoming. America's political culture has parallel strands and inconsistent traditions, but to become reacquainted with these sources is essential, I think, for anyone concerned with the future of American foreign policy.

My purpose here is to assess American foreign policy needs in the new international era in light of several principal convictions: first,

---

*This chapter, originally published in *Foreign Policy* during 1976, reflects, in essence, the mood and outlook just prior to Jimmy Carter's presidency. It stands now primarily to document the retreat on all fronts from the rhetoric and stance of liberal internationalism.

that the United States finds itself in a new and still indistinct geopolitical situation; second, that the Jeffersonian perspective on America's role in the world is suggestive, although no more than that, for those who favor a value-oriented foreign policy with roots in the historical past and that can yet respond to likely discontinuities in the probable future; third, that the effort of "liberal internationalists" to redirect American foreign policy has failed to make adjustments in behavior commensurate with either the character of the new geopolitical challenge or their own aspirations to revive America's role as a moral force in the world; finally, that appropriate adjustments called for on both geopolitical and normative grounds can be illustrated by reference to concrete policy to show what is meant by a new foreign policy alive to the Jeffersonian perspective. The four sections of this chapter correspond with these four concerns.

A GEOPOLITICAL PERSPECTIVE

Americans have always been "self-conscious" about their status in the world of sovereign states. This self-consciousness has focused upon the special destiny of the United States, upon the behavior of globally dominant states as "great powers," and upon how the United States should relate to the main interactions among these great powers. The United States did not begin its national existence as a great power; on the contrary, it was initially a relatively weak and remote state with the singular, vital interest of safeguarding its independence. However, with the passage of time, the United States improved its relative and absolute position in the world and expanded the geographical reach of its "vital interests." The United States became, of course, a great power and, in time, the greatest of great powers.

Geopolitics is concerned with the conditions of "order" in a world of sovereign states.[1] In Western juridical thought, order in international relations is associated with the basic doctrines of international law. These doctrines embody in legal language the fundamental concepts that underlie the modern state system: territorial sovereignty, the state as the sole subject of the system, the equality of states, nonintervention, and the right of states to act in self-defense. However, although these legal notions are universally affirmed, in reality they are not the principal sources of order in the world.

International order has been largely created and sustained by the role great powers have played outside their territories. Thus, the geopolitical perspective emphasizes inequalities among states, zones of domination, patterns of intervention and penetration, alliances, conflict formations, and the role of military force. As is evident, juridical conceptions of order are inconsistent with and subordinate to geopolitical forms of order. This subordination is manifest in the legal confirmation of colonial title to territory or in the validity of "peace treaties" that legalize the territorial gains of aggression.

American foreign policy has always exhibited ambivalent attitudes toward geopolitical forms of order. The United States initiated its existence through victory in a war of national liberation waged against one of the great powers of the time. The geographical isolation of the United States from the main arenas of hostile interaction among these great powers also was formative.

The last 200 years of American history can be divided into four main geopolitical phases. A brief discussion of each phase suggests the relevance of the geopolitical situation to the various alternative roles currently available to the United States as the most affluent, experimental, and powerful but embattled of all sovereign states.

Renouncing Geopolitics (1789–1917)

The initial prime motive of American foreign policy was to avoid getting drawn into the geopolitical maelstrom of its era. Having won its struggle against England with the help of France, the United States was particularly anxious to avoid getting drawn into further wars as a consequence of Anglo-French rivalries. The early years of the nineteenth century demonstrated that the United States depended for commercial reasons on interaction with Europe and would not, in turn, be left altogether alone to pursue its independent path.

Nevertheless, America's geopolitical posture was plain in this period. Its most celebrated formulation was George Washington's Farewell Address of 1796, a document that won the shared endorsement of both Thomas Jefferson and Alexander Hamilton, polar rivals in their day on many fundamental questions of national policy. The essence of American foreign policy in this period was to opt out of great power diplomacy, to remain detached from the geopolitical nexus of the day. This tactical stance of detachment was reinforced by a moral judgment that European political rivalries were despotic and led to an endless chain of warfare. America, by its position and its ideology, could and should remain detached, partly to ensure its evolution as a virtuous nation.

Complementary American strategies of expansionism, illustrated, for instance, by the Spanish-American War of 1898, impinged upon geopolitical structure and qualified the purity of detachment. Jefferson, despite his vaunted passion for decentralization and small-scale government, was the chief architect of America's continental expansion via huge territorial acquisitions (Florida and the Louisiana Purchase) concluded during his presidency. But more than this, the United States moved toward the proclamation of a custodial role for the entire Western hemisphere. On one level, such a proclamation (formalized in the Monroe Doctrine in 1823) merely extended the benefits of detachment to Latin America, the United States playing the self-appointed role of keeping the hemisphere off-limits to the acquisitive great powers of Europe.

When asked by President James Monroe to comment on the proposed doctrine, Jefferson called it "the most momentous which has ever been offered to my contemplation since that of Independence." Jefferson believed that Monroe's proposal would complement existing efforts to maintain America's geopolitical detachment by extending the benefits of detachment to Latin America. He reaffirmed the notion of detachment from European affairs as the cornerstone of American foreign policy. And in turn, Jefferson defended this geopolitical orientation by stressing his belief in America's moral superiority. The American objective would be "to make our hemisphere that of freedom" in contrast to Europe, "the domicile of despotism."[2]

It wasn't long before the attempt to contain European colonial expansion blended into the development of a curiously distinctive anticolonial American brand of expansionism. As Samuel P. Huntington suggests, the anticolonial ideology of the United States has not extinguished the imperial impulse, but merely channeled that impulse into economic and cultural forms of penetration rather than territorial or juridical forms of transnational penetration and control, ranging from notions of custodial intervention in Latin America to the maintenance of an "open door policy" to assure economic access in the Far East.[3]

Especially because this special variety of imperialism was partially motivated by the positive mission of providing others with widely admired features of the American experience, it is almost impossible for Americans to strip away the veil of self-righteousness that envelops their foreign policy. Indeed, this dual geopolitical heritage underlies all subsequent efforts by the United States to spread its influence, while simultaneously adding to its affluence by reconciling its immense power and wealth with an abiding special sense of national virtue, a self-proclaimed "exceptionalism."

Emergency Geopolitics (1917–1947)

The reluctant decision to enter World War I to sway the course of the war in favor of France and Great Britain marked a decisive shift in America's relationship to the geopolitical nexus of the world system. Of course, the United States had earlier ventured beyond the Western Hemisphere, perhaps most prominently in the "opening" of Japan in 1853 and the annexation of the Philippines at the close of the century. Entry into World War I, however, represented a partial repudiation of the diplomacy of detachment, which had presupposed that the outcome of warfare among the European powers was not a vital interest of the United States. In effect, when the United States entered World War I, it was serving notice that under certain exceptional circumstances, it would make its weight directly felt, even at the cost of American lives, in the traditional geopolitical arena of Europe.

The fact that Woodrow Wilson was the American president at the time was significant. Wilson coupled America's entry onto the European stage with a strenuous effort to transform geopolitics and shift its character to conform more closely to a juridical conception of international order. Much to the distress of European leaders, Wilson proclaimed American support for the ethos of national self-determination, thereby strongly encouraging anticolonialist tendencies throughout the world. Wilson also lent credence to the idea that traditional geopolitics based on balance of power diplomacy was corrupt and inevitably led to highly destructive international wars. To overcome such a condition, in Wilson's view, classical geopolitics must be gradually superseded by the formation of organized community procedures capable of providing genuine security and modes of peaceful change in international life. The creation of the League of Nations was one expression of this Wilsonian urge to transform geopolitics. In a sense, the United States under Wilson attempted to extend the notion of hemispheric liberty to the entire world.

However, Wilson underestimated the strength of America's traditional commitment to geopolitical detachment. The American refusal to join the League of Nations can be explained in a variety of plausible ways, but surely one factor was that the United States was far from ready, no matter what the circumstances, to assume a permanent role either in keeping the geopolitical balance among the great powers or in transforming the geopolitical nexus in a Wilsonian direction.

At the end of World War I, the triumph of Leninism in the Soviet Union countered the American tendency to resume fully its earlier posture of geopolitical detachment. Wilson was as committed to making the world unsafe for socialism as he was to making it safe for democracy, and unlike the idealistic part of his diplomacy, this ideological and confrontational side persisted as a durable element in American foreign policy. The United States joined with France, Great Britain, and others in the allied intervention after World War I, seeking by military means to reverse the outcome of the Russian Revolution.[4] Although the intervention ended in failure, the United States stubbornly refused to recognize the Soviet government until 1933.

Such a policy exhibited the American view that revolutionary socialism was an illegitimate form of governance that deserved to be undermined and combatted. Such an ideological view of self-determination introduced a tension into the traditional American position of opposition to colonialism and added an important element to American foreign policy.

World War II, coming after a period of prolonged tension and economic decline, accentuated many of these earlier tendencies. Again, the United States sought at first to remain detached from the European arena of struggle even though Hitler's threat to the established geopolitical order went far beyond merely upsetting the balance among the great powers of Europe. By 1941, the United States was still not adequately prepared for a major war and finally joined as a full participant only after Japan attacked (Japan, significantly, like the United States, evolved as a great power outside the traditional geopolitical nexus of power) and Germany declared war. In its wartime role, the United States sided with and helped the Soviet Union defeat Germany, thereby suspending its ideological opposition to communism as a world movement. This wartime collaboration, expediential for both sides, was to create disagreement and confusion among Americans about the opportunities for order and justice in the postwar world that emerged in 1945.

Whereas World War I weakened Europe's control over geopolitical structure, World War II shifted geopolitical organizing energy away from Europe altogether. Like Wilson before him, Franklin Roosevelt was firmly convinced that a durable peace depended upon effective international arrangements that would move toward the substitution of juridical forms of order for geopolitical maneuverings of states. The United Nations continued the League of Nations approach of providing institutional reinforcement for the juridical promise of international law; it was also the bearer of that promise "to save succeeding generations from the scourge of war," contained in the preamble of its own charter. The location of this global institution in New York symbolized the transfer of geopolitical capacity to the United States and also represented a successful attempt to forestall a recurrence of the isolationist sentiment that had kept the United States from joining the League of Nations.

Our rapid demobilization after the war suggests that the traditional American desire for geopolitical withdrawal was still operative. But the next context meant that the desire no longer corresponded to the objective situation. The United States, for better or worse, had become the principal source of order in the world, both as a great power and as an advocate of increased respect for juridical arrangements. The advocacy was suspect from the outset, to the extent that it coincided with American political capacity to dominate the activities of the United Nations. The idealistic impulse had not been tested in relation to traditional geopolitical goals of power and influence. When these tests occurred in succeeding decades, as a consequence of the global scale of the cold war and through the formation of an anti-Western group of Third World countries, the idealistic impulse did not significantly persist except as "a cover story." The United States increasingly behaved like a European great power of the eighteenth or nineteenth century, that is, like the states against which it had earlier defined its own identity.

Imperial Geopolitics (1947–1973)

The United States played the principal role in reconstituting a viable international order in the years following World War II. No posture of geopolitical detachment was sustainable in the face of the Soviet-led communist challenge taking shape at a time when the traditional great powers of Europe were on the defensive. Once again the juridical view of order was quickly superseded by geopolitical exigencies. The United Nations became a partisan arena in which majorities could be routinely mobilized in support of American political goals.

In American foreign policy thinking, the need to contain communist power took priority over legalistic considerations and idealistic hopes, especially after 1949 when Mao Tse-tung's forces achieved their spectacular victory in the Chinese Civil War. In the Korean War (1950–1953), the United Nations sided with South Korea, conferring the blessings of a globalist mandate on America's military role. From 1953 onward, the United States gave major aid to French efforts to defeat the independence movement in Indochina. When the French cause seemed lost, the United States came close to intervening militarily itself.

In short, during the period following World War II, anticommunism became the principal guideline for American policy-makers. This was peculiarly evident during John Foster Dulles's tenure as secretary of state in the Eisenhower years and was dramatized by his ceaseless travels to foreign capitals to form a global network of American-led alliances against communism. The foreign policy of the cold war was also deeply influenced by the adverse lessons of appeasement associated with Britain's attempt to accommodate Hitler at Munich. American foreign policy-makers identified Stalinist Russia as a revolutionary danger to the minimum geopolitical structure in the same sense that Hitler's Germany was dangerous. Therefore, the United States was determined to take early action rather than be faced with a major war later on. The notion of deterrence, then, was expanded from its literal relationship to national security to encompass a much broader context of geopolitical security. In effect, any international development that encouraged Moscow to pursue its revolutionary objective of spreading communist influence (which was perceived as identical with Soviet imperial influence) was perceived by Washington as adverse, an occasion for opposition.

The anticommunism crusade became fully manifest in the course of America's long involvement in the Vietnam war. The United States added to its abandonment of geopolitical detachment the renunciation of its traditional commitments to anticolonialism and national self-determination. The image of "the free world" was never much more than an anticommunist mobilizing concept. It was totally incompatible with Jefferson's vision of the United States as bearer of liberty in contrast to the despotism of other societies. But neither was Jefferson's ideological heritage explicitly renounced. Indeed, America pressed hard to assure the trappings of democratic government in societies where its own involvement was deep. Nothing was more ludicrous, or more revealing, in this regard than American pressure on South Vietnamese leaders of the 1960s to establish a constitution, allow political parties, and organize elections. Of course, this pressure also flowed from a practical need to sustain domestic support in the United States by convincing the American people that some positive goals were being achieved.

In the postwar period, American global leadership was also expressed in economic terms. The Bretton Woods arrangements rested world monetary policy on the commanding strength of the dollar. The General Agreement on Tariffs and Trade (GATT) established an American-conceived framework for the encouragement of trade. And, most of all, the American corporation became a transnational phenomenon that penetrated foreign societies. This economic role thus reinforced the geopolitical one. America's world position rested upon maintaining political stability in countries that received foreign capital and upon the willingness of such governments to protect capital against expropriation.

Even more to the point, the overall growth of corporate capitalism on a global scale also tacitly depended on inhibiting Socialist development strategies. Therefore, quite independent of "containment" strategies devised for purposes of national security, there arose an interventionary impulse to prevent the dynamics of self-determination from eventuating in socialist societies. Because this impulse to intervene contradicted the American juridical creed of respect for national sovereignty, it tended wherever possible to be channeled into covert operations and indirect means of influencing foreign societies. The latter repertoire included training officers of Third World countries in anti-Marxist counter-insurgency roles, as well as using foreign aid for political purposes rarely acknowledged in public.

In this period of flourishing American imperialism, idealistic pretensions coexisted with the ambitious spread of influence and control. John F. Kennedy's simultaneous enthusiasm for the Peace Corps and the Green Berets aptly reflected this characteristic American attempt to do good while doing well. As long as a foreign society appeared to be developing along lines the U.S. government regarded as appropriate, then aid and support were forthcoming. However, if American policy-makers concluded that a particular society was moving toward socialism, then strong interventionary practices by the United States were likely to ensue. This pattern was especially evident in domains of traditional American influence.

American efforts in Central America—the anti-Arbenz coup in Guatemala (1954), the anti-Castro Bay of Pigs Operation (1961), and the Dominican intervention (1965)—are good examples of this pattern. The anti-Allende "destabilization program" in Chile (1970–1973) was conducted more discreetly, partly because it was physically more remote and situated at the periphery of America's hemispheric sphere of influence.

Increasing numbers of countries achieved political independence in the 1950s and 1960s. Many of these "new nations" were as fearful of getting embroiled in diversionary and debilitating geopolitics as the United States had been in the nineteenth century. Consequently, many authentic leaders of these countries sought to safeguard their independence by forging a new diplomacy of geopolitical detachment. But now, the United States, as geopolitical leader and as the guarantor of peace and security in the face of communist aggression, was deeply hostile to these new assertions of geopolitical detachment—hence, Dulles's distaste for efforts by such leaders as Nehru, Sukarno, and Nkrumah, to promote "nonalignment" and "neutralism." With the foreign policy priorities characteristic of this era, America stressed its support for strongly anticommunist governments on the periphery of Soviet power, ranging from the Rhee regime in South Korea to the shah's imperial government in Iran. Indeed, as in Iran, American covert intervention was responsible for an earlier governing group that failed to uphold national rights. These anticommunist leaders generally welcomed an American commitment, even if it meant bringing American troops into the country and offering rights to maintain military bases.

Later in this period, as the Communist bloc split into pro-Soviet and pro-Chinese camps, a process of partial "de-ideologization" of world politics began. Indeed, the new configuration of great powers, now including China, produced, over time, a dramatic reversal of affinities. China became increasingly concerned about the Soviet menace, until in the late 1960s it reached out to support many anti-Soviet actors in the world, including even the European NATO alliance. In 1971, through Nixon's trip to China, the United States finally entered into diplomatic relations with the second socialist superpower in the world, although it has still not fully disentangled itself from its earlier commitment to Chiang Kai-shek. With the advent of a détente posture in U.S.-Soviet relations, the ideological dimension of geopolitics further diminished (but has far from disappeared and is now experiencing a revival). The arms race continued at high levels, considering the relative absence of international tension. The rationale for interventionary diplomacy provided by the cold war was severely eroded by the difficulties encountered in Vietnam, by the vigorous dissent engendered among the American people, and by the disintegration of a unified Communist challenge emanating from a monolithic ideological stance.

Also relevant was the steady rise to prominence of European and Japanese economic competition challenging the pre-eminence of the dollar. American military paramountcy persisted, due to the dominance of the United States in nuclear and nonnuclear weaponry, but it was no longer reinforced to nearly the same extent by economic paramountcy. American paramountcy largely persisted as an objective condition, but its substance was being eroded abroad and its policy implications re-examined at home.

In addition, a new roster of concerns associated with population

growth, resource depletion, and planetary pollution began to complicate the traditional geopolitical agenda, and these provoked concerns
about an international laissez faire economic and political system in
which each state pursues its own interests with only the most minimal
regard for the well-being of other states or of the system as a whole.
The onset and evolution of the nuclear age created a widespread
feeling that human survival itself might be threatened. But however
much the apocalyptic imagination flourished, the disinclination of the
nuclear superpowers to disarm, the absence of nuclear warfare despite several decades of recurrent international crises and abiding
tension, and the apparent rationality of strategic deterrence, all contributed to the belief that it was futile, perhaps unnecessary, and
possibly dangerously destabilizing, to challenge the war system based
on national military establishments.

Managerial Geopolitics (1973–   )

The era of American paramountcy has largely come to an end, partly
through international developments and partly through a process of
domestic disenchantment with the burdens and consequences of the
earlier role. Many factors played a part. Already in the Kennedy and
Johnson years, American foreign-policy-makers had consolidated the
bureaucratic reins of power, relied on secrecy and deception, used
"national security" as a rationale for infringing upon citizens' rights,
and undermined the credibility and trust so essential for a healthy
democratic political order. The Vietnam defeat, of course, played a
major role in bringing this era to a close. The Vietnam experience,
especially in conjunction with the further reverberations caused by
Watergate and the CIA disclosures, substantially, if only temporarily,
diminished the American ardor for empire.

The United States has also found itself increasingly isolated on
principal symbolic issues of the day: the cause of Palestinian nationalism, the liberation of southern Africa, and the construction of a new
international economic order. In relation to each of these issues, the
United States is perceived as a principal source of resistance to
change. Its wealth and power are associated with exploitation and
regressive policies. These perceptions have been heightened as the
noncommunist world of advanced industrial states has lost its cohesion and as leftward political tendencies have emerged in several key
European countries. As matters now stand, the United States is more
envied and resented than respected and feared.

Part of this negative attitude toward the United States arises from the central role of American capital and corporations in the world economy. Capitalist strategies of economic development in Third World countries appear to combine receptivity to foreign investment and multinational corporations with brutal repression of domestic political opponents. The multinational corporation neither causes nor advocates such repression, but governments which have decided to maximize growth via private sector development rather than promote equity have also decided to defer mass economic development.

In Brazil and South Korea, for example, such decisions have produced high rates of economic growth, and significant profits for a small number of foreign and domestic entrepreneurs, in tandem with persisting large-scale poverty and persistent economic inequality. Leaders in such societies are often understandably nervous about potential opposition movements and are inclined to squelch such movements before they acquire mass support. Hence, there does seem to be a correlation between capitalist-style economic development, the denial of human rights, and the persistence of poverty. Also, there are no real counterexamples. While Socialist governments also imprison and frequently mistreat opponents, somehow these abuses are less offensive to world public opinion because they seem incidental to acceptable programs of social and economic development. Furthermore, the socialist path of development does not lead either to major repatriations of profits outside territory or to growing income disparities. The point here is that the United States is perceived by most of the world as the leader of reaction, opposing mass economic development for the Third World, resisting self-determination for many national peoples, and refusing to contribute sufficiently toward the creation of a new international economic order.

Many other factors have also altered the geopolitical context. It is not that the old quest for national control and economic advantage has vanished, but that new realities of complexity and vulnerability have created additional geopolitical dimensions. To advocate isolationism in this situation is either illusory or misleading if the intention is a revival of geopolitical detachment. At best, isolationists are anti-interventionist in cases like Vietnam, Chile, or Angola, i.e., exhorting compatriots to support policies of noninvolvement in foreign struggles of national self-determination. In addition, some who are called isolationists advocate reducing or eliminating the U.S. military presence by phasing out overseas commitments or bases. Isolation in this sense means taking unilateral moves to realize juridical ideas about a world of states allowing each to experience the risks and rewards of territorial sovereignty and political independence. Of course, such unilateral initiatives rest finally on the willingness of other great powers to withdraw from foreign entanglements to a roughly comparable degree.

But such a constrained view of American security as confined to our territory can no longer imply geopolitical detachment as it did in the early decades of the republic. The complex realities of interdependence preclude any such option. To deal with economic, technological, cultural, and ecological dimensions of national existence requires unprecedented participation in global arenas. Indeed, if geopolitics is primarily the art of sustaining order among great powers, it then seems appropriate to identify the emergence of a new species of geopolitics that is managerial in character.[5]

One managerial goal is to coordinate national policies in ways that reduce certain forms of national and global vulnerability. Whether the issue is pricing of raw materials, oil spills in the oceans, airport terrorism, or drought-induced famine, there is a growing agreement among American leaders that advanced planning of transnational scope is certainly desirable and probably necessary. Whether adequate managerial capacities can be evolved within the classical framework of geopolitics remains very much in doubt. The struggle to negotiate a new treaty for the oceans is one major test of whether governments can agree on managerial needs and, if they can, whether their agreement will be effective in practice and generally protective of global, as well as national, interests.

Phenomena as dissimilar as oil embargoes, terrorism, and ozone depletion suggest both the vulnerability of individual states, even the most powerful, and the fragility of the system as a whole. The United States is often the favorite target of those who are politically weak but driven to desperate acts by their sense of grievance and deprivation. To select Americans for kidnapping often will achieve a maximum impact; and besides, the United States is so often involved, or seems to be, in upholding the status quo against which the group is struggling. The United States, then, has a strong, often contradictory, incentive both to manage the various dimensions of global interaction in the quest for order and to satisfy the grievances of those who are most distressed by the status quo.

The set of concerns arising from poverty, repression, or territorial dispossession, whether raised in connection with ocean rights, Special Drawing Rights (IMF), or the right to eat, goes far beyond the mere functional requisites of order. The new concerns involve questions of justice and equity in international relations. One novel and hopeful feature of the present world setting is a growing conviction that order cannot be sustained unless there is widespread belief that justice is also being realized at a satisfactory rate. Whether most governments are fit instruments for the pursuit of a just world order is another and highly problematic issue, given the degree of internal repression and exploitation that exists in so many of those very states whose leaders are most vociferous in their calls for more equitable international arrangements.

In this new setting, the United States occupies a commanding but far from impregnable position. With so much to lose, the United States has the highest stake in promoting and fulfilling the need for "the management of interdependence." However, the managerial potentialities of the world system, unlike its imperial potentialities, depend very largely on the voluntary participation of governments with very different degrees of power, wealth, and ideological concern. Hence, the extent of participation will depend on whether or not governing groups believe such efforts will serve their own national interests. In this respect, managerial geopolitics more closely corresponds with the juridical postulates of the state system than do any of the three earlier geopolitical approaches relied upon during the course of American history.

Americans are unsure how to act under these new geopolitical conditions. There are four main groups contending for influence, and each exerts some influence at this stage.[6]

1. *Isolationists*—those who seek to restore the tradition of American detachment from geopolitical concerns. Their nostalgia is irrelevant outside the security area, for in the altered geopolitical setting the United States is too vulnerable, interpenetrating and interpenetrated to make a posture of detachment possible. The contemporary choice is one of selecting values to guide various modes of unavoidable participation.

2. *Imperialists*—those who identify various categories of barbarians at the gates and seek to bar their entry. Proponents of this position applaud the pre-eminence of the United States, emphasize military prowess, are critical of all attempts to appease those who complain, and oppose any national move that seems to renounce or reduce America's imperial role. Ultimately, imperialists rely upon military force to firm up a disintegrating geopolitical order. Imperialists tend to underestimate the leverage of the weak and largely overlook the inability of power to deter the desperate. This position, like the isolationist position, also fails to appreciate the significance of

nonmilitary forms of geopolitical power that arise from growing complexity amid interdependence. Finally, imperialists discount the adverse effects of a sustained imperial posture on democratic values and procedures at home.

3. *Managers*—those who would entice the dissatisfied to join with the satisfied in a single world system based on explicit procedures and structures for the management of interests. This position favors striking a series of world order bargains on critical issues. It also generally favors expanded participation in global policy-making settings to include all important actors in the world; thus, conferral of great-power status on non-Western states (e.g., Brazil, Iran, Nigeria, Saudi Arabia, Indonesia) is a likely feature of this position. At heart, the managers are seeking practical patterns of accommodation on mutually acceptable terms. Some who hold this position are enthusiastic about the possibility of entrusting international institutions with expanded roles, especially in relation to the new agenda of environmental, economic, and social issues.

The managers underestimate the depths of antagonism, often overlook the intolerable domestic systems of the new great powers, exaggerate the negotiability of the main issues of geopolitical concern, and presuppose the efficacy of moderation and a spirit of compromise. The underlying failure of the managerial perspective, naturally allied to a technetronic interpretation of modernity, may be its confidence in reason and the spirit of reasonableness as a basis for just order. A related failure is a tendency to define justice in a broad, abstract way that is divorced from the domestic condition of real people.

4. *Transformers*—those who argue that a new system of world order must be created to avoid a situation of growing planetary danger. Spokespersons for this position usually assume the need for both equilibrium and equity in global society. Transformers, confronted by the magnitude of their task and the prospects of scant support, are often pessimistic about the current framework of states to realize either equilibrium or equity on a wide variety of agenda items. Others are naively optimistic about the ease of bloodless, drastic reforms in the near future.

Most thoughtful transformers adopt a time frame of at least several decades and may regard it as expedient to join forces with the managers in the short run. Transformers usually assess geopolitical trends by reference to a series of values. They are generally convinced that an immense potentiality for change exists but are skeptical of any approach to national well-being that is resigned to the durability of the state system. The greatest weakness of transformers is their inability to mobilize widespread support partly, perhaps, because of their difficulty in depicting a credible transition process and partly because those with vested interests in existing arrangements have immense resources with which to shape or at least confuse public opinion on prospects and effects of transformation. Furthermore, transformers, by their insistence on fundamental change, are alienated by style from the policy-making mainstream in the United States, which is overwhelmingly gradualist in approach and scornful of any kind of "grand design" to solve the problems of the world.

The more sensitive American policy-makers are at present groping toward a synthesis based on a mix of these four positions. The relative weight of these positions will vary from issue to issue and evolve in response to international experience and domestic public opinion. More time is needed before we can confidently interpret this relatively new geopolitical situation and the emerging responses to it. One thing is already apparent, however: the earlier geopolitical preoccupations with territory and space (as expressed by notions of withdrawal and expansion) are far less important than they used to be. Even control seems less central to the agenda of complex functional management than do reliable patterns of coordination.

The idealistic component of American diplomacy is represented by the transformers, who regard a shared set of values as the essential basis of viable geopolitics. Of course, one element in the current debate about policy has to do with the presentation of "reality." Who are the utopians? Those who think the traditional system of states will persist for the indefinite future, or those who are convinced that this system will be overcome (for better or worse) in the course of the next several decades?

THE JEFFERSONIAN MODE

Thomas Jefferson had strong convictions about the future of America and its relation to other countries. The Jeffersonian perspective has attracted supporters and fascinated historians of ideas throughout American history. Hence, the Jeffersonian outlook belongs in the repertoire of indigenous political traditions available to contemporary architects of change who seek to explain their positions in a way that does not seem "alienated" or "anti-American."

The Jeffersonian perspective is elusive. Jefferson never systematically formulated his main ideas, but set them forth in letters and papers prepared over the course of a long and varied life. As a result, Jefferson failed to develop a coherent position. In many respects, Jefferson balanced within his own sensibility some contradictions that have persisted in American political culture—he owned slaves, yet condemned the institution of slavery; he had great admiration for Indian cultural achievement, yet contributed to the destruction of Indian culture; he advocated juridical virtue in international relations, yet was an expert practitioner of conventional geopolitics; he spoke eloquently of liberty and of national self-determination, but was among the first American statesmen to envisage and advocate a foreign policy based upon America's hemispheric interests.

Nevertheless, despite the elusiveness and inconsistencies, Jefferson stands for an important set of ideas that continue to be active in American political thought, if only by contrast with those of Alexander Hamilton. Hamilton was skeptical of the citizenry, well-disposed toward privilege, cynical about human nature, and insistent on effective patterns of governance. Such an outlook led Hamilton to support strong government based on political and fiscal centralization, to be very opportunistic about international diplomacy, to distrust moralizing in foreign policy, and to associate the nation's prosperity with the rapid expansion of its urban manufacturing sector.

Jefferson, in contrast, was optimistic about the capacities of educated citizens to play a critical role in the political life of their country. "I am persuaded that the good sense of the people will always be found to be the best army."[7] Whereas Hamilton feared that chaos would result from insufficient government, Jefferson worried that despotism would arise from excessive government. Jefferson was willing to accept some measure of disorder, even a small rebellion every now and then, to prevent bureaucratic tendencies from ossifying vital social and political impulses. Writing from Paris in 1787 about Shay's rebellion, he declared:

We have 13 States independent for 11 years. There has been one rebellion. That comes to one rebellion in a century and a half, for each state. What country before, ever existed a century and a half without a rebellion? And what country can preserve its liberties, if its rulers are not warned from time to time, that this people presume the spirit of resistance? Let them take arms, the remedy is to set them right as to facts, pardon and pacify them.[8]

Jefferson was, in theory at least, an early advocate of "continuous revolution" and preferred to accept the risks of popular accountability than to incur the costs he associated with higher levels of governmental control and efficiency.

In many respects, Jefferson placed his hopes and faith in the idealistic, special character of America as a country devoted to liberty as well as to independence. Hamilton and Adams were characteristic of those who felt that once independence was acquired, the people could best be governed from above in a conscientious but rather elitist and insistent fashion. Jefferson, on the other hand, was convinced that such centralism would degenerate into some form of despotism of the sort prevalent among the states of Europe. Only the people, Jefferson believed, were capable of upholding their liberty through time and it was thus critical for the nation's future to institutionalize within its political framework a suspicious attitude toward official power and governing bodies.

Despite Jefferson's ascendancy in his own day, the evolution of America has proceeded primarily, many would also say appropriately and unavoidably, along a Hamiltonian path. The bureaucracy has become immense; there has been a spectacular rise in centralized fiscal and industrial power; the governing bodies have added incrementally to their own governing power; American behavior in the world has been largely based on standard geopolitical calculations involving wealth, power, and prestige, but often misleadingly disguised by American anticolonial reluctance to acquire extrahemispheric territorial possessions. Despite this reluctance, however, a steady course of territorial expansion has occurred through the course of American history.

One ingredient of Jefferson's outlook was widely shared at the country's inception and figured in George Washington's farewell address—namely, the domestic rationale for adhering to a foreign policy based on geopolitical detachment. Washington argued that detachment would avoid "the necessity of those overgrown military establishments which, under any form of government, are inauspicious to liberty, and which are to be regarded as particularly hostile to republican liberty." No one agreed more strongly than Jefferson. He too felt that a permanent military establishment would emerge if the United States became a regular participant in Eurocentric geopolitics and was firmly convinced that there was no way to reconcile standing armies with his image of America's proper line of national development and destiny.

The application of a Jeffersonian perspective to contemporary U.S. foreign policy would lead in two main directions: First, it would call into question the domestic consequences of an American global role based upon permanent geopolitical attachment (whether the imperial mode or the managerial mode of coordination). Second, it would emphasize the extent to which American national identity was based on normative as well as purely materialist aspirations associated with wealth, power, and size.

To cope with permanent geopolitical attachment, unavoidable in the present world situation, requires added vigilance of citizens against further encroachment on traditional liberties. The modes and extent of such attachment should also be minimized and confined to those roles most compatible with the values we proclaim for ourselves. The tension between global policy and domestic freedoms is greatest when we seek to inflict on other societies forms of governance that we purport to abhor for ourselves. In this sense, it matters little whether interventionary diplomacy is overt, covert, or indirect.

All policies designed to "stabilize" repressive governments or to "destabilize" progressive ones place similar strains on our domestic polity and, of course, tarnish our self-image as a traditional supporter of national self-determination.[9] In the contemporary situation, the United States is almost everywhere led to define its interests in opposition to successful and popular movements for national self-determination, especially if these movements include a serious social and economic program for achieving a more equitable economy.

Jefferson's importance today is, of course, symbolic rather than literal. For Jefferson represents, above all else, a willingness to trust the people and to grasp the extent to which development depends upon change, including those changes that may have to be forced upon institutions and elites by the expression of rebellious energies from below.

Jefferson also believed that liberty was associated with a balanced social and economic order in which rural, agrarian lifestyles were not displaced by urban industrial patterns. Although anti-industrial and anti-urban in his earlier phases, Jefferson eventually came to appreciate the need for indigenous industrial capability to avoid a crippling dependence on foreign societies. Nevertheless, he prophetically foresaw the dangers implicit in the materialistic cult of progress. In this respect, Jeffersonian ideas also serve as an inspiration for those social forces now questioning the postulates of industrial civilization.

Jefferson warned, in a letter to James Madison dated December 20, 1787, that "When we get piled upon one another in large cities, as in Europe, we shall become corrupt as in Europe, and go to eating one another as they do there." The woeful condition of American cities, despite the amazing prosperity of the society as a whole, argues for taking seriously Jefferson's anxiety about an urban-dominated America.

In relation to foreign policy, the question raised is whether America now requires a cultural revolution within its own boundaries if it is to free itself from the economic and political compulsions associated with industrial growth in a crowded world of increasingly integrated consciousness, afflicted by massive poverty, and constrained by a variety of ecological limits. The countercultural emphasis on agrarian virtue, on solar energy, on communal-scale polities, and on environmental prudence represents a contemporary rediscovery of this earlier Jeffersonian conception of what fulfillment might mean for America.

THE LIBERAL INTERNATIONALISTS' OUTLOOK

Although several ideological positions are prominent in this early phase of the era of managerial geopolitics, the position of liberal internationalism has had predominant influence on American foreign policy throughout the 1970s. The outlook for liberal internationalism seems clouded for the 1980s, especially given the bipartisan consensus on the decline of U.S. power and the renewed urgency of cranking up the war machine to meet the fused challenges of Soviet power and Third World turbulence. Liberal internationalists have more or less controlled the drift, or at least the rhetoric, of American foreign policy since the end of World War II, with a brief interregnum during the Nixon-Kissinger-Ford years. But as genuine conservatives argue, even these republican years seemed indistinguishable from their democratic, professedly liberal counterparts, especially given the Nixon-Kissinger stress on détente, Chinese normalization, ending the Vietnam War, and major arms control agreements. Although liberal internationalism exhibits some of the moral concern associated with the Jeffersonian outlook, it is more accurate to regard this position as an expression of Hamiltonian ideas of governance and foreign policy. Ironically, perhaps, the Jeffersonian heritage may be more active both on the conservative right, with its dislike of political centralization, and on the progressive left, with its receptivity to change and deep concern with values. Alongside militarists and conservatives applauding the Mayaguez recapture, advocating anti-OPEC adventures, and resisting adjustments in America's status in the Panama Canal Zone are antimilitarists and progressives urging the abolition of the CIA, the withdrawal of American ground forces from overseas bases, the renunciation of nuclear weapons options and interventionary diplomacy.

However, neither conservatives nor progressives are likely to shape the future of American foreign policy, although the former have far better prospects than the latter. The conservative influence arises from its strong position in big business, in much of the media, and within the bureaucracy (especially in the Treasury and the Pentagon), from its dominance in certain regions of the country, and from its many adherents among American leadership groups. And the conservative voice has been strengthened further by the apparent drift of recent global development adverse to U.S. imperial interests. Progressive influence is insignificant within American policy-making circles, and progressives do not command significant resources with which to influence these main arenas of decision.

It does not yet appear likely that conservatives will control foreign policy in the years ahead. Rather, U.S. policy will more likely be controlled by a broad coalition of outlooks that can be labeled "liberal internationalist." This foreign policy perspective is exemplified in the output of such influential projects as the Trilateral Commission or "The 1980s Project" of the Council on Foreign Relations. Essentially bipartisan in spirit, these projects typify the effort to shape a consensus that corresponds to the dictates of "managerial geopolitics." The tone and substance is moderate, and the goal is to effect a reconciliation among America's material interests, the adversary interests of the Third World, and the collective needs of the planet as a whole.

The liberal internationalists' credo has several dominant strands. Its adherents generally believe that industrial growth can persist indefinitely if intelligently regulated and that the main challenge is to find ways of spreading its benefits rapidly and widely. They are generally friendly to the multinational corporation, regarding it as a bearer of American technology and productive capacity. On the other hand, liberal internationalists are ambivalent toward military power, seeking to restrain but not drastically alter the basic patterns of defense spending, prevailing commitments, or strategic doctrines. Liberal internationalists generally seek to reassure conservatives about their own commitment to stability and patriotism, as well as to the traditional range of national interests. Hence, they often clarify their position by rejecting contending positions to the left.

In this sense, Richard Holbrooke's observation that "the left's critique of America's role in the world has taken on some ominous overtones" is a typical liberal internationalist's indictment, as is his closely related complaint that the left is guilty of making "extreme extrapolations" from some specific American mistakes in policy. Holbrooke acknowledges that it is appropriate to condemn "some evil things" America has done, but sees the contention that "America is itself an evil force in the world" as an example of extreme extrapolation.[10]

In fact, the liberal internationalist resists extrapolations altogether and tends to regard each specific failure of policy as a mystifying occurrence that calls for a detailed and separate explanation. Generalized conclusions are rarely drawn, patterns of response are seldom discerned, recurrent structures of behavior are almost never depicted. In this respect, the liberal internationalist wants another chance "to muddle through," especially by bringing "the best and the brightest" back to power, and is deeply convinced that the United States can still exert a beneficial leadership role in the world despite the "evil things" it has done in recent decades.

A Benevolent Role

One particular appeal of liberal internationalism is its confidence in the capacity of the United States to play a benevolent role in the world without having to sacrifice any of its power and wealth. Conservative critics charge liberal internationalists with sacrificing real geopolitical interests by weakening the resolve and capability of the country to hold onto what it has. At the same time, progressive critics accuse liberal internationalists of adopting a hypocritical stance of decency and moderation that obscures a tenacious determination to uphold selfish geopolitical positions almost regardless of human consequences.

Liberal internationalists have a range of ideas about how to revive America's capacity to play a benevolent world role. There is agreement among them that a revival is needed and desirable. Zbigniew Brzezinski's belief that the "overall impact of America is to stimulate change" enables him to call contemporary America "the world's social laboratory."[11] Brzezinski's conclusion is based upon the premise that growth-oriented industrial civilization is the cutting edge of change in the world. He believes it is America's leadership in mixing electronics and technology, the components of what he calls "the technetronic age," that makes the American experience particularly important at this juncture for the rest of the world.

The major defect of Brzezinski's assessment of creative potential is that it fails to respond to the global priorities of most people. The changes that currently capture the popular imagination are those associated with overcoming poverty and political impotence. China, not America, is thus properly perceived as "the world's social laboratory." China's creative initiative arises from its apparent success in mobilizing its huge population to meet the society's most fundamental needs. China's example has raised the hope that the hardships of poverty can be eliminated from the Third World in a relatively short period of time and, furthermore, that societies who succeed at this task will command respect and exert influence in the world system.

The American technetronic initiative, on the contrary, if applied to a society that suffers from mass poverty, tends to concentrate its benefits upon the advanced industrial sectors and accentuate pre-existing patterns of social and economic distortion. This approach may result in higher growth rates and a larger GNP, but not in appreciable social or economic gains for the bottom 70 percent or more of a Third World society. It also draws the countryside into the large cities, the industrial dynamism of the urban sector acting as a magnet; the consequence is urban sprawl of the most depressing sort, widespread hardship, as well as high rates of unemployment and underemployment. The governments of South Korea and Brazil do regard the United States as the main social laboratory. Their interrelated features of high growth, continuing poverty, and systematic, militarized repression seem characteristic of the overall effects upon a Third World country if it chooses to go the American way.[12]

The technetronic strategy remains dominant in America and is clearly connected with the extent of its external influence; but its rewards are being increasingly questioned, even by Americans. This strategy is associated with an entire ethos of development based on endless technological innovation to achieve an ever-larger productive output. The very success of this strategy in America makes it easier to grasp the accompanying defects, such as persisting hardship for the poor and deep malaise for all strata of society. It is hard to conclude that America is a happier, safer, or more enlightened nation than it was 200 years ago, despite its extraordinary, sustained industrial growth.

The various manifestations of withdrawal from and reaction to the drift of the technetronic age are what give the United States some claim to be a social laboratory for the world. The impulse toward change in America is most apparent in the so-called "counterculture," a diverse, uneven social movement that includes the upsurge of spiritualist interests, social experiments in new rural settlements, greater self-sufficiency based on low and medium technology, the expansion of organic farming, and the growing popularity of diets based on natural foods. The counterculture embodies many of the values associated with Jefferson's image of America: simplicity, decentralization, antibureaucratism, and reverence for nature. Unlike Jefferson, however, the counterculture is suspicious of reason and education as sources of enlightenment and looks more favorably upon religious and spiritual sources for inspiration and guidance.

This counterculture ethos has taken shape in a national setting in which the powers of rationality and the institutions of formal learning have been appropriated by the prophets of a technetronic civilization.[13] Of course, the counterculture is still a subordinate aspect of American life, but it is developing rapidly in size, maturity, and even political potency (especially in New England and in the Pacific states). Still, the counterculture represents America's only genuine claim to provide the world with some imagery of positive change. This imagery, importantly, need not be arcadian and antitechnological; solar and wind energy, cable TV, or even the space program with its implications for planetary unity and human solidarity can serve the ends of progressive politics and spiritual development.

The important consideration here is that because liberal internationalism emanates from the wellsprings of technetronic culture, its proponents invariably tend to either ridicule, resist, or dismiss the potentialities for change that come from within the counterculture. If this continues to be the case, the liberal internationalists will not be able to provide the leadership needed to make managerial geopolitics a positive force in human history.

Speaking in 1901, at the celebration of the one hundred and twenty-fifth anniversary of the Battle of Trenton, Woodrow Wilson asked, "What did it mean that the greatest Englishmen should thus cheer us to revolt at the very moment of our rebellion?" It certainly did not mean admiration for military power or technological achievement. It meant, of course, that enlightened people everywhere supported the American struggle to achieve independence and liberty.

In the era of its birth, America was indeed the great social laboratory of the world, because its revolution gave rise to social and political arrangements that satisfied popular needs and aspirations in new, exciting ways that seemed capable of generalization beyond national boundaries. In this sense, the admiration for America in its early decades resembles some of the enthusiasm that has greeted the Vietnamese or Chinese achievements of unity and independence. Just as the American revolutionaries proved the vincibility of the English colonial monarch, triumphing on native soil despite their distinct technological and military inferiority, so the Vietnamese victory is widely celebrated throughout the world as a dramatic sign that the geopolitical center of the world system can be challenged by a defiant and courageous opponent operating at the periphery.[14]

America's Credibility

America's credibility as a progressive force in history has been slow to wane. Writing in 1869, Mikhail Bakunin, the great Russian libertarian socialist, called the United States ". . . the finest political organization that ever existed in history." Even after World War II, despite the evident permanence of the Communist revolution and America's flagrant antisocialist diplomacy, the United States retained the mantle of progressive leadership for most of the world. As Franz Schurmann points out in *The Logic of World Power*, "The dilemma the Communists of the world faced in 1945 was that the one great revolutionary vision came not from socialist Russia but from capitalist America." The leaders of independence movements in the colonial world, including Ho Chi Minh, looked to Washington, not Moscow, for their inspiration. And yet, Schurmann continued, "As the cold war progressed, America lost the ideological struggle, and with the Vietnam war, lost even the capacity to understand ideology."

But such shifting perceptions and roles do not tell the whole story. The disposition toward repression in American foreign policy is mainly a matter of structure, not will. Many American leaders still believe in the protection of human rights. The United States continues to be a favorite sanctuary for political exiles. And prominent liberal critics of foreign policy seem sincere in their belief that the United States can and should resume a progressive role.

For instance, Bayless Manning muses that "It is now obvious to all that our Vietnam policy was a blunder; one cannot help but wonder, too, how different and better a world it would be for the United States today—and for everybody else—if we had worked more actively for the last 30 years to assist the forces for change in the Third World."[15] But was this option ever really available to U.S. foreign policymakers?[16]

In the colonial world of Asia and Africa, and to some extent Latin America, the political possibilities tended to be extreme. These peoples could decide to consolidate power and wealth in a tiny elite (whether traditionalist or modernizing) that could win nominal independence but would then probably maintain the social and economic status quo. Or, such peoples could try to bring off a social revolution that produced a new ruling elite increasingly likely to adopt some form of socialism. The moderate middle choice was not generally available, although India, until recently, symbolized both its possibility and its frustrations.

Given such choices, the United States drifted toward the right in its patterns of Third World alignment. In the main, these alignments were reluctantly endorsed by American leaders of both parties, on the widely shared belief that anti-Soviet and anticommunist geopolitical considerations must come first. This was the cement that kept American foreign-policy-makers together and engendered high levels of bipartisan public support. But the communist challenge was magnified beyond all reality, so that when the communist world system began to break apart, the evidence was widely ignored for years after the fact. To understand these distortions, it is necessary to examine the explicit, acknowledged, negative mission of *containment* alongside the implicit but unacknowledged positive mission of *expansion* and *control* that has been identified here as imperial geopolitics.

Protecting Human Rights

Liberal internationalists believe that the United States must remain active in the world system. They believe we should reestablish the nation's credentials as a country that is sympathetic to change and concerned with protecting human rights everywhere. But liberal internationalists stop short of drawing structural inferences. Bayless Manning insists that "the surest way for the United States to influence for the better the ideological future of mankind everywhere is by being sure that we present an unwavering example of commitment to our principles at home." But it is naive to assume that this goal can be achieved so long as American involvement in foreign societies is linked to the triumph of principles antagonistic to our own.

Manning goes on to argue that the "United States should continuously speak out internationally to reassert its ideological stance on individual freedom and expression." But nowhere does he suggest that we get out of the business of destabilizing and stabilizing foreign governments, nor does he demonstrate much awareness of just how suspect our credentials have become. More pertinent still, Manning does not even consider dismantling the capabilities or denying the budget that make covert activities virtually irresistible. After all, CIA operatives overseas have to do something with their vast but secret budgets. Even assuming benign intent, careers are at stake, reports have to be filed, money spent. But on what?

Only the naive would believe that a multibillion-dollar budget is needed to gather information necessary for our security (as distinct from upholding our vast network of political, economic, and military interests). In the nuclear age very little information is required to assess the possibility of military attack, and that particular information is reliably available through satellite surveillance of rival military installations and conventional intelligence activity. Secondary realms of political struggle in foreign societies have no bearing on our own territorial protection or national security, and such struggles can be adequately understood without deploying a vast intelligence apparatus.

Critics charge American policy-makers with hypocrisy on human rights, alleging that our words do not correspond to our alignments. In response to such charges, liberal internationalists advise that we speak out still louder and more often against human rights violations and other foreign abuses, enter international agreements, and the like. But such counsel will become credible only when it is coupled with a renunciation of the interventionary diplomacy that helps create the political conditions giving rise to the abuses. Why do liberal internationalists always stop short of politically fractious proposals?

Richard Ullman, another leading liberal internationalist, argues that American foreign policy should be realigned to embody a more credible concern with human rights. He therefore urges the United States to break with repressive regimes wherever possible. However, he pointedly exempts South Korea, "where weakening the American embrace might lead either to a major war or else toward the substitution of one repressive regime for another—in the Korean case, a repression of a more far-reaching, systematic, and ruthless nature."[17] Ullman offers no evidence of why a weakening of the American embrace would lead to war, nor why he is convinced that North Korean repression is worse than South Korean repression.

The case of South Korea is important because America has already fought a costly war on its behalf, because the Seoul regime during the Park era engaged in brutal repression including systematic torture (verified by an Amnesty International special report), because the United States has deployed troops and nuclear weapons on South Korean territory, and because international public opinion is increasingly more sympathetic to the position of North Korea in the overall dispute. The Korean issue, then, has major symbolic overtones, and it is difficult to grasp how the United States can change its real international role or image while continuing to reaffirm commitments of this character. And what about Chile, Brazil, Indonesia, and the Philippines? Ullman does not indicate how, if at all, our relations with these countries would be transformed by the policies he advocates.

The truth—and the trouble—is that there is no "cheap" way to achieve the goals that such liberal internationalists proclaim. Some economic and geopolitical costs will have to be paid, and if they have to be paid they should be made explicit first. Can the world be made more humane, for example, without being made less profitable for multinational corporations? If a humane world would be less profitable, as I believe it would for reasons set forth earlier, then to make such a choice will provoke strong domestic repercussions from many influential sectors of American society.

In essence, liberal internationalists reaffirm their faith in a positive role for the United States, but their proposals are unconvincingly rhetorical—at once too easy and too feeble. The shift from imperial geopolitics to managerial geopolitics can take a variety of forms, but the liberal internationalists' approach does not seem capable of effecting the real substantive changes in American foreign policy that could help promote the emergence of a more peaceful and just system of world order. The liberal internationalists' stance seems pathetically weak by comparison to the entrenched military, geoeconomic, and politically conservative support structures that created American dominance in the preceding epoch of imperial geopolitics.

In other words, the key to change is not words, but deeds. The precondition of progressive geopolitics is a real rather than a rhetorical or instrumental shift of role and identity toward an entirely new conception of national goals.

Zbigniew Brzezinski, in his article "America in a Hostile World," is correct in arguing that "nothing could be more destructive than for the United States to position itself as the ultimate shield of the remnants of white supremacy in Africa at a time when racial equality is coming to be accepted as an imperative norm. This would rally all of Africa and much of Afro-Asia against us."[18] But such a *tactical* argument, based again on playing the geopolitical game as effectively as possible under altered conditions, is hardly very exalting. The question of how the United States itself regards the norm of racial equality needs to be *felt* as a primary ingredient of policy, rather than made a contingent (and self-serving) afterthought.

In that respect, if liberal internationalists believed in their own values on an operational level, it would be as unthinkable to support regimes that practice racial oppression or torture their opponents as it would be to consort with such policies and politicians within our own political order. To make a tactical adjustment in southern Africa, but simultaneously to embrace the Shah of Iran as our geopolitical partner, is to exhibit cynicism of the worst variety.

I do not contend that it is an easy matter to reconcile geopolitics with human rights in the current world setting. Quite the contrary. No major state in our time has successfully made the reconciliation. But to pretend that difficulties don't exist is to invite both a failure of policy and a loss of moral credibility. Conservatives, in a sense, were correct to be *morally* appalled by the way we ditched the Thieu regime in South Vietnam once it was perceived to be a "loser." Principled foreign policy must either be abandoned altogether or else it must find coherent ways to transcend merely *expediential* choices. To side with winners and abandon losers may be sensible from a pragmatic viewpoint, but such policies have only an accidental and most unconvincing connection with moral purpose.

The refusal of liberal internationalists to confront difficult choices arises also from an inherent skepticism about fundamental reform. Thus, they are comfortable only with minor shifts that can be made by moderate means, that will not be viewed as too threatening to selfish interests, nor as purely sentimental. Such predispositions make liberals especially vulnerable to charges of hypocrisy. They are not content to vindicate foreign policy by calculations of advantage but piously insist upon the moral contributions that result from their approach. Ultimately, however, the marginal policy changes they advocate can only be decided upon in terms of national advantage narrowly calculated by reference to power, wealth, and prestige. And here is the rub. Such calculations will never add up to more than the most episodic and marginal support for human rights, mass economic development, redistribution of global wealth and income, or genuine national liberation.

ADAPTING TO MANAGERIAL GEOPOLITICS

A new managerial geopolitics is emerging, one that will set some limits upon American foreign policy initiatives. This section indicates some of the concrete adjustments in American foreign policy that would express a sensitive shift toward the progressive ideology that I have associated with the Jeffersonian heritage. The readjustments advocated here pose fundamental challenges to established cultural assumptions and values. I believe that such measures would make the emergent geopolitical system more responsive to the following specific world order values: peace, economic well-being, social and political justice, and ecological balance.[19]

American foreign-policy-makers, whatever their ideological persuasion, face very real dilemmas because there is no assured way to revive the American role as a progressive force without incurring some heavy short-term geopolitical costs. Dominant interest groups in the United States—labor, business, military, bureaucratic—seem primarily concerned with satisfying their immediate interests and are not inclined to compromise these interests for the sake of a safer, fairer, and more satisfying foreign policy. Therefore, the practical prospects for a progressive foreign policy are exceedingly poor.

But to dwell on obstacles alone is as misleading as are liberal exaggerations of how easy it would be to achieve a normative reorientation of American foreign policy. The indigenous Jeffersonian tradition is still meaningful for a significant section of the public; in particular, certain aspects of the tradition dealing with decentralization of power and wealth command widespread support at present. A leader connected to this tradition would not be perceived as "radical" or "alien." Furthermore, the Indochina defeat has created, temporarily at least, a national mood of suspicion about military involvement in the political affairs of foreign societies. This mood could spur a serious reaffirmation of Jeffersonian ideas about the nourishing value of rebellion, the populist bias of progress, and the right of national self-determination as the moral basis of foreign policy.

The growing complexity and interdependence of economic, social, and ecological subject matter leave little doubt about the practical need for globalist solutions and structures. This complexity and interdependence is also related to a growing awareness of increasing national vulnerability—hence, the widely shared acceptance of managerial geopolitics. A progressive leader could relate these developments to the evolving sense of planetary wholeness that arises from many different sources and underlies metaphors such as "spaceship earth" or "the global village." This sense of planetary wholeness could also serve as a basis for planetary ethics; the new ethics could be expressed as a serious American commitment to ensure the fundamental human right to eat, to take only one obvious example, and could be lent credibility by the enormous North American control over that portion of the world's grain production available for export.

If these various strands of support for a shift in behavior were drawn together in a coherent ideology, the cumulative result could be a social movement for a just world policy that would quickly assume transnational importance. This result would generate public excitement by responding in a positive spirit to historical tendencies that lead toward some form of global integration. A national leadership that moved in such directions would be likely to find support from unexpected quarters as well. There are individuals within the bureaucracy, and even within the leadership of those vested interest groups most threatened by change, who would share the vision or could be persuaded that a progressive outlook was nationally beneficial at this stage of history.

It remains necessary to consider what specific shifts in policy could be made by a hypothetical leader who possessed this outlook and who sought a value-oriented U.S. foreign policy as a prelude to long-range global reform. One crucial aspect of effective progressive leadership would be its timing—specifically, its ability to move with urgency and clarity, but not so far ahead of the public mandate as to provoke desperate resistance by threatened elites. On this basis, three sets of recommendations for foreign policy reform are offered.

Nuclear Policy

The cutting edge of America's geopolitical position in recent decades has been its nuclear weapons superiority, backed up by a publicly announced readiness to use such weapons for the sake of "vital security interests." The development of a vast nuclear capability has brought America's revolutionary slogan "don't tread on me" to its logical and most terrifying conclusion. But America's nuclear superiority may also be its eventual undoing, by making this nuclear technology available to many nations and groups who desperately want to change their position in the world. Reliance on nuclear deterrence also constitutes a permanent genocidal threat to essentially innocent civilian populations who have no means of controlling the provocative behavior of their governments.

At present, new weapons systems like the MX missile, Trident, and cruise missile technology suggest renewed pressure among military planners to retain a first-use strategy and option. Hence, for both pragmatic and normative reasons it is vital to begin moving back from the nuclear brink. Nonproliferation goals must be reinforced by a complementary set of initiatives that deal with denuclearization. A symbolic initiative of great magnitude would be a "no-first-use declaration." Such a declaration could perhaps be formulated in stages, emphasizing at the outset a pledge never to use nuclear weapons against a nonnuclear state, and then proceeding to a total renunciation of national discretion to use nuclear weapons as legitimate instruments of war except in self-defense against a nuclear attack. Hence, a no-first-use policy could be linked to an international pledge to regard the initiating use of nuclear weapons as a crime against humanity. On the basis of this first step, especially if coupled with canceling or delaying the MX and Trident, the process of arms reduction and the goal of comprehensive disarmament could be, at last, approached in a serious and practical spirit instead of as a propaganda exercise.

The issues associated with nuclear weapons are also deeply affected by the status accorded civilian nuclear energy. As matters now stand, there is a Catch-22 relationship between advocating the nonproliferation of weapons capabilities and the export of nuclear technology that enables recipient states to develop their own national nuclear energy programs. Such technology has an implicit military capability, as the Indian test explosion of 1974 demonstrated. And, indeed, American nuclear salespeople have been pushing nuclear reactors, in part, by emphasizing their latent military potential. This sales pitch has now almost become an economic necessity, as the commercial attractiveness of nuclear power has diminished markedly for all but the largest of nonnuclear states.

However, if we unilaterally cut off foreign nuclear sales, we will not only be opting out of a profitable export market and eroding the capital basis of our domestic nuclear industry, but we will also be reneging on the Treaty on Non-Proliferation of Nuclear Weapons itself. In Article IV of the Treaty, the United States promises to provide nonnuclear signatories with the peaceful advantages of nuclear energy, once these nations renounce the military option. Thus, the goal of nonproliferation will be undermined whether we supply or whether we withhold nuclear technology. To withhold only the elements of the nuclear fuel cycle most susceptible to diversion for illicit purposes (reprocessing and enrichment facilities) is a stopgap approach. If the United States, European, and Soviet vendors succeed in their current attempt to organize a supplier cartel, they will only underscore the discriminatory character of the nuclear club.

Ultimately, the hope of avoiding nuclear catastrophe depends on the reciprocal renunciation of nuclear power, both military and nonmilitary, by *all* states. Denuclearization in both military and nonmilitary spheres depends, in turn, on progressively eliminating the advantages (or, rather, the perceived advantages) associated with nuclear weapons or nuclear reactors. Fortunately, from this point of view, the inherent dangers of civilian nuclear power (vulnerability to accident, difficulty of waste disposal, encroachment on civil liberties, and the dangers of diversion, blackmail, or terrorism) are beginning to generate social movements within principal nuclear powers (except possibly in China, India, and the Soviet Union) against reliance on nuclear power to satisfy energy needs. The stakes of the nuclear controversy are enormously high because the scale of investment will deeply influence the political future of the planet, and thereby the prospects for averting—or inviting—the worst implications of the technetronic destiny.

Governments all over the world will be watching with particular interest to see which way the nuclear controversy is decided in America: the only country to have ever used nuclear weapons in war, the leading advocate of nonproliferation, the dominant exporter of nuclear technology (over 70 percent of the entire market), the leading developer (along with Japan and Brazil) of civilian nuclear energy programs for peaceful purposes, the staging area of a growing and increasingly militant antinuclear movement. All these considerations heighten the global significance of American nuclear policy. On the nuclear issue, as elsewhere, the border between foreign and domestic policy is artificial. What happens in the American civilian power controversy is likely to shape the global outcome to a considerable extent.

Naturally, there are some limits to what national political leadership can do to reverse the momentum of the nuclear spread. But limits need not become excuses for resigned acceptance. Progressive leadership could begin to articulate the choice between a nuclear world of great vulnerability and a more secure, less nuclear world. Nonutopian voices could dissipate the illusion that we, as a nation, can have the benefits and added leverage of nuclear status without disproportionate risks.

To stimulate the rationality of the democratic process, at least the artificial subsidies given technetronic options should be removed: Congress should repeal the Price-Anderson Act that severely limits private liability in the event of nuclear accident; the Nuclear Regulatory Commission should be constituted so as to build confidence in its ability and willingness to safeguard the public interest to the extent that it collides with that of the nuclear industry; utilities that ostensibly serve the public interest should be forbidden to pay for pronuclear lobbying and media campaigns or else be compelled to publicize both sides of the nuclear controversy; a rational energy policy for the world should be actively pursued under international auspices; the mindless technetronic myth that technological momentum is irresistible regardless of the human consequences should be challenged and repudiated in relation to nuclear policy (and in other contexts, such as genetic engineering, as well).

Interventionary Diplomacy

A progressive American president could achieve dramatic results by the timely formulation of new foreign policy doctrines, especially if his words seemed to be backed by credible intent. Many factors suggest the plausibility of converting the international legal norm of nonintervention into a central ingredient of American foreign policy: the Vietnam defeat; the CIA disclosures of covert operations; the emergence of rightist military regimes following American interventions against the left; the spread of militarist rule, human rights violations, and reliance on torture; the failures of Soviet-led interventions to shape the political future of Third World countries.

Proclamations of nonintervention are no more than empty rhetoric without specific acts of implementation. Only concrete measures can give proof of a genuine shift in America's foreign policy direction. We could begin by eliminating the CIA's mandate for covert operations, as well as staff college training and assistance programs in counterinsurgency warfare for foreign military officers; pursuing a policy of reconciliation in Indochina by normalizing diplomatic relations, resuming trade, permitting access to the United Nations, and delivering pledged reconstruction aid.

Parallel to reconciliation in Vietnam, we should welcome war resisters back to American society, regarding them as citizens who gave priority to their moral impulses at great personal sacrifice. Never was the Jeffersonian insistence on governmental mildness toward "rebels" more apt than in dealing with our own antiwar militants who refused conscription, left the country, deserted while in service, or intentionally earned less than honorable discharges. As a country we need to encourage rather than stifle such decentralized populist "checks" on the abuse of centralized governmental power. By removing counterinsurgency capabilities and the remaining foreign and domestic stains of the Vietnam experience, new leadership could set the stage for a credible American renunciation of interventionary diplomacy.

Long-range Foreign Policy Planning

A further step in these recommended directions would involve the creation of a long-term perspective, reinforced by bureaucratic practice. In other words, foreign policy must come increasingly to be perceived in terms of decades rather than four-year electoral cycles.

The Pentagon has achieved longer time-horizons for its major weapons programs, but similar lengthening of the policy planning process is needed in the domain of foreign policy. This aim of lengthening the time spans for policy planning is integrally connected to the pursuit of world order goals, as distinct from the geopolitical maneuvering characteristic of traditional statecraft. The citizenry requires presidential leadership that articulates (1) longer-term values and goals, (2) images of world order systems that are stable and equitable, and (3) conceptions of transition that chart the most beneficial pathways from "here" to "there."

It is complacent to suppose that busy policy-makers in a crisis-laden world can pause to contemplate the future or that by reading good newspapers the public can evolve a sufficiently well-informed attitude on the risks and potentialities of change. A more serious, contemplative process of reflection and initiative must be institutionalized, perhaps through some of the following ideas:

—world order impact statements comparable to environmental impact statements could routinely accompany contemplated foreign policy decisions;
—an institute within the Washington bureaucracy could be entrusted with long-range world order design and staffed with humanists and ethicists as well as futurologists and operations analysts;
—a nonpartisan and transnational citizens commission on the future of world order could review American foreign policy from the perspective of longer-range goals and proclaimed values;
—a national and global educational effort, perhaps stimulated by a series of United Nations forums and conferences, could promote a consensus as to the goals, values, and transition strategies relevant for global reform.

The assumptions of these illustrative suggestions is that the course of American foreign policy can be positively readjusted through a combination of leadership initiative and public pressure. No world order "quick fix" is imaginable. As the Vietnamese often stressed in the course of their struggle against the French and the Americans, "patience is a revolutionary virtue." But as has also often been observed, even the longest journey must begin with a single step.

POSTSCRIPT 1980

Much of the context of the analysis in this chapter has been shaken by recent developments—the Iranian Revolution, the persisting Western energy supply and price crisis, the deepening of economic conflict within the Western alliance, the Soviet move into Afghanistan, the extended and severe global recession, and with it all, an emerging, apparently conservative political mandate in the United States for the early 1980s. Most of the strictures directed here at liberal internationalists apply even more forcefully, I believe, to the conservatives who are more reluctant to acknowledge foreign policy inhibitions flowing from either the dangers of nuclear war or the limited utility of military responses to revolutionary nationalism in the Third World. Whether these differences in proclaimed outlook will give way to a coherent set of implementing policies, and how these may alter prospects for peace, justice, and ecological balance, remains uncertain. It is well to remember that liberal internationalism, at its peak during the Camelot years, was coupled with the decisive early steps toward the Indochina intervention, a militarist approach to East-West relations, the Cuban Missile Crisis, which took the world to the brink of nuclear war, and an array of bizarre CIA plots to overthrow or assassinate foreign leaders. Perhaps "the checks and balances" of the American temperament, as well as the antinuclear grassroots surge, will push a conservative president to show concern for world order values, but perhaps not, especially given the high geopolitical stakes of conflict in the Middle East.

NOTES

1. Order refers here to stable arrangements of power. An arrangement is stable if it can be maintained without large-scale violence. Of course, order is a matter of degree, of more or less rather than of kind.

2. Letter to James Monroe dated October 24, 1823, from Thomas Jefferson, *The Life and Selected Writings of Thomas Jefferson,* ed. Adrienne Koch and William Peden, (New York: Modern Library, 1944), p. 708. As Walter Lippmann has argued, the hidden underpinning of the Monroe Doctrine was the assured support of British sea power that shared with the fledgling United States a vital interest in containing the ambitions of the Holy Alliance. See Walter Lippmann, *U.S. Foreign Policy: Shield for a Republic* (Boston: Little, Brown, 1943), pp. 16–22.

3. Samuel P. Huntington, "Transnational Organizations in World Politics," *World Politics* (April 1973): 342–347.

4. American participation was also designed—some argued primarily so—to

assure that Japan did not expand her sphere of East Asian interest through her role in the intervention.

5. A parallel argument to this effect is made by Marina von N. Whitman in "Leadership Without Hegemony," *Foreign Policy* 20: 138–160.

6. This section is heavily influenced by Fouad Ajami, in conversation and his unpublished papers.

7. Letter to Colonel Edward Carrington, dated January 16, 1787, from Thomas Jefferson, *Life and Selected Writings*, p. 411.

8. Letter to Colonel William Stephens Smith, dated November 13, 1787, from Thomas Jefferson, *Life and Selected Writings*, p. 436.

9. It is true, of course, that undisclosed interventions are not assimilated by the public as a whole and the domestic effect is corrosive precisely because the government is itself hiding the character of its controversial behavior from its citizenry.

10. Richard Holbrooke, "A Sense of Drift, A Time for Calm," *Foreign Policy* 23: 99.

11. Zbigniew Brzezinski, "America in a Hostile World," *Foreign Policy* 23: 92.

12. Repression is not structurally implied if the country is exceptionally well endowed with resources and can combine a capitalist style of growth with a distribution of benefits that appears satisfactory to the poorer sectors. Also, the industrial revolution that brought prosperity to Europe, North America, and Japan did not presuppose repression because the masses were more inert, expected far less, and were less susceptible to mobilization by political radicals.

13. W. I. Thompson, *At the Edge of History* (New York: Harper and Row, 1971); Theodore Roszak, *Unfinished Animal* (New York: Harper and Row, 1975).

14. In this regard, Third World solidarity in relation to OPEC, to the Indian nuclear explosion, and to Cuba's involvement in the Angolan war of independence are all quite "rational" if interpreted primarily as events that demonstrate the potency of the geopolitical periphery and the vulnerability of the geopolitical center. This form of rationality seems quite formidable and engenders support even from governments in the periphery whose welfare is closely linked to support from and coprosperity with the geopolitical center of the world system.

15. Bayless Manning, "Goals, Ideology and Foreign Policy," *Foreign Affairs* 54 (January 1976): 281.

16. The moderate forms of governance established in Germany and Japan under the sway of American military occupation suggest the genuineness of the liberal internationalists' claims of preference for constitutional democracy and give substance to the further contention that cooperation with rightist elements has occurred as a reluctant necessity (i.e., in response to overriding geopolitical priorities).

17. Richard H. Ullman, "Washington versus Wilson," *Foreign Policy* 21: 121–122.

18. Zbigniew Brzezinski, "America in a Hostile World," *Foreign Policy* 23 (summer 1976): 96.

19. For extended development of this point of view, see Richard A. Falk, *A Study of Future Worlds* (New York: Free Press, 1975).

CHAPTER 7

What's Wrong with Henry Kissinger's Foreign Policy*

> A *Hero of Our Time*, gentlemen, is indeed a portrait,
> but not of a single individual;
> it is a portrait composed
> of all the vices of our generation
> in the fullness of their development.
>
> Mihail Lermontov
> "The Author's Introduction"
> *A Hero of Our Time* (1958)

PRELIMINARIES

My purpose here is to criticize the workings of the state system in the latter part of the twentieth century. One means of doing so is to examine the role of its most exemplary practitioner, Henry Kissinger, during the early part of his policy-making career. There is much to admire in Kissinger's role as foreign policy architect. He has helped moderate tensions among the superpowers and used his formidable intelligence and energies to work toward the settlement of the most dangerous international conflicts. Indeed, Kissinger has dramatically

*It should be stressed that this chapter was originally written in 1975 prior to the many damaging disclosures about Kissinger. If written in 1982, it would be far less generous, far less willing to treat Kissinger as an exemplary practitioner of statist geopolitics. I have resisted the temptation, however, to revise the original version in any serious way because I think it best serves one thesis of this book—namely, to show that statism, even taken at its best, fails world order at this juncture in history. On another occasion, a harsher portrait of Kissinger and Kissingerism may be in order, including the apparent opportunism of seeking to mend whatever fences might otherwise have kept him from serving a new Republican president. From the vantage point of 1982, there seems to be no presidential aspirant who is so far to the "right" that he offends Kissinger's geopolitical scruples.

revealed how much peacemaking can still be done by way of traditional diplomacy.

Given these achievements, it may seem almost perverse to single Kissinger's foreign policy out for critical attack. Indeed, Kissinger has realized the dream of every political figure—to become so valuable a public servant that it seems irresponsible to criticize him; in almost every part of the world, including those most anti-American, Kissinger appears to stand above criticism.[1] Of course, this widely shared appreciation of Kissinger may not last; it is precarious and could vanish as soon as U.S. diplomacy turns hard into an unpopular direction. For there is no doubt that Kissinger's activities have been predicated on what is good for the U.S., and not necessarily on what is good for the world. Nevertheless, Kissinger seems to be the only diplomat whose skill and stature are so great that his services appear indispensable to the cause of moderation and peace among sovereign states.

I am not out to shatter this Kissinger myth, only to discuss its geopolitical significance for the central problems confronting an increasingly tormented mankind. My main point is decidedly not that Kissinger has been a worse spokesman for U.S. foreign policy than his principal predecessors William Rogers, Dean Rusk, or John Foster Dulles. Nor am I implying that a politically feasible successor to Kissinger, regardless of which party prevails in the 1976 elections, is going to be an improvement. Quite the contrary. I believe that Kissinger has been about the best that the U.S. political system can produce under the circumstances, given the prevailing political beliefs and consciousness. Nor do I wish to imply that governments in most other large states have been, during this time, capable of pursuing a consistently more progressive foreign policy.[2] I find no evidence at all to suggest that the Soviet Union or Japan or most European countries would not have gladly exchanged their current foreign ministers for national equivalents of Kissinger.

I also do not in any sense want to make the more limited point that Kissinger has been contaminated by Watergate involvement or by his close association with now a discredited president (although there is room for argument that Kissinger should have quit, or at least that he compromised himself by exhibiting the Watergate mentality to the extent of wiretapping his own staff). But I am prepared to go along with the view that Kissinger was obliged to this degree of participation in the Nixon ethos in order to sustain his own effectiveness, and that this effectiveness was and remains far more important to the country and the world than any conceivable expression of indignation through acts of opposition or resignation.

On a more problematical basis, I concede that my condemnation of Kissinger for his willingness to implement and justify cruel and illegal U.S. policies in Indochina would not necessarily destroy his capacity for constructive foreign-policy-making in general. Kissinger's public endorsement of the 1972 Christmas bombings of Hanoi, after peace agreements had already been negotiated, manifested Kissinger's Vietnam role in its most objectionable form. This role persists. Kissinger received a Nobel Peace Prize for negotiating the Paris Peace Agreement of 1973, which he allowed (perhaps even encouraged?) Saigon to repudiate in numerous ways before the ink was even dry. In addition, Kissinger led the political fight to sustain high levels of U.S. military and economic aid for the Thieu regime and shares some responsibility for the various covert means used by the United States to avoid the obligations solemnly assumed in Paris.

I do not want to emphasize Kissinger's personal frailties either. His personal biography is only relevant to the extent that it helps us understand his access to power and his broad political support despite his identification with the dramatic efforts to end, or at least moderate, the Cold War. Kissinger has achieved diplomatic success mainly because of structural features of the contemporary world and also because he has put his intelligence, energy, and charm to work on behalf of an essentially correct reading of diplomatic possibilities presented by this structure during this time. This assessment, based on Kissinger's early White House years, is far too generous on a tactical level. Subsequent disclosures about Kissinger's relation to the destruction of Cambodia, the downfall of Allende, and the conflicts in southern Africa disclose a dark, destructive geopolitical temperament, quite worthy of condemnation without recourse to the longer-term claims of world order.

My principal aim is to show that Kissinger's foreign policy, successful as it seems, has not sufficiently addressed the central task of our time—namely, the need to evolve a new system of world order based on principles of peace and justice. Kissinger's effort to settle international conflicts which threaten large-scale warfare has certainly been admirable from almost any point of view, but it may be dangerously deceptive if it is not compared to a wider program of global reform. Indeed, Kissinger's historical importance may have been to provide a specious stability to a disintegrating state system on behalf of the few states that are both powerful and rich. This policy reflects a global ideology of domination that embodies indifference to the poor and weak. It is a foreign policy based on the presumption that the governments of sovereign states can achieve security and prosperity for their populations, despite the growing interdependence of life on the planet. In essence, I am arguing that Kissinger's foreign policy is oblivious to the deeper self-destructive tendencies and inequities of the state system and hence to the need for and desirability of adapting geopolitics to an emergent global situation of *de facto* integration.[3]

Another preliminary issue of a related nature is the extent to which Kissinger's influence on foreign policy should be regarded as a reflection of Richard Nixon's outlook. I believe that Nixon and Kissinger shared an interpretation of the dynamics of the state system and of the main targets of diplomatic opportunity that existed in 1969. I do not mean that Kissinger has always been in agreement with the tactical judgments of Nixon, only that for our purposes we can ignore the fact that Kissinger has acted on behalf of Nixon. While Nixon's view of the state system seems indistinguishable from that of Kissinger, Kissinger's diplomatic flair has probably added a measure, perhaps a decisive measure, of effectiveness to what Nixon might have achieved with ordinary as distinct from exemplary execution of his policies.

ELEMENTS OF KISSINGER'S APPROACH

As a matter of background, it is helpful to examine Kissinger's approach to foreign policy developed over the years when he was a university professor.[4] His scholarly work exhibits an unusual single-mindedness of purpose. From the time Kissinger was a graduate student at Harvard he seemed preoccupied with the achievement of stability in international society. It is, perhaps, not surprising that someone who had spent the formative years of his life in Nazi Germany would be concerned with stability and its concomitant affirmations of the status quo and moderation. It is even less surprising, I think, that Kissinger should identify revolutionary actors, whether from the left or the right, as the main threat to stability. Despite this apparent rejection of *all* revolutionary actors, Kissinger's work actually deals mainly with the threat from the left. There are several apparent explanations. Kissinger obviously believes that the Soviet challenge is historically paramount. As his career progressed, Kissinger came to write more and more with the outlook of a U.S. geopolitician rather than that of a social scientist; and increasingly, he seemed to regard U.S. opinion leaders and policy-makers as his most significant audience.

In his earliest work Kissinger's approach was oriented toward the discovery of "crucial" truth in a relatively detached manner. In that spirit Kissinger found it most useful to understand the present and the future by penetrating an analogous setting in the past.

As he put it in his Harvard doctoral dissertation:

> The success of physical science depends on the selection of the 'crucial' experiment; that of political science in the field of international affairs, on the selection of the 'crucial' period. I have chosen for my topic the period between 1812 and 1822, partly, I am frank to say, because its problems seem to me analogous to those of our day.[5]

Kissinger has sometimes been accused of modeling himself on the nineteenth-century Austrian diplomat Metternich. I think Graubard is correct when he writes that "Kissinger's interest was not in a historical personage, Metternich, but in the problems that Metternich was compelled to deal with. He chose the Napoleonic period because he believed it resembled his own."[6] The modern resemblance arises from Metternich's successful confrontation of revolutionary France under Napoleon and the creation of a moderate, war-free period of international diplomacy. Kissinger himself, in his famous interview with Oriana Fallaci,[7] has made it plain that he does not regard Metternich as a *model* for his own statesmanship:

> Most people associate me with Metternich. And that is childish . . . there can be nothing in common between me and Metternich. He was chancellor and foreign minister at a time when it took three weeks to travel from Central Europe to the ends of the Continent. He was chancellor and foreign minister at a time when wars were conducted by professional soldiers and diplomacy was in the hands of the aristocracy. How can one compare such conditions with the ones prevailing in today's world, a world where there is no homogeneous group of leaders, no homogeneous internal situation and no homogeneous cultural background?[8]

What Kissinger admired was Metternich's understanding of the revolutionary character of the Napoleonic challenge and his leadership in bringing about a new era of international stability after Napoleon's military defeat.[9] But Kissinger never intended such admiration to be understood as proposing a Metternichian recipe for the solution of comparable contemporary problems.

In his *A World Restored*, Kissinger examines the efforts of Metternich and Castlereagh to rebuild the international order of Europe after the revolutionary challenge posed by Napoleonic France had been turned back. Kissinger's backward glance at history was intended as an acerbic commentary on post-World War II, U.S. diplomacy which, in Kissinger's view, had not clearly enough come to terms with the revolutionary nature of the Soviet challenge.

What was implicit in *A World Restored* became the central argument of *Nuclear Weapons and American Foreign Policy*,[10] the book that made Kissinger an academic celebrity. Kissinger states his case in strong terms that link revolutionary challenges by Napoleon and Hitler with the contemporary challenge posed by the Soviet block:

Time and again states boldly proclaim that their purpose is to destroy the existing structure and to recast it completely. And time and again, the powers that are the declared victims stand by indifferent or inactive while the balance of power is overturned. Indeed, they tend to explain away the efforts of the revolutionary power to upset the equilibrium as the expression of limited arms or specific grievances, until they discover—sometimes too late and always at excessive cost—that the revolutionary power was perfectly sincere all along, that its call for a new order expressed its real aspirations. So it was when the French Revolution burst on an unbelieving Europe and when Hitler challenged the system of Versailles. So it has been with the relations of the rest of the world toward the Soviet bloc.[11]

Kissinger argues that Soviet (and, under Mao, Chinese) words and deeds exhibit an unswerving commitment to revolutionary objectives which are antithetical to the realization of his own utopia—namely, international stability in the face of revolutionary challenges.[12] In this regard he is openly scornful of those who think that a more forthcoming attitude by the liberal democracies would be rewarded by a more pliant and moderate Soviet foreign policy. In a sense, Kissinger's whole approach is an attempt to learn and teach the lesson of Munich in the altered setting of the nuclear age. He believes that the liberal democracies are inherently complacent about safeguarding stability against major challenges. He is critical of the failure of the United States in the 1950s to evolve the only sort of military strategy that he believed capable of averting either World War III or some sort of political catastrophe for the noncommunist world. For Kissinger, the inadequate response to Hitler confirms his anxiety: "In 1936, no one could know whether Hitler was a misunderstood nationalist or a maniac. By the time certainty was achieved it had to be paid for with millions of lives."[13]

Kissinger even turns on its head the argument that Soviet leaders seek nothing more than defensive security. He acknowledges that Soviet leaders were "probably sincere" about feeling threatened, but he notes: "the point to bear in mind is that nothing can reassure them."[14] Extending this line of reasoning, Kissinger arrives at the startling conclusion that:

Because their doctrine *requires* them to fear us, they strive for absolute security: the neutralization of the United States and the elimination of our influence from Europe and Asia. And because absolute security for the USSR means absolute insecurity for us, the only safe United States policy is one which is built on the assumption of a continued revolutionary struggle, even though the methods may vary with the requirements of the changing situation.[15]

This assessment of the Soviet system was frequently reiterated by Kissinger, even in an article published shortly before he joined the Nixon administration in early 1969.[16]

Given this perception of the international setting, the only way to turn back the revolutionary challenge was to mobilize military capabilities on behalf of status quo interests.[17]

In *The Necessity for Choice*, published in 1961, Kissinger in even more pointed terms emphasizes the danger to American interests that arises from the Soviet challenge. Indeed, he begins his book on an alarmist note:

The United States cannot afford another decline like that which has characterized the past decade and a half. Fifteen years more of a deterioration of our position such as we have experienced since World War II would find us reduced to Fortress America in a world in which we had become largely irrelevant.[18]

Kissinger's main argument is for a policy that involves a strategy for coping with the Soviet-led challenge. Because he feels that, above all, it is necessary to understand the revolutionary character of the challenge, he does not see the Soviet challenge as likely to be dissipated by the domestic evolution of the Soviet system nor by a change in the fundamental outlook of its leadership. Indeed, Kissinger's reading of history stresses military responses: a revolutionary movement subsided "when such a movement came to be opposed with equal fervor or when it reached the limits of its military strength."[19] On this basis, Kissinger urges upon the United States a determination to fight throughout the world where and when it is necessary, rather than rest its security upon a capacity to deter a nuclear attack upon itself.

At the same time, Kissinger acknowledged that the prospects for world peace could be improved because of the apparent rationality of the communist side, at least with respect to avoiding all-out mutually destructive nuclear war. For this reason, Kissinger believed, for instance, that if "the free world gains in purpose, cohesion, and safety," then it may be possible to negotiate seriously with communist leaders on "how to reduce the tensions inherent in an unchecked arms race."[20] When confronted with strong political and military opposition even a revolutionary actor may be willing to strike certain bargains with his status quo adversaries, and the quality of international stability will thereby be enhanced. Kissinger seemed to believe that the possibility of such bargaining, even during a revolutionary phase, constituted one of the distinct effects of nuclear weaponry on the international system. However, Kissinger qualified his receptivity to bargaining with a revolutionary Soviet actor by insisting that negotiations deal with concrete issues on the basis of mutual interest and that negotiating initiatives derive from strength rather than from false rhetoric of harmony.

In *The Necessity for Choice,* Kissinger's analysis already showed a shift in emphasis from the revolutionary actor to the revolutionary situation. By broadening his analysis, Kissinger meant to emphasize several rapid changes in the international setting—the spread of communism, the rise of new postcolonial nations, and the proliferation of nuclear weapons—that made it appropriate to regard "our period as an age of revolution."[21] The struggle with communism remains at the top of the agenda, but these additional factors complicate the maintenance of stability, which is, we should remember, the *sine qua non* for Kissinger of an acceptable world order structure.

In 1968 this shift in focus becomes even more central to Kissinger's interpretation of the international scene and apparently reflects his mood at the time he entered policy-forming arenas. As Kissinger depicts this revolutionary background of international relations:

The revolutionary character of our age can be summed up in three general statements: (a) the number of participants in the international order has increased and their nature has altered; (b) their technical ability to affect each other has altered; (c) the scope of their purposes has expanded.[22]

As a result of the Sino-Soviet split, the rise of Afro-Asian states, and the weakening of the Western alliance, multipolarity has generally superceded bipolarity. The nature of the revolutionary challenge, even the identity of the challenger, may differ from context to context. Such issues as resource flows, monetary relations, and military security suggest the variances that occur in a multipolar setting. As a consequence, a statesman needs to be more flexible and sophisticated than in the simpler circumstances of earlier centuries. In Kissinger's words:

Many of the elements of stability which characterized the international system in the nineteenth century cannot be re-created in the modern age. The stable technology, the multiplicity of major powers, the limited domestic claims, and the frontiers which permitted adjustments are gone forever. A new concept of international order is essential; without it stability will prove elusive.[23]

What is revealing about this statement, especially when compared with his earlier analyses of international situations, is that it anticipates a diplomatic stance that is post-Cold War in character. Having become antagonists of one another, the Soviet Union and China become potential (if limited) partners for the U.S. This option of partnership available to an adept U.S. diplomat provides geopolitical leverage in meeting a revolutionary challenge from a given national source. Still, Kissinger remains wary of the Soviet Union.[24] He is impressed by its political absolutism and hostile propaganda toward the West and skeptical of any short-term prospect of fundamental change, although he urges that "a serious endeavor to resolve concrete disputes" be undertaken.[25] The Nixon-Kissinger diplomacy of the past few years has made this serious endeavor but, given Kissinger's earlier arguments, at the cost of generating undue and premature optimism about the future of Soviet-U.S. relations.

Détente diplomacy has proceeded cautiously, testing the extent to which Soviet-U.S. tensions can be moderated. Although conservatives are uneasy about the new approach to the Soviet Union, Kissinger has made it clear by both words and deeds that the U.S. government has no illusions about Soviet liberalization or about the permanence of the détente atmosphere.

The fracturing of the world communist movement and the U.S. failure in Indochina created an international atmosphere where both sides were eager to compromise their differences and enter into specific negotiations across a wide spectrum. True, Nixon and Kissinger, as well as their Soviet counterparts, have sustained a posture of wariness and a willingness to resume antagonistic postures, as in the Middle East, when their interests clashed.[26] Nevertheless, the Nixon-Kissinger "structure of peace" is based on the conviction that no substantial revolutionary threat is at work in world affairs and that, therefore, present international disputes can be settled by negotiations among the great powers—especially if they defer to each other's zones of imperial or hegemonial control over the Third World and other areas.

To Kissinger it makes almost no difference whether a revolutionary is red or white.[27] Both are equally dangerous to international stability, which is the overriding, virtually the exclusive, objective of a statesman. Thus, any kind of ideological or moralistic posturing by a government or its leaders is abhorrent to Kissinger. For this reason, he dislikes the liberal wing of the American establishment, because it tends to confuse the quest for stability with reforming the character of international order. Presumably for this reason also, although he nowhere says so, Kissinger is not concerned as a statesman with domestic repression in a foreign country.[28] It is not that he necessarily likes the Greek or Chilean juntas, but he believes that they do not pose the sort of threat to international stability that is created by governments such as those of Castro's Cuba or Allende's Chile, which tend to be anti-United States and espouse solidarity with oppressed peoples everywhere. The attractiveness of Kissinger's approach derives, in part, from its simplicity and clarity. As soon as issues of dignity and equity are taken into account, matters of choice and policy involve a more complex, ambiguous frame of reference.[29] It is difficult for either conservatives or liberals to oppose the moderation of conflict in international relations; Kissinger's tendency to remove the moral question from the sphere of international diplomacy is a tremendous asset in the search for domestic political support within the U.S.

There is a further element in Kissinger's approach. It is his tragic view of human nature. He repeatedly asserts that it is the man of good will and idealistic fervor who brings bloodshed and grief into the world: "Rousseau killed a lot of people with optimism which resulted in the French Revolution. . . . When you know history, how many tragedies have been touched off by good will, you have to admit the tragic elements of existence."[30] Similarly, Kissinger rails against those antiwar Americans who demonstrated their disapproval of the U.S. invasion of Cambodia in 1970, castigating them as "those short-sighted professors, partisans and ideologists, incapable of maturity or objectivity in reaching judgment."[31] In contrast, Kissinger believes that the man alive to the evil aspirations of others and prepared to do whatever is necessary to thwart them is likely to exert a beneficial force in world history.[32] The warmaker becomes the only reliable peacemaker. This basic belief was, perhaps, gloriously confirmed for Kissinger when he served as the main model for Dr. Strangelove in Stanley Kubrick's film and then received a Nobel Peace Prize a decade later.

Kissinger believes that Americans exhibit a peculiar susceptibility to the flow of optimism that it is his special vocation to be on guard against. As he puts it, "Nothing is more difficult for Americans to understand than the possibility of tragedy. And yet nothing should concern us more."[33] Before entering the government Kissinger was concerned about the tragedy of general nuclear war. He believed that this tragedy was more likely to take place if Americans did not anticipate it as a plausible prospect. To prepare for nuclear holocaust, he thought, it was necessary to be strong and to manifest a readiness to fight with nuclear weapons in quite destructive limited wars.[34] In essence, it was necessary above all else to avoid any impression of appeasement whenever revolutionary conditions existed in international life; if such conditions should disappear, then an international atmosphere of "reasonableness"—the bargaining of differences— might be possible.[35]

A final element in Kissinger's approach is to plan for the future: "I admire people who don't try to monkey around with the present, but see further than that and do all they can to set up the future."[36] Such a futuristic perspective should be understood in relation to Kissinger's preoccupation with international stability. Kissinger thinks that threats to stability can be dealt with less destructively if they are identified and countered as early as possible. Achieving a *stable* world order, for Kissinger, requires that great powers feel content with their status, that leaders avoid ideological fervor or grand designs, and that dominant states and alliances stay strong and militant enough to avoid any revolutionary temptation on the part of those who are dissatisfied.[37] He is therefore sensitive to "the lesson of Versailles" as well as to "the lesson of Munich," namely, that the purpose of force is to remove the revolutionary element in world society but not to humiliate or dismember a major constituent state. To impose excessive burdens on a defeated country, as was done to Germany at Versailles after World War I, is to plant a revolutionary seed in the soil of the defeated enemy. The defeated society harbors resentment against the international status quo and becomes more receptive to an extremist like Hitler who promises to regain the nation's rightful place in the world system. Again, Kissinger should be seen as rather singleminded. The role of war as an instrument of nonrevolutionary diplomacy (that is, by status quo or dominant states) is *exclusively* counterrevolutionary. It has few ulterior ends, whether moral or geopolitical.

There is an important confusion embedded in Kissinger's academic writing. This confusion derives mainly from Kissinger's intermingling of neutral analysis of the conditions of international stability with policy analysis of the conditions of U.S. geopolitical primacy. As a consequence of this intermingling, it is difficult to analyze why Kissinger is mainly preoccupied with exposing the destabilizing effects of radical politics, while in his theoretical and historical expositions (of Bismarck, for instance), he makes no distinction, as noted, between the revolutionaries of the left and of the right. At the same time, Kissinger is no mere geopolitical maximalist, since he is sensitive to the dangers of overreaching by the U.S. and he believes that geopolitical rationality generally conforms with the requirements for international stability. My point is that Kissinger has never clearly resolved the relationship between a national interest (or foreign policy) perspective and a world order perspective.

There is one other point of qualification. Kissinger's career as a public servant seems more responsive to considerations of diplomatic climate than his academic writing would lead one to suspect. In part, this may reflect a concession to the Nixon presidency with its overall obsession with public relations. But I suspect it more directly reflects Kissinger's appreciation of the extent to which bargaining possibilities in diplomacy are increased by an atmosphere of "good feelings." Of course, this side of Kissinger's public image is quite at odds with the apparent message of his earlier writing to the effect that raising public hopes about friendly relations with geopolitical rivals tends to undermine the morale and, hence, the security of a liberal democracy like the U.S. And it is precisely on this kind of point that Senator Henry Jackson has led a domestic counterattack against the détente diplomacy of Nixon and Kissinger.

THE MIRACLE OF HENRY KISSINGER

Why has Kissinger been so effective and celebrated as a statesman? What has made him the most dramatic diplomat on the contemporary scene? Why, especially, has he been so successful and admired at a time when the world prestige of the United States is at a low ebb?

The American columnist James Reston has written of "the miracle of Henry Kissinger," implying that his success defies any rational explanation. In a later section we shall challenge the view that Kissinger's overall impact has been benign, much less miraculous, but here my interest is in giving an account of his undeniable potency as a statesman.

The first point to note is that there is nothing distinctive about his vision of world affairs. He understands and accepts the logic of the state and in this sense, despite his protestations, belongs to the Machiavellian tradition of statesmen.

He accepts balance of power mechanisms and political pluralism and is willing to use force, if necessary, and diplomacy, if possible, to settle international conflicts. This orientation hardly differs from that held by many other diplomats on the world scene, including such prominent Americans as John Foster Dulles, Dean Acheson, Jr., and Dean Rusk, who were active during the period when the United States had more leverage to exert in international relations than it has had during the Kissinger years. It seems clear, then, that Kissinger's influence cannot be understood by reference to some new set of ideas about either the means or goals of foreign policy.

Coherence

Although Kissinger reflects conventional wisdom on the conduct of foreign relations, he has a deeper penetration of its nuances and characteristics than other major diplomats. In that sense his orientation is reassuring to others, and yet its greater coherence lends to its exposition a quality of authoritativeness. Kissinger's background of study and reflection adds a dimension of personal assurance, as well as historical depth and precision, to his perception of diplomatic possibilities. In this regard, his stature as a former Harvard professor has been consciously underlined by references to him as "Dr. Kissinger." This kind of professional claim has not been asserted by other academics in the American government; for example, Schlesinger, Galbraith, and Rostow, all of whom tried to play down the egghead connotations of their intellectual background as much as possible.

Whereas an academic background has usually been a liability in the upper echelons of American government and was particularly scorned during the Nixon presidency, Kissinger turned it into an asset. First of all, his academic qualifications seemed to contribute directly to the discharge of his governmental responsibilities; the claim of expert status made on his behalf had an unusual degree of plausibility. Secondly, Kissinger's approach was not at all threatening to the main power brokers in the Pentagon or elsewhere in Washington. His advocacy of a strong defense posture had been a consistent ingredient of his policy advocacy through the years. Thirdly, he brought to his job none of those threatening forms of morality or idealism that Washington professionals associate with liberal academicians. On the contrary, he tended to support in an effective way their own amoral approach to geopolitics. Furthermore, his dislike of ambiguity or uncertainty, as well as the focus on revolutionary danger, made him temperamentally akin to the military and business mentality so prominent in U.S. government circles during the Nixon years.[38]

The main point is that Kissinger has a coherent view of the state system, which allows politicians and policy-makers to pursue their interests without fear of moral encumbrance or judgment. It would not occur to anyone to accuse Kissinger of false sentimentality. He has demonstrated a stomach for power, whether it entails the mindless bombing of Indochinese peasants or wiretapping his own personnel.

Kissinger's flexible view of the state system presents a more positive side of his diplomatic role. Although his approach to international relations resembles that of his predecessors, it is less ideological in two respects. First, he has been more willing to regard the Cold War as a phase rather than a condition in international affairs. Kissinger's historical studies seem relevant to this posture. Metternich believed that the objective of diplomacy was to neutralize a revolutionary challenge with as little dislocation as possible and not to mount an ideological counteroffensive aimed at disabling the revolutionary state. By this reasoning, it would be far more preferable to induce the Soviet Union to exchange revolutionary policies for beneficial participation in the world economic and political status quo than to endure a persisting confrontation among nuclear superpowers. Second, Kissinger's indifference to domestic conditions in foreign societies has enabled him to forego judgments about the inequities or indecencies of other national systems, as long as repressive governments renounce their revolutionary stance. In this sense, Kissinger has been able to bargain without ambivalence with governmental leaders from any part of the world. Since many powerful governments do have skeletons in their closets, they welcome this nonjudgmental appreciation of the limits of diplomacy in the state system. Part of Kissinger's international success, therefore, arises from this very unconcern with human rights and from the extent to which this unconcern is a shared premise of mainstream statecraft.

Timing

Given his views, Kissinger arrived on the diplomatic scene at a very opportune moment. The Sino-Soviet split, U.S. weariness with Vietnam, common dangers from an unchecked arms race, and the growing difficulties of the world economy created unusual opportunities for diplomatic maneuver. Kissinger prudently took advantage of this situation to generate a new political climate of great power relations. The Cold War mentality no longer seemed plausible to many Americans, and its ideological overtones were not accepted by Kissinger. Leaders in China and the Soviet Union, preoccupied with domestic problems and with one another, were much more concerned with moderating their relations with the United States than with pursuing revolutionary goals by continuing the tactics and rhetoric of confrontation. A few years earlier, neither American nor Western public opinion would have been ready, nor would leaders in Peking or Moscow likely have been so responsive. In the earlier world setting Kissinger probably could not have succeeded, and might not even have tried, to moderate great power conflict. Therefore the timing of his access to power was perfectly adapted to the search for new modes of international stability in a phase of great power relations of diminished ideological and revolutionary intensity.

Kissinger has been a credible diplomat. He has been backed by a president who shares his essential interpretation of the world scene and who seemed able, until Watergate, to generate bipartisan public enthusiasm for his international policies. Nixon had such impeccable Cold War credentials that his Chinese and Soviet overtures could be undertaken without fear of provoking substantial accusations of being soft on communism.

Kissinger has been similarly reassuring. He is one of the few prominent American intellectuals with a long period of identification with the Republican Party. For several years he worked closely with Nelson Rockefeller, known even in his former period of relative domestic liberalism for his hawkish views on national security and the Cold War. Kissinger's earlier intellectual mentors were also ultraconservative.[39] More significantly, Kissinger credibly has presented himself as a man virtually free from human compassion—the quality that so often antagonizes conservatives in the United States, either because they regard such sentiments as hypocritical or because they fear that they are not. Kissinger's role is compatible with the dominant neo-Darwinian ethos that is the inversion of the ethics of empathy characteristic of the world's great religious and humanistic traditions. As for the liberals, they found Kissinger's geopolitical initiatives so constructive that they were even almost willing to go along with Nixon on "peace with honor" in Vietnam. As a consequence, the main thrust of the Kissinger diplomacy gained domestic credibility across a wide political spectrum; this base of bipartisan domestic support greatly strengthened Kissinger's international bargaining power. The Kissinger-Nixon initiatives were unlikely to be rebuffed by Congress or a hostile public opinion, or even to be repudiated by subsequent elections.

Edgar Snow noted long before Nixon that Chinese leaders indicated a preference for dealing with a conservative American administration, feeling that any understandings reached would be more durable than if made with a liberal American government that was negotiating ahead of its domestic public opinion. The solidity of Kissinger's domestic position undoubtedly has strengthened his credibility as he approached leaders in foreign capitals. I believe, also, that Kissinger's Machiavellian posture has been a welcome relief to many foreign statesmen who have developed a distaste for and suspicion of the self-righteous pretensions of U.S. diplomacy since the time of Woodrow Wilson. Kissinger at least has been playing "the game of nations" as it is and should be played—that is, to maximize the player's advantage. Such a style encouraged focus on specific negotiating bargains that could be achieved in various international settings; less rhetoric, more results. As the time was ripe for bargaining toward détente, the results appeared spectacular. In other settings where the contours of bargains are not yet apparent, as in Euro-U.S. or Japan-U.S. relations, the results have been less promising. The impact of Kissinger's diplomacy on the Middle East is not yet clear, although Kissinger's energy and skill have been well deployed as a designer of reasonable bargains, that is, of conceiving and proposing settlement terms which neither party can reasonably turn down. To the extent that governments want a settlement, then, such an intermediary role has been invaluable, as it has liberated the antagonists from ideological entrapment.

Kissinger has been effective wherever the game of nations can be pursued without ideological or moral imperatives. He has been ineffectual elsewhere, as for instance in overcoming any of the more extreme patterns of injustice in the Third World areas, even in parts of the international system where the heavy hand of U.S. influence is strong. It is not only that Kissinger has been silent about the abuses but that he evidently supports the covert and indirect moves of U.S. diplomacy used to maintain or create such injustices. This observation may appear to slip over into an appraisal, but it is not yet so intended. My point here is that Kissinger's effectiveness has arisen from his capacity to deal with foreign governments without making any unpleasant representations about their domestic indecencies. One can almost visualize Kissinger justifying embarrassed representations to the Soviets on Jewish emigration policy not by the human rights at stake, but because Congress would otherwise interfere with the Administration's efforts to achieve trade liberalization. Statesmen can accept this language of gains and losses without feeling threatened.

The Kissinger Style

It would be a mistake to assume that Kissinger has been only an opportunist. Indeed, I accept his own protestation: "I'm intelligent, true; but that's no source of pride to me. But I am proud of having character."[40] Kissinger has never wavered. He was uncomfortable with liberal administrations in Washington and held back from identifying himself with their efforts. He believes there is no place for morality in foreign policy beyond the overarching morality of securing as much stability as the system will really permit at a given time. His genius, if this is the term, lies in his deep understanding of what is possible and in his ability to ground that understanding on a strong domestic political base. Furthermore, foreign statesmen who grasp Kissinger's view of things can enter the game fairly confident of what it is they are bargaining toward. There are no illusions, hence few disappointments.

Perhaps the North Vietnamese were somewhat deceived by Kissinger's negotiating posture, but it is more likely that they expected the United States not to implement the Paris Agreement of 1973.[41] In that setting, Kissinger probably had the narrow task of negotiating the return of American POWs in exchange for an end to a direct U.S. military role. Although the Paris Agreement promised much more by way of converting a military struggle into political competition between the Provisional Revolutionary Government of South Vietnam and the Saigon Administration, this promise was clearly dependent on either Saigon's good faith (for which there was no hope) or Washington's willingness to pressure Saigon into compliance (for which there was virtually no hope). Therefore, in his most celebrated negotiations for which he was awarded the Nobel Peace Prize, Kissinger probably did not purport to do much more than was achieved—that is, provisional narrowing of the military struggle.[42] To call such an outcome "peace" is of course grotesque, given the high casualty rates after the settlement came into effect at the end of January 1973. That the Nobel Committee should celebrate such an illusion provides a revealing insight into the low state of contemporary statecraft.

But was the Paris Agreement an illusion when it comes even to the issue of peace? Yes, if you count Indochinese corpses, or if you count American corpses; no, if you consider "peace" to involve only relations among great powers. Kissinger succeeded in removing the obstacles to détente posed by the continuing U.S. combat involvement in the Indochina War. The so-called structure of peace involved moderating great power relations so as to reduce the danger of general warfare by cutting tensions and slowing down the arms race. It did not promise to eliminate violence from international relations, and especially not from those marginal sectors (that is, the entire Third World) in which exploitation and mass misery are the norms of existence.

WHAT'S WRONG WITH HENRY KISSINGER?

As indicated at the outset, Kissinger embodies, in exemplary form, the strengths and weaknesses of the existing international system. Those who approve of the system or think that it defines the realistic outer limits of what can be achieved tend to applaud Kissinger's role and accomplishments. Those who believe the system is deeply flawed by injustice and imperialism or by an avoidable escalation to self-destruction powered by the war machine and its technological and ecological accompaniments tend to view Kissinger as either a dangerous throwback to nineteenth-century diplomacy or an evil genius who is inflicting such brain damage on the collective wisdom of the human race that people increasingly believe war is peace and injustice is justice. In the middle are those of liberal persuasion who believe that a moderate balance of power is the best we can hope for in international relations but also believe it is possible, desirable, perhaps even necessary, to display a bit more concern than Kissinger shows for small-power politics and for the impoverished billions in the Third World. Such a position tends to praise Kissinger for seeking to end the Cold War and to resolve the dangerous intergovernmental conflict in the Middle East but criticize his do-nothing posture on Third World issues.

The remark attributed to Kissinger by García Márquez, "I am not interested in, nor do I know anything about, the southern portion of the world from the Pyrenees on down,"[43] may not actually have been said, but it undoubtedly expresses the Kissinger outlook. As far as I know, Kissinger has given virtually no thought to the world food crisis that, according to the latest UNICEF figures, threatens as many as 500,000,000 children in Africa and Asia with famine, disease, and deformation. Kissinger is not alone among world leaders in passing over such a massive human tragedy, but he is part of a conspiracy of silence that is directed by the rich and powerful with regard to the deprivations of the poor. It is inconceivable that afflictions of this magnitude in the northern hemisphere would not be perceived as a catastrophe of historic significance. Kissinger cannot be held accountable for this discrepancy, which is more properly attributable to the hegemonic dimension of the state system, but his behavior does provide important evidence for our appraisal of the system's adequacy in meeting human needs. Kissinger's outlook presupposes that it is possible to manage international relations mainly by moderating conflictual relations among governments in the northern hemisphere.[44] This conviction is the underlying conceptual flaw in Kissinger's approach to global reform.

Kissinger's strategies for accommodating revolutionary challengers and stabilizing great power relations in moderate phases presuppose the continuity of the state system that has dominated international society since the Peace of Westphalia in 1648. However, in my view, international society can learn a far more relevant lesson from the *pre-Westphalia* context, because it was a period in which the system itself was undergoing a fundamental transition from *nonterritorial central guidance* of Medieval Europe to the *territorial central guidance* of post-Westphalia Europe.[45] This regional system became the nucleus of the world system because cultural, economic, and political forms of imperialism eventually gave it a global outreach. At the present stage of world history, as a result of increasing *interdependence* and a rediscovery of resource scarcity and limits to growth, we are beginning to experience the early stages of a new transition process that is moving the world political system toward some form of nonterritorial central guidance.[46] What matters now is which actors will control this process of transition for what ends and with what effects. Will it be the multinational corporation operating a global market? Will it be a coalition of powerful governments? Will it be an alliance of governmental and corporate actors? Will poor countries succeed in creating significant centers of power capable of sharing in the central guidance process? Will it become possible to organize a transnational populist movement seeking to orient central guidance processes around humanistic world order values?

Kissinger has been participating in this transition process by apparently seeking to establish a cooperative directorate among great powers. Such a vision of the future is short-sighted in the sense that it will not work at all, or at least not for long. It is also stultifying so far as human potentialities are concerned. It accepts as inevitable the persistence of large-scale misery and repression. It enables the disfavored many to be kept under control by the favored few. The global structure of control that Kissinger envisages and endorses tempts change-minded groups to adopt some variant of "desperate politics" to achieve their goals of liberation from social, political, and economic oppression.

Any conception of international relations that is confined to actions among principal governments is profoundly deficient. It is insensitive to the historical forces that are enlivening human awareness of inequities and that are shifting the locus of authority toward a nonterritorial center. It is the choice of options surrounding the shape and orientation of that center that is the major global issue of the day. Kissinger's approach solidifies the position of neo-Darwinian ethics—the rich and strong are entitled to prevail because they are the most fit—and is likely to be embodied in a scheme by which the great power governments forge a working alliance with the major multinational corporations. For those of us who fear or oppose such a new world order, the impact of Kissinger's diplomacy is an occasion for alarm. At the same time we can acknowledge the importance in the nuclear age of his major premise if it could be relegated to the position of minor premise in an adequate movement for global reform, that is, it is desirable to moderate conflict among great powers while a process of transition (the major premise) is shaping the world order system to foster peace, equity, dignity, and ecological balance for the world *as a whole*. Without an ethics of global concern, the attempt to merely smooth out relations among great powers is a recipe for disaster.

NOTES

1. At the same time, there is a widespread uneasiness generated by Kissinger's role. As Irving Kristol notes, Kissinger "is a much admired and much distrusted Secretary of State. . . . The anxiety as to the meaning of Kissinger pervades the entire political spectrum—right, left, and center." Kristol believes that "this widespread apprehension" arises because there is a "dim but nagging recognition that he has a new conception of American foreign policy." I. Kristol, "The Meaning of Kissinger," *The Wall Street Journal,* April 12, 1974, p. 11. Nevertheless, I think that for the present the admiration clearly overshadows the uneasiness.

2. The criticism is directed mainly at the rich and powerful states of the most industrialized sector of world society. Such other large and important states as China and India have pursued a more progressive course in foreign policy on global issues, partly because they have a natural basis for solidarity with the poor and weak and seek a more equitable distribution of wealth and income in the world.

3. In effect, it is not enough to restore "balance" to the relations among principal states; this traditional search by prudent statesmen assumed the sufficiency of decentralized control over the main life and wealth processes of planetary existence. My

argument is that objective conditions are producing circumstances of global integration and interdependence that require some mode of central guidance; see Richard A. Falk, *This Endangered Planet: Prospects and Proposals for Human Survival* (New York: Random House, 1971) and Richard A. Falk, *A Study of Future Worlds* (New York: Free Press, 1975).

4. The best comprehensive treatment of Kissinger's *pregovernment* thinking is by his friend and academic colleague, Stephen Graubard, *Kissinger: Portrait of a Mind* (New York: Norton, 1973).

5. Ibid., p. 10.

6. Ibid., p. 14.

7. Oriana Fallaci, "An Interview with Oriana Fallaci: Kissinger," *New Republic*, Dec. 16, 1972, pp. 16–21.

8. For a more intellectual formulation in which Kissinger displays his awareness that the problems for the statesman of today are dramatically different from those confronting Metternich, see Henry Kissinger, *American Foreign Policy* (New York: Norton, 1969), p. 57.

9. Henry Kissinger, *A World Restored: Europe After Napoleon* (New York: Grosset and Dunlap, 1954).

10. Henry Kissinger, *Nuclear Weapons and Foreign Policy* (Garden City, N.Y.: Doubleday, 1958).

11. Ibid., p. 43; also, on the "dynamism of the Soviet system in relation to its revolutionary objectives," see pp. 47–48.

12. Ibid., pp. 50–51 and generally, pp. 44–80. He says, "From Lenin, to Stalin, to Mao, and to the current Soviet leadership, the insistence on superior historical understanding, on endless and inevitable conflict with non-Soviet states, on ultimate victory, has been unvarying."

13. Kissinger, *American Foreign Policy*, p. 14.

14. Kissinger, *Nuclear Weapons*, p. 77.

15. Ibid., p. 77.

16. Henry Kissinger, "Central Issues of American Foreign Policy," in K. Gordon, ed., *Agenda for the Nation* (Washington: Brookings Institute, 1968).

17. Kissinger, *Nuclear Weapons*, p. 76.

18. Henry Kissinger, *The Necessity for Choice: Prospects of American Foreign Policy* (New York: Harper and Row, 1961), p. 1.

19. Kissinger, *Nuclear Weapons*, p. 76.

20. Kissinger, *The Necessity for Choice*, p. 7.

21. Ibid., p. 2.

22. Kissinger, *American Foreign Policy*, p. 53.

23. Ibid., p. 57.

24. Ibid., pp. 85–90.

25. Ibid., p. 89.

26. In the 1968 essay, "Central Issues," Kissinger writes: "The obsession with Soviet intentions causes the West to be smug during periods of détente and panicky during crises. . . . The West is thus never ready for a Soviet change of course; it has been equally unprepared for détente and intransigence." Kissinger, *American Foreign*

Policy, p. 89. Since beginning his career as policy-maker, Kissinger has sought to be steadfast both in pursuing lines of convergent interest (i.e., readiness for détente) and in sustaining a firm defense posture (e.g., the willingness during the October 1973 crisis in the Middle East to put U.S. nuclear forces on a global alert so as to dissuade the Soviet Union from sending troops to Egypt to implement the UN cease-fire).

27. See Henry Kissinger, "The White Revolutionary: Reflections on Bismarck," in D. A. Rustow, ed., *Philosophers and Kings: Studies in Leadership* (New York: Braziller, 1970), especially p. 317 where he quotes approvingly the German liberal Bamberger who wrote, with Bismarck in mind, "People are born revolutionaries. . . . The accident of life decides whether one becomes a Red or a White revolutionary."

28. Recalling Kissinger's quest for stability, he seems only to regard domestic political orientation as a factor if it embodies a missionary ideology. Of course, it is not quite so simple, because Kissinger perceives the requirements of stability primarily from the U.S. outlook. Thus an anti-United States Latin American dictatorship of the left is perceived as an "adverse" development whereas an anticommunist dictatorship is not.

29. This kind of analysis is perceptively presented in F. Ajami, "The Global Populists: Third World Nations and World Order," Research Monograph No. 41, Princeton University, Center of International Studies, May, 1974.

30. This was attributed to Kissinger in a rather illuminating account of her infatuations and impressions by French television journalist Danielle Hunebelle, *Dear Henry* (New York: Berkeley, 1972), p. 24.

31. Ibid., p. 174. In contrast, when asked about the military, Kissinger responded, "Oh me, I'm an agnostic where the military is concerned. . . . I'm neither for nor against on that score. . . ." p. 16.

32. Over and over again Kissinger refers to the paradoxical relationship between the quest for and the attainment of a peaceful world order. One characteristic formulation is in the introduction of *A World Restored:* "But the attainment of peace is not as easy as the desire for it. Not for nothing is history associated with the figure of Nemesis, which defeats man by fulfilling his wishes in a different form or by answering his prayers too completely. Those ages which in retrospect seem most peaceful were least in search of peace," p. 1. Kissinger starts *Nuclear Weapons and Foreign Policy* on the same note: "In Greek mythology the gods sometimes punished man by fulfilling his wishes too completely. It has remained for the nuclear age to experience the full irony of his penalty," p. 1. See also the same idea in his essay on Bismarck, "The White Revolutionary," p. 319.

33. Kissinger, *The Necessity for Choice,* p. 1.

34. Such a posture attracts establishment support as it reconciles the rhetoric of decency and concern for peace with the necessity for high rates of defense spending and an aggressive foreign policy.

35. But by characterizing the age as "revolutionary," he stresses the importance of military strength and wariness as constant ingredients of a rational foreign policy.

36. Hunebelle, *Dear Henry,* p. 26.

37. Two assertions by Kissinger further illuminate his view on the conduct of foreign relations. In his Bismarck essay he writes: "The bane of stable societies or stable international systems is the inability to conceive of a mortal challenge," Kissinger, "The White Revolutionary," p. 348. In other words, stability collapses when its ar-

chitects grow too self-assured. In his general appraisal of the world scene in 1968, Kissinger writes: "We will never be able to contribute to building a stable and creative world order unless we first form some conception of it," Kissinger, *American Foreign Policy*, p. 97. Kissinger opposes the *ad hoc*, antidoctrinal, anticonceptual cast of mind that has so often dominated U.S. policy-making in world affairs. He favors general interpretations that are realistic and establish a basis for coherent behavior across a series of contexts and through a period of time.

38. According to Hunebelle, Kissinger actually regarded Nixon as a personal confidant during his early years at the White House. Kissinger is quoted as saying that it is "too dangerous" to keep a personal diary: "Suppose I died or got robbed. . . . Even so, when you're permanently under pressure and in control of yourself, you really feel like opening up sometimes. So, at night, I often go up and chat with the President," Hunebelle, *Dear Henry*, p. 43. Little did Kissinger realize that while he was "opening up" Nixon was evidently taping their conversations!

39. Kissinger attended Harvard at the suggestion of Fritz Kraemer, a Pentagon official whom Kissinger describes as more conservative than himself; see Hunebelle, *Dear Henry*, p. 46. At Harvard he worked mainly with William Y. Elliott, the most conservative member of the Government Department, to whom Kissinger dedicated his first book, *A World Restored*.

40. Hunebelle, *Dear Henry*, p. 27.

41. For a revealing account of the Paris negotiations that details Kissinger's role in misleading North Vietnam (and others), see Tad Szulc, "Behind the Vietnam Cease-Fire Agreement," *Foreign Policy* 15 (1974): 21–69.

42. As Anthony Lewis puts it on the basis of the evidence contained in Szulc, "Behind the Vietnam Cease-Fire Agreement," the record is clear that the United States backed off an agreement, then bombed the other party to mollify a recalcitrant ally. Whatever other diplomatic accomplishments history credits to Henry Kissinger and Richard Nixon, that episode will forever blacken their names, and their country's."

43. Gabriel García Márquez, "The Death of Salvador Allende," *Harper's Magazine*, May, 1974, p. 46.

44. Such indifference to Third World needs and aspirations has been accentuated, not alleviated, by Kissinger's new effort at an idealist rhetoric of compassion and concern. His statements, part of the role of a U.S. Secretary of State, have created confusion because the right phrases are used but no behavioral consequences seem to follow. Nothing illustrates this pattern better than Kissinger's effort to foster good relations with Latin America based on what he calls "a new process of collaboration and inspired by a new attitude—the spirit of Tlatelolco." (Address before General Assembly, Organization of American States, April 20, 1974).

45. I have developed this analysis in some detail in a series of lectures delivered at Yale Law School in March 1974, a mimeographed copy of which is available upon request. The reference to "territorial" and "nonterritorial" models of world order has to do with the connections between *authority, control, and physical space*. The Catholic Church, the Holy Roman Empire, the World Communist Party, the multinational corporation, and the organs of the UN are all examples of nonterritorial actors whose orbit of authority is not based upon jurisdiction over events in space, whereas the sovereign state or its political subdivisions enjoy degrees of authority and control that are operative within boundaries fixed in space.

46. See Miriam Camps, *The Management of Interdependence: A Preliminary View* (New York: Council on Foreign Relations, 1974). For a more normative and political response to the challenge of interdependence, see the principal manuscripts published under the auspices of the World Order Models Project and the volume of essays from the Project cited in Chapter 5.

CHAPTER 8

The Decline of International Order: Normative Regression and Geopolitical Maelstrom

The notion of "decline" is elusive. My usage implies three dimensions: the risk of general war; the degree to which statecraft is militarized; and the diminishing extent to which world order values are realized. The first two seem reasonably clear, although criteria of risk and of militarization are difficult to make precise. The third dimension, involving world order values, is of little significance without specification. In brief, the phrase "world order values" as used here refers to peace (violence-avoidance), economic well-being, human rights, and ecological balance.[1]

The central thesis of this analysis of international order is that international order is declining in quality with respect to each of these dimensions. The attempt here will be to provide a reasoned basis for reaching such a conclusion. It would be useful, in addition, to reinforce such reasoning with a careful compilation of evidence, a process that would move an interpretative argument of this sort closer to a demonstration.

Underlying this inquiry into the downward drift of international order is a hopeful posture toward a longer-term political future. There is nothing inevitable about the course of politics on a global scale. If the proper climate of concern can be created, a new kind of survival-oriented political leadership could emerge on the state level.[2] One way of expressing this prospect is to project a leadership for vital international actors oriented around the promotion of human interests rather than national interests.[3] Another way is to anticipate a citizenry who gradually complement a statist orientation with a globalist orientation, one in our terms, concerned about the fuller realization of world order values for all peoples.[4]

Of course, such reorientations are not imminent. Whether their prospect is several decades away or longer, perhaps much longer, is impossible to predict even in loose terms. We can, however, take account of a multidimensional process of globalization that has itself been going on since the close of the last century, if not longer.[5] The content and completion of this great transition will depend upon many variables, including especially the avoidance of large-scale catastrophe.[6] The current decline of international order can also be expressed as a growing receptivity to catastrophic modes of transition, involving rising public expectations of nuclear war.

Also, it should be evident that globalization is not necessarily positive from the viewpoint of world order values. In fact, considering the evidence at our disposal, the most probable forms of globalization are likely to represent a further deterioration in the quality of societal life on the planet. More hopeful futures, to be realistic, cannot be derived by projection from the existing world.[7] Hopeful, credible futures must posit "a mutation," whether in the form of axial upheaval or spiritual awakening.[8]

Finally, with respect to orientation, this interpretation of what might be ahead takes comfort from "a hypothesis of latent discontent."[9] In effect, this hypothesis posits that beneath the surface of the old, obsolescent, yet still predominant affinities is a growing alienation from the conventional and increasing receptivity to new, adaptive outlooks.[10] The distribution of power currently favors old ways to an overwhelming extent, but their security of tenure may be deceptive. Suppressed is a radical challenge, especially in the developed countries, that is waiting to be activated on a mass scale. To illustrate the notion, but not the content of latent discontent, let us consider the surprising course of recent Iranian politics. As late as 1976, perhaps 99 percent of Iranians, or more, considered the Shah's rule impregnable for the remainder of the century. Two years later more than 90 percent of the Iranian people were united, according to knowledgeable observers, in an unarmed struggle that successfully toppled the Shah. What was overlooked in the 1976 setting that erupted in 1978? To say, retrospectively, that certain elements of Iranian political culture were at the pre-eruption stage in 1976 is to explain nothing, but it does express the earlier reality of revolutionary potential.

There are obviously no facile analogies to be drawn here. The simple argument is that the conventional international order is in serious decline, that the experience of decline has been registering on human consciousness in a variety of ways for several decades, and that out of such an encounter come new possibilities, some awful, some hopeful.

My analysis of the decline of international order is divided into two parts: first, some consideration of the normative manifestations of the latest phase of this decline and, second, some discussion of the specific danger that arises from normative deterioration in a setting of intensifying militarism.

NORMATIVE REGRESSION

The image of "normative regression" implies a base point in the past. The analysis here proceeds from the general context of post-World War II, say 1945 to 1960. Also, the inference of "regression" is an aggregate, or net, inference, assessing a balance sheet of developments with varying normative weights. It is, in a sense, necessarily subjective. For instance, how do we appraise the weight of a continuing arms race as against a generally successful decolonialization process? To some extent, the appraisal process is inevitably from a perspective, reflecting priorities and preoccupations especially characteristic of the advanced industrial countries in the early 1980s.[11] Since part of the position, however, avows a human interest conceived from a global perspective, the overall content of the normative outlook adopted here is not easily classified. Perhaps it is useful to acknowledge that the agenda is shaped by provincial considerations of time, place, and class, whereas the envisioned lines of positive response, although not entirely separable, aspire to greater universality.

Erosion of Legal Inhibitions on Aggressive War

A major normative enterprise initiated after World War I has been devoted to the effective outlawry of aggressive, that is, nondefensive, war. The Pact of Paris ("Kellogg-Briand Pact") of 1928 engaged the major governments of the world in a renunciation by treaty of aggressive war. The condemnation of the Axis Powers proceeded on this basis, as did the prosecution of the defeated leaders of Germany and Japan as war criminals.[12] The United Nations Charter carried forward this normative idea, although with admitted ambiguity, prohibiting recourse to force (Article 2[4]) except in instances of self-defense (Article 51), and only then, to the extent authorized by the Security Council. Throughout this period a major effort was made to achieve an agreed upon definition of aggression so as to specify more carefully the orbit of prohibition.[13]

This normative enterprise was from the beginning subject to sharp criticisms. It was attacked as vague, subject to gigantic loopholes, and self-justifying.[14] Furthermore, its major punitive applications were widely criticized as "victors' justice," as hypocritical and impersuasive.[15] Finally, international practice was alleged to depart frequently from these restraints without any reliable method to secure compliance. Peacekeeping based on normative propriety has never been consistently undertaken by the organs of the United Nations or any other organization. All along, the main international effort under United Nations auspices has been, at best, to prevent war and then, if possible, to restore peace, rather than to render effective the central normative idea that aggression must be resisted, regardless of political consequences, by the collective strength of international society. The eruption of the Cold War in the late 1940s decisively weakened the prospects for collective security at the global level and made it almost impossible, aside from exceptional cases, for collective machinery to operate in conflict-resolving, war-peace settings.[16]

At the same time, governments using force or involved in international conflicts have generally given "lip service" to these normative notions. India was widely criticized by the West in the Security Council because it broke with these contentions when it forcibly took over the enclave of Goa from the Portuguese in 1962. The United States, in particular, has been a leader until recently in these efforts to present its own uses of force as "defensive" and those it opposes as "aggressive." Its diplomatic justifications of involvements in the Korean War and the Vietnam War were centrally keyed to the basic claim that its adversaries were aggressors.[17] In 1956 the United States Government even lined up with Nasser's Egypt to protest against the military attack initiated by England and France, its principal allies at the time. Part of the motivation appeared to be the importance the United States government continued to attach to the prohibition, however imperfectly implemented, on aggressive war.

Thus, it is notable that there has been a falling away of this tradition in recent years. True, uses of force by adversaries are attacked in normative terms as vigorously as ever; for instance, consider the normative outrage directed against the Soviet Union for its use of military forces in Afghanistan since the end of 1978. However, if only *adversary* uses of force are condemned, then normative discourse in international affairs is properly located in the domain of propaganda rather than that of law and morality or even in a mixture of the three. Furthermore, armed attacks upon unpopular or isolated governments have been tolerated without any effort to demonstrate "defensive" intentions. The most obvious instances are China's attack on

Vietnam (1979), Tanzania's 1978 attack on Amin's Uganda, and most recently, Iraq's attack on Iran.

The normative silence in the United Nations, and elsewhere, has been deafening. The Iraq/Iran War is a spectacular confirmation of this new trend toward geopolitical primacy. Iraq's large-scale attack was militarily unprovoked, and the Iraqi pretension that its use of force sought only satisfaction of a border claim was manifestly false. Of course, Khomeini's Iran (like Vietnam and Amin's Uganda) was isolated and unpopular, and the attack occurred during the middle of the hostage incident, pitting Iran against the United States. In addition, Iran's Islamic Revolution was feared by most governments in the region, as well as opposed by both superpowers. The original expectation of these governments evidently was that Iraq would sweep Iran clean of the Khomeini movement, or at the very least detach the Arab-populated, oil-producing province of Khuzistan. The main point relevant here is that Iraq's undisguised war of aggression failed to engender any kind of normative condemnation in the United Nations or elsewhere on behalf of the victim state: The United States and the Soviet Union both declared themselves uninvolved and adopted a posture of neutrality. It should be clear that neutrality as a mode of response is incompatible with aggression/self-defense views about the propriety of military power that form the cornerstone of the normative assault on the discretionary status of recourse to war.

United States diplomacy is especially significant in these regards. It was, after all, the United States that had championed the normative approach in the first instance. Without U.S. support there seems to be little strength behind the basic Charter claim of prohibition, and a lapse into cynicism and undisguised *realpolitik* was bound to occur.

This normative retreat by the United States (and others) is part of a broader pattern, one that relates to shifting geopolitical circumstances. Some comments on this shift will be made in section II, but for now it can be summarily said that the United States, its allies, and even its principal Northern rival are increasingly convinced that military options are needed for security purposes, especially in connection with protecting the resource base in the Persian Gulf that underlies Western economic ascendency.[18]

The Nuclear Weapons Challenge to International Law

Even before atomic bombs were developed and used, weapons innovations earlier in this century put great pressure on the law of war as a moderating force. The submarine and the bomber were powerful weapons whose optimal use defied the traditional limiting notions of international law as applied to wartime uses of force. These problems, however, have become so acute as a result of nuclear weaponry as to draw the entire enterprise of the law of war into doubt.[19] As is generally known, the classical legal tradition codified to a great extent at the Hague Conventions of 1899 and 1907 rested on the central idea that warfare could be conducted within a framework of restraint and that the permissible range of means to injure a belligerent enemy were not unlimited. The main legal restraint, derived from far-earlier just-war notions, insisted that legitimate uses of force be directed against military targets in a discriminate manner so as to avoid civilian and non-military damage. Even discounting hypocrisy and battlefield pressures, a restraining effect seemed to arise from these endeavors of international law. At least, the pretension of adhering to the law of war enabled a reconciliation of sorts between war as a social institution and ideas of civilizational concern for ethical standards of behavior.

Nuclear weapons challenge such a reconciliation in fundamental ways. The prospect of millions of casualties, devastated cities, and the dissemination of cancer-producing radiation in epidemic proportions suggests a weapon that is, *in its essence,* indiscriminate and cruel.[20] The seriousness of the normative damage is heightened by the central role played by nuclear weapons in the security policy of the superpowers and their alliances. Nuclear weapons are not solely weapons of last resort, retained as a way to discourage others from ever making use of such weapons or to stave off the destruction of a country's sovereign reality. For the superpowers, and this is plainer in the case of the United States, nuclear weapons are contemplated for a variety of contexts, both to deter "provocations" of an unspecified character and to achieve battlefield results by way of "limited nuclear warfare." Deterrence doctrine, made credible by actual weapons deployments, continuously threatens massive indiscriminate danger. This threat, endorsed through alliance arrangements by powerful governments, flaunts in the most fundamental ways the minimum claims of the law of war.

Of course, such a condition has existed in some form ever since 1945. Recently, its seriousness has grown evident as the number of nuclear weapons states and range of weaponry increases and their contemplated roles become more provocative. Such trends cumulatively increase the prospect of nuclear warfare. In that sense, the normative vacuum created by the unwillingness of the relevant governments to renounce the legitimacy of even first uses of nuclear weapons against non-nuclear adversaries is notable. If there is no normative inhibition on such holocaustal violence directed at civilians and their surroundings, then lesser normative undertakings seem meaningless at best, at worst, diversionary.

Lowering the Nuclear Threshold

Another central tenet of the normative environment has been the informal prohibition upon recourse to nuclear weaponry except as a matter of ultimate resort.[21] True, nuclear threats had been made from time to time by the superpowers, and during the Dulles era of American foreign policy, the doctrine of massive retaliation seemed to indicate a willingness to use nuclear weapons in response to a whole unspecified series of Soviet challenges to American interests around the world. In actuality, the American doctrine was never tested, and in 1960 was abandoned in favor of a policy that deemphasized nuclear weapons except as ultimate weapons. The expansion of the role of nuclear weapons in the geopolitical strategy of the United States commenced after the Vietnam defeat in 1975 and was especially associated with the statements made about American defense policy by James Schlesinger during his tenure as Secretary of Defense.

A mixture of changing circumstances and new technical capabilities continue to lower the nuclear threshold. As with other aspects of this analysis, the main testing-ground is the Persian Gulf, although concerns are mounting about Europe as well, especially when connected with the prospective deployment of Pershing II and cruise missiles on the American side and MIRVed SS-20 (intermediate range missiles) and backfire bombers on the Soviet side.[22] Increasingly, the United States's position seems to be one of threatening to unleash nuclear war in the event that its hegemonial relationship to the oil producers is any further weakened. Presidential Directive 59 and the enunciation of the Carter Doctrine in the aftermath of the Afghanistan intervention by Soviet troops tended to codify this expanded role for nuclear weapons in the security policy of the United States. Early Reagan defense policy goes even further in these directions. In this central Persian Gulf application of military policy, there is an appreciation that subnuclear capabilities cannot assure Western interests against either a large-scale internal challenge in a key producing country or an external attack. Conventional forces in the region are, at most, a tripwire.

This lowering of the nuclear threshold is augmented by popular discussions of nuclear war scenarios, especially if constructed by "specialists" in military matters, which reinforce anxieties about plausible nuclear war prospects.[23] Especially in an international atmosphere of raised tensions and pervasive uncertainty, there is some disposition to increase the role of nuclear weapons as a way of imposing a kind of order upon the chaos of international relations. Also relevant is the spread of nuclear weapons capabilities to additional countries; in addition to the seven states that are accepted as nuclear weapons states (all, save Israel, having exploded a device), many states are near-nuclear powers by virtue of their access to nuclear technology.

Finally, the nuclear arms race contains a new anxiety about surprise attacks, retaliatory credibility, and first strike options. As a result, there seems to be diminishing confidence that a crisis confrontation could be handled without unleashing a cycle of escalation, resulting in widespread mutual destruction, possibly on a scale of societal annihilation.

Disappearance of Disarmament and, Lately, Even Arms Control from the Active International Agenda

As with the campaign to outlaw aggression, until recently there has been support, at least at the rhetorical level, for disarmament as a negotiating goal for all countries.[24] Such a disarmament campaign has never, true enough, gotten very far, but it has been on the international agenda since World War I, and really before that. What happened in the 1970s was the removal of disarmament from the serious negotiating agenda of the superpowers, a conclusion only slightly qualified by the 1978 United Nations Special Session on Disarmament, an occasion that made few ripples and was virtually boycotted by leading states.

In the 1970s the SALT process of bipolar arms control displaced the headier objectives of disarmament.[25] The arms control argument was based on attainable objectives, placing ceilings on some categories of weapons system, cutting down on incentives to take wasteful and destabilizing steps (such as, for instance, the antiballistic missile), and building confidence for further steps, including arms reduction. The central case, however, was built on stabilizing the US/Soviet relationship.[26]

The American failure to ratify the SALT II Treaty and the election of an anti-SALT president in 1980, has effectively removed arms control, as well as disarmament, from the international agenda. Such a development directly violates the pledge made by the nuclear weapons states in the Non-Proliferation Treaty to pursue in good faith arms control and disarmament negotiations.[27] It also creates a normative vacuum with respect to the arms race at a time when budgetary outlays for defense are rising in absolute and relative terms, a trend with broad social and political implications in a context of reduced public service spending and concern. To sustain support for this militaristic drift requires an atmosphere of international tension, including even a heightened fear of nuclear attack in the event that our side's guard is let down.

The Falling Stature of the United Nations

The United Nations, as successor to the League of Nations, was established to sustain human hopes in normative progress, especially in the area of war and peace.[28] Again it was the West, particularly the United States, that viewed the United Nations as the chrysalis of a new statecraft, one that renounced pure unilateralism and balance of power approaches in favor of collective action and peaceful settlement procedures. As of 1945, and through the first decade of its existence, the United Nations was a compliant arena for the pursuit of United States-led Western foreign policy. Subsequent to the Korean War, however, the Cold War split the organization into immobilizing factions, as the Soviet bloc battled more effectively to prevent the United Nations from being used against its interests. More serious, perhaps, was the effect of the decolonializing movement on the composition of membership in the United Nations. As non-Western, ex-colonial states began to dominate the General Assembly, the agenda changed and the perception of the organization shifted. For one thing, the United Nations became an arena for Third World economic demands often stridently stated. For another, from 1967 onwards the United Nations took an increasingly tough anti-Israel line, a development that considerably reshaped its image in liberal eyes, especially in the United States, earlier its main bastion of financial and ideological support.[29]

In effect, then, the United Nations has receded from view; its normative character has been compromised in some critical quarters, and there is almost no disposition by important state actors to endow the organization with important missions. The United Nations has become distinctly a sideshow in the global political stage, and even public pressure to enhance its role is almost never evident now. But such a diminished stature for the United Nations could be rapidly reversed in the event that the superpowers should decide to entrust the organization with the resolution of a prominent issue.

The Decline of Idealistic Elements in the Foreign Policy Process

In the earlier years of the postwar period, important idealistic and humanitarian undertakings seemed to form a genuine part of the foreign policy process, especially as assessed in relation to the United States, leader of the Western alliance. To some extent, the pattern has oscillated back and forth over the years, varying considerably with the condition of the world economy and with the climate of domestic politics, including the orientation toward internationalism of the most prominent political leaders of the day. Nevertheless, since the mid-1970s, there has been a dramatic decline in support for redistributive approaches to poverty and inequality among states. This decline can be understood by comparison with earlier achievements. First of all, there was the effort to help Europe and Japan recover from the ravages of war. Second, there were the foreign aid programs designed to give poorer countries help in achieving developmental goals, including self-sustaining growth. Third, there were attempts, especially popular in the United States during the Kennedy presidency, to send young people to Third World countries as sources of help with practical problems of health, education, and food production. Fourth, there were varying attempts, including the recent one by the United States Government early in the Carter Administration, to insert human rights into the foreign policy process; the rapid sequence of embrace and abandonment of this emphasis on human rights raised and then shattered expectations about a normative element in foreign policy. Fifth, there was a widespread willingness, especially in Western Europe and Japan, to work toward various accommodations with the Third World in order to forge a compromise new international economic order.

Without detailed discussion, suffice it to say that there has been disillusionment with each of these efforts. The world political system is moving back toward an embrace of statist selfishness as the dominating basis of foreign policy. Such a normative retreat can be exaggerated and interpreted as "a new reality" when, more accurately, it is only a temporary readjustment. There always were, of course, pragmatic motives underlying the supposed benevolence of "the donor," whether "the gifts" were money, advice, or ideological guidance. Nevertheless, idealistic pretensions, and possibly accomplishments, at least created some impression of a nascent world community. This erosion of normative content in foreign policy tends to underscore the reality of a fragmented political order containing states grossly unequal in all respects. Such an image of conflicting hierarchy becomes the dominant, almost the uncontested, image of the character of international order. The debt dependency of the poorer countries, including virtually the entire Third World except for the major oil producers, now adds up to an amount in excess of $500 billion, fostering a situation that points to the fragility of the monetary foundations of international order and the new forms of postcolonial subordination that are the experience of most of the non-Western world.[30]

A NOTE ON THE GEOPOLITICAL MAELSTROM

This interpretation of international order emphasizes the retreat on the levels of discourse and policy from any serious expectations of normative growth. The evidence of this retreat is heavily influenced by the shift in the United States's orientation over the years. The power, wealth, and prominence of this single country is very important to the overall tone of international relations. Hence, the advent of the Reagan presidency is both the most recent and blatant confirmation of this basic assertion of normative decline, an explicit repudiation of idealistic initiatives.[31] The new American leadership places its emphasis on a conflicting view of international relations, a view in which the only outsiders that count are friends, that is, allies in the wider geopolitical struggle for dominance. The provisional decision by the Reagan leadership to hold up on the negotiation of a final version of a law of the seas treaty, because of the wealth-sharing provisions that bear on ocean mining, is indicative of a skeptical attitude toward cooperative approaches to international issues. Its vigorous, overt support for the counterinsurgency regime in El Salvador augurs a stepped-up emphasis on military approaches. Finally, the wonderfully symbolic claim that a campaign against terrorism will serve as a substitute in the Reagan Administration for the campaign on behalf of human rights in the Carter years (a campaign, incidentally, that even Carter virtually abandoned in the last two years of his presidency) is not only ideologically revealing but suggestive of a new escalation of "double think" discourse, considering that antiterrorist tactics often involve reinforcing repressive regimes.

What also seems evident is the absence of any idealistic substitute for United States leadership. Western Europe and Japan, although perhaps comparatively more prudent at this stage on East-West issues, at least with respect to military power and intervention, are without any serious tradition of normative concern on an international level. Scandinavian countries, especially Sweden, are a partial exception to the preceding generalization, but Sweden lacks the weight to exert much of an impact on the overall tone of international relations. The Soviet group adopts a more ideological rather than normative approach, although by virtue of its position and outlook it seemed a progressive force, especially in the Third World during the decolonialization process. This favorable impression of a Soviet role has all but vanished in recent years. The massive Soviet military intervention in Afghanistan sealed this negative impression. Finally, the OPEC group, as a Third World formation, could have used a fraction of its extraordinary wealth and dollar surplus to raise the hopes of the world as a whole. These oil producers, although not acting more selfishly than most rich states, have not put forward any normative claims in a strong way aside from a vague and weak endorsement of the Third World call for a new international economic order, and some routine contributions by way of development assistance. These oil producers have been overwhelmingly preoccupied with their own security and development and have not attempted to halt the process of normative decline.

As might be expected, the normative decline has been accompanied by an accentuation of militaristic tendencies. World military spending is expected to top $600 billion in 1981, with pressures mounting at all levels to go still higher. A series of careful books warns about the growing danger of nuclear warfare.[32] The *Bulletin of Atomic Scientists* has moved the minute hand on its renowned clock closer to the midnight of nuclear war, going from seven minutes before midnight to four in its January 1981 issue.[33] What is worse, perhaps, is a revival of limited nuclear war thinking, implying that nuclear wars are fightable, even winnable, without placing the heartland of the superpower in jeopardy. These attitudes have been translated into new strategic doctrines and feverish weapons acquisition and deployment plans.[34] The prospects of limited nuclear wars in such vital theaters of geopolitical concern as Europe and the Persian Gulf are now widely discussed. Such a drift of superpower thinking has led to the formation of a strong grass-roots antinuclear weapons movement in Europe over the last year or so that is beginning to worry the NATO-oriented leadership.[35]

Another indication of this antinormative trend is the growth of grand strategy as a background for national foreign policy. Ray Cline, a former CIA high official, is taken seriously when he writes a neo-Mahanian tract proposing a twenty-two nation, all-oceans alliance to counter the combined weight of the Communist countries, including those currently antagonistic to one another.[36] More modest grand strategies call for an all-out effort to defend the Persian Gulf against any and all contingencies, whether the threat is mounted from within or without.[37] Again, this worldview is being embodied in a broadened conception of security requirements, in this instance, a justification for an all-oceans naval presence, reinforced by basing rights and widespread deployment of contingents of troops.

Finally, of course, this new militarism, producing anxiety and fiscal burden, requires justification to receive and retain public support. Such support in the West depends on whipping up fears of Soviet expansionism among the citizenry. A very fully orchestrated effort along these lines over the past few years has reshaped the post-Vietnam neoisolationalist political climate in the United States.[38]

On the Soviet side, this impression is reinforced. Soviet military spending, direct and indirect involvements in the internal politics of foreign societies, and failure to produce new leadership all foster the impression of a fortress mentality, as well as a conception of security reliant on military intervention to suppress popular movements in countries along the Soviet periphery. This mentality feeds also on the American militaristic drift, thereby creating a feedback loop that accelerates the destructive spiral of the arms race. These militaristic patterns may also be reinforced by the failure of either superpower to solve domestic economic problems; there is an oft-noticed tendency in the political life of major states to exaggerate international dangers so as to discourage scrutiny of domestic failures. Such a destructive dynamic, concentrating on military prowess, was impeded during the détente years (roughly 1972–78), at least symbolically, by other contrary undertakings, including especially arms control negotiations, but also trade and cooperative ventures such as cultural exchange and joint space activities. Removing these moderating aspects from the bipolar context leaves one with the strong sense that the Cold War has "heated" up again, quite possibly in a more dangerous way because of the political and military preparations for nuclear war, the overall precariousness of the world economy, and the sharpening global struggle for resources, markets, and capital.[39]

NOTES

1. Such a specification has been elaborated by the World Order Models Project (of the Institute for World Order) in various settings. See, for example, Saul H. Mendlovitz, ed., *On the Creation of a Just World Order* (New York: Free Press, 1975); my own

elaboration can be found in Richard Falk, *A Study of Future Worlds* (New York: Free Press, 1975), pp. 11–48, and chapters 4 and 5 in this volume.

2. See the important and innovative discussion in Robert C. Tucker, *On Political Leadership* (Columbia, Mo.: University of Missouri Press, 1981), especially chapter 4, entitled "Leadership and Man's Survival," pp. 114–157.

3. This distinction is developed clearly and comprehensively in Robert C. Johansen, *The National Interest and the Human Interest* (Princeton, N.J.: Princeton University Press, 1980), especially pp. 3–37.

4. For a creative consideration of this prospect, see Harold D. Lasswell, "Future Systems of Identity in the World Community," in Cyril E. Black and Richard Falk, eds., *The Future of the International Legal Order* (Princeton, N.J.: Princeton University Press, 1972), pp. 3–31.

5. Culminating this process has been identified by some seminal figures as the great challenge of our time. See, for example, Pitrim A. Sorokin, *The Crisis of Our Age* (New York: E. P. Dutton, 1941); Kenneth Boulding, *The Meaning of the Twentieth Century* (New York: Harper and Row, 1964); Albert Bergeson, "From Utilitarianism to Globology: The Shift from the Individual to the World as a Whole as the Primordial Unit of Analysis," in Albert Bergeson, ed., *Studies of the Modern World-System* (New York: Academic Press, 1980), pp. 1–12; and Pierre Teilhard de Chardin, *The Future of Man* (London: Collins, 1964).

6. For instance, in Sorokin, *The Crisis of Our Age*, the author writes that "the final outcome of this epochal struggle will largely depend upon whether mankind can avoid a new world war. If the forces of the decaying sensate order start such a war, then, dissipating their remaining energy, these forces can end or greatly impede the creative progress of mankind." See also Sorokin's final statement in the book, along similar lines, p. 326. Such apprehensions are quite typical for those authors who perceive our age as a time of "great transition." For an overall assessment, see Richard J. Barnet, *The Lean Years* (New York: Simon and Schuster, 1980).

7. Trend projections that suppose the crisis to be on the plane of *things* rather than on the plane of values do not respond to the deeper forms of malaise, do not raise hopes, and, despite their optimism, are but another manifestation of despair. Along these lines, see F. M. Esfandiary, *Optimism One* (New York: Popular Library, 1970); F. M. Esfandiary, *Up-Wingers* (New York: Popular Library, 1973); H. Kahn et al., *The Next 200 Years*(New York: William Morrow, 1976); at this stage, even the most institutionally optimistic auspices, that is, governments, are beginning to acknowledge the deteriorating situation. See, for example, *Global Report 2000* (Washington, D.C.: U.S. Government Printing Office, 1980).

8. See conceptual and historical assessments in Lewis Mumford, *The Transformations of Man* (New York: Collier, 1956).

9. In addition to a negation of dominant trends, there are diverse indications of newly emergent values, beliefs, and life styles that could provide the cultural foundation for a postmaterialistic, even a postmilitaristic civilization. See, for example, Marilyn Ferguson, *The Aquarian Conspiracy* (Los Angeles: J. P. Tarcher, 1979); R. Inglehart, *The Silent Revolution: Changing Values and Political Styles Among Western Publics* (Princeton, N.J.: Princeton University Press, 1977).

10. See, for example, Theodore Roszak, *Person/Planet* (Garden City, N.Y.: Doubleday, 1978); there is also an equivalent emphasis on mutation by the recovery of lost wisdom in Gary Snyder, *Myths and Texts* (New York: New Directions, 1978); Wendell Berry, *The Unsettling of America* (New York: Avon, 1977).

11. The appraisal process here endorsed is based on world order values as a mechanism for identifying the content of the human interest. As such, it contrasts with geopolitical calculations seeking to maximize the national interest of a given actor or those associated with managing intraimperial and interimperial rivalries.

12. The essential material is intelligently collected in Leon Friedman, ed., *The Law of War*, 2 vol. (New York: Random House, 1972).

13. For a comprehensive presentation, see Benjamin B. Ferencz, *Defining International Aggression*, 2 vol. (Dobbs Ferry, N.Y.: Oceana Publications, 1975).

14. A comprehensive attack along these lines is to be found in Julius Stone, *Aggression and World Order: A Critique of United Nations Theories of Aggression* (London: Stevens, 1958).

15. For the fundamental criticism, see Richard Minear, *Victors' Justice: The Tokyo War Crimes Trial* (Princeton, N.J.: Princeton University Press, 1971); Eugene Davidson, *The Nuremberg Fallacy: Wars and War Crimes Since World War II* (New York: Macmillan, 1973).

16. For an excellent conceptual and historical survey of recent international relations in light of the low disposition toward collective diplomacy, see I. Clark, *Reform and Resistance in the International Order* (Cambridge, England: Cambridge University Press, 1980), especially pp. 133–168.

17. See, for example, William L. Standard, *Aggression: Our Asian Disaster* (New York: Random House, 1971); Roger H. Hull and John C. Novogrod, *Law and Vietnam* (Dobbs Ferry, N.Y.: Oceana Publications, 1968); Richard Falk, *The Vietnam War and International Law*, 4 vol., especially vol. 1 (Princeton, N.J.: Princeton University Press, 1968).

18. This line is persuasively spelled out in Robert W. Tucker, "The Purposes of American Power," *Foreign Affairs* 59 (winter 1980/1981): 241–274.

19. So discussed in Michael Walzer, *Just and Unjust Wars* (New York: Basic Books, 1977), pp. 269–283.

20. A powerful indictment developed out of the just war tradition can be found in James W. Douglass, *The Non-Violent Cross* (New York: Macmillan, 1968); for later development and radicalization of Douglass's response to the nuclear weapons challenge, see *Lightning East To West* (Portland, Oregon: Sunburst Press, 1980).

21. Richard Falk, Lee Meyrowitz, and Jack Sanderson, "Nuclear Weapons and International Law," World Order Studies Program, Occasional Paper No. 10, Center of International Studies, Princeton University, Princeton, N.J., 1981.

22. A discussion of European implications and response in this evolving strategic context can be found in Edward P. Thompson, "The END of the Line," *Bulletin of the Atomic Scientists* 37 (1981): 6–12, especially 10–12.

23. For example, General Sir John Hackett, *The Third World War: August 1985* (New York: Berkley Books, 1979); see also Shelford Bidwell, *World War 3* (Englewood Cliffs, N.J.: Prentice-Hall, 1978).

24. See, for instance, the "Joint Statement of Agreed Principles for Disarmament Negotiations" ("McCloy-Zorin Agreement"), text in Burns Weston, Richard Falk, and Anthony D'Amato, eds., *International Law and World Order* (St. Paul, Minn.: West Publishing, 1980), pp. 404–406; but note skepticism about disarmament in the officially sponsored study, Arnold Wolfers et al., *The United States in a Disarmed World* (Baltimore, Md.: Johns Hopkins University Press, 1966).

25. See, along these lines, various contributions to *Daedalus* 104, no. 3 (summer 1975): i-214, on the theme "Arms, Defense Policy, and Arms Control."

26. See contributions by Joseph J. Kruzel and Richard Burt to *Daedalus* (winter 1981): 137–158, 159–178; see also Christoph Bertram, "Rethinking Arms Control," *Foreign Affairs* 59 (winter 1980/1981): 352–365.

27. The pledge is contained in Article VI of the NPT: "Each of the Parties to the Treaty undertakes to pursue negotiations in good faith on effective measures relating to cessation of the nuclear arms race at an early date and to nuclear disarmament, and on a treaty on general and complete disarmament under strict and effective international control."

28. But see Clark, *Reform and Resistance,* p. 133f, for a view that the collective impulses underlying the United Nations were weak, or even absent, from the outset of its existence in 1945.

29. See the generalized attack so derived, in A. Yesselson and A. Gaglione, *A Dangerous Place: The United Nations as a Weapon in World Politics* (New York: Grossman Publishers, 1974).

30. See Richard F. Janssen, "Third World's Debts, Totaling $500 Billion, May Pose Big Dangers," *Wall Street Journal,* January 28, 1981, pp. 1, 27.

31. See, for instance, Hobart Rowen, "A U-Turn Away from the Third World," *Washington Post,* March 5, 1981, p. 419.

32. For example, Louis R. Beres, *Apocalypse: Nuclear Catastrophe in World Politics* (Chicago: University of Chicago Press, 1980); Nigel Calder, *Nuclear Nightmares* (New York: Viking Press, 1979); see also J. A. Leonard, "Danger: Nuclear War," *Monthly Review* 32 (1981): 23–34.

33. See the lead editorial, Bernard T. Feld, "The Hands Move Closer to Midnight," *Bulletin of the Atomic Scientists* 37 (1981): 1.

34. See the interview with Daniel Ellsberg, "Nuclear Armaments," published as a pamphlet (1980).

35. For important statements, see Edward P. Thompson, "Notes on Exterminism; the Last Stage of Civilization," *The New Left Review,* no. 121 (1980): 3–31; Raymond Williams, "The Politics of Nuclear Disarmament," *The New Left Review,* no. 124 (1980): 25–42.

36. This is spelled out in Ray S. Cline, *World Power Trends and U.S. Foreign Policy for the 1980s* (Boulder, Colo.: Westview, 1980); see also Colin S. Gray, *The Geopolitics of the Nuclear Era* (Chicago: Crane, Russak, 1977).

37. Most carefully argued in Robert W. Tucker, "Purposes of American Power," *Foreign Affairs* 59 (1981): 241–274; see also *Challenges for U.S. National Security: A Preliminary Report* (Washington, D.C.: Carnegie Endowment for International Peace, 1980); Karl Kaiser et al., "Western Security: What Has Changed? What Should be Done?" a published report by directors of four foreign policy institutes (New York: Council on Foreign Relations, 1981); "The Geopolitics of Oil," Staff Report, U.S. Senate Committee on Energy and Natural Resources (Washington, D.C., December 1980).

38. See the excellent study of this mobilizing dynamic in Jerry Sanders, "Peddlers of Crisis" (Ph.D. diss., University of California, Berkeley, 1980).

39. Even the most judicious assessors are driven toward these conclusions. See, for example, Michael Howard, "Return to the Cold War?" and George W. Ball, "Reflections on a Heavy Year," in *Foreign Affairs* 59 (1981): 459–473; 474–499.

PART FOUR

Problems

CHAPTER 9

Nuclear Policy and World Order: Why Denuclearization?*

THE RELEVANCE OF WORLD ORDER

The quality of world order lies in the eye of the beholder. In discussions of nuclear policy within the United States, world order considerations are typically invoked to underscore the wisdom of confining the spread of nuclear weapons to the narrowest possible extent.[1] Underlying these nonproliferation goals, which combine traditional U.S. foreign policy concerns with a broader commitment to the avoidance of nuclear war, is the conviction that the fewer nuclear actors the better. Increasingly, this arithmetic image of proliferation is reinforced by explicit anxieties that nuclear weapons will come into the hands of "irresponsible governments," namely Third World rulers, as well as nongovernmental and especially terrorist groups.[2] Both these fears and the "world order concerns" they provoke have intensified recently, because nuclear technology now appears within easy reach of virtually all governments and nongovernmental actors as well. One reliable source estimates that by 1985 as many as 50 countries could "produce enough plutonium each year for at least

*An earlier, much shorter, version of this chapter was published in *International Security* I (1977): 79–93. Although many individuals have made useful comments, I would like especially to thank Fouad Ajami, Graciela Chichilnisky, and Ali Mazrui for their valiant efforts to prevent me from succumbing to First World provincialism. On no issue of global concern is this failure to acknowledge the biased filter of time and place more prevalent and more pernicious, I believe, than with respect to nuclear weapons policy. Such a comment applies with particular force to Americans who lead the world with respect both to reliance on nuclear weaponry and to sermonizing on the evils of such reliance. Of course, I have not escaped my identity as an American in assessing these issues or in my understanding of what is most "irrational" and "dangerous" about them; however, I have tried to be guided by my identity as a planetary citizen as well as my narrower identities as a North American, as a white male, as a father of young children, and so forth. In my view, learning to feel, think, and act like a planetary citizen is what world order studies are all about.

several dozen nuclear explosives."[3] An even more immediate danger, say other analysts, is that "economic competition among nuclear suppliers today could soon lead to a world in which twenty or more nations are but a few months away from a nuclear weapons force."[4]

Three developments have created this disturbing situation:

• the rush of many governments around the world to develop nuclear power facilities as a consequence of rising oil prices, the unreliability of existing supplies, and the realization that all natural stocks of petroleum will eventually dwindle in any event;

• the actuality of India's nuclear explosion in May 1974, which demonstrated that states with civilian nuclear programs can simultaneously but surreptitiously develop their own nuclear weapons capability;

• the intensifying competition among supplier nations for foreign nuclear sales, which has highlighted the incompatibility between nonproliferation goals and the pursuit of national commercial advantage. Essentially, this reality has emerged from a break in the U.S. monopoly over civilian nuclear technology, and the willingness of France and Germany to provide desirous buyers with *all* elements of the nuclear fuel cycle, including enrichment and reprocessing facilities. In terms of global political impact, the commercial equivalent of India's explosion has been the German-Brazilian deal worth at least $8 billion.[5]

Such increasingly broad access to nuclear technology raises the alarming prospect that beleaguered governments or desperate political actors of any sort may acquire, and possibly even use, nuclear weapons for their own political purposes. This potential has already been demonstrated by Israel's semi-overt reliance on a secret nuclear arsenal which apparently numbered thirteen weapons at the time of the 1973 October war. These nuclear weapons were reportedly assembled after Israeli leaders had been informed by their military commander on the Suez front that Egyptian forces might soon break through Israeli defense lines.[6] South Africa, South Korea, and Taiwan are also beleaguered states whose ruling groups face adverse regional and/or domestic balances of power, and who are obviously strongly tempted to acquire their own nuclear weapons capability— not only for its value as a deterrent but also as a military option of ultimate resort. These countries provide plausible settings for future military conflict in which the "losing" side (in conventional terms) may be tempted to rely, however self-destructively, on nuclear weapons.

Another category of nuclear aspirants consists of states which seek a new and stronger lever in international relations, often in the context of shifting regional balances. India initiated its nuclear program partly to offset the effects of China's nuclear status. Pakistan may, in turn, be motivated to counter India's nuclear advantage, thereby leading Iran, perhaps, to invoke that development as justification for setting off a nuclear explosion of its own. The Shah of Iran was once quoted as saying that "If every upstart in the region acquires atomic bombs, then Iran must have them as well."[7]

Iran, Brazil, and possibly Indonesia and Saudi Arabia are all examples of states whose incentives to acquire nuclear status are linked to foreign policy goals of achieving regional or subregional hegemony. With the decline of the American imperial presence, such opportunities for regional dominance now exist, waiting only to be seized by nations willing to invest in the necessary weapons capabilities. Of course, such developments might well lead to nuclear arms races on regional levels; if Brazil were to develop nuclear weapons, would Argentina be far behind? As the technological and economic inhibitions continue to fall, additional states will very likely come to associate their own prestige and autonomy with the development of national nuclear capabilities.

Disturbing as all these possibilities may be, there is no doubt that the current nuclear states are most alarmed by knowing that now even "irrational" Third World leaders can secure nuclear weapons of their own. John Phillips, a Princeton undergraduate with no special training, has demonstrated that a crude atomic bomb can be made for as little as $2000 and with the appropriate *unclassified* information. Other evidence indicates that with sufficient money and will power, it is no more difficult to obtain enriched uranium or plutonium than it is to buy bulk quantities of heroin.

In this context, Libya's Col. Muhammed el-Qaddafi is usually presented as the extreme or worst-case example. First, there is the fear that Qaddafi is personally "maniacal" enough to pursue his dreams of advancing Islamic unity and Libyan national goals by actually using nuclear weapons if once obtained. Moreover, Libya's emergence as a nuclear power would undoubtedly cause a regional chain reaction extending at least as far as Egypt and Israel. It would also definitely end all doubts about the ease with which *any* actor, whether governmental or not, could join the nuclear club if so determined.[8] Consequently, when the Libyan leader tried to purchase atomic weapons from France and China, it caused an international tremor, as did his apparent subsequent effort to assemble enough scientists and engineers to put together a few bombs.

Whether these particular fears are justified or not, it seems self-evident by any standards that the problem of nuclear proliferation presents ample grounds for concern, even alarm. Although the risks of nuclear war cannot be associated in any mechanical fashion with the number of nuclear actors, it does nevertheless seem logical to make some rough correlations between the extent of proliferation and the likelihood of nuclear war.[9] Conventional world order thinking in the United States (and elsewhere in the Trilateral world) has therefore moved virtually automatically from the dangers of proliferation to a desperate search for new ways to halt proliferation. Recently, there has been a surge of writing on "safeguards" and on incentives (such as better technology sharing or security guarantees from the nuclear powers) to make non-nuclear states forego their tentative nuclear aspirations.[10]

Other suggestions focus on improving the Non-Proliferation Treaty by extending safeguards covering of all elements of the nuclear fuel cycle (not merely reactors), and by giving the administering agency, the International Atomic Energy Agency, enforcement functions in addition to its present detection role.[11] One popular line of nonproliferation thought, encouraged slightly by the London Conference of Nuclear Supplier Countries held in 1975 and inspired by the tantalizing image of a "nuclear OPEC," is for nuclear suppliers to cooperate more closely among themselves.[12] Still another popular proposal involves creating a multinational regional nuclear fuel center (as if a permanently reliable site existed), designed to give non-nuclear countries assured access to nuclear fuel without the need for them to establish enrichment and reprocessing facilities on their own soil. Currently, international controversy centers on the dispute between the United States and its European competitors, France and West Germany, over whether or not it is reasonable to sell the most proliferation-prone components of the nuclear fuel cycle (enrichment and reprocessing facilities). Indeed, in 1976 the United States induced South Korea to cancel its purchase of enrichment facilities from a French concern. In other settings, notably Iran and Pakistan, the United States has applied similar leverage in its role as a major supplier of conventional arms. In fact some analysts believe the United States would be more reluctant to sell ultrasophisticated weapons to certain Third World countries if it did not attach such priority to the goals of slowing, as well as halting, nuclear proliferation.

A cynical interpretation of America's stress on nonproliferation emphasizes the present competitive edge which France and Germany enjoy in the more advanced phases of nuclear technology. In this view, the United States wants time for its own technology to catch up, in order to compete more successfully when the export market expands from reactors to complete fuel cycles.

Occasionally, America's priority on nonproliferation is translated into actions which even limit the discretion of existing nuclear powers. Attempts to limit the parameters of the arms race through the Strategic Arms Limitation Talks (SALT) process, for example, are often described as an earnest of good faith by the superpowers. At least as of now, however, this interpretation is inaccurate; SALT has rechanneled arms competition rather than deescalated the arms race, and has not yet initiated moves toward nuclear disarmament. Unilateral arms restraints like President Carter's decision not to develop the B-1 bomber at this stage are also invoked as evidence of good faith on the part of the United States. Here too, however, such optimistic assessments are off the mark. In reality, steps which supposedly aid deescalation are in fact accompanied by compensatory forms of escalation, and are primarily motivated in any event by considerations of cost effectiveness rather than arms control. In this case, for example, more strategic value could be obtained with the cheaper Cruise Missile than with the more expensive B-1 bomber, and in any event, even the restraints widely proclaimed may not endure a shift in administration, as the renewed commitment to proceed with the B-1 illustrated.

In the available literature, some importance is attached to a comprehensive test ban which would preclude further nuclear explosions by all states.[13] Also mentioned frequently is the possibility that nuclear powers might pledge never to use or threaten to use nuclear weapons against a non-nuclear weapons state that has ratified the Nuclear Non-Proliferation Treaty.[14]

In fact, however, at the NPT Review Conference in May 1975 the nuclear powers seemed unwilling to take even these modest steps in diminishing the *discriminatory* character of the NPT system. At most, then, the nuclear powers have merely sought new ways of moderating, and disguising, the discrimination within the international system against non-nuclear weapons states. Mainstream policy analysis rarely acknowledges the dubious validity of a world order system based on the inherent discrimination which flows automatically from the distinction between nuclear and non-nuclear states.[15]

Much of world public opinion seems justifiably suspicious of the way in which the West, especially the United States, harps on the nuclear danger. Why are other comparable dangers given so little attention? For instance, deadly biological weapons of mass destruction are easy and cheap to produce, and their possession, moreover, is difficult to detect. Why has this danger not alarmed those who stress the risks of possible nuclear proliferation? Indeed, as terrorist activity suggests, all modern societies are vulnerable to determined opponents—who need only poison the water supply or destroy key bridges and tunnels.

What makes the nuclear danger so special, it would seem, is the fact that some governments insist on retaining the right to have, develop, and use nuclear weapons, while at the same time seeking ways to prevent most others from doing the same. In effect, it is the frequent use of nuclear weapons—as actual instruments of war during World War II, and as political or psychological tools ever since—which endows these weapons with a certain legitimacy that biological weapons and deadly poisons do not share. Paradoxically, then, it is the relative *legitimacy* of these weapons which makes their possession by others seem so alarming—especially by those who seem to have the smallest stake in helping the present system to survive.

Furthermore, the existing system of global security depends on letting each of the superpowers rely on their respective nuclear capabilities in their own spheres of influence. If the overall system is to work, these roles for nuclear weapons must be preserved in particular arenas, for instance, in South Korean and Europe. U. S. reliance on nuclear weapons as a geopolitical instrument has been more overt than Soviet reliance. Nevertheless, the Soviet relationship with China has been very much shaped by the way in which the Kremlin has used its nuclear advantage. Significant forms of proliferation will interfere with existing international arrangements, although, as Chinese acquisition of a nuclear capability suggests, the shift from an absolute nuclear advantage to a relative one may not be as significant as the antiproliferation forces fear.

One of the more suspect elements in nonproliferation sensibility is its preoccupation with what might happen if "irrational" Third World leaders obtained nuclear weapons. One would think that Hitler and Mussolini—or, for that matter, Stalin and Nixon—were prehistoric figures. On the contrary, modern history shows that desperate leaders are likely to emerge in all societies which experience severe pressures. There is no evidence that Third World countries are to be feared especially in this regard. Beyond this, irrationality is often associated with unfamiliar cultural forms. When an African leader joins in a native dance, his behavior strikes us as "wild." When an American President calls a football coach in the middle of the night with a play for the big game the following day, as Richard Nixon once did, or insists on briefing his advisers while seated on the toilet, as Lyndon Johnson reputedly did, their actions seem to express harmless enthusiasm. The desperation of leaders in powerful states—even, or perhaps especially, when reinforced by platoons of strategic thinkers bearing reams of computer printouts—is far more menacing to human destiny and nuclear peace, in my opinion, than is the alleged "irrationality" of Third World leaders. It is chastening to recall that the first use of nuclear weapons, at Hiroshima and Nagasaki, was vindicated by "rational" arguments about saving lives. Who could not devise similar arguments again, as long as no one questioned whether the underlying goals themselves were legitimate? Eminently "rational" advisers were waiting in the wings throughout the Vietnam war, ready to make a moral case for using nuclear weapons.

Finally, if one considers the potential *global* side effects of a nuclear war between the superpowers, then the prospect that modest nuclear capabilities may proliferate within the Third World for purposes of regional security becomes a matter of distinctly secondary concern. Even if we project Third World scenarios where nuclear weapons are used, horrifying as such eventualities would certainly be, the orbit of their effect would be geographically circumscribed, and local recovery prospects at least relatively favorable. In East-West relations, on the other hand, nuclear conflict could disperse lethal fallout throughout the planet, permanently wrecking the world economy and creating chaos and panic everywhere. When seen in this light, state visits by American leaders who counsel nuclear forbearance to their Third World counterparts appear as pious mischief, or worse.[16] The emphasis on nonproliferation, as distinct from denuclearization, is a geopolitical confidence game being played for stupendous stakes. Therefore, it should not be particularly surprising to find the United States—by far the greatest proliferator of nuclear weapons: its own—as the most passionate advocate of nonproliferation. What is surprising is that this dual reality has not been more widely noticed and challenged.

In view of the genuine danger of nuclear war and the growing salience of nuclear weapons in all modes of international relations, a far-reaching global policy on nuclear weapons is long overdue. This chapter outlines such a policy within the wider framework of world order analysis with particular reference to four specific values, the balanced attainment of which I believe would characterize a just world order: peace, economic well-being, social and political justice, and environmental quality.[17]

More concretely, the goal of this analysis is to suggest a global nuclear policy which would allow these world order values to be realized, at least in some minimal way, by all the peoples of the world within the next few decades. In addition to being informed by specific values and adopting a long-range outlook, this perspective also assumes the necessity of *structural change*. By this, I mean a coherent series of fundamental reforms in the institutional arrangements and patterns of authority which currently characterize international relations. Such a thoroughgoing change is required, I believe, because, although the sovereign state and the state system itself remain beneficial for certain parts of the world and for particular normative purposes (for instance, to achieve equality among peoples, deepen the independence of Third World nations, and eliminate imperialism), these arrangements are not able to realize world order values for the planet as a whole.

As the studies stimulated by the World Order Models Project suggest, interpretations and policy prescriptions can differ widely within a common framework of world order values.[18] The distinguishing feature of world order analysis from this perspective is that it views nuclear policy as one aspect of a wider search for stability and equity in the world. Studies of nuclear policy whose conclusions differ from my own—such as those of T. C. Schelling[19]—also qualify as world order analyses.

QUESTIONING THE POSTULATES OF NONPROLIFERATION DOCTRINE

One line of attack on nonproliferation doctrine emerges from the bosom of the nuclear industry itself. Writing in *Fortune,* Tom Alexander declares that "it seems clear that we are sacrificing too much of our foreign policy on the altar of nonproliferation."[20] In effect, Alexander is indicting U. S. foreign policy, not only because it is futile so far as nonproliferation is concerned, but also because it is self-defeating as well—merely shifting important shares of the export market to foreign competitors who have less concern for nonproliferation goals than we. It also saturates the export market with more proliferation-prone technology (for example, Canada's CANDU reactor, the wastes of which are fissionable without reprocessing). Given the logic of the competition, on the one hand, and the priority of security, on the other, American policy regarding international nuclear transactions is indeed implausible in a sense. Why shouldn't French or German competitors strive for a larger share of a lucrative market estimated to be worth $295 billion over the period 1971–1985?[21] Why shouldn't Brazil or South Africa acquire a nuclear option to satisfy the drive for a first-rank power status or as a hedge against future contingencies? Whether the issue be whales or nuclear bombs, all governments are primarily motivated by relatively short-term calculations of national economic and political self-interest. Their willingness to sacrifice any portion of that self-interest out of deference to world community well-being is purely rhetorical, if, and to the extent that, it exists at all. On nuclear policy specifically, America's apparently greater concern with nonproliferation does not display a more evolved world community consciousness but rather reflects its geopolitical position as a global security manager. As Hedley Bull puts it, implicit in the superpowers' choice "of proliferation as the danger to peace and security that must be curbed now—rather than, say, the danger inherent in the growth of their own weapons stockpiles—is the perception that curbs in this area will restrict others and not themselves."[22] It is hegemony which is jeopardized by proliferation, because the spread of nuclear weapons makes it harder for the superpowers to control the boundaries and predict the outcome of regional conflicts in which they themselves have some involvement. In other words, both geopolitical control and bipolar stability are distinctively superpower preoccupations. Hence, it is not surprising that the United States aspires to reconcile its geopolitical and commercial goals at the altar of nonproliferation.

At the same time, I also agree with Richard Betts that "the full cost of preventing a country from going nuclear has to be weighed against contradictory goals. Senator Ribicoff to the contrary, strategy has to accommodate to the fact that the United States has other interests in foreign policy besides prevention of nuclear spread."[23] One can add, of course, that so have other nuclear powers. These interests include export markets, political influence, regional balance, and rivalry between great powers. There is simply no painless way for any of the nuclear supplier states to implement a strategy of nonproliferation, and even American policy-makers do not necessarily agree among themselves that nonproliferation deserves absolute priority over all other foreign policy goals. For instance, if key countries like Iran, Saudi Arabia, or Turkey credibly threatened to shift their geopolitical allegiance away from the West unless they were allowed to achieve nuclear military status, American leaders would probably cease to insist on nonproliferation in strategically sensitive cases.

Nevertheless, if the nuclear suppliers can reach an agreement on common ground rules, then both the superpowers will be able to pursue their global geopolitical strategies without losing ground in the lucrative commercial market. Although the Soviet Union is more exclusively concerned with geopolitics than the United States, both countries seem to be moving toward a similar set of policies on nuclear issues (as was evident at the NPT review conference), and have even supported and taken part in the London supplier conferences. A common superpower position on nonproliferation seems to be emerging without any explicit concert of action.

An additional factor sets the nuclear superpowers apart from other supplier nations. The United States and the Soviet Union are both concerned with maintaining "first use options" in situations other than the ultimate self-defense of homeland. Consequently, nonproliferation goals provide a convenient means of protecting existing military advantages for the present owners of nuclear weapons. For example, by threatening to defend South Korea with nuclear weapons during the Kissinger era, American officials sought a cheap option (compared to that pursued in Vietnam) of intimidating a non-nuclear Third World country with the specter of nuclear devastation.

Of course, such diplomacy itself undermines efforts to curtail proliferation, by demonstrating how vulnerable non-nuclear states are to such one-sided blackmail. Precisely because such a menacing posture brings the inherent discrimination of the NPT system into the open, it is criticized by moderate arms controllers. Generally "liberals" and "rationalists" understand that it could be costly to undermine the calculus of gains and losses associated with non-nuclear status.[24] However, the liberal critique is directed only to the excess of discrimination, not to its *existence,* nor to its underlying structure.

According to a less sentimental perspective on proliferation policy, the discrimination issue is only a red herring, an illustration of "the moralist's fallacy," which alleges that moral considerations have an important influence on behavior (in this instance, decisions to acquire nuclear capabilities), when the evidence seems to favor other explanations (namely, self-interest as related to fear and ambition). One analyst of this persuasion contends that "stressing the discriminatory immorality of Soviet and American maintenance of large nuclear arms capabilities is analytically wrong, prescriptively quixotic, and a dangerous misdirection of effort."[25] Although its tone is strident, the statement does contain a grain of truth. Liberal attempts to blunt such "discriminatory immorality" do tend to underestimate the logic of self-interested behavior, which is, after all, the dominant feature of the statist system of world order.

At the same time, I strongly applaud all efforts to stress discrimination within the existing international order, if such efforts form part of an overall assault on the primacy of state interests and the war-based security system, on the hierarchical and hegemonical features of the state system, and on statist logic altogether. If our perspective is one of system change rather than system reform, then the acknowledged discrimination of nuclear weapons distribution within the present system is both a mobilizing focus and a primary target. This emphasis is especially appropriate if our primary audiences are not policy-making elites but more flexible and open-minded sectors of public opinion.

Even in the terms of statist logic, a geopolitical strategy that goes no further than nonproliferation is questionable on both pragmatic and principled grounds. On pragmatic grounds, it is unlikely to work because there is no basic reason why those who want nuclear weapons should forego them, so long as some states insist upon their right to retain and develop such weapons further. Moreover, so long as civilian nuclear power continues to expand, there can be no reliable assurance that any given state has not acquired a covert or latent nuclear weapons capability. From a statist perspective, the most effective approach to nonproliferation would probably require a maximum extension of superpower roles. However, that outcome would itself conflict with the geopolitical goals held by the most intense advocates of nonproliferation. As Betts argues, "There is no free lunch in nonproliferation policy . . . the biggest price would be the reaffirmation or extension of protective alliances which would relieve the insecurities" of those states tempted by their national situation to acquire nuclear weapons.[26] Betts specifies this price tag in suggestive ways. It is worth stationing American troops on Israeli soil to obtain Israeli adherence to the NPT, he argues; worth acquiescing in South Korean repression; worth incurring India's displeasure by aiding Pakistan in non-nuclear respects; worth letting China choose whether it wants the United States to guarantee Taiwan against invasion or would rather risk having a nuclear Taiwan; and worth abandoning South Africa with the warning that the United States will support the armed struggle of black Africans if Pretoria ever threatens its adversaries with nuclear attack.[27] What is evident, whether or not one goes along with these policy prescriptions, is that there is no way within the state system to reconcile nonproliferation goals with other widely endorsed world order values such as nonintervention, human rights, and peace. It is self-deceiving to claim otherwise.

On principled grounds, the morality of the state system is built around the primacy of state interests as conceived by governmental leaders. It is instructive to recall how enthusiastic our highest officials became upon being told in July 1945 that the atomic bomb would soon be definitely available to the United States—as a weapon of war (against Japan) and as an instrument of diplomacy (against the Soviet Union and, to a far lesser extent, Great Britain).[28]

True, once the horrible effects of atomic power became clear, there was some attempt (the seriousness and reasonableness of which still are difficult to assess) to rid the world of nuclear weapons for all time. Nevertheless, the main patterns of behavior suggest that the use, development, and role of nuclear arms have been almost entirely determined by considerations of state power. Hence, there is little reason to suppose that such considerations will not prevail in the future, as they have in the past, in determining whether additional governments will decide to develop, deploy, and use nuclear arms. Government leaders may pursue self-destructive policies based on the narrow interests of their ruling groups and may, further, be entrapped within horizons of time and security which are far too short even from the perspective of national well-being. Nevertheless, such leaders are the only effective policy-makers on nuclear matters, given the structure and political realities of the state system. Furthermore, in a world system that has been victimized by imperial patterns of exploitation, there is little rational and even less emotional appeal in positions which are premised upon inherent discrimination between states which do and do not possess nuclear weapons at a given moment of time. The identity of "responsible states" and "terroristic elements" may seem crystal clear to George Ball and Henry Kissinger, but not at all so to the leaders of a wide variety of Third World nations, wherein more than two-thirds of humanity reside. Hence, a major conclusion of a world-order analysis guided by the values already enumerated is that nonproliferation goals can become persuasive ingredients of global policy only when they are integrated into a credible program of total denuclearization.

TOWARD MILITARY DENUCLEARIZATION

Military denuclearization means the process of progressively eliminating nuclear weapons. The goal is a non-nuclear world in which nuclear weapons are neither legitimate nor possessed by any state. In the context of denuclearization, nonproliferation is obviously an integral but secondary goal. From this perspective, the gravest dangers are presented, not by those international actors who *may* acquire nuclear weapons, but by those who already possess them, who rely on their active role in a variety of security situations, and who have continued to deploy and "improve" upon nuclear weapon systems.[29]

In world order terms, the argument for denuclearization is again both pragmatic and principled. From a pragmatic perspective, denuclearization is the only way to overcome the inherent discrimination of the present world order system and, in particular, the most extreme manifestation of that discrimination—namely, the capacity of nuclear states to decisively affect the security of non-nuclear and lesser nuclear states under a wide variety of circumstances. Moreover, the state system derives its moral legitimacy from the juridical premise of sovereign equality. From a principled perspective, then, denuclearization would constitute a fuller realization of statist logic, which would in turn provide a positive basis for moving beyond the state system at some future time. Hence, whether the ultimate goal is to *reform* the state system or to actually *transform* that system, denuclearization would have a decisively beneficial effect. Nonproliferation divorced from denuclearization, by contrast, is at best ambiguous from both perspectives: it could possibly make the system more stable, but might well stabilize it in an imperial fashion.

Assuming, then, that denuclearization is a positive goal, is it also a feasible one? If so, to what extent? Even those who favor the approach disagree among themselves here. If denuclearization is to gain any momentum, far-reaching changes in the political climate must first take place within the leading nuclear nations. The prospects for denuclearization, at least in the decade ahead, will depend largely on domestic politics and partly upon the interactive behavior and perceptions of the two superpowers. So long as the goal of genuine denuclearization lies outside the mainstream political debate in the United States and the Soviet Union, it has virtually no hope of getting started, at least this side of nuclear catastrophe.

Does the present atmosphere permit at least *modest* steps toward denuclearization? Unfortunately, even limited efforts in this direction are more problematical than is generally supposed. So long as the statist logic persists, government bureaucracies will be inherently incapable of endorsing policies which reject the endless search for military advantage. Hence, small steps like signing the ABM treaty or cancelling the B-1 program seem positive only when viewed in isolation, but not if evaluated in their full bureaucratic contexts. In such cases, as we have seen, alternative weapons systems at least as lethal are accelerated "to fill the vacuum." This process is especially misleading to the general public. Encouraged to focus on dramatic and well-publicized concessions to "peace," most citizens can hardly help overlooking the technical diversion of funds to other weapons programs. Significantly, when President Carter vetoed the B-1 bomber, his explanation did not seem influenced at all by world order goals.[30] Only a visionary leader willing to mobilize populist support could circumvent powerful special interests and the structures of bureaucratic politics. And then it is not evident whether such a leader could survive, physically or politically. Existing political elites seem genuinely trapped and cannot provide credible leadership to achieve even modest world order goals.

Despite these caveats, several promising steps toward denuclearization could be taken right now. For instance, top government officials can and should repudiate the loose talk about using nuclear weapons in Third World contexts or against non-nuclear weapons states. Perhaps the main nuclear powers could even pledge never to use nuclear weapons first against a signatory of the NPT or against non-nuclear powers. Such pledges might be reinforced and given credibility by shifting patterns of nuclear deployment (for example, nuclear weapons could be removed from Korea and from forward positions in Western Europe). However, such denuclearization steps, desirable as they are, might also be viewed as nothing more than attempts to restore the prospects of nonproliferation. In this respect, such forms of denuclearization are of a piece with various proposals designed to extend the so-called nuclear shield to non-nuclear states or to work out contractual arrangements for peaceful nuclear explosions.[31] With all such proposals, nonproliferation is the essential goal and modest denuclearization is viewed—usually implicitly—as a tactic, virtually as a bargaining chip.

In some instances, admittedly, denuclearization and nonproliferation appear to work at cross purposes. For example, in 1977, South Korea's President Park Chung Hee declared that his country would acquire its own nuclear arsenal, if the United States followed through on President Carter's plan to remove nuclear weapons and American troops from South Korean territory.[32] How seriously should such a threat be taken?[33] Suppose South Korea does develop nuclear weapons in the wake of American withdrawal? Is the process of denuclearization worth the dangers of short-term proliferation? In another context, advocates of the neutron bomb (the so-called enhanced radiation weapon) contend that its deployment in Europe will enhance NATO's credibility and make the outbreak of nuclear war less likely.[34] In the short run, the logic of strategic thinking cuts deeply into arguments for denuclearization.

A comprehensive test ban treaty (CBT) would represent a more momentous step down the denuclearization path because it could substantially inhibit further nuclear weapons innovations—provided, of course, that it was imposed before accuracy, reliability, and throw-weight (payloads of warheads) goals already had been attained. Here again, CBT is generally viewed as an element of reciprocity required to make nonproliferation credible in a world of self-assertive states. However, its implications could be more systemic, especially if linked to shared commitments by Moscow and Washington, first, to renounce limited nuclear war options and, second, to limit the role of nuclear weapons to mutual deterrence of nuclear aggression.

A comprehensive no-first-use pledge would be another constructive step. Such a declaratory measure could provide important symbolic acknowledgment that nuclear weapons are illegitimate weapons of war, much as poison gas or biological weapons. To be credible, a no-first-use pledge would have to be coordinated with programs to redeploy nuclear weapons away from frontiers and to augment conventional capacities, thereby signaling specific second-use intentions for nuclear weapons. Such a no-first-use declaration, if solemnly made and implemented, would have immense value as an educational experience that would, in turn, support more drastic forms of denuclearization. Ironically, in the present world setting, it is not the superpowers but the pariah states vulnerable to armed attack who may prove the most reluctant to make such declarations. These pariah states are the only ones who face a severe security threat, but who do not seem capable of evolving any substitute for nuclear weapons.[35] Nevertheless, even if pariah states should remain outside the no-first-use orbit, the step would be a promising one, as it touches upon the geopolitical nexus of the existing system.

If we are to move beyond these secondary declaratory steps, however, the continental divide which separates nonproliferation thinking from denuclearization thinking must sooner or later be crossed.[36] Up to this point, the two perspectives overlap and conflicting interpretations are plausible for any given step. As suggested already, unambiguous denuclearization presupposes a domestic political shift of values and priorities within the principal nuclear states. It is difficult to depict the precise character of this value shift, but it would almost certainly have to involve a societal commitment to the pursuit of drastic global change, based on the sort of world order values outlined above.[37] This shift need not entail a commitment to world government nor to any other specific structure. In fact, I personally favor world order solutions based on political and economic decentralization combined with functional centralization.

A value shift would finally clear the path for genuine nuclear disarmament, to be accompanied at later stages by conventional disarmament as well (beginning with high technology weapons like precision-guided munitions). Nevertheless, it is likely that steps toward nuclear disarmament will be offset—and perhaps even more than offset—by compensatory moves which augment conventional weapons both quantitatively and qualitatively. In other words, even if the denuclearization divide has been clearly crossed, the disarmament divide will still remain. In time, the value shift needed to cross the first may generate sufficient momentum to carry the political process across the second as well. However, this optimistic possibility is by no means assured. So long as policy-making elites in powerful states adhere to conventional notions of national security, the outlook for disarmament is bleak indeed.[38]

During the transitional periods when each of these major divides are being traversed—from nonproliferation to denuclearization and finally to general disarmament—political leaders are bound to feel that their national security is being eroded. Coping with these fears and with the counterproductive behavior they may incite will present critical challenges to advocates of drastic global change. The problem can hardly be solved until new concepts of national security and positive visions of comprehensive change find their way into the ruling circles of the major powers.

When the governments of the world at last begin to lay down their nuclear arms and then their conventional weapons as well, it will probably be useful to establish a supranational police/military capability to serve on both regional and global levels. An institution of this kind could help enforce the disarming process and could also play a transitional role as supranational "manager" for maintaining global peace.[39] To prevent new incarnations of the war system from emerging, an appropriate constitutional framework will also be needed, with particular emphasis on checks and balances, separation of powers, compromises between efficiency and accountability, and, most of all, a new image of national security that does not depend on military might.[40] Deep in such a disarming process lies the question of whether a supranational security agency should itself possess nuclear weapons as a residual deterrent against cheating, nuclear rearmament, terrorism, and the like. If and when the time comes, this will be an extremely vexing issue, but it is not one which can be predetermined in the present global setting. (Even should a supranational security agency be armed with nuclear weapons, presumably that decision would be a conditional and temporary one hedged by elaborate constraints.)

IS MILITARY DENUCLEARIZATION ENOUGH? A CASE FOR CIVILIAN DENUCLEARIZATION

The history of civilian nuclear power is a twisted one. It is closely associated with the sense of guilt felt by those who first developed the atomic bomb, and who subsequently tried to make partial atonement by putting the atom to constructive use. Their hope was that the civilian nuclear spin-offs, once perfected, could be lifted from their military context, put to good domestic use, and then transferred abroad through the Non-Proliferation Treaty, which would yield lucrative foreign markets for U.S. industry in the process. However, the hope that atomic power could serve peace without being tarnished by the horror of Hiroshima fostered an artificial separation between the military and civilian nuclear programs. The catch, and it is a Catch - 22, is that there is no way to spread nuclear technology without inevitably spreading weapons capability right along with it.[41] It took India's nuclear explosion to bring this reality home. Before then, nations with civilian nuclear programs were indiscriminately put in the category of non-nuclear states, for military and international legal purposes, unless they had actually tested a nuclear bomb. This view reinforced the illusion that only military proliferation as such was evil, but that civilian nuclear spread was beneficial (or at least neutral) from the perspective of international stability.

In recent years, however, far more sophisticated measures of nuclear capability have emerged. They include the possession of basic nuclear knowledge, the number and kind of fuel-cycle facilities, access to fissionable material, the extent of technological engineering and managerial know-how, and so forth.[42] More generally speaking, the link between civilian nuclear proliferation and the proliferation of nuclear weapons has now passed into conventional wisdom.

Three major strategies have evolved in response to this insight, but all with only the limited goal of halting the spread of nuclear arms. In other words, the principal lines of thought all represent extensions of the nonproliferation approach to international security. The first such strategy involves a moratorium or even an outright ban on commercial nuclear power. In part, this approach is an offshoot of the general Western anxiety about nuclear weapons falling into "wrong" hands.[43] Responding to "the terrifying prospect of atomic bombs almost everywhere," Daniel Yergin cites the abandonment of civil nuclear power as possibly "the decisive step" in the struggle against proliferation. In view of his overall assessment of nuclear power, including its declining commercial appeal, Yergin calls for an

American moratorium on "the new development of conventional fission nuclear power."[44] In several major countries there is already growing support for this approach, motivated largely by the belief that civilian nuclear power facilities simply cannot be safeguarded well enough to permanently deter or foil nuclear theft. Lovins, an antinuclear spokesman, explains: "The fundamental reason that nuclear theft cannot be prevented is that people and human institutions are imperfect. No arrangement, however good it looks on paper, and however competently and devotedly it is established, is proof against boredom, laxity, or corruption."[45]

Those who adhere to an opposing line of thought insist that it is misleading to lump all civilian nuclear technologies together. They point out that there are, in fact, several distinct variants already in existence and even more are in the offing. Therefore, their approach to nonproliferation is to discourage the most proliferation-prone technologies (those having to do with breeder reactors and plutonium recycle) and to encourage those that are most resistant to use for weapons production.[46] This camp has always found fusion technology especially attractive, since it produces no weapons-grade material as a byproduct, and the attendant problems of accident, radioactive hazard, and waste disposal seem smaller than in the case of fission. However, certain serious environmental and security problems do exist with fusion. Moreover, fusion reactors require astronomical outlays of capital that would centralize energy production to an even greater degree than a large-scale fission program. It has been estimated that $20 billion would be needed in the research and development phase "before commercial use could be contemplated."[47] Moreover, the technical obstacles to commercial nuclear fusion remain so formidable that they may well prove impossible to overcome. At best, it seems implausible to expect fusion technology to be available until well into the next century, if at all.[48] Finally, the most probable line of fusion development would embody the worst features of breeder technology, including its susceptibility to proliferation. For technical and economic reasons, "the first generation of fusion reactors would consist of fusion-fission hybrids designed to breed plutonium."[49] Hence, all things considered, nuclear fusion appears to be an impossibly difficult or at best an exceedingly long-term and costly energy option which, in all probability, would not even achieve the goal of curbing weapons proliferation.

Up to now, the United States has been pursuing a third strategy: attempting to strike a compromise between nonproliferation objectives and economic energy goals. This official approach centers on internationalizing those elements of the fuel cycle most susceptible to illicit diversion.[50] Its essence, however, is to regard inherent discrimination as a permanent feature of international relations and to assume that the global spread of civilian nuclear power facilities is inevitable and irreversible. For this reason, the prevailing goals, as expressed in nonproliferation terms, are to bring the pace of nuclear spread into line with "realistic" expectations. The most we can hope for, in this view, is to avoid the emergence of twenty and fifty nuclear powers by the year 2000 and to prevent illicit acquisition altogether. For example, the Aspen group's positive image is a world with no more than ten nuclear powers by 2020; George Quester suggests that one more nuclear power each decade would be acceptable.[51]

Perhaps the most notable aspect of the twin debates over civilian nuclear spread and over nuclear proliferation in the military realm is their relative isolation from one another. So far, domestic discussions of nuclear power have largely ignored international security questions, focusing instead on matters of safety, health, environmental quality, political centralization, and civil liberties.[52] Failure to link these two sets of issues seems foolishly shortsighted because both the capital requirements and the lead times needed to readjust energy systems make civilian nuclear power a world order issue of first magnitude. To be more specific, the heavy investments demanded by a large-scale nuclear energy program would set critical—even though not yet generally evident—limits on the prospects for realizing world order values.

This chapter, however, limits itself to exploring whether meaningful and permanent denuclearization can be achieved in the military sphere as long as governments continue to pursue the civilian nuclear energy option. In other words, if we are to rid the world of atomic weapons forever, must we repudiate the "peaceful atom" as well? The answer seems clear, given the impact of a global civilian nuclear power program. First of all, the rapid spread of reactors in the years ahead (SIPRI estimates a fourfold growth from 99 reactors in 15 countries in 1970 to 405 reactors in 28 countries by 1980) vastly increases the global potential for weapons proliferation.[53] If that potential should be rapidly translated into weapons capability, then the movement toward denuclearization is likely to be thwarted and perhaps irreversibly so. The mere attempt to discourage the surreptitious manufacture of nuclear weapons would require significant degrees of surveillance and intrusive inspection, as well as changes in export policies of all nuclear suppliers. Surely, the prospects for denuclearization, already doubtful in a world of persisting inequality and conflict, would be even more vulnerable to disruption at an increasing number of points in a world of ubiquitous nuclear power plants. Clearly, there is something incoherent about trying to get rid of nuclear weapons while simultaneously disseminating the techniques and materials that make their acquisition ever easier.[54] More important still, the prospects for denuclearization presuppose broad social movements within many societies around a series of interrelated value goals. These goals include some loosening of centralized political controls over national populations, but that possibility is virtually precluded by civilian nuclear power with its terrorist potential, its high degree of energy centralization, and its concomitant need for equally centralized political control.

All nuclear facilities, whether civilian or military, must be vigilantly guarded. Recent studies in the United States and elsewhere emphasize the vulnerability of these facilities, especially in view of the inadequacy of present security standards.[55] Better protection, extending to lines of supply, shipments of nuclear fuel and, possibly, spent fuel and wastes, requires a virtual paramilitary capability with extensive authority to handle suspects and threats. Democratic procedures and associated civil and political rights are too fragile to withstand such intense security pressures.[56] Given a world order perspective that emphasizes the interrelations of values, it is important to assess energy and security policy choices with reference to their impacts on prospects for humane governance. On this basis alone, nuclear power appears unacceptable.

Symbolically and psychologically, the movement against nuclear power must be comprehensive, encompassing its military and civilian dimensions alike, if it is to achieve real mobilizing power. Lovins puts this well in arguing that the combination of elements in the overall denuclearization process produces "a psychological synergism that is essential to their success."[57] In effect, the linkage between nuclear weapons and nuclear power produces mutually reinforcing patterns of support, as the coherent possibility of life-affirming, alternative approaches to security and energy becomes more credible. A comprehensive antinuclear movement draws upon the vital energies of peoples devoted to keeping the earth safe and secure for future generations. To repudiate nuclear technology in all its forms would be to withdraw from a nuclear bargain that should never have been struck in the first place. The human species is not so constituted that it can achieve the infallibility and societal performance that nuclear safety presupposes, just as it is not able to achieve the perfect rationality presupposed by deterrence-based security programs.

Is it feasible to eliminate commercial nuclear power from the world scene? Current trends certainly lead in the opposite direction, and to reverse them would require at least momentous decisions by the United States and other advanced industrial countries. In the short run, while alternative energy sources and decentralized social systems are being developed and deployed, some oil-dependent, balance-of-payment deficit countries may feel that they are locked into the nuclear option. However, recent research shows that even nations as dependent on imported energy as Japan could actually become energy independent, through a combination of rigorous conservation measures and the use of renewable, decentralized fuels.[58]

In view of the costs and dangers of nuclear energy, soft energy alternatives, the viability of which has been sufficiently demonstrated, deserve serious commitment. Even the prestigious Ford Foundation study of 1977 concludes, despite its acceptance of the inevitability of nuclear power, that "there is enough solar energy to meet any foreseeable needs for electrical energy. The question is one of price." Essentially because of this question of price, the study concludes that solar energy "may provide a significant fraction of energy in the United States, but not until rather far into the twenty-first century, and with a price premium over nuclear or coal power."[59] Other assessments of solar potential are far more encouraging in respect to both time and cost. For instance, Feiveson and Taylor contend that "the prospects are excellent that solar energy can be developed and implemented on a large scale in a period of time comparable to that required to develop fully safeguarded breeder systems."[60] Even a government-sponsored study of solar energy, which shares the conventional wisdom about high energy requirements, concludes that "solar energy is not a cure-all for our energy problems; but combined with a larger strategy that includes energy conservation, cascading, and some sacrifice of convenience, solar energy does offer the option of a society based upon a renewable source of energy."[61]

In a sense, these assessments of solar potential are only minimal statements, based on technical and economic considerations. More positive and ambitious scenarios for the energy future of the world are now being projected. Writes Denis Hayes:

About one-fifth of all energy used around the world comes from solar resources: wind power, water power, biomass, and direct sunlight. By the year 2000, such renewable energy sources could provide 40 per cent of the global energy budget; by 2025, humanity could obtain 75 per cent of its energy from solar sources. Such a transition would not be cheap or easy, but its benefits would far outweigh the costs and difficulties.[62]

During the period of transition, coal and conservation techniques (in building codes, automobile designs, and many industrial processes) could play an enormously constructive role in assisting us to move from our current reliance on finite reserves of oil and natural gas, to renewable energy sources. Lovins envisions an "energy income economy by 2025" (that is, one based on renewable resources) and argues that this goal can be implemented without great strain if "the sophisticated use of coal, chiefly at the modest scale" is encouraged to relieve the pressure on oil and gas during the transition period.[63] Full-scale arguments on the viability of renewable fuels and possible transition strategies are enormously complex, of course, and are not all equally convincing. Nevertheless, authors like Hayes and Lovins have effectively shifted the balance of persuasion to those who persist in their belief that nuclear power is necessary and/or inevitable.

The changing economic realities pertaining to nuclear power, too, make its elimination more feasible than is generally supposed. The original case for peaceful nuclear power was based on the extravagant claim that it would be "too cheap to meter." But recent trends reveal a steadily increasing price per nuclear kilowatt hour, as well as a deteriorating cost picture relative to other energy sources. A careful analysis of U.S. fuel costs shows that in all regions of the country, coal is now cheaper than nuclear power, although the degree varies from two percent less in the northeast, to forty-nine percent in the Mountain Pacific northwest region.[64] Although nuclear power is often justified on economic grounds by those who believe we cannot afford to forego its cost advantages while basic needs go unmet around the world, the reality of rising nuclear costs undermines the validity of such economic rationale for proceeding down the nuclear path.

It is necessary to consider briefly the impact of these proposals on the economic prospects for poor Third World countries. Of course, the renewable energy potential of a given country varies according to geographical location, wind and geothermal resources, and hydroelectric potential. On the whole, however, Hayes maintains that "in the Third World, enormous strides can be made with relatively modest investment if those investments are made wisely. For example, two percent of the world military budget for just one year could provide every rural Third World family with an efficient stove—doubling overnight the amount of useful work obtained from fuel wood, and reducing the pressure on the world's forests accordingly." On the other hand, to the extent that Third World development is culturally or economically tied to energy strategies in the industrial world, the pressure to import nuclear technology will remain strong. At one stage, renewable energy systems were viewed as second-rate solutions that no self-respecting Third World country would adopt. More recently, however, especially in the wake of the OPEC experience of 1973–1974, Third World countries have shown a great deal more interest in evolving indigenous capabilities for energy production. As Hayes notes, these "indigenous technologies born of the new capability may prove to be more compatible with world needs than borrowed machines and methods." He goes on to point out that "Brazil's large methanol program, India's gobar gas plants, and the Middle East's growing fascination with solar electric technologies can all be read as signs of an interest in renewable energy resources that bodes well for the future."[65]

Furthermore, renewable energy systems tend to be far more labor intensive and decentralized, thereby encouraging productive use of the labor surplus which characterizes most poor countries and also disengaging the economies of these countries from their expensive dependence on imported energy, capital, and technology. In this regard, goals of equity and self-reliance associated with world order values seem to be tangibly facilitated by soft energy options.

Finally, even double denuclearization—eliminating nuclear weapons and civilian nuclear power—will not be enough to assure the success of the wider program of global changes envisioned here. The process of getting the nuclear genie back in the bottle must be associated with and sustained by a social movement organized around the interrelated pursuits of peace, economic well-being, social and political justice, and ecological balance, held together by an emergent sense of human community and planetary identity.[66] Such a movement need not be dedicated to global federalism. However, I personally hope that it would emphasize the deconcentration of wealth and the dispersal of authority at the national level. Presumably, some modes of central guidance will be required, but the preferable organizational dynamic would be dialectical, weighted toward the greatest possible decentralization of societal functions which still allows for the satisfaction of basic human needs. Separate state sovereignties, although still often useful to redress grievances within the existing frame of world politics, cannot be trusted to protect long-run human or overall planetary interests. I do not suggest that the state as actor will *disappear*, but that it will be *displaced* to varying degrees on various issues in varying places by functional arrangements (international and transnational actors) which augment the roles of individuals, groups, and international institutions. (It is important to stress the unevenness of this displacement process. For example, the state may play a diminishing role in advanced industrial countries at the same time that it is augmenting its functions within many Third World countries.)

IS DRASTIC GLOBAL REFORM TOO FAR OUT?

The influential Ford Foundation study on energy structures its proposals and analysis on the basis of two assertions:

(1) "Nuclear energy is now a fact of international life and will provide a significant portion of the world's electricity by the end of the century."

(2) "In our view, the most serious risk associated with nuclear power is the attendant increase in the number of countries that have access to technology, materials, and facilities leading to a nuclear weapons capability. . . . If widespread proliferation actually occurs, it will prove an extremely serious danger to U.S. security and to world peace and stability in general."[67]

These premises betoken a marginalist view of societal potential. Implicit throughout the study is the assumption that speculation concerning social policy must always be constrained by "the given." On the basis of this operating assumption, small adjustments alone merit serious consideration. Thus, nuclear-based security is taken for granted, as is the viability of commercial nuclear power. The policy recommendations which can be made within these confines include the deferral of nuclear reprocessing, a slowdown of research and development on breeder reactors, strengthening controls over the export of enrichment technology, and, of course, an extensive program to improve safeguards and security capabilities against nuclear theft or terrorism.

The Ford study is bound to influence U.S. policy-makers. It has the unanimous backing of prestigious and respected experts, and offers the hope that everything will be fine if only some minor adjustments are made. The report points out that these required adjustments may bruise some domestic interest groups while favoring others, but on balance the study's recommendations call for no major alterations in the nation's plans, values, assumptions, policies, or outlook.

The advice the report gives may provide short-term reassurance, but, by underestimating the context of danger, it correspondingly constricts the arena of appropriate choice. Accepting the Ford study prescription would mean reinforcing the principal tendencies of the present world situation, including the pressure to nuclearize in both military and civilian domains. The need, on the contrary, is to arrest and reverse these trends in the only time still left—perhaps no more than a decade—to reorient security and energy policies in positive directions. At best, the Ford study is a prudent assessment of the short-term interests of the United States as the primary economic and security manager of the world. In my judgment, this effort to shape conventional wisdom on nuclear policy, however competent the analysis, is a gross example of unintentional mystification and misdirected energy. It does not help us understand what is needed, what is desirable, or what is possible. Conventional wisdom, such as that represented by the Ford study, despite its good intentions, encourages us to relax in the sinking vessel at precisely the moment when we should all be lowering the lifeboats.

Conventional wisdom often embodies what C. Wright Mills defined as "crackpot realism."[68] The presumed permanence of inherent discrimination within the international political order and of civilian nuclear power as an irreversible fact of life are largely unexamined instances of contemporary "crackpot realism." Precisely because the deficiencies of modern civilization are so fundamental, the resistance to honest examination of these deficiencies is intense and emotional. Those who adopt skeptical views and project alternative visions of the future are dismissed as "utopian" or "romantic," so many Don Quixotes riding into battle to tilt at windmills. The condescension in establishment circles also derives, in part, from a materialistic view of history which associates human progress with technological inevitability. Those who adhere to this worldview regard proponents of demilitarized, decentralized security and energy systems as reactionaries, naifs, or peculiar dreamers who seek to "go back" to something primitive. My argument is premised upon a different and, I believe, a more positive image of historical and cultural evolution. In my view, progress evolves in a more elusive fashion, according to spiral forms, going back to earlier patterns but at a higher level, in a different setting, acting through rediscovery that builds upon the insufficiencies of what preceded. In this view, the future is neither a projection of the past, nor a series of repetitions, but is rather a sequence of ascending spirals which exhibits a complex interplay of recurrence and innovation.[69]

NOTES

1. See, for examples, Lincoln P. Bloomfield, "Nuclear Spread and World Order," *Foreign Affairs* 54, (July 1975): 743–755; George H. Quester, "What's New on Nuclear Proliferation?" *Aspen Institute for Humanistic Studies Occasional Paper* (Aspen, Co., 1975), pp. 1–23. Alton Frye, "How to Ban the Bomb: Sell It," *(New York Times Magazine,* January 11, 1976, pp. 11–12ff; and Michael Nacht, "Nuclear Energy and Nuclear Weapons," *Aspen Workshop on Arms Control, Aspen Institute for Humanistic Studies Occasional Paper* (Aspen, Co., 1975), pp. 1–22. The most comprehensive inquiry along these lines is by William Epstein, *The Last Chance: Nuclear Proliferation and Arms Control* (New York: Free Press, 1976). See also Daniel Yergin, "The Terrifying Prospect: Atomic Bombs Everywhere," *Atlantic Monthly* April 1977, pp. 46–65.

2. George Ball, *Diplomacy in a Crowded World* (Boston: Atlantic, Little, Brown, 1976).

3. U.S. Congress, "Approaches to Arms Control and Disarmament," *24th Report of the Commission to Study the Organization of Peace,* July 1976, p. 31. President Ford's report to Congress on the subject estimates that 40 countries will have a weapons-producing potential by 1985.

4. Stephen J. Baker, "Nuclear Proliferation: Monopoly or Cartel?" *Foreign Policy* 23 (summer 1976): 202–220; and Thomas C. Schelling, "International Security," *Foreign Policy* 23 (summer 1976): 77–91.

5. Norman Gall, "Nuclear Proliferation: Atoms for Brazil, Dangers for All" *Foreign Policy* 23 (summer 1976): 155–201.

6. This military eventuality never came to pass and, hence, nuclear weapons played no explicit role in Israeli diplomacy. For an account, see "Special Report: How Israel Got the Bomb," *Time,* April 12, 1976, p.39. For more background, see Howard Kohn and Barbara Newman, "How Israel Got the Bomb," *Rolling Stone* 1 (December 1977): 38–40; and "U.S. Documents Support Belief Israel Got Missing Uranium for Arms," *New York Times,* November 6, 1977, p.3.

7. Quoted by Yergin, "Terrifying Prospect: Atomic Bombs Everywhere," *Atlantic Monthly* 239, no. 4 (April 1977): 54.

8. This prospect is well substantiated by Albert Wohlsletter, "Spreading the Bomb Without Breaking the Rules," *Foreign Policy* 25 (winter 1976–1977): 88–96.

9. At the same time, linear rationality is probably not very instructive in assessing risks, costs, and effects of varying nuclear policies. For all we know, a spirit of proliferation, perhaps accompanied by relatively small-scale threats or accidents or uses would trigger a nuclear disarmament movement of such force as to create for the first time in the nuclear age a genuine prospect of drastic global reform.

10. For a useful summary, see Ted Greenwood, "Discouraging Proliferation in the Next Decade and Beyond," in Ted Greenwood et al., *Nuclear Proliferation, 1980s Project* (New York: McGraw-Hill, 1977), pp. 1–122.

11. Well summarized by Yergin, "Terrifying Prospect," p. 63.

12. Baker, "Nuclear Proliferation: Monopoly or Cartel?"

13. The United States and the Soviet Union signed a treaty in 1974 prohibiting test explosions in excess of 150 kilotons (or ten times the magnitude of the Hiroshima bombs). The treaty has not been ratified, but its provisions established such a high threshold that current test programs could be continued without interference. The

rationale for a high threshold is to assure that test explosions can be detected and identified in order to permit peaceful nuclear explosions (so-called PNE's) for building dams and canals or for redirecting rivers. What the treaty does prohibit is any large-scale test explosion of the sort which would be set off by a new nuclear state lacking the more refined technology needed for testing large weapons through smaller explosions. This example is typical of arms-control measures with purported bilateral restraints whose inhibiting effect would be felt mainly by others. As recently as October 1977, there were indications of Soviet-American receptivity to the idea of a total prohibition of nuclear explosions, at least for a trial period of three years. Such a step would have closed off at least one dimension of the strategic arms race. At present, there is some uncertainty and controversy as to whether further testing is required to proceed with various kinds of weapons innovation.

14. Nacht, "Nuclear Energy and Nuclear Weapons."

15. One exception in the serious literature is "Approaches," *24th Report of Commission to Study the Organization of Peace*, which connects nonproliferation goals with a revived concern for overall disarmament, including general and complete disarmament (GCD).

16. See, for instance, accounts of Secretary of State Cyrus Vance's visits to Argentina and Brazil in November 1977, when he exacted pledges from the leaders of these countries to restrict nuclear programs (for example, *New York Times*, November 22, 1977, p. 3 and November 23, 1977, p. A9). More plausible diplomacy would enact the process of persuasion more or less in reverse. When the giant insists that the midget remain unarmed for the safety of all, we are inhabiting a "surrealistic" security zone.

17. For a discussion and exposition of these world order values, see Saul H. Mendlovitz, "General Introduction," in Richard A. Falk, *A Study of Future Worlds* (New York: Free Press, 1975), pp. xvii–xviii and chapter I.

18. The range of approaches is indicated in Saul H. Mendlovitz, ed., *On the Creation of a Just World Order* (New York: Free Press, 1975).

19. Schelling, "International Security." See also the study, *Nuclear Energy and National Security* for Committee on Economic Development (New York, 1976) of which Schelling was the Project Director.

20. Tom Alexander, "Our Costly Losing Battle Against Nuclear Proliferation," *Fortune* 92 (1975): 142–150.

21. Stephen J. Baker, "Commercial Nuclear Power and Nuclear Proliferation," *Cornell University Peace Studies Program Occasional Paper*, No. 5, May 1975, pp. 1–66.

22. Hedley Bull, "Rethinking Non-Proliferation," *International Affairs* 51 (1975): 175–189.

23. Richard Betts, "Paranoids, Pygmies, Pariahs, and Non-Proliferation," *Foreign Policy* 26 (1977): 157–183.

24. See the Aspen Institute's criticisms of "loose talk" by James Schlesinger (then secretary of defense) on possible uses of nuclear weapons by the United States. As Michael Nacht puts the views of the conference participants, "The right person to speak on questions of nuclear weapon use is the President and the tone should be one of awe." Nacht, "Nuclear Energy and Nuclear Weapons," p. 15.

25. Betts, "Paranoids, Pygmies, Pariahs, and Non-Proliferation."

26. Ibid.

27. Ibid.

28. The news of the successful test explosion at Alamogordo came to American leaders along with Soviet and British heads of state as they were attending the Potsdam Conference on the settlement of World War II. Churchill observed that the news cheered up Truman to such an extent that "he was a changed man." One interpreter of the period reports that "the reassuring news about the bomb wrought a complete reversal of U.S. goals for the conference." Daniel Yergin, *Shattered Peace: The Origins of the Cold War and the National Security State* (Boston: Houghton Mifflin, 1977), pp. 115–123.

29. Research and development (R and D) innovations pursued especially by the superpowers have been undertaken in a competitive pursuit of "superiority" rather than to assure the stability of deterrence. In other words, one cannot even argue convincingly that existing nuclear powers behave "responsibly" within the framework of stable deterrence. In the current context of international relations, the nuclear arms race—with only its few mutually agreed upon "constraints," such as arms control measures—seems every bit as "irresponsible" as the acquisition of nuclear weapons by additional governments. In essence, there is no particular reason to believe that today's nuclear powers are any more reliable than future nuclear states (in the Third World or elsewhere) would be. The evidence suggests that virtually all states are highly irresponsible when it comes to issues of national security.

30. As Bernard Weinraub, Pentagon correspondent for the *New York Times*, concludes: "It is evident that Mr. Carter's impulses were based by and large on military considerations." See Weinraub's persuasive analysis of this B-1 decision in *New York Times*, July 3, 1977, p. E1.

31. In this light, I have in view the various proposals and incentives to forego nuclear weapons put forth in Bloomfield, "Nuclear Spread" and Frye, "How to Ban the Bomb."

32. See Rowland Evans and Robert Novak, "Korea: Park's Inflexibility," *Washington Post*, June 12, 1976, p. A19.

33. Of course, the tendency toward self-nullifying actions should not be ignored. After President Carter declared that he was planning to remove nuclear weapons from South Korean soil, he reaffirmed their possible use by air or sea launch in the event of a Korean War (*New York Times*, May 30, 1977, p. 2). The result is the worst of both worlds: nuclear deterrence in Third World contexts is perpetuated, and South Korea is induced to acquire nuclear weapons of its own. In cases like this, liberal statists do more to subvert stability in the present world order system than do their more conservative counterparts. Later the reports suggested that the Carter Administration might not, after all, remove nuclear weapons from Korea, or might do so slowly and tentatively over a period of four to five years. William Beecher, "Carter May Keep Tactical Nuclear Weapons in Korea," *Boston Globe*, July 10, 1977. Late in the Carter Administration and in the early Reagan period there was every reason to believe that nuclear weapons would remain indefinitely in South Korean territory.

34. Bernard Weinraub, "Pentagon Hopes to Deploy Neutron Weapons by 1979," *New York Times*, July 8, 1977, p. A7.

35. It is possible to imagine security guarantees that would substitute for the residual threat to use nuclear weapons. Such guarantees have been proposed in the United States on behalf of Israel. However, to guarantee the security of a pariah state means trying to freeze a status quo, which seems unacceptable to most of the world. The very offer of a guarantee entails high social costs, and its controversial character probably makes the guarantee itself unreliable. The pariah state, sensing this unrealiability, would still, I suspect, be hesitant to renounce an ultimate nuclear option even if it

received a strong guarantee of its present borders. Similarly, in such contexts political compromises may not appear available to the parties, and hence there would be no alternative to armed struggle. In such a conflict, the parties will not often be prepared to renounce any weapon or tactic that might prove useful under some set of circumstances. But in such a case official renunciation would not seem reliable any way.

36. For a world order analysis of the Vladivostok Accord, see Robert Johansen, "The Vladivostok Accord: A Case Study of the Impact of U.S. Foreign Policy on the Prospects for World Order Reform," Center of International Studies, World Order Studies Program Occasional Paper, No. 4, (Princeton, N.J., March 1976), pp. 1–114.

37. See Falk, *A Study of Future Worlds.*

38. For a persuasive depiction of institutional barriers to disarmament on the national level, see Richard J. Barnet, *Roots of War* (New York: Atheneum, 1972).

39. One proposal along these lines may be found in Robert Johansen and Saul H. Mendlovitz, "Global Enforcement of Just Law: A Transnational Police Force," *Alternatives* 6, no. 2 (July 1980): 307–338.

40. For some creative research and analysis along these lines, see Adam Roberts, *Nations in Arms: The Theory and Practice of Territorial Defense* (New York: Praeger, 1976).

41. For documentation, see Wohlsletter, "Spreading the Bomb."

42. Lewis A. Dunn and William H. Overholt, "The Next Phase in Nuclear Proliferation Research," *Orbis*, summer 1976, pp. 497–524.

43. Theodore B. Taylor and Mason Willrich, *Nuclear Theft: Risks and Safeguards* (Cambridge, Mass.: Ballinger, 1974).

44. Yergin, "Terrifying Prospect," pp. 46–65.

45. See William Sweet, "The Opposition to Nuclear Power in Europe," *Bulletin of the Atomic Scientist* 33 (December, 1977): 40–47; see also the international opposition to nuclear power in Denis Hayes, "Nuclear Power: The Fifth Horseman," *Worldwatch Paper* No. 6 (May 1976): 8–10. See also Amory B. Lovins, *Soft Energy Paths: Toward a Durable Peace* (Cambridge, Mass.: Ballinger, 1977), where Lovins portrays the situation as follows: "Nuclear expansion is all but halted by grass roots opposition in Japan and the Netherlands; has been severely impeded in West Germany, France, Switzerland, Italy, and Austria; has been slowed and may soon be stopped in Sweden; has been rejected in Norway and (so far) Australia and New Zealand, as well as in several Canadian provinces; faces an uncertain prospect in Denmark and many American states; has been widely questioned in Britain, Canada and the USSR; and has been opposed in Spain, Brazil, India, Thailand, and elsewhere" (p. 52).

46. In this regard, see Harold Feiveson and Theodore Taylor, "Alternative Strategies for International Control of Nuclear Power," in Greenwood *et al., Nuclear Proliferation, 1980s Project* pp. 123–133, especially the discussion on the thorium option (generating power by using thorium as the basic fuel), which the authors allege is easier to safeguard against diversion than fission technology. But see Lovins, *Soft Energy Paths*, for the contrary view that the thorium cycle uses a mixed oxide from which plutonium can easily be extracted.

47. *Nuclear Power: Issues and Choices*, Report of the Nuclear Energy Policy Study Group, the Ford Foundation (Cambridge, Mass.: Ballinger, 1977), p. 147.

48. See Michael Kenward, *Potential Energy: An Analysis of World Energy Technology* (Cambridge: Cambridge University Press, 1976), pp. 118–132; Amory B. Lovins, *World Energy Strategies* (San Francisco: Friends of the Earth International, 1975), pp. 74–76 and G. Tyler Miller, Jr., *Living in the Environment: Concepts, Problems and Alternatives* (Belmont, Ca.: Wadsworth Publishing, 1975), pp. E148–E150.

49. Hayes, "Nuclear Power: The Fifth Horseman."

50. See Baker, "Commercial Nuclear Power and Nuclear Proliferation"; see also Bloomfield, "Nuclear Spread and World Order," *Foreign Affairs* 53, no. 4 (July 1975): 749, who says: "Our puzzle is how to change the system enough to get a better political-psychological base under nonproliferation without having to work a total transformation in man or in the basic geometry of his political world." This basic geometry appears to include the retention, and even the continuing development, of nuclear weapons by the existing nuclear powers. See also a list of proposed steps to undergird NPT system in Nacht (1975); see also Wohlsletter, "Spreading the Bomb."

51. Quester, "What's New on Nuclear Proliferation?"

52. Richard A. Falk, "A Non-Nuclear Future: Rejecting the Faustian Bargain," *Nation*, 13 (March 13, 1976): 301–305, and Hayes, "Nuclear Power: The Fifth Horseman."

53. See *The Nuclear Age*, Stockholm International Peace Research Institute, (Cambridge, Mass.: M.I.T. Press, 1974), p. 45.

54. As Wohlsletter in "Spreading the Bomb" notes, a non-nuclear recipient of nuclear technology can come to the very verge of weapons capability without violating any legal obligations under the Nuclear Proliferation Treaty. He illustrates this with the starting assertion that a nonweapon state can come closer to a plutonium weapon today than the United States could in 1947 when the assembly of bombs required many hours for fusing and wiring components together.

55. Lovins, *Soft Energy Paths.*

56. R. Ayres, "Policing Plutonium: The Civil Liberties Fallout," *Howard Civil Rights—Civil Liberties Law Review* 10 (Spring 1975): 369–443.

57. Lovins, *World Energy Strategies.*

58. Amory B. Lovins, "Energy Strategy: The Road Not Taken?" *Foreign Affairs* 55 (October 1976): 65–96.

59. The text goes on to argue that "the capital cost per kilowatt of peak capacity for most methods of converting solar energy to electricity in central-station facilities is estimated to be more than double that of nuclear power, a figure that must be multiplied by another factor for additional costs of energy storage" p. 137. This cost assessment seems unduly pessimistic; it presupposes a continuing need for centralized electrical energy systems, and overlooks important cost savings (most obviously, of course, on fuel supplies and pollution control). On the availability of solar energy, the figures in the study are reassuring: "The amount of solar energy falling on the United States is enormous: 44,000 quads per year. The present annual U.S. consumption of electrical energy could be supplied by 0.15 percent of this solar energy, if it could be used at 10 percent efficiency" (p. 130). The Ford Foundation study was published under the title *Nuclear Power: Issues and Choices* (Cambridge, Mass: Ballinger, 1977).

60. After considering the sort of economic obstacles which the Ford study finds decisive in the intermediate period, Feiveson and Taylor in *Nuclear Proliferation* (New York: McGraw-Hill, 1977) conclude, "We are more optimistic about solar energy than most people and are encouraged by the increasing rate at which promising new concepts are being proposed and assessed. The biggest uncertainty about solar energy, in our minds, is how long it will take to implement its use on a large scale. However, it is not at all clear that this time will be significantly longer than the time required to develop worldwide fission breeder reactor systems that are effectively safeguarded against diversion of nuclear materials to destructive purposes."

Note, also, that breeder technology is a virtually inevitable sequel if we opt to rely on fission power, because uranium is expected to run out by the end of the century. Of course, even if the United States does not resort to breeders, plutonium will be present in large quantities by the early 1980s in many other countries.

61. *Solar Energy in America's Future—A Preliminary Assessment,* Stanford Research Institute, Report for U. S. Energy and Research Development Administration, (Stanford, Ca., January 1977) p. xvii.

62. Denis Hayes, *Rays of Hope: The Transition to a Post-Petroleum World* (New York: Norton, 1977).

63. Lovins, *World Energy Strategies.*

64. Testimony by Charles Komanoff on the costs of nuclear power before the House Subcommittee on Environment, Energy and Natural Resources, September 21, 1977 (mimeographed); see table on relative costs of coal and nuclear power in different regions of the United States, p.1.

65. Denis Hayes, "Energy for Development: Third World Options," *Worldwatch Paper No. 15,* December, 1977, p. 5.

66. Amory Lovins advocates a three-part strategy for the United States: (1) abandoning nuclear power, (2) reallocating resources in the direction of making soft-energy paths based on solar, wind, and geothermal energy courses viable at home and abroad, and (3) treating nonproliferation, control of civilian nuclear technology, and strategic arms reduction "as interrelated parts of the same problem with intertwined solutions." He maintains that these three steps provide "a universal, nondiscriminatory package of policies" that "would be politically irresistible to North and South, East and West alike." This approach very closely parallels the argument of this chapter, but with two significant differences. First, I believe that the total elimination of nuclear weapons capabilities is essential to any process of strategic arms reduction. Secondly, I believe that denuclearization and energy policy must be related to the wider social and economic issues of global reform. Of course, there is a tactical advantage in presenting the smallest credible package in order to make the process of adjustment appear as manageable as possible. My own assessment, however, is that the package will not be credible unless it is enlarged in the ways I have indicated. Lovin's proposals are sufficiently integrated and bold to start us down the right path. Once firmly on this path, we may be able to widen it along the lines discussed above, but I am fearful of mounting a radical argument that is not convincing on its own terms.

67. *Nuclear Power: Issues and Choices,* pp. 5, 22.

68. C. Wright Mills, *The Causes of World War Three* (New York: Ballantine, 1960), pp. 89–97.

69. For a discussion of the spiral image as an alternative to linear thinking, see Jill Purce, *The Mystic Spiral* (New York: Avon, 1974). The same perspective underlies the work of Theodore Roszak, *The Unfinished Animal* (New York: Harper and Row, 1975), pp. 152–181.

CHAPTER 10

Arms Control, Foreign Policy, and Global Reform*

A CRITIQUE OF THE PREVAILING APPROACH

Advocacy of arms control has centered upon the control of the arms race and the prevention of nuclear war. These objectives are obviously interrelated, as some weapons deployments and strategic attitudes present more of a threat than others to the goal of avoiding nuclear or large-scale conventional warfare. Some features of the arms race have even been consistent with overall prevention goals. Particularly where international tension has a strong ideological component, adversaries premise their security on possessing sufficient unilateral capabilities to inflict unacceptable damage and on being perceived as having the will and capability of doing so. As ideological tensions wane or disappear, technical considerations grow more prominent, and actual and potential weapons capabilities are viewed with more mutual understanding. During the Nixon-Ford-Brezhnev tenure, bipolar relations became generally more cooperative, and this development has certainly been reflected in a continuing search for bipolar arms control agreements.[1] But, at the same time, bipolarity has also been significantly eroded and even superseded by emergent multipolarity and interdependence in such domains as trade, money, and natural resources. China's independent path in foreign policy, India's acquisition of nuclear status, the enormous currency surpluses of the main oil producers, the weakness of the dollar, the shaky domestic political conditions prevailing in most of the principal non-communist states, and the increasing tactical skill and bargaining leverage displayed by Asian, African, and Latin American countries

*The author wishes to thank the following readers of earlier drafts for editorial and substantive suggestions: Robert Art, Harvey Brooks, Abram Chayes, Janet Lowenthal, George Rathjens, and Leonard Rodberg. The initial composition of this chapter in the mid-1970s reflects an earlier context, but the main argument of substance continues to express my position.

are all elements that complicate the setting within which arms control negotiations must now take place.

In part the complexity arises from the widely held suspicion that diplomatic cooperation is included in the secret agenda of Soviet-American arms negotiations, often masquerading (or appearing to do so) under the ritual affirmation of alliance loyalties. The resulting situation is best understood as being ambiguous rather than sinister, although the evidence is such that either perception can seem reasonable;[2] it is doubtful that either Soviet or American leaders have themselves fully sorted out their true schedule of priorities with regard to acknowledged arms control objectives and unacknowledgeable ambitions for geopolitical management. In any event, in both countries these schedules are bound to be unstable because the ranking of priorities also depends on interactions that are difficult to assess—Soviet governance being such a secretive operation and American governance having been for so long substantially immobilized by the combined impact of Watergate and Vietnam.[3] Furthermore, there are also indications that neither leadership group has fully decided on a clear geopolitical course of action for the years ahead.

Perhaps it has been Henry Kissinger, more than any other commentator on Soviet-American relations, who has over the years counseled both doves and hawks against an overly ideological approach to arms control negotiations.[4] Kissinger's argument is that American leaders should make "a serious endeavor to resolve concrete issues" rather than become sidetracked by discussions of Soviet intentions or by prospects for liberalizing the harsh Soviet system of domestic rule.[5] Because Kissinger is pessimistic about the latter two issues, he does not want them to become stumbling blocks to the concrete bargains that the superpowers can and should reach to reduce the prospect of nuclear conflagration. To strike a bargain does not require friendship, although a lessening of tensions and increased cordiality among leaders do help sustain a negotiating atmosphere and encourage popular expectations that agreements can, will, and should be reached.

Despite ambiguities and complexities, certain features of the recent American approach to arms control negotiations can be discerned with sufficient clarity to enable reflection and analysis. Richard Nixon, in his fourth annual report on foreign policy issued in early 1973, expressed the basic character of the Soviet-American approach to arms control in the early seventies:

There is mutual agreement that permanent limitations must meet the basic security interests of both sides equitably if they are to endure in an era of great technological change and in a fluid international environment. There obviously can be no agreement that creates or preserves strategic advantages.[6]

Of course, some of this language can be discounted as propaganda; each side would gladly accept whatever advantages the other side was willing to "negotiate away." But it is a significant assertion, because it discloses a parity-oriented rather than a superiority-oriented approach.

The report went on to specify that any acceptable arms control agreements would have to accomplish the following five objectives:

—establish an essential equivalence in strategic capabilities among systems common to both sides;
—maintain the survivability of strategic forces in light of known and potential technological capabilities;
—provide for the replacement and modernization of older systems without upsetting the strategic balance;
—be subject to adequate verification;
—leave the security of third parties undiminished.[7]

These five requirements express mainstream opinions and conventional wisdom about national security in the nuclear age; they also illustrate the extent to which prenuclear statecraft continues to dominate arms control thinking. If these requirements are a checklist of critical considerations that any responsible government would take into account, then they are unexceptionable. But if they represent conditions regarded as sufficient in themselves, then they provide opponents of disarmament with authoritative arguments for resistance. Indeed, it is the inherent and readily discernible ambiguity of these requirements that arouses concern and invites suspicion, especially given the "hard-line" background of Richard Nixon and Gerald Ford and their support within military and business circles. The first requirement emphasizes the extent to which "balance" or "equivalence" is relied upon to maintain peace between states with possibly conflicting foreign policy goals; if one takes this approach, the mutual deterrence of nuclear war becomes nothing more than an important special case in the standard nation-state approach to national security.[8] The second and third requirements listed by Mr. Nixon seek to sustain "equivalence" through time, despite the dynamism of modern weapons technology and asymmetries in relative military capabilities and concepts; they are thus elaborations of the first requirement. The fourth requirement, of "assured verification," can only mean either normal prudence or a kind of generalized

Machiavellian reminder that trust and good faith have no place in serious diplomacy. The fifth requirement, which may be the most questionable in terms of real—as distinct from proclaimed—policy, seeks to reconcile superpower diplomacy with alliance diplomacy. Both the United States and the Soviet Union have provided frequent elaborate, but not altogether convincing, reassurances to their allies on this subject, but there is an inevitable ambiguity of intention that arises from ending the Cold War (or appearing to end it, at least provisionally) at a time when there is considerable economic rivalry among advanced industrial states with market economies and intense hostility among various strands of the world Communist movement.[9] It is not clear, and perhaps there is as yet no internal consensus in either superpower, whether this new form of bipolarity is bipolistic in spirit and designed primarily to keep secondary states under control, or whether the earlier bloc rivalry continues to dominate their geopolitical maneuverings, but in muted form. In either case, Nixon's fifth requirement acknowledges the alliance side of geopolitics in the state system and seeks to reconcile alignment interests with arms control policy, both allegedly to contribute to "balance" within the system as a whole.

The other side of this view of arms control is a strong emphasis on the continuing usefulness of force, and of its threatened use, to attain American foreign policy goals other than those of national defense. Mr. Nixon's words and policy made this clear. He contended, "In a period of developing détente, it is easy to be lulled into a false sense of security," and further,

Military adequacy is never permanently guaranteed. This Nation cannot afford the cost of weakness. Our strength is an essential stabilizing element in a world of turmoil and change. Our friends rely on it; our adversaries respect it. It is the essential underpinning for our diplomacy, designed to increase international understanding and to lessen the risks of war.[10]

More concretely, such an orientation implies a special role for the United States in the state system: "The United States cannot protect its national interests, or support those of its allies, or meet its responsibilities for helping safeguard international peace, without the ability to deploy forces abroad."[11] These so-called forward deployments are associated with the main global security missions that the United States undertook in the Cold War—to protect countries in Western Europe and East Asia against communist expansion or communist-led insurgencies.

The American presence in Europe and Asia is essential to the sense of security and confidence of our friends which underpins all our common endeavors—including our joint efforts in the common defense. Our forces are deployed to provide a responsive and efficient posture against likely threats.[12]

In the aftermath of Vietnam, such global foreign policy aims encourage the development and deployment of non-nuclear weapons that can strike at a distance and thus minimize the risk to American combat personnel. The Nixon Doctrine—applied "in its purest form" in the air war in Cambodia waged up through August 15, 1973, we were told by the president (in a news conference, November 12, 1971)—was a *doctrinal* expression of this posture; the electronic battlefield, "smart bombs," defoliation campaigns, meterological warfare, and saturation bombing were among its *technological* embodiments.

The problem of interpretation is formidable. Are we confronted by a situation in which American (and Soviet) leadership is so wary of the other side that the risks of agreement generally outweigh the risks of virtually unrestrained competition in arms development? Or is the element of wariness mainly a pretext for refusing to curtail freedom of choice in foreign policy and to cut back on military-industrial influence at home? Or, more likely, is there a bewildering mixture of these mutually reinforcing attitudes? It should be emphasized that SALT I, like other arms control agreements since World War II, had no effect whatsoever on "deployed levels of armaments." Indeed, as the Associate Director of the Livermore Laboratory observed, "Both sides agreed to retain what they had and to do without systems that they did not want."[13]

Despite the general impression that conflict among principal states in the world had entered a moderate phase, it is difficult to discern any modification of foreign policy objectives and world order design implicit in the Nixon-Ford-Kissinger-Brezhnev diplomacy. For reasons I hope to make clear, this essential continuity was unfortunate and had a particularly dampening and distorting effect on the prospects for arms control. There are two principal themes in American thinking:

1) *Foreign policy continuity:* Despite the spirit of détente, the drift of Cold War diplomacy remains unchanged and continues to include massive forward deployments of weapons in Europe and Asis, as well as an occasional willingness to undertake counter-insurgency missions in the Third World.[14]

2) *World order continuity:* Despite the new ecological awareness

and the prominence of economic interdependence, deference to statist logic remains the cornerstone of analysis and planning for the
future of world politics.[15]

In my view, these persistent features have been too little stressed
in most recent arms control literature. I believe that the presumed
adequacy of the state system is dangerous to national and global well-
being and that arms control analysis needs to be guided by viable
conceptions of foreign policy and world order that are more responsive to our national situation and to the world-historical context.
Otherwise, ambitious proposals for arms control are inherently unconvincing because they fail to question the underlying dynamics of
the war system, manipulated by what are now the most powerful and
ambitious governments.

THE RELEVANCE OF FOREIGN POLICY PERSPECTIVES

An appropriate foreign policy for the United States ought to satisfy
four requirements:

1) It must provide for national defense in all plausible contingencies where the United States or its principal allies could be the
victims of direct military attack.[16] In the nuclear age, this requirement
entails some form of credible deterrent. The acceptable form and
reach of such deterrent capabilities are properly the central issues of
arms control policy, and their resolution depends on the approach
that the principal adversaries take to these same issues.

2) Its main precepts must generate a bipartisan consensus, so
that they will not be subject to the vagaries of party politics. Mr. Nixon
and Secretary Kissinger were generally successful in generating a new
bipartisan consensus for their geopolitical initiatives, especially their
effort to mute the Cold War and to replace it with an active form of
détente, but they were not able to generate a consensus on the need to
sustain extensive alliance commitments in the Third World.[17]

3) It must embody the revered norms and tradition of the society. In particular, the United States government cannot hope to
endorse and support antidemocratic governments abroad while endorsing the means and ends of democracy at home. Precisely those Americans most directly in touch with the values our society is supposed to
stand for will perceive the immorality of interventions on behalf of
undemocratic regimes. This, I believe, is the most important lesson of

the antiwar movement generated by the Vietnam War. And it was the fear of such opposition that led in the past to secrecy, deceit, manipulation, and finally outright repression, when that, too, was felt to be necessary. Any stable political system resorts to a certain amount of hypocrisy to reconcile contradictory pulls of policy and to meet emergency pressures, but, if carried very far, either the government begins to repress its domestic opponents or the society becomes so badly split that an effective foreign policy is impossible.

4) It must generally respond to the minimum requirements of world order. These requirements have long been set by the logic of the state system, and have traditionally been satisfied by relying on costly processes of readjustment. The search for balance or control presents alternative ways for a principal government to maintain world order. Even the existence of nuclear weaponry has not undermined this system. Indeed, the prospect of nuclear war raises the stakes of security so high that the search for "balance" is more intense than it has ever been before.[18] What has imperiled the traditional quest for minimum world order is a combination of factors arising from the growing interdependence of all phases of global activity and from a series of dangerous pressures on the biosystem associated with what might be called "the ecological challenge." We do not yet possess enough information on the increasing interdependence or the seriousness of the ecological challenge to know whether minimum world order can be maintained by a continuing reliance on the state system, or whether some more centralized system of authority will prove essential. But ominous warnings suggest that we should no longer take for granted a world order based on present statist foreign policy dynamics.

The acceptance of these four conditions would determine the orientation of United States foreign policy, but the conditions themselves do not constitute a program. Specific applications would still have to be worked out in the face of complex and often inconsistent domestic and international considerations.

The suggested reorientation might have profound consequences for arms control, although conjecture is difficult because so much depends upon how we perceive the behavior of principal foreign adversaries and on the relative influence of the military within national policy-making arenas. Nevertheless, a new impetus in arms control could be confidently expected from such a reorientation, even if progress is at first confined to a series of unilateral initiatives and negotiated bargains designed to cut down surplus capacity of various kinds. I believe that rising ecological awareness will make governing groups everywhere (but especially in the United States, because of its disproportionate demands on the world's resources) sensitive to the present waste of resources and the fundamental importance of adopting conservation strategies. Effective arms control is a particularly attractive conservation strategy for a number of reasons, and it offers enterprising politicians many opportunities.

The superpowers might agree to undertake a series of parallel unilateral steps that would proceed in mutually reinforcing directions. These steps would in turn create an appropriate context for negotiating proposals to minimize the scale and scope of deterrence and to limit, at least to some extent, its awesome orbit of devastation, while sustaining its relative safety, enhancing its reliability, and even increasing its flexibility.[19] Arms control efforts by nuclear superpowers could appropriately concentrate upon securing the cheapest, safest, most reliable, and least inhumane form of deterrent capability. To sustain this objective it would also be necessary to pursue vigorously, and on a global scale, arms control policies designed to restrict the role of nuclear weapons to the narrowest possible situation, namely, nuclear response to nuclear attack. In the absence of effective global protection for international boundaries (for example, through permanent, internationally supervised buffer zones and retaliatory military capabilities),[20] this objective would not provide adequate security for states such as Israel, Taiwan, and South Africa, which feel threatened by vigorous and widely supported revisionist strategies.[20] Such a security system—unconditionally acknowledging the international legitimacy of state boundaries—would be an unacceptable endorsement of the status quo unless it was combined with an international toleration of the internal dynamics of self-determination (including small-scale and covert cross-border support activities) and with effective procedures for peaceful change.[21] The reformist logic on security here set forth need not be tested by its capacity to control these most troublesome of all international situations, where the local stakes of conflict are irreconcilable and where the beleaguered government is committed to an all-out struggle for survival. Our main concern over the next several decades is to improve international relations in situations where conflict is negotiable or its stakes marginal. It is in such situations that the diplomacy of denuclearization, including such declaratory steps as nonaggression pacts and renunciation of first-use options, might be expected to achieve a desirable reorientation of arms policy.[22]

THE RELEVANCE OF WORLD ORDER PERSPECTIVES

Arms control policies since World War II have done little to mitigate the horrors of the war system, to reduce arms spending, or to inhibit the proliferation of non-nuclear weapons technologies. Arms control measures have served mainly to ratify the bipolar dominance of international politics and to maximize the stability of this dominance from a managerial standpoint. Agreements have simply expressed, in treaty form, those steps that the respective governments were prepared to take on a unilateral basis in any case. So-called disarmament proposals were propaganda exercises, cast in terms never intended to gain adversary acceptance; indeed, if acceptance had been forthcoming, the proposals probably would have been reformulated by the original sponsor. In essence, the traditional centrality of the war system in international politics has not been challenged by arms control, but has only been adapted somewhat to certain special characteristics of nuclear technology and to the participation in international affairs of many more centers of independent authority. This adaptation of the war system to new realities has been a generally beneficial process, given the widespread acceptance and inevitable persistence of the state system as it operated from the Peace of Westphalia (1648) to the end of World War II.

The most fundamental challenge to this apparent continuity has to do with the cluster of considerations that can be subsumed under the rubric "the ecological challenge." The limits-to-growth debate and related developments have given potency to a serious world-wide discussion of this problem. In essence, the ecological crisis, if accepted as genuine, requires an adjustment of much more fundamental proportions than that necessitated by the nuclear threat, although the character and timing of this adjustment remain controversial and undefined.[23] There are two main lines of coherent response: coercive, imperial centralization (i.e., a global structure of authority brought about and maintained by force) and voluntary, contractual centralization (i.e., a global structure of authority brought about by agreement and basically sustained by consent of national governments). There is also a third—and incoherent—response, which is to sustain the fragmented, nationalistic world order system that operates in accordance with statist logic.[24] This third response continues to dominate most of our thinking, although there are some signs that its inadequacy is beginning to be more widely recognized.

These three analytic conceptions are ideals, whereas concrete situations in the world demand intermingled strategies, especially during the present period of transition, when the extent of the ecological challenge and its links to the structure of world order are themselves the subjects of vigorous debate in which relatively strong evidence can be adduced to support conflicting views.[25] A minimum expectation during this period of uncertainty would be the initiation of a serious study of comparative systems of world order.[26] Within the confines of this essay, it is possible only to sketch the prospects for global reform in general terms. We should take note of three constructive strategies of global reform, each of which is appropriate to certain conditions of public understanding and great power attitudes and inappropriate to other conditions. The scholar concerned with policy should attempt to clarify the contexts in which each of the following three reform strategies could be constructively applied.

1) *Reforms within the state system:* If optimistic assessments of technological prospects prove to be correct—including the development of cheap, abundant, and nonpolluting energy sources, and given sufficient willingness to suppress or regulate tactics that disrupt complex technology, it may be possible to defer almost indefinitely any fundamental world order changes that might otherwise have been neecessitated by the ecological challenge. However, such potentialities for reforming the state system will depend upon enlightened leadership in the governments of the world on matters of population policy and economic development. The implementation of such potentialities will also require effective compromise among states with vastly diverse interests, technological capacities, and socio-economic statuses on matters as crucial as allocating ocean resources and sharing many of the fruits of new technologies. Earth resource satellite surveys, weather surveying, information storage and dispersal, and nuclear power are only some of the areas in which it will be important to spread the benefits of technological advances. To create and sustain such an atmosphere of international cooperation would require, in my view, a substantial dismantling of the war system, as well as a far more successful mobilization of national resources to meet human needs than we have seen to date. To some degree, the multinationalization of business operations, with its claims to represent a "new globalism" rather than a *"new imperium"* might provide some of the inspiration needed for achieving drastic global reform.[27] Also of some importance is the rapid growth of international private (i.e., nongovernmental) institutions in a wide variety of areas like the Ger-

man Marshall Fund, the Japan Fund, Amnesty International, the International Commission of Jurists, the Club of Rome, and so on.

2) *Coercive, imperial centralization as a new world order system:* Pressure brought about by increasing scarcity of land and resources could easily induce national leaders to adopt imperial methods in their efforts to stabilize the world situation. Indeed, such a trend may already be operating at the present time, as the rich and powerful seek to harmonize their own interests and relationships, while policing the poor and weak—but numerous and desperate—with various counterinsurgency techniques. From this perspective, a bipolar détente (with the possible inclusion of other power centers) could be regarded as the incubus for a domineering world-state structure. The control of nuclear weaponry would probably require that the system have at least two capitals, but a limited number of existing governments could seek to centralize global policy on resource use and to achieve minimum conservationist and environmental quality goals without jeopardizing existing patterns of privilege and stratification. The severity of the scarcity and the ethos of the controllers would determine the extent to which the new world order became openly despotic and repressive. If a spirit of humanity (that is, a stress on peace and equity in human relations) were to prevail and be sustained by favorable technological developments, such a new *imperium* could perhaps be made acceptable, especially if it relied on indirect rule and minimal governance.[28] Perhaps such a consolidated world order system could limit itself to policing the technological capacities of the world against misuse or disruption.

Unfortunately, such an eventuality is not very likely to materialize. The formation of this kind of *imperium* is only likely to come about in time of acute scarcity and in an atmosphere of ecological alarm. It may also be abetted, or even caused, by expectations that rise faster than the domestic capacities to meet them; such a gap between expectations and capacities has already often led to domestic repression and abrupt changes in international relations. Coercion and repression seem integral to the process of establishing and maintaining a system of global supervision based on domination by great powers.

In any case, the most powerful states may come to feel extremely vulnerable to disruption by escalating terror tactics. In this eventuality, such governments may actively undertake to control the weaker and poorer regions of the world, subjecting their disarmament to rigorous forms of imperial administration, including surveillance and suppression of any threatening mode of deviance.[29] It seems likely that such a global strategy, by its very character, would necessarily be preceded by the destruction of democracy in the United States. Such a precedent is already being set in an increasing number of countries where consensual government has been forcibly replaced by repressive forms of policy and military rule (for example, Brazil, Chile, South Africa, and Rhodesia). In such circumstances, governance would involve protracted counterrevolutionary warfare on a global scale, since popular sentiment would be strongly aligned with insurgent goals. To offset its universal unpopularity, the constituted authorities would come to rely on terror and military repression, both at home and abroad.

3) *Voluntary, contractual centralization:* This third response to the ecological challenge seems the least likely to come about but also the most desirable. Its prospects depend on a long period of preparation that would allow the necessary value changes to occur in the principal societies of the world. The foreign policy proposals outlined earlier in this essay are partly intended to facilitate this necessary development of public awareness, at least in the United States. The sooner a transnational movement for voluntary global reform takes shape, the better the prospects for a gradual, nonviolent transition to some variant of voluntary, contractual centralization; in other words, intergovernmental agreements will provide the foundation for a program of drastic global reform.

There are some signs that such a movement is emerging and will be strengthened in the years ahead:

—a growing awareness of the fundamental character of the ecological challenge;

—a growing effort by transnational groups—the Club of Rome, editorial board of *The Ecologist,* Institute for World Order—to devise both systematic and politically serious responses to the ecological challenge.

—a realization that world poverty is endangering the well-being of hundreds of millions of people, many of whom are unable to obtain enough food even to sustain basic health;

—widespread disillusionment with the state system arising from the horror of modern war and the vulnerability of all societies to military attack;

—the growth of a global cultural perspective associated with the greater mobility of people, things, and ideas, and the dissemination of the "Apollo Vision" of the earth as an island spinning in space;

—the economic organizational drive to create a single all-embracing market with minimal distortion from national policies, and the technological capacities (e.g., computers and jet travel) to administer such a system;

—strong functional pressures for global patterns and structures of cooperation in relation to environmental policy, ocean-resource development, suppression of terrorism using satellite broadcasting;

—a movement by politically moderate, medium-sized national governments to make it more generally understood that a coercive global tyranny is likely to emerge unless a voluntary system of central guidance is made effective.

ARMS CONTROL POLICY AND WORLD ORDER REFORM

Two premises underlie my approach to arms control and world order reform:

1) the ecological challenge has been sufficiently substantiated to warrant the serious study of world order options;

2) any given option is worthy of endorsement only if it can be brought into being through voluntary and contractual means.[30]

In the light of these major premises, I propose that we consider arms control objectives as though we were operating late in the life of the state system. The first issue is not whether there will be a new world order system, but whether the one that emerges will come about convulsively (by catastrophe), coercively (by conquest and domination), or voluntarily (by a consensus of opinion). The second issue concerns the design of a future world order system that can both meet the ecological challenge and allow the human species to overcome the forces that now appear to threaten its well-being, even its survival.[31] I would like here to stress the importance of designing voluntary transition plans and world order models with a normative consensus on the primacy of minimizing war, poverty, oppression, and environmental decay.[32] At the very least, such a program for global reform should eliminate the more serious drawbacks of the present world order system, but it could also include more positive goals. However, at this point any emphasis on far-reaching goals (such as individual and group self-realization) would be both premature and distracting. Global reform should be a continuous process; any successful reform should serve to extend the horizon and bring new goals to the fore.

This approach to the analysis of global prospects can be briefly depicted in schematic terms: Let S_1 represent the existing world order system, S_2 and S_3 future world order systems, and S_0 the present point of origin; the location of S_0 near to the end of S_1 expresses a personal judgment as to the relative durability of S_1.

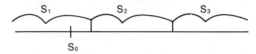

The interval from S_0 to S_2 is denoted as the transition interval, and for convenience this period of transition is divided into three stages:

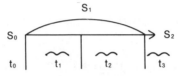

T_1 will be characterized primarily by changes in political awareness in the leading centers of existing power and authority, that is, domestic arenas of principal sovereign states; t_2 is associated with mobilization for action; t_3 with institutional transformation. This transitional sequence is intended only to convey an expected pattern of emphasis; the transitional process in real time will be overlapping and cyclical, most likely resembling a spiral rather than the linear form that this analytical scheme suggests.

An effort should be made toward t_1 to build public understanding and support for global reform on the basis of the four minimization goals and on the premise that the existing world order system must be changed by voluntary means within the next several decades. Even given these design constraints, there is an array of S_2 options, ranging from a highly differentiated federal structure to a loose confederation. These various options cannot be discussed in detail here, but in my judgment a preferable model for S_2 would rely on a form of "central guidance" that meets the demands of the ecological challenge while involving a minimal bureaucratic buildup and a maximal dispersal of power and authority.[33] This preferable model of S_2 would try to combine functional specialization with elaborate checks and balances in political supervision.[34] The potentialities of information and communications technology would make it possible to develop efficient structures of authority during the transition process (from S_0 to S_2) that have a minimal dependence upon hierarchical organization.[35]

Within such a movement for drastic global reform there would be a specific role for arms control advocacy within the United States, a role shaped also by the foreign policy assessments made in the section on the relevance of the foreign policy perspective. The principal opportunity to promote global reform during t_1 lies in awakening public consciousness to the need, feasibility, and character of a positive S_2. There are also other reform missions in t_1, including the stabilization of relations among governments in S_1 to allow more time for the transition and for the emergence of a global consensus on the nature of peace, justice, and governance in S_2.

In t_1, arms control advocates can help build the sort of public awareness needed in this country by supporting specific policies and lines of approach, including:

—declaratory measures of weapons renunciation, especially first-use options with respect to nuclear weapons;

—redesign of second-use deterrence systems to minimize damage and civilian casualties, vulnerability to accident and miscalculation, and waste of scarce resources;

—creation of standby war-prevention and conflict-confinement capabilities, partly under international auspices; such capabilities would not be dependent upon ad hoc intergovernmental consensus;

—adoption of unilateral measures to initiate and accelerate a reverse arms race at the strategic level and to negotiate arms-spending ceilings throughout the world;[36]

—declaratory and negotiated restraints on the sale of arms;

—strengthening procedures for peaceful change and the settlement of disputes so that legislative alternatives to war begin to gain strength.

My point is that, from the perspective of world order, arms control advocacy and discussion can play a major educational role. Global reform, engineered by voluntary planning and reinforced by popular and leadership support, depends upon what is essentially a learning process that will be characterized in its early stages by value changes and altered states of political awareness. A great deal of debate will be necessary before the renunciation of first-use options or the redesign of second-use systems becomes politically feasible; this debate will itself have great educational value because it will create direct controversy between those loyal to the state system and those who advocate drastic world order reform.[37] Such a discourse could help shape a consensus on whether or not S_1 was durable enough to deal with mounting pressures against it. Because arms policy is so central to the functioning of the state system, efforts to replace the logic of laissez-faire rivalry by a more cooperative policy could become central dramas of immense historical significance. The outcome cannot be confidently predicted at this time, but the early enactment of such a drama within the United States would undoubtedly raise the question for other societies as well. In t_1, the period immediately ahead, two elements of global reform should be understood:

—the world order learning process will be primarily internal, especially for principal states, although directions of response in one domestic arena will generate transnational effects in the others.

—such a segment learning process, adapted to the immense diversities of national and group situations, could have a number of results. It might produce convergent attitudes, although not yet a global consensus, regarding both the inevitability of a transition from S_1 to S_2 and the desirability of creating S_2 by voluntary (contractual) means as soon as possible. On the other hand, the learning process could lead to a generally approved and well-substantiated dismissal of the ecological challenge as an issue in international affairs, on the grounds that its significance has been exaggerated.[38]

THREE POSSIBLE OBJECTIONS

I should now like briefly to consider three of the most important objections to this approach to arms control. First of all, it may be argued that the gap between academic problem-solvers and governmental problem-staters has been broadened to unmanageable proportions. Arms control negotiations inch forward, based on a painful process of intragovernmental and intrasocietal consensus that is, at best, rather delicate. To encumber this process with an array of concerns arising from the credibility of the ecological challenge is not desirable. My response is simple: A scholar-citizen working on this subject needs to depict the situation objectively. He may sacrifice some short-term influence on the policy-makers, but, to the extent that his statements of the problems adhere to the facts, the evidence will eventually bear out his appraisals and ultimately come to influence policy. A time of transitional crisis may be identified, in part, by the size of the gap between problem-solvers and problem-staters, but only thought-control advocates or extreme cynics would want to narrow that gap out of deference to the meager capabilities of governmental problem-solvers. For the moment, the immediate objective is to reform *behavior* in the realm of foreign policy (i.e., national strategies of participation), but only *attitude* or orientation with regard to the broader issues of world order.

A second objection is that an analysis of this sort tends to overstate the role of reason and reasonableness in governmental and human behavior. In essence, no appeal to evidence is likely to be influential in the realms of power, where bureaucratic factors of habit, interest, and pressure prevail. I would agree that the reasonableness of an argument does not very frequently account for basic behavior. However, a persuasive argument based on evidence may strengthen the position of members of the elite already amenable to change, or support the tactics and strategies of counter-elites.[39] In any event, analysis and evidence are fundamental to education, and education in global reform should be given high priority in the present period of turmoil and confusion.

A third objection might be that, if a nation such as the United States prematurely accepts the case for drastic world order reform, it may become particularly vulnerable to the rapacity of some less enlightened states. It, along with other more enlightened states, would then be risking exposure to a known evil for the sake of pursuing an uncertain good. Again, this anxiety seems at least premature. A learning process that would include acute sensitivity to the behavior of possible rivals should provide sufficient reassurance. Loyalists to the state system—a commanding majority for the foreseeable future—would also lose no opportunity to publicize any evidence of attempts by other powers to take unfair advantage of shifts in foreign policy position and world order perspective.[40] Especially in the area of arms control, the huge overkill arsenal of weaponry provides an enormous safety factor that insures a long period of virtually risk-free experimentation with global reform postures.

In short, each of these objections contains some partial truths, but neither separately nor cumulatively do they convincingly refute the case for drastic global reform. It still seems essential to advance the case for foreign policy and world order reform in emphatic terms and to clarify the link between the two in the setting of arms control policy.

CONCLUSION

This chapter has made two main points: First, the present foreign policy of the United States is sustaining old patterns of behavior at a time when fundamental changes are both possible and necessary. The possibility has been provided by the ending of American combat in the Indochina War and the muting of the Cold War. The necessity has been created by the damaging domestic and global consequences of sustaining a counter-revolutionary mission in many parts of the Third World and by a continuing large investment in military capabilities during a period of national peace and relative international stability.

Second, foreign policy reforms of the sort specified above need to be supplemented by a serious consideration of the pressures building up against the existing world order system dominated by interacting states. These pressures are inducing a variety of globalizing tendencies, especially manifest in new geopolitical patterns of great powers and in the extraordinary surge of multinational corporate activity. These tendencies fall short of an adequate response to the pressures on the state system, because they neither deal directly with the ecological challenge (pollution and shortage of resources), nor do they provide a response to the great blights of poverty, war, oppression, and waste.

These two dimensions of appraisal influence our assessment of arms control policy. In the first instance, arms control policy is, and should be, an integral part of a rational foreign policy for the nation; it should not be considered autonomous (except for bureaucratic reforms) or be subject to inviolable domestic political constraints. Therefore, it is important that the United States take both the unilateral and the cooperative (i.e., negotiated) actions necessary to implement the possibilities for arms control that would be implicit in a renunciation of counterinsurgency military options and in other concrete steps to move beyond the hostile confrontations associated with Cold War tensions. These arms control steps involve the relationship of the United States to the Third World conflict as well as our strategic arms competition with the Soviet Union. Arms sales, military and policy training and aid programs, foreign bases and deployments, and defense spending are among the areas appropriate for creative, bold arms control activity. More ambitiously, perhaps, this may now be the time to revive the consideration of "deep disarmament" and even "general and complete disarmament." The war system is more dangerous than ever but rarely succeeds in translating battlefield victories into political settlements; the dangers of the future are bound to become greater as the technology of mass destruction is dispersed around the globe to governing elites and even to desperate counter-elites. In addition, arms spending squanders resources at a time of growing resource depletion and deepening poverty. The failure to consider drastic disarmament may become one more depressing confirmation of an unsuspected kinship between the human species and the lemming.

With respect to reforming the world-order system, our immediate emphasis must be upon education; several key tenets should be central to this educational campaign:

1) the state system is not able to deal with the agenda of human concerns very successfully;
2) a large number of attractive alternatives to the state system exist, some of which do not involve concentrating power and authority in a governmental center;
3) the process of transforming the state system should and could proceed by nonviolent and voluntary means;
4) global reform needs to be conceived as a continuous learning process;
5) a consensus favorable to drastic global reform must initially be shaped simultaneously in various national arenas throughout the world; and
6) while the war system is the Achilles' heel of the state system, the new awareness may become more closely associated with insights into the ecological unity of the planet.

From an arms control perspective, global reform is, for the moment, in an educational rather than a structural phase. Renunciation of specific military options—first-use of nuclear weapons, counterinsurgency roles, excessively cruel weaponry—would revitalize the vague renunciations of aggressive force contained in the United Nations Charter. In essence, arms control thinking needs to subvert the role of force in the pursuit of national goals. It should emphasize the degree to which the war system drains national treasuries while providing only the most fragile sort of security shield, a shield which, if punctured, threatens those that it protects as well as those it is designed to menace with virtual extinction.

High priority, then, belongs to the conceptualization and study of alternative systems of world order in which the war system is eliminated or drastically curtailed. No longer is such a futurist inquiry a utopian exercise for a questing imagination. It should be relevant to the practitioners of power who govern our destiny as a nation and as a species. If arms control thinking breaks this new ground in the decade ahead, then it will have fulfilled a basic function in history.

NOTES

1. The persisting Soviet role in the Middle East certainly dampened American enthusiasm for détente and discouraged the widely held sentiment in this country that the improvement in Soviet-American relations was so fundamental as to be virtually irreversible. Mr. Nixon's political collapse, Soviet repression of prominent dissenters and anti-Israel posture, renewed turbulence in China, the election of a pro-American government in France, and, perhaps most of all, Soviet resentments over Congressional attempts to condition economic relations on Jewish emigration rights are among the developments early in Nixon's second presidential term that made the future of Soviet-American relations much more problematic than it had been at the end of his first. These adverse trends were temporarily obscured by Secretary Kissinger's bipartisan stature as peace-maker and architect of United States foreign policy.

2. The tentative Soviet-American understanding reached at Vladivostok in 1974 to put a cap on the offensive arms race illustrates the problem of perception. Is this agreement to be considered a breakthrough, as officials of the negotiating governments maintain, or is it better understood as a mystifying gesture made in the name of arms control, but with no dampening effects on war risks or defense costs? A positive claimant can point to the historic establishment of upper limits. On the skeptical side, it can be pointed out that the agreed limits place almost no constraints, as the ceilings are higher than existing arsenals and, in any event, the limits simply legitimize a shift from quantitative arms buildup to qualitative competition. On balance, it would seem that the cynic's view of arms control has by far the better side in the argument, at least vis-à-vis the Vladivostok outcome.

3. Addressing the conference Pacem in Terris III in October 1973, even Henry Kissinger called for a national debate on America's world role as a necessary prelude to crystallizing a new domestic consensus for foreign policy purposes. Because domestic factors so often predominate, it is clear that no given course for United States foreign policy is likely to succeed over time unless it has a domestic mandate. Obviously, non-democratic societies can conduct a foreign policy without such a mandate, although analogous requirements for agreement probably exist. It is quite probable that no such consensus on American foreign policy goals will be achieved in the years just ahead, because isolationist-versus-interventionist issues will not be resolved for some time. But I think it safe to conclude that the appropriate role of direct and indirect military activity by the United States in foreign conflicts is likely to remain both controversial and central to forming American foreign policy.

4. See Henry A. Kissinger, "Making Foreign Policy," *The Center Magazine,* 7 (1974): 34-39, especially p. 39.

5. Henry A. Kissinger, *American Foreign Policy* (New York: Norton, 1969), p. 89; for a fuller discussion along the same lines, see Henry A. Kissinger, *The Necessity for Choice: Prospects of American Foreign Policy* (New York: Harper and Row, 1961), especially pp. 169–339.

6. Richard M. Nixon, *U.S. Foreign Policy for the 1970s—Shaping A Durable Peace: A Report to the Congress by Richard Nixon,* May 3, 1973 (Washington, D.C.: Government Printing Office, 1973), p. 202.

7. Ibid., p. 204.

8. Note that this Nixonian formulation of balance does not allow for equivalence in capabilities achieved by different weapons systems but seems to depend instead on

equivalence of the weapons systems themselves. Such a definition of "balance" results in great inflexibility, complicating and constraining arms control prospects still further.

9. Undoubtedly, the purpose of this fifth requirement also is to reassure China that bipolar arms control agreements are not being concluded at her expense.

10. Nixon, *U.S. Foreign Policy for the 1970s,* p. 18.

11. Ibid., p. 180.

12. Ibid., p. 187.

13. Michael M. May, "SALT: Two Possible Approaches," *Wall Street Journal,* May 24, 1974, p. 10.

14. Admittedly, it is not easy to alter abruptly the drift of American foreign policy in a responsible fashion. Alliances may remain constructive in some regions of the world. In any event, the withdrawal of superpower involvement should be undertaken with care and in an evenhanded fashion. There are two distinct concerns: first, asymmetrical withdrawal might expose allies to pressures or even to attack, inducing adversaries to make miscalculations, conceivably leading to warfare, and thereby generating more dangerous and costly forms of reinvolvement; secondly, it might have destabilizing consequences on the internal, public order systems of those states previously dependent on American credibility for their security, as manifested through forward deployment. At the same time, there is no plausible argument for sustaining the American posture of support for counterrevolutionary regimes nor for the American role in planning, training, and executing counterinsurgency missions. This Third World role has been thoroughly discredited by involvement in Indochina. In an atmosphere of détente the Cold War arguments for Third World involvement are no longer valid, and it is almost impossible to furnish an acceptable rationale of security for our past and continuing embrace of reactionary regimes. The only convincing rationale remaining would have to involve the protection of American world economic interests, a rationale our leadership has so far refused to provide.

15. The issue here, too, is whether there are reasonable policies leading to global unity that responsible national leaders can support. Such support could be manifested in official attitudes toward the United Nations and other international cooperative endeavors. Our leaders could begin to create a political conscience founded on human solidarity and upon the need for global planning and sharing as the sole viable basis for upholding the security of Americans. See Lester R. Brown, *World Without Borders* (New York: Random House, 1972); Barry Commoner, *The Closing Circle* (New York: Random House, 1971); Barbara Ward and René Dubos, *Only One Earth* (New York: Norton, 1972); Louis René Beres and Harry Targ, *Reordering the Planet* (Boston: Allyn and Bacon, 1973); Edward Goldsmith et al., *Blueprint for Survival* (Boston: Houghton, Mifflin, 1972); Richard A. Falk, *This Endangered Planet: The Prospects and Proposals for Human Survival* (New York: Random House, 1971); Richard A. Falk, *A Study of Future Worlds* (New York: Free Press, 1975).

16. There is ambiguity surrounding the conception of "direct attack." The core idea is clear—a major military attack against the United States must be deterred by all possible means. But what of attacks against close allies? Can the United States abandon these allies if they are the victims of such attacks? If not, is it not preferable to be clear about the intent to respond in order to deter direct attacks on American allies? And if this is the case, then cannot one defend the logic, although perhaps not the extent, of forward deployment? And, finally, is there any prospect of inducing the Soviet Union to cease to include within its definition of national security the defense of its close allies against direct attack? In effect, it becomes difficult for the United States to leave the

mainstream of geopolitics in any dramatic way without incurring greater costs than it now incurs. Therefore, a rational foreign policy for the United States seems to require a combination of marginal adjustments to cut the risks and costs of geopolitical patterns and a major effort to transform mainstream geopolitics from a statist to a global (that is, world order) perspective.

17. The United States has never considered itself responsible for guaranteeing the status quo everywhere. Indeed, it has welcomed shifts to the right brought about by coups and illegal violence, although in larger Third World countries it has generally limited itself to exerting marginal influence through diplomatic and economic levers.

18. The nuclear dimension, indeed, makes a more serious case for the earlier claim that national military capabilities are primarily concerned with keeping the peace among states. The mutuality of deterrence has very likely prevented a third world war from arising, as the prospect of nuclear devastation makes recourse to war a very desperate last resort, rather than the result of probable costs and benefits. The stabilizing effects of nuclear weaponry among the central powers has not prevented either warfare in the periphery of the international system or the military involvement of the central powers in these peripheral wars. Perhaps the most impressive argument along these lines is to be found in Robert E. Osgood and Robert W. Tucker, *Force, Order, and Justice* (Baltimore: Johns Hopkins University Press, 1967).

19. See McGeorge Bundy, "To Cap the Volcano," *Foreign Affairs*, 48 (1969): 1-20; Fred Charles Iklé, "Can Nuclear Deterrence Last Out the Century?" *Foreign Affairs*, 51 (1973): 267-285; Herbert York, "A Proposal for a Saner Deterrent" (mimeographed); Wolfgang K. H. Panofsky, "The Mutual-Hostage Relationship between America and Russia," *Foreign Affairs* 52 (1973): 109-118.

20. It is unclear whether it would be possible, or even desirable, to build a consensus among governments on the renunciation of war, even in the face of widely endorsed revisionist goals. At present, despite the provisions of the United Nations Charter, no such consensus exists.

21. One underestimated difficulty with war prevention schemes is their failure to take account of the traditional role of force in accomplishing social and political change. Without nonviolent alternatives to war, it is unrealistic to expect any legal framework for prohibition to succeed, nor is it necessarily in the human interest that it should. Obviously, the line between what is tolerable in the name of self-determination and necessary prohibition in the name of world peace is exceedingly difficult to specify in the abstract. In practice, the need to determine on which side of the line a given issue falls should help to sensitize governments to the importance of separating local tests of strength from wider global systems of geopolitical equilibrium.

22. I have attempted a rationale for comprehensive no-first-use pledges as an arms control measure in "Renunciation of Nuclear Weapons Use," in Bennett Boskey and Mason Willrich, eds., *Nuclear Proliferation: Prospects for Control* (New York: Dunellen, 1970), pp. 133–145.

23. A substantial ecological challenge can be met successfully only by some reliable mechanism for global administration, which would assure that the planet as a whole is not imperiled by the behavior of any of its parts. Such managerial globalization need not be hierarchical or governmental in structure, but it must be capable of effective and efficient coordination where standards of behavior or allocations of scarce resources are necessary. Structures of central guidance can be designed with safeguards for diversity in economic, social, and political organization.

24. Contractual centralizational and nationalistic world order responses may dif-

fer more in tone than in substance. Voluntary, contractual centralization accepts the need to globalize planetary management, whereas the fragmented, nationalistic world order system is generally confident about the capacities of the state system to endure, provided enlightened leadership emerges to meet the ecological challenge.

25. I have developed this line of analysis of prospects for global reform in "The Logic of State Sovereignty Versus the Requirements of World Order," *Yearbook of World Affairs* (London: Stevens, 1973), pp. 7–23.

26. World Order Models Project is described in Thomas Weiss, "The WOMP of the Institute for World Order," *Peace and Change*, 2 (spring 1973): 1–2; Ian Baldwin, Jr., "Thinking About a New World Order for the Decade 1990," *War/Peace Report*, 10 (1970): 3–8 and chapters 3 and 4 of this book. The World Order Models Project is the first comprehensive effort by scholars to design a plausible and desirable future world order system. Each of the eight groups of scholars arrives at its own independent judgment on world order problems and solutions, supplying the intellectual diversity that is needed at this stage of international awareness.

27. It is difficult to evaluate the relative importance of the rise of the multinational corporation to world order and in world affairs. Does the multinational corporation promise to provide economic prosperity for all peoples living where it operates, or does it offer such a promise mainly to existing enclaves of a small, wealthy upper stratum? Is the multinational corporation generally a substitute for governmental forms of imperialism, or is it a genuine alternative that is increasingly successful in its claim to possess an anational identity? Will multinational corporate growth help sustain the war system by building "military industrial complexes" wherever it operates, or will these multinational corporations come to favor dismantling the war system to assure stable operating conditions in a market that embraces as much of the world as possible? Can a profit-seeking corporation contribute effectively to social reform and human well-being in a world beset by mass poverty and extreme inequality?

28. The proponents of economic growth, larger foreign aid programs, and an expanded developmental role for international lending institutions all share a belief in the capacity of the present global system to evolve in a manner ultimately beneficial for mankind, often combined with a profound distrust of, or antipathy to, alternative global designs (regarding them as utopian, in the sense of being unattainable).

29. As has so often been the case with unpopular methods of control, elaborate efforts to disguise them would be attempted. The imperialism of the duopoly may be hidden beneath attractive labels—"controlling regional arms races," "arms control and disarmament," and "international peacekeeping." The Soviet-American role in the Middle East deserves careful study in this respect. Is this role an experiment in duopolistic management, where arms buildups are encouraged to establish influence and are then followed by the imposition of settlements designed to assure stability of influence? How else, except through Soviet and American guarantees, can a Middle East settlement be reached? How else can guarantees be relied upon except by introducing elements of a military presence? The mystification process reaches its fullest embodiment when the victim countries of the world call for such solutions.

30. Other world order options, whose origins would be neither voluntary nor contractual, should also be studied and understood, especially since their emergence seems more likely at the present time.

31. Among the requirements for a coherent world order design are the following: normative goals of universal application; a time horizon that extends for several decades, perhaps even for centuries; a systematic framework of inquiry that embraces

all principal elements relevant to the process of change; a conception of transitional tactics and strategies; images of a preferred world.

32. These minimizing objectives are not always reconcilable in specific contexts of choice; tradeoffs will have to be made between, say, improving the distribution of wealth and preserving environmental quality. Nevertheless, a program of global reform, if it is to succeed fully, would have to make cumulative progress over time in all four areas. See Garrett Hardin, *Exploring New Ethics for Survival: The Voyage of the Spaceship Beagle* (New York: Viking, 1972); Van Renssalaer Potter, *Bioethics: Bridge to the Future* (Englewood Cliffs, N.J.: Prentice Hall, 1971).

33. These ideas are set forth in more detail in my essay "Toward a New World Order: Modest Methods and Drastic Visions," in Saul H. Mendlovitz, ed., *On Creating a Just World Order* (New York: Free Press, 1975).

34. Functional specialization refers to the distribution of tasks in different areas of international life to specialized agencies organized on a regional and global basis (for example, health, food, environment, ocean resources, space, and disarmament). Elaborate checks and balances would be designed to frustrate efforts to concentrate power in the general-purpose institutions needed both to assure some political direction in matters of global policy and to coordinate functional activities. The relationship between efficiency and protection from global tyranny would be the principal constitutional problem for designers of models for drastic global reform.

35. Breakthroughs in information technology have such radical significance because they permit efficient organization without hierarchical structure. These breakthroughs may allow the world order system to develop mechanisms of coordination and procedures for mutual guidance without building up the sort of institutional "critical mass" that is associated with "world government" conceptions. This administrative possibility would become politically attractive if it were combined with social and technological breakthroughs (e.g., greatly reduced energy costs) that would alleviate, if not altogether eliminate, world poverty. For a creative consideration of noncentralized sanctions, see W. Michael Reisman, "Sanctions and Enforcement," in Cyril E. Black and Richard A. Falk, eds., *The Future of the International Legal Order*, Vol. III (Princeton, N.J.: Princeton University Press, 1971), 273–335.

36. A "reverse arms race" refers to the interactive dynamics of reductions in arms spending, military posturing, and the demilitarization of foreign policy. As a government proceeds in this direction, cautiously at first, it reinforces comparable tendencies in adversary societies, or at least it provides such tendencies with an opportunity for further development. This type of arms control "methodology" lies somewhere between formal arms control measures negotiated and embodied in treaty form and unilateral initiatives undertaken for purely domestic reasons (e.g., reforms in weapons procurement practices or constraints on presidential war-making powers).

37. Of course this discourse will also be shaped by differing assessments of the existing intergovernmental setting, especially judgments made about the intentions and capabilities of major rival governments.

38. Note that such a choice does not envision agreement on the character of S_2 at this stage, but only on whether it is necessary, and if it is, on the further necessity of achieving transition by peaceful and voluntary means. The next stage of the discourse would proceed to the shape of a new system of world order that would be both desirable and attainable within a given period.

39. Consider, for instance, the role of Marx and Lenin in the world communist movement. Critics of the state system must develop a persuasive ideology that can effectively convey their fears and preferences to others.

40. The shift in American geopolitical posture from Cold War to détente provides a constructive analogy. Cold War diehards, such as Senator Henry Jackson, require that advocates of détente vindicate their interpretation of events at every step along the path. The need to sustain a popular and governmental consensus requires advocates of reform—détente, in this instance—to demonstrate continuously that the old assumptions about Soviet behavior are no longer applicable. A policy shift is not an event in time, but a process through time that can be slowed down, speeded up, and even reversed.

CHAPTER 11

Satisfying Human Needs in a World of Sovereign States: Rhetoric, Reality, and Vision

INTRODUCTION

No Quick Solution to World Poverty

The enigma of world poverty continues to baffle people of good will. Why are there so many poor people despite a long period during which the gross planetary product has steadily increased? Some blame capitalism or imperialism; others stress selfish leaders and ruling groups; some talk of the ignorance, corruption, and inefficiency of governments or the backwardness of societies; still others point to nefarious money managers and to obscure machinations by multinational corporations; some suggest that the *real* problem is a result of unchecked population growth; and some contend that poverty remains entrenched because the planet is running out of cheap resources.

Of course, there are elements of truth in each line of explanation, and yet we lack the knowledge to assert with any real confidence that a single line of explanation is conclusive. We are faced with a reality: grinding poverty for the mass of humanity. And we posit a goal: a world economic and political order that produces enough goods and services and distributes them in such a way as to satisfy the basic material needs of everyone. The gap between reality and goal is what defines the scope of our inquiry.

At the outset, it seems important to assert that there is no technical way to close this gap rapidly. It exists, not out of necessity, but because of the way in which states and the system of states are organized. To change organizational patterns on this scale is a complex, difficult, perhaps impossible undertaking that depends on shifting patterns of perceived interests and on changing value formations. It is a formidable challenge to our institutions and traditions and calls for a wide range of responses. It calls, especially, on our religious heritages to provide us with clues as to what is wrong and what to do about it, as well as with inspiration to strengthen our resolve.

New Stress on Needs Is Ambiguous

The stress on "needs" is, at once, obvious and problematic. It is obvious because the poorest people in the world are numerous and miserable and because the overall arrangement of wealth that allows such disparities to persist is an assault upon our most basic ethical sensibilities. It is problematic because it encourages a kind of patronizing philanthropic concern about doing something for "others," conceived as helpless objects, and therefore resists the understanding of poverty as a "structural" consequence of the way in which power and wealth are and have been deployed. Nevertheless, we shall focus on needs because that is the way people are thinking about meeting the challenge of world poverty. This stress on needs proceeds from a nonphilanthropic outlook that asks how we must transform domestic and international structures to enable *all* people to enjoy a satisfying life; it does not isolate "the poor" as a distinct category.

The diagnostic question is why it seems so difficult to achieve distributive patterns that satisfy the basic material needs of all people. How should we understand and explain this difficulty? This chapter argues that the principal difficulty arises at the interface between politics and economics on both national and international levels. It also argues that a denial of human needs of the masses is not inevitable, but results from the contingent structures of inequality existing between and within states. This can be rectified, although only after an intense and prolonged struggle.

The therapeutic question is what to do to achieve distributional patterns that are designed to satisfy basic material needs. The argument sketched here is that political structures will have to be fundamentally transformed by struggle, one that is facilitated by cultural innovation, and pursued according to a variety of nonviolent strategies ranging from education to mass civil disobedience, general strikes, and the like. Values constitute the core of what the struggle is about, in reality translating the great religious vision of what has been ethically presupposed for humanity into the actualities of political, economic, and social arrangements. Such an imperative is reinforced by the apocalyptic dangers of persisting with behavioral and organizational patterns premised on the acceptability of *exploitation* (giving rise to personal and collective inequality, including deep poverty for large numbers) and of *fragmentation* (associating well-being with a part—territory, class, race, or religion—rather than with the whole of the human species). The possibility of a positive human destiny depends upon suffusing activities with a vivid and intensifying sense of human solidarity on all levels of societal interaction.[1]

Obviously, such a vision of the future can only begin to be approximated after a long process of change. The process can be initiated immediately in appropriate forms within every possible setting. We can begin now, and, given the urgency of the undertaking, there is no time to lose. Yet we cannot expect to achieve rapid results except within domains under our direct control. The length of time needed for a cumulative shift of structures may be as short as several decades or as long as several centuries. We have no way of knowing, or even of assessing the probabilities. The correctness of the stand, and not its rewards, provides us with the basis for action. At the same time, the present rewards are tangible because the experience of transformation is palpable. We can realize now the emergent future order to some extent by putting into practice the principles and values of humane governance in as many activities as our strength and our circumstances allow.

Overview

Structural and Ideological Impasse. In this chapter, I shall pursue these themes by considering the current impasse over methods to reduce world poverty and diminish the disparities between rich and poor countries. Given the prevailing secular structures and their supportive ideological outlooks, there is no way to circumvent this impasse. Furthermore, frustration occasioned by this impasse is likely to grow even more acute, resulting in a violent cycle of repression and resistance. Violence on both sides, repressive violence by those who would manage the status quo versus revolutionary violence by those who would change it, will increase.

Such a cycle leads to a political dynamic that is futile for both sides, as one side fails to achieve "order" and the other side fails to achieve "justice." Without greater consciousness of what is necessary, the conception of what is possible will remain excessively modest, dooming the revolutionary attempt, even if successful, to shifts in policy and personnel and failing to break through the cycle of violent and inhumane governance. The effects of the Soviet Revolution are illustrative.

Of course, structural constraints are not everything. The particular orientation of individuals and elites toward global policy issues may be more or less generous, imaginative, and effective. These variations of outlook could make the difference between a relatively steady voyage into the future and a disastrous shipwreck. At the same time, the constraints on official leadership arising from the demands of domestic social forces, from the influence of perceived interests, and from traditions of behavior associated with national security and sovereignty are so great as to make it highly unrealistic to expect much aid and comfort for transformative demands emanating from the centers of established power and authority.[2]

Evolution of Consensus. There is encouraging evidence of the evolution of a consensus on what is needed to devise patterns of humane governance for the planet. This consensus is gradually forming despite the practices and tendencies of constituted power. In effect, we cannot, at this stage, expect most official institutions and governing groups, given their sense of priorities, to support a social movement for planetary renewal, although individuals serving in these structures will be influenced by the movement to varying degrees, and may keep the processes of governance from veering to extremes.

Uneven Process of Renewal. This transnational movement of renewal will proceed unevenly. In the advanced industrial countries, the crux of the problem lies in the interplay between runaway technology and the apparatus of state power. The state is too large for humane governance, and yet too small to cope functionally with the planetary agenda. Overcoming the predominance of the state presupposes a dialectical unfolding toward values that are on the one hand more communal and personally felt and produce decentralization and values that, on the other hand, are more universal and functionally successful and, as such, require greater centralization of organizing structures.[3] Decentralizing potentials are more significant than centralizing ones because it seems so essential to reduce to the furthest extent possible the intrusion of bureaucratic ways and means on people's lives.

In less industrialized countries the emergence of strong state structures is part of the phenomenon of "catching up," and provides some assurance that political independence can be safeguarded and that global issues will be dealt with in a fairer way. Statism as a short-run response to imperialism enables Third World societies to make effective their quest for national self-assertion, including achieving greater participation in international arenas and more regulation of foreign penetration in their own societies. Such nationalistic strategies interfere with interim, stopgap globalist adjustment processes (inhibiting, for instance, formation of an enlightened law of the oceans), and may have some unfortunate domestic effects, such as a tendency to smother the domestic self-determination dynamic beneath an effective machinery of repression.

Overall, however, it remains a matter of letting history run its course. The dynamic of self-determination at the national level and of globalization at the international and individual levels are both reinforced by the weight of social pressures to such an extent that efforts of resistance must choose more and more desperate tactics. These pressures may make the interval and process of transition a dangerous and confusing one, as well as making its outcome uncertain. These pressures also establish the specific context in which religious and cultural perspectives possess their greatest relevance: to facilitate transition by reorienting consciousness toward the satisfaction of human needs and the fulfillment of human potential for individual and group development.

THE MAINSTREAM DEBATE ON THE WORLD ECONOMIC SITUATION

Some widely accepted generalizations can be set forth to provide a normative sense of direction:

—a large and growing number of peope live near or below subsistence;

—the overwhelming concentration of these poor people is among nonwhite populations located in Asia, Africa, and Latin America;

—a much more rapid and relative rate of population increase exists among the nonwhite poor of the world than among the white population;

—a widening gap exists between the per capita GNP of rich and poor countries currently estimated as 11:1 or 12:1;

—an even more rapidly widening income gap exists within poor countries, resulting in the relative, and in some instances the absolute, decline in the purchasing power of the poorest 40 percent or so of the population despite overall societal growth;[4]

—a corresponding absence of influence and power on the part of poor countries in international economic and political arenas;

—a disproportionate use of scarce resources by the rich countries of the North relative to their population, perhaps at a ratio of 15:1 on a per capita basis, affecting price and availability or resources required to meet basic needs;

—a strong correlation since 1945 between the poorest sectors of world society and the location of most instances of large-scale collective violence, including warfare;

—an equally strong correlation between the rich sectors of the world society and outlays for defense spending;

—an intensification of arms race behavior, including nuclear weapons innovations by superpowers, the spread of nuclear capabilities to many additional countries, and the rise of arms spending for sophisticated conventional weaponry; this dynamic increases the likelihood of the outbreak of various forms of warfare, including nuclear war;

—an intensification of authoritarian tendencies, especially throughout the Third World, signifying the decline of moderate politics;

—a mood of growing despair in the rich countries about their economic and political prospects as a consequence of energy costs and options, sustained unemployment and inflation, environmental pressures, terrorist activities, increasing protectionism, and spreading mass disaffection among all social classes.

These elements of the international situation are not meant to be exhaustive. The purpose of this enumeration is to clarify the grounds of concern about the workings and prospects of the international system. In addition to these various factors, two kinds of linkages, the first between political and economic strategies, and the second, between the domestic political order and the international order, are of fundamental importance.

Idealistic Rhetoric

My analysis proceeds from the conviction that political factors severely constrain available economic policy choices within unacceptably narrow limits and vice versa. These narrow limits reflect a certain stress upon selfish, short-term, domestic concerns that dominate governmental policy-making procedures and make it unrealistic to anticipate any major voluntary adjustments in the international system that could result in substantially greater satisfaction of basic human needs. Put differently, despite idealistic rhetoric as well as a sense of what needs to be done, altruistic motivation is an exceedingly weak premise for any meaningful program of global reform, and perceived selfish motivations are not likely to work for the benefit of the poor.[5]

The only way to avoid this assessment is to envision a reorientation of domestic elites around a more planetary interpretation of national interests coupled with the success of populist politics that successfully revises the domestic allocation of income and wealth. Neither shift is remotely plausible without prior drastic changes in the prevailing political consciousness. This will include the emergence of new belief/value orientations that reflect a simultaneous emphasis on the worth of the individual person, on the solidarity of humanity, and on the value of human persistence and evolution.

Such shifts are already underway to some extent, but it will take several decades at least until they become dominant; in the interim, stiffening resistance from more traditional and conservative conceptions of human nature and political practicality will be encountered. Only by careful examination of prevailing configurations of political power, including their economic dimensions, can we begin to appreciate the magnitude of creating an overall social order on a planetary scale that endows all classes and peoples with the opportunity to satisfy basic human needs, a goal more dynamic and ambitious than the elimination of poverty.[6] Poverty could, in theory, be virtually eliminated by welfare payments on an international level without creating a social environment where people have their basic needs, including their sense of dignity, satisfied. Our concern rests with the more organic attainment of a development process that encompasses everyone, providing work as well as sustenance, dignity as well as material wherewithal, participation as well as benefits.

This insistence on grounding inquiry within the realm of power is especially important where normative concerns are as prominent as they are here. There is often a tendency in international relations to substitute high-minded intentions and words for policy and behavior, or to assume that benevolent adjustments in economic relationships can somehow be achieved by the right technical "fix." The issue of world poverty and the related "development gap" are especially prone to simplistic rhetoric and mechanistic proposals.

Leaders of both rich and poor countries, for a variety of pragmatic reasons, endorse the goals of eliminating poverty as rapidly as possible from the face of the earth. President Jimmy Carter of the United States exhibited a characteristic understanding of this view in a major foreign policy address delivered at Notre Dame University on May 22, 1977: "More than 100 years ago, Abraham Lincoln said that our nation could not exist half slave and half free. We know that a peaceful world cannot long exist one-third rich and two-thirds hungry."[7] To similar effect is a statement by Julius Nyerere, President of Tanzania: "If the rich countries go on getting richer and richer at the expense of the poor, the poor of the world must demand a change, in the same way as the proletariat in the rich countries demanded change in the past. And we do demand change. As far as we are concerned the only question at issue is whether the change comes by dialogue or confrontation."[8]

The formal consensus seems virtually unanimous at such levels of abstraction. Rich and poor leaders alike accept the normative and pragmatic case for a world campaign against both poverty and global disparities. The extent of formal support is also disclosed by the virtually unanimous approval given to the postulates of the new international economic order in key votes at the United Nations; disagreement emerges as soon as action proposals are put forward on such issues as debt cancellation, indexing of commodity prices, and national control of foreign investment.

Southern Perspectives

However, even the apparent consensus on goals is deceptive, as sharp disagreement becomes quickly evident on the level of explanation and remedy. Third World representatives, regardless of political orientation, tend to put blame for Third World poverty on the rich countries and naturally expect these countries to bear the moral and material burdens of rectification. As Adam Nsekela, an African World Bank official, puts it: "Why are the poor states poor? The answer is that they are poor because they have been colonized, dominated, drained of their surpluses, locked into bondage in which they are poor and are becoming ever poorer because the rich are rich and are becoming relatively richer."[9] Such a perspective leads, at the very least, to an insistence that a feature of any new international economic order that emerges be that states in the poor sector are helped to become economically more secure. In Mr. Nsekela's words, "The New International Economic Order is about distribution: the distribution of world production, the distribution of the surpluses derived in any country and the distribution of economic power."[10] The standard proposals to achieve these results are outside the scope of this paper, but do include such measures as debt relief, stabilization of commodity prices, increased direct assistance, indexing of prices for primary and finished goods, increased Third World voting power in international economic institutions, and improved terms of trade.[11]

Whether or not such a Southern perspective also includes a transformation of distributive patterns within the state is, of course, a more sensitive issue. To look outward at other governments or global institutions for capital, technical assistance, or social reform may be to invite intervention that endangers political autonomy. In many instances upholding autonomy is a national goal that is as important as and, on occasion, more important than, economic development. To look inward at inequity is to challenge the legitimacy of the state as currently constituted in a political setting where opposition and dissent are increasingly regarded as criminal activities by the leadership of the society. The more radical positions on social change have certainly concentrated upon the need for drastic restructuring on the domestic level and have regarded international restructuring as desirable, but definitely subsidiary. Whether this domestic restructuring is, in effect and unavoidably, a call for some variety of socialism is an important issue. Can governments that rely on private domestic and foreign capital for development purposes, in other words, achieve distributive justice if they are, indeed, operating from an initial circumstance of mass poverty? How?[12]

Northern Perspectives

The governments of rich countries respond to Third World claims in several ways. The most sophisticated and euphemistic line of resistance is to emphasize the automaticity of mutual benefit created by the positive linkage between "growth" for the North and the South, contending that only adjustments based on the imagery of "mutual gain" are politically feasible, economically effective, and morally persuasive. Such an outlook argues against placing additional burdens on the North that will retard its engine of growth to any extent, on the morally self-serving ground that such an effect would be especially harmful to the South. As a consequence, large-scale transfer or redistribution proposals are rejected as "counterproductive" and "irrational." Perhaps the most authoritative statement of this convenient outlook is contained in the Communiqué of the Economic Summit Meeting held in London during May 1977, and issued on behalf of the seven leading "industrial democracies":

The well-being of the developed and developing countries are bound up together. The developing countries' growing prosperity benefits industrial countries, as the latter's growth benefits developing nations. Both developed and developing nations have a mutual interest in maintaining a climate conducive to stable growth worldwide.[13]

Even if one grants this dubious premise, what remains to be accounted for is the assessment of whether or not the character of such growth projected for the South is likely to benefit the poorer countries and the poorer segments of these countries. Growth of what? For whom? And over what time period? These critical normative questions are rarely addressed by liberal internationalist advocates.

The more moderate versions of this mutual gain position argue that the prosperity of the North is the key to market outlets for the products of the South, and that the poor countries are poor for reasons disconnected with their colonial heritage. The essential point in the argument is that these countries would be no less poor had they not been colonized, and that the rich countries would be as rich (or richer) even if there had been no colonial system. (For example, Sweden and Switzerland had no colonies and are rich; Portugal had colonies and is relatively poor.)[14]

Some Northerners go further and provide an even more self-vindicating account of economic disparities. For example, the British economists Peter Bauer and John O'Sullivan write that: "Surely the principal reason [for global disparities] is that nations, peoples, tribes, communities are not equally endowed with those qualities which mainly determine economic achievement."[15] That is, the inequality of result in the world of the late 1970s is an inevitable reflection of the inequality of endowment, and to allege exploitation and injustice is to offer a rationalization for poverty ungrounded in fact or evidence. Bauer and O'Sullivan go on to attack Northern statesmen for their fatuous acquiescence to the Southern indictment. They argue that indigenous failures of leadership in poor countries are generally responsible for the mass economic plight of their peoples.

This debate about causation and tactics remains intense and inconclusive. A focus on the level of argumentation tends to overlook more critical issues of political will and capability. The North lacks both the *will* and the *capability* to depart significantly from what it has been doing. Domestic demands for jobs, profits, and inflationary control are predominant, and equalizing concessions to the South are perceived as needless exercises in self-sacrifice for which there is no domestic political constituency of any consequence.

SOME PERSPECTIVES ON REFORM

There are a variety of approaches to global economic reform. The strengths and weaknesses of the principal approaches will be examined in this section.

Capital Transfers and Reallocations

A Painless Economic Fix? Many Northerners continue to believe it is possible to help the South with massive capital transfers, coupled with domestic reallocations of investment priorities. Barbara Ward, for instance, proposes "a planetary bargain" between the North and South comparable to the Marshall Plan. As of 1947, the United States made large resource transfers (up to 2 percent of U.S. GNP per year) for a period of years to stimulate European economic expansion. The result, point out its enthusiasts, has been twenty-five years of mutually beneficial growth. Arguing that a comparable growth potential exists for North-South trade, Barbara Ward calls for a similar resource transfer, but at the level of .7 percent of GNP (compared with the current .3 percent for a sustained period), perhaps for several decades. Her economic case rests on the view that legitimate demand for goods among the Trilateral countries is largely saturated, leading to increasingly destructive competitive interactions, whereas the demand potential in the Third World remains mostly undeveloped; ("There is no doubt where marginal productivity is highest—among still undeveloped people, areas, and resources.")[16]

The incentive for Northern [in conjunction with the Organization of Petroleum Exporting Countries (OPEC)] action is the lure of mutual benefit associated with the prospect of major increases in the productive capacity and purchasing power of the poor. This kind of economic thinking, the liberal dream of fusing "rationality," "decency," and "self-interest," is expected to come true and provide the world economy with a painless apolitical "fix." The catch, however, is that there is virtually no chance of winning support for such an approach in most rich countries, and even if such support could be found and the plan put into effect, there is no reason to expect poor countries or poor sectors of societies to benefit to any large extent.

The analogy drawn between economic conditions in post-World War II Europe and in the contemporary Third World is unconvincing. First of all, Europe in 1947 had a disabled industrial capability damaged by war that could be rebuilt by an efficient, generally disciplined work force provided only that the capital became available. In contrast, much of the Third World has an industrial sector that is restricted to a small physical area, that involves only a fraction of the labor force, and that lacks a large reservoir of skilled labor to draw upon for purposes of rapid economic expansion. Third World poverty tends to be concentrated in the rural sector, and its alleviation

would require dramatic shifts in public investment priorities so as to
stimulate overall rural development that would benefit the rural
population as a whole.[17] Second, the governments of Europe after
World War II were genuinely determined to rebuild their economies
in an efficient manner, whereas governments in Third World countries are often unable to organize themselves for large-scale undertakings, being disabled as much by corruption as by capital shortages.
Third, the short-term effects of such a stimulus of Third World productive capacity would be to export trilateral jobs and markets in a
period of rising economic nationalism and protectionist sentiment in
the North. Fourth, there is no assurance that such a growth spurt,
even if it occurred, would bring substantial benefit to the really poor
segments of Third World societies—especially the rural poor.

The tensions extend even further. If investment, for instance,
was heavy in agricultural development of the sort required for food
self-sufficiency, then it would deprive North American farmers of
part of their market for exportable grains and cereals, depress world
prices, and cause severe domestic problems. In fact the situation of
the U.S. farmer is already described as worse than it has been at any
time since the depression, and steps have been taken by the government to cut back wheat production by as much as 20 percent. These
steps have been taken, incidentally, at a time when famine conditions
exist in Laos, Mozambique, and elsewhere.

Among others, Arthur Lewis has shown that "mutual gain" based
on North-South trade, especially in exports of primary goods, does tie
the economic hopes of the South to the prosperity of the North. The
tie is not mutual, however, because of the extreme dependence of the
South on the stability of commodity markets in the North, and because of the absence of any comparable Northern dependence on
Southern prosperity. Lewis favors stimulating the growth of South-
South trading relationships, as well as diversifying the productive
capacities of Southern countries to reduce their import requirements
and overall dependency. These policies, Lewis argues, would be
beneficial in promoting viable forms of development in the South.
Lewis's analysis is powerful, in part, because it proceeds within the
confines of liberal economic analysis to clarify why present structures
of North-South relations are exploitative even if growth rates appear
to move in tandem.[18]

Naive "Econometric" Solutions. Another kind of "fix" is to abstract
the quantum of resources needed to overcome world poverty. Roger
Hansen, for instance, reports "that two estimates resulting from dif-

ferent approaches and methodologies suggest that absolute poverty could be virtually ended within ten to fifteen years at a cost of $125 billion (in 1973 dollars); and that an asset-transfer policy to assure the 'forgotten 40 percent' of a firm floor above that level in the future might cost approximately $250 billion." As Hansen notes, such a program could be financed for $10-13 billion per year for fifteen to twenty years, "depending on the thoroughness of the job." Since the present flow of aid from OECD countries is at the level of $13.6 billion, with much of it going to middle level countries or for purposes unrelated to basic needs, it would be possible, Hansen contends, to reallocate this amount around the priorities of the basic human needs approach without even necessitating increases in aid totals.[19] This contention seems so simple that it raises the obvious question, why doesn't it happen?

Hansen also points out that according to a World Bank estimate "a 2 percent annual transfer from the upper classes to the bottom 40 percent of the populations of the developing countries could successfully finance both the short-term and the long-term goals of the strategy over a twenty-five year period."[20] Again, we are intrigued by the apparent triviality of the effort as compared to the grand character of the promised effect; and again, as with an international transfer, the political constraints emerge when we ask, "Why doesn't this happen?" Here, as well, the technical vision is flawed: resource transfers by themselves will not induce self-sustaining growth.

How does one get the capital to the countryside intact and then invest it in such a way as to meet the human needs of the poor, including infrastructure deficiencies, in a manner that will generate a dynamic of productive growth? Without convincing scenarios, targets and numbers are misleading, diverting us from an appreciation of the structural difficulties of rural development in a polity where the capital allocation process is generally dominated by growth-oriented technocrats and profit-oriented urban industrial capitalists. Such arithmetic targets are useful to the extent that they underscore the availability of economic capabilities to meet human needs and call attention to the structural distortions of priority and control that make these reallocations highly implausible. However, to the extent that such "econometric" solutions are meant to provide a *real* solution via an appeal to the good faith rationality of policy-makers, they are naive about the nature of power, as well an insensitive to the exploitative character of human relationships implicit in capitalism. As Fernando Henrique Cardoso puts it, "Because they fail to recognize the banality—social and economic exploitation of man by man, of one class by another, of some nations by other nations—so-called 'counter-élites' often go round in circles, dreaming of technical solutions."[21]

The Bariloche Model. On a different level of seriousness, large-scale economic models project ways to help the poor and/or eliminate disparities. Perhaps, the most significant initiative to date is the Bariloche inquiry into the kind of development strategy appropriate for the realization of basic human needs. Unlike "the fix" of resource transfers, the Bariloche model examines scenarios that involve indigenous Third World investment reallocations designed to produce a needs-oriented development path.[22] Stress is placed upon the kinds of productive outputs needed to satisfy distributional minima for the poorer sectors of the population, as well as on activating demand from those who are now enduring severe levels of deprivation. The model demonstrates, essentially, that a needs-oriented, demand-pulled "engine of growth" is technically feasible when appropriate resource reallocations are made.

This formal demonstration that needs could be satisfied fulfills an educational function, as well as creates a political instrument of criticism and advocacy. The fact that the Argentinian government has withdrawn support from the Bariloche Foundation, evidently in reaction to the publication and widespread discussion of the model (with its implicit critique of GNP-maximation development strategies that tend to skew investment patterns in directions that perpetuate and even intensify income inequalities), is one indication that rigorous demonstrations of alternate development paths are politically threatening to the extent that they make a needs approach appear feasible.

. The technocratic, reactionary regimes in the South claim that their approaches to developmental choices possess "objectivity" and that the toleration of continued poverty is unavoidable for the present. Such approaches dismiss criticism calling for greater equity as sentimental or polemical or misguided. The Bariloche model, with its increasingly rigorous methodology, erodes these official claims to speak objectively and therefore helps to expose the ideological and class character of prevailing developmental policy. As such, it is naturally perceived as dangerous by ruling groups, as it weakens the legitimacy of governmental claims to be doing as well as possible on the most explosive of all issues in the South.

Such a drastic critique of prevailing policies cannot easily be dismissed as a Marxist effort to overthrow the existing order. Indeed, such model-building is often attacked by those who insist that Marxist categories of perception are the only adequate tools for understanding what is going on at the interface between economics and politics. In this regard, those who favor humane development patterns and yet are disillusioned by hardened ideological claims can take heart. The Bariloche approach seeks to create a knowledge base that can make it possible for policy-makers to shape developmental patterns in ways that meet the needs of the poor. However, the demonstration of economic feasibility should not be confused with demonstrations of political feasibility. The latter demonstration depends on understanding the basis of the governing coalition in a given country and the extent of discretion that exists among the leaders to alter the bases of support for that coalition within the bureaucracy and in relation to public opinion.

Coercive Transfers

OPEC, since 1973, has achieved a massive North-South transfer of resources without producing a war, although a rising level of threat occurred during the period of embargo. The bulk of these resources, however, have benefitted only a few countries. Most of the additional oil revenues have been recycled in the North and have been financing huge arms puchases to build up powerful military establishments in several oil-rich countries, especially Iran and Saudi Arabia. Such a use of the market mechanism to achieve rapid international *redistributive* outcomes is certainly effective, but it does not appear to be generalizable beyond oil, nor does it assure a contribution to international equity, as measured by human effects. Recycling of earnings in safe, productive sectors of the world economy is self-interested behavior by OPEC members. The diversion of resources to poor country economies would almost certainly lead to a global depression, provoking an atmosphere of crisis and danger, as well as depriving the oil producers of their best customers. The OPEC strategy is not, in any event, generalizable because oil has special properties. It is a critical resource for which no available substitute exists in sufficient quantities in the short-run. No other commodity is nearly as vital as oil, although some gains for the South can surely be achieved in other trading contexts by a concerted and intelligent assessment of the market.

It is not realistic to envision the OPEC-strategy as capable of solving the challenge of other disparities of poverty. It is true, however, that the radicalization of Iran and Saudi Arabia could make a sizeable difference in the international climate, possibly sufficiently reinforcing more militant overall demands for a new international economic order to make some genuine restructuring begin to happen.

Nevertheless, there is no reason to suppose that domestic radicalization will produce solid benefits for people other than those living within those state boundaries, although the reality of such benefits might stimulate revolutionary activity elsewhere. In essence, the secondary effects of coercive transfers (via resource cartels) are not likely unless the main militant governments themselves move toward socialism, which in itself is not a likely prospect for the immediate future, or unless, an even less likely prospect, the overall international economy is restructured along non-capitalist lines.

International Institutional Arrangements

There are some possibilities for wealth sharing that exist at the frontiers of technology. The mineral wealth of the ocean sea bed, for example, was for a time conceived to be a part of "the common heritage of mankind," which could be largely administered by international institutions. Most of the income derived could then be distributed according to equity criteria, giving resource-poor Third World countries a source of capital that came without strings or with an interventionary presence, provided only that the recipient governments were pursuing a development strategy of benefit to the society as a whole.

What is now apparent is that ocean idealism has been superseded by selfish pressures to divide up ocean wealth according to criteria of geopolitical clout, technological capability, and availability of venture capital. The expected result is that the richest and most powerful countries will acquire most of the economic benefits, either because a treaty arrangement favorable to their interest is negotiated, or because it isn't, and exploitation then proceeds on the basis of relatively unregulated competition.

Statist imperatives have been in the foreground of the ocean negotiations, exhibiting the extent to which each government seeks the best possible deal for its country regardless of effects on other less favored states. This kind of statism implies that there is no real prospect of getting a progressive distributive arrangement based on relative societal need, but that each state will bargain for its "fair share" based on its size, ingenuity, and capability. What becomes more important is that behind these governmental positions have been the special economic interests of the multinational corporations, which have pressured their particular governments to create investment incentives that include assurances that the lion's share of economic reward goes to developers.

Here again the main point is that the existing structures of power in global society will be generally reflected in the arrangements that are likely to emerge to govern ocean mineral wealth. Even new sources of wealth are not significantly subject to redistributive pressures. The idealism associated with such global negotiations is subordinated, in practice, to the persisting selfishness of governmental outlooks. This generalization includes the behavior of the Soviet Union (as well as its group of dependent socialist countries), which has taken a position similar to that of the United States on ocean minerals, and seeks an arrangement that will reward its superior developmental technology and its supportive polity. Although the South has so far resisted this solution, it has done so on behalf of Third World governments as a whole, rather than on behalf of equitable arrangements designed to channel profits from ocean mining to the governments of poor societies.

What is evident here is the same pattern that can be discerned everywhere—namely, the predominance of statism. There are small variations among governments as to the degree to which global interests are incorporated, but official behavior seems generally designed to maximize state interests and to conceive of international negotiations as interstate bargaining situations, rather than as a cooperative search for a global solution expressing human or planetary interests. Given the diffusion of state power associated with the spread of formal independence and with political and military capabilities, there are some international redistributive effects arising from statist logic, but the intranational impacts are barely discernible.

Multinational Corporate Globalism

In a recent full-page advertisement in the *New York Times,* an investment banking firm epitomized the new globalistic perspective of big business by a huge picture of electronic equipment dwarfed by four huge globes in the background. The caption read in bold letters: "THE ROOM IS NOW GLOBAL." Underneath was an explanation: "Why? Because the needs of the corporations, governments, and institutions we serve are now global."[23]

Beneath this public display lies the dynamic of corporate growth reinforced by electronic capabilities now available to manage operations spread around the globe almost as efficiently as if their geographical extent was confined to a single city. The particular pattern of interests varies from industrial sector to industrial sector, even from firm to firm. In some areas where the domestic market is being encroached upon by foreign competition there is a growth of economic nationalism in the form of protectionist sentiment. Occasionally, this position is advocated by a coalition of labor (fearing an export or loss of jobs) and management (fearing losses of domestic markets and profits).

Overall, the Multinational Corporations (MNCs) seek to deal with the world, or with as much of it as possible, as a single market. One tendency, evident in textiles and electronic assembly, is to locate productive facilities where taxes and labor costs are low and environmental regulations minimal. South Korea and Taiwan have been beneficiaries of such policies. It is alleged that the expansion of MNCs weaves a network of trade and investment interests that erode conflicts at the political level and make for a more peaceful world. IBM's motto expresses the wider MNC global ethos: "World Peace Through World Trade."

More relevant, however, are MNC claims that jobs, capital, and technology are being beneficially transferred to poor countries. Indeed, spokespeople for the MNC outlook applaud the noninterventionary contributions being made to economic growth throughout the Third World. Such a positive interpretation of MNC roles remains unconvincing. First of all, the beneficiaries of the MNC are a tiny proportion of the work force, who tend to be concentrated among the most skilled and already well-off workers. Second, in countries with mass poverty, MNC operations depend on the creation of stable political conditions, which often require a deliberate effort to eliminate drastic challenges from below. The search for "discipline" to reduce the economic costs of social uncertainty inevitably leads to the denial of human rights, to repression and to suppression of populist claims for redistribution, full employment, and the like.[24] Indochina, Argentina, Indonesia, the Philippines, and Thailand are among the countries that illustrate political solutions of a highly authoritarian character that can be explained, in part, by the priority their leadership attaches to attracting foreign capital (including loans from international financial institutions). At least for the short-run, this insistence upon discipline tends to mean that increased activity by MNCs is not likely to result in greater satisfaction of basic needs of poor peoples. Indeed, the bargaining leverage of the poor may be cut down by government policy to assure an attractive investment climate for MNCs and national capitalists.

Third, economic nationalism in the Third World may be a more important force than the benefits derived from MNC operations. The Brazilian government seems willing, during this present period of its history, to complicate the lives of MNCs so that it can fulfill nationalistic goals, including the reduction of foreign encroachment.

Fourth, the markets for MNC output have tended to concentrate on the goods that could be purchased by those people with disposable income, i.e., the middle classes. Necessities associated with nutrition, housing, health, and education are impossible to mass produce for profit when most potential customers lack purchasing power. As a consequence, most MNC production related to the domestic markets of Third World countries is associated with luxury items, thereby widening the consumption gap.

As matters now stand it is difficult to be positive about MNCs as agents of social change and reform. Their direct impact seems concentrated among favored strata of the population, and their generally unintended but definite influence is to encourage repressive tendencies by placing a premium on domestic stability. Such stability in a context of mass poverty tends to close off avenues of domestic reform for a long time. Also, the technological sophistication associated with MNC operations is often extended to police administration in these countries, although this "modernization" of law enforcement procedures may occur in the absence of MNCs. In any event, there is no positive example of a country where high levels of MNC operations have yielded dramatic distribution gains for the poorest sectors or where income disparities have narrowed. Even resource-rich Third World countries have adopted no policies designed to achieve domestic equity.

Domestic Radicalism in the South

Economic Achievements of Socialist Regimes. It seems correct to credit socialist governments in the Third World with substantial achievements, at least with respect to intranational equity. To the extent that resource capabilities exist, the basic needs of the population are met, and internal disparities reduced. External penetration is reduced as well, either by way of corporate behavior or by foreign governments, and economic structures of self-reliance are generated. The tradeoffs have involved relinquishing political diversity, as socialist governments in the Third World have severely inhibited oppositional politics of every variety. Bureaucratic elites have also emerged, threatening to evolve into "a new class" and give rise to domestic disparities. Despite these difficulties, the economic achievements of China, Cuba, and Vietnam suggest that the material needs of Third World populations can be rapidly and substantively satisfied by socialist regimes.

Lessons of the Allende Experience. These socialist success stories, however, have all involved triumphant revolutionary movements in a position to reshape the apparatus of state power after a prolonged armed struggle. The contrary experience of the Allende period in Chile (1970–1973), and possibly of Portugal since 1974, confirms the previous observation. A mandate for structural reform—to shift income to the poor and to orient economic planning around needs—engenders resistance from a state bureaucracy dominated by military officers and civil servants wedded to the old order. Such resistance makes it difficult, if not impossible, to carry out a program of domestic reform in an effective manner.

This resistance poses a serious dilemma for a progressive leadership that does not have its own people in dominant positions throughout the state bureaucracy. If the program can be blocked by hostile forces within the official hierarchy, then it can be discredited as "incompetent"; on the other hand, if the program is effective despite resistance, then counterrevolutionary forces are mobilized. Allende's experience involved a mixture of these elements: strong bureaucratic resistance, considerable popular success despite obstacles, and a counterrevolutionary takeover justified by the alleged incompetence of Allende's government and necessitated by its persisting popularity, which evidently was understood to mean that it was unlikely that Allende could be unseated by constitutional means.

External factors, of course, reinforced this pattern. The United States Government, via the Central Intelligence Agency (CIA) and other intelligence agencies, mounted a campaign of "destabilization" designed to foster an impression of incompetence on the part of the Chilean government. The powerful MNCs, especially International Telephone & Telegraph (ITT), did their best to keep Allende from power and then harassed the government during his tenure. Furthermore, by means of CIA actions and a variety of intergovernmental military relationships, the United States maintained contact with and gave encouragement to the counterrevolutionary leadership in Chile. It remains difficult as yet to assess the cumulative effect of the U.S. role in this period. Pressure was also successfully used at American initiative to deny Allende the benefit of loans and credits from international financial institutions, including the World Bank. These institutions are dominated by OECD capital and voting power, lack any countervailing socialist participation, and, therefore, tend to resist any kind of radical redistributive policy by a national government despite the degree to which such policy does what virtually everyone says is desirable.

A final factor involved the failure of the Soviet Union to take protective action on behalf of Allende to offset the effects of American pressure. Soviet motivation is difficult to fathom, but some speculations are possible. One interpretation suggests that the Soviet expense of offsetting American economic pressure on Cuba may have been as much as the Kremlin was willing to accept for the sake of securing "friendly" governments in Latin America. Another view maintains that Allende was "a Marxist" rather than "a Communist" and, consequently, was not sufficiently deferential to Moscow to engender Soviet support. Finally, détente may have been a factor, especially when considered together with the deference the superpowers had been giving to each other's spheres of influence. Soviet leaders may have regarded Chile as within the American sphere and that serious pro-Allende support would have destroyed détente and its related economic relations.

Whatever the causal sequence accounting for Allende's bloody downfall and the harsh military rule that has befallen Chilean society since 1973, it has tended to reinforce the Leninists' insistence that socialism cannot be introduced except as a sequel to a prior armed struggle. This realization is a grave setback for those social forces in the Third World seeking a nonviolent path to a socialist political economy.

Cultural Revolution in the North

Together with the notion of helping the South is a new and quite autonomous appreciation that the North itself is suffering from a mixture of pressures that have been provocatively labelled "overdevelopment." Such a term suggests that the alienating and dangerous character of postindustrial civilization is to be partly associated with unchecked technological momentum. In effect, the argument is that above a certain threshold of affluence, "more means worse."

Disintegrating Impact of "Overdevelopment." The idea of "overdevelopment" is vague and needs some elaboration. The notion derives from the realization that the food we eat, the air we breath, the water we drink, and the lives we lead are contaminating our bodies and spirits in ways we have yet to understand. A recent scholarly paper concludes that malnutrition from affluent diets is taking almost as great a toll in life expectancy as do protein deficient diets.[25] Along similar lines, a report concludes that at least one of four industrial workers in the United States is exposed, without precaution to hazardous disease-producing conditions as part of routine work.[26] A great deal more than physical health is at stake, however. There are numerous signs of the breakdown of values, institutions, and morale. These signs include the weakening of family ties, the corruption and incompetence of government, the rise of crime, incredible rates of hard drug use, the loss of neighborliness and community sentiments, and widespread evidence of despair and alienation. It is an extraordinary commentary on the breakdown of civility to note that the richest cities in the richest countries are the most dangerous for the unwary.

Overdevelopment, of course, is compatible, especially in the United States, with deep pockets of poverty, as well as with high levels of unemployment, specifically among minority youths in the cities. Serious deficiencies associated with race, region, and class persist in most so-called rich countries. These rich polities, as an aggregate, nevertheless waste resources in large quantities on fashions, luxury consumption, planned obsolescence, and weapons. This waste by the rich occurs during a period of rising consciousness about satisfying basic needs and, more keenly, at a time of an emerging concern about "limits to growth," not necessarily mechanical limits but limits to destructive forms of growth and their environmental effects.

Ecological Ethos—A Rising Social Force. The ecological ethos—a measure of deference to nature—is a rising social force, especially in Western Europe, where green, not red, is becoming the color of radical politics. Its potency is revealed by the expansion of a militant antinuclear movement throughout the democratic societies of the industrial world. This movement gains support from many sources, but its principal strength arises from the conviction that official institutions are no longer to be trusted with the protection of human interest, especially where fundamental issues of choice and risk are concerned.

In the nuclear context, many people seem prepared to forego, perhaps eagerly, additional energy in exchange for a healthier, more humane environment. The prospects of economic growth are no longer as tantalizing as they once were to large numbers of people, especially if the cost is reliance on technologies that are serious health hazards and that result in further centralization of economic and political activities. On a scale less spectacular than the antinuclear movement is the rising resistance throughout the West to dams, highways, and bridges, which reflects a growing skepticism about the benefits of progress defined in overly materialistic terms.

This skepticism has even penetrated official institutions to varying degrees in different countries, although the dominant consensus in these institutions emphasizes the management of environmental concerns in a fashion that is consistent with rapid domestic growth. A bigger pie—and not a more equitably distributed or more stable pie—remains the major premise of economic policy in every society where the quest for profits and higher aggregate production structures are accepted goals. This growth bias is especially strong in recent years because profits and net output must be sustained in an atmosphere of sharply escalating costs.

In the background of overdevelopment thinking lie varying degrees of guilt or anxiety about the annual allocation of world resources. One assessment suggests that 85 percent of the world's resources is being used each year for the benefit of less than 20 percent of the world's population; the people who comprise this 20 percent are mainly white Northerners.[27] The overdevelopment prescription adopts the inverse view of "the mutual gain" perspective of liberal internationalists. It suggests that the rich should cut back on their use of scarce resources and allow the poorer countries to have a larger share. This outlook would require drastic changes in domestic economic policies and new trade and monetary relations to become operative without inducing severe disruption. It is not an immediately practical alternative. Nevertheless, the overdevelopment outlook is increasingly endorsed by those who seek an economics with a humane and an ecological face.

Skepticism Toward Scientific Rationalism. The values challenge directed at current affluence patterns is also expressed in affirmative ways. There is a remarkable surge of interest in spiritual possibilities of all kinds, bearing witness, I think, to a widespread refusal to accept the reign of scientific rationalism. Science and technology are generating the kind of skeptical reaction that had been directed toward religion in earlier generations. The interest in Eastern religions and practices throughout the West expresses, also, a demand for a deeper religious experience than is currently available in most established religious institutions. This spiritual impulse has been complemented by a variety of questionings directed at the viability of affluent life styles based upon mainstream careerism. There is an immense growth in various modes of "voluntary simplicity" in these parts of the world, especially in the United States. In these cultural gropings there is much that is faddish, immature, and quixotic, but there is also impressive evidence of serious quests for more satisfying and more suitable new cultural forms.[28]

A relevant line of conjecture goes as follows: if voluntary simplic
ity grows in scope and depth, becomes politically potent via its role in
consumer and antinuclear causes, then it may create a new normative
climate for political leadership. In this new climate territorial boundaries may come to mean less than what one author has called "earth-
manship."[29] Whether such a drastic shift of consciousness can emerge
without violent convulsions is, of course, problematic. Recent descriptions of antinuclear activity in Europe suggest, for instance, a pattern
of intensifying violence. Last summer at a large demonstration in
France, one protester was killed and several others maimed by highly
armed national guard security forces. There appears to be an escalating cycle of militance in the confrontation between the state and its
opponents on these issues of technological choice.[30]

Shifts in Life Styles and Religious Outlook Could Make a Difference. In
essence, then, shifts in life style in the North could cut domestic disparities as well as make a greater proportion of global resources available for the satisfaction of basic needs of other societies, provided, of
course, that viable ways to sustain the world economy are found. For
such a movement to succeed, it would have to draw upon spiritual
energies that reformulate the conditions of happiness and development, to include the satisfactions of simplicity.[31] The positive
character of this conception would have to prevail against the whole
mobilization and manipulation of highly individualized tastes based
upon the accumulation of goods, high style and fashion, and the
identification of success with luxurious living. The rise of such alternative life styles would have to displace the widely held presumption
that virtually all sensible people seek to enjoy the energy-intensive
middle class life style associated with the United States. As one influential commentator puts it, "Attainment of middle-class style of life
is what constitutes development in countries as widely separated geographically and ideologically as Brazil and USSR."[32] It would require
a reversal of the prevailing policy-makers' view that Brazilians on the
whole are better off than, say, the Chinese, or more aptly, to entertain
the possibility that the Chinese model of development, if perfected,
might do more to satisfy the total needs of people than can the perfec-
tion of the Brazilian model. The value shift, in effect, would depend
upon "less being better," provided "less" is enough to satisfy basic
needs, and that the nonmaterial benefits of community solidarity,
socialist consciousness, and equality were made available and widely
dispersed.[33]

It is difficult to determine the strength and durability of these
tendencies toward voluntary simplicity and associated spirituality. To

influence the overall economic condition of the world such tendencies would have to evolve much further and begin to influence policy-making on global economic issues. Such an impact cannot be expected for another several decades, although it is worth noting that the late E. F. Schumacher built a large following for ideas associated with decentralization, simplicity, and appropriate technology. Influential political leaders, at least privately, have indicated an appreciation for his kind of approach. It is also relevant that Schumacher's position and influence was infused by a deeply held religious outlook that seems organically related to the radical view of development that he espoused.

A PERSPECTIVE ON TRANSFORMATION: SOME TENTATIVE COMMENTS

Perhaps more than social science or even fiction, children's literature has the clearest and most direct insight into the present situation. A familiar theme in recent children's books is the restoration of the earth after it has been plundered by human activity.

The Earth Belongs to Everyone

One such story, called *Dinosaurs And All That Rubbish,* tells of a man who caused great ruin on earth so that he might have a rocket built for a visit to another planet. After he leaves a totally polluted planet behind, some dinosaurs, sleeping for ages underneath the earth, awake and fix things up so that landscapes become green again. The man in his rocket, in the meantime, discovers that the distant star of his dreams is barren, so he looks elsewhere. He finds, finally, a planet that is green and beautiful and is astonished to discover that this beautiful habitat is the same earth that he had abandoned in disgust. He pleads, then, with the dinosaurs to be allowed to have some land to live on:

"Please may I have a small part of it back?" he asked. "Please, just a hill, or a tree, or a flower?"

And here is how the dinosaur responds:

"No," said the dinosaur.
"Not a part of it,

but all of it.
It is all yours
but it is also mine.
Remember that.
This time the earth belongs to everyone,
not parts of it to certain people
but all of it to everyone,
to be enjoyed
and cared for."[34]

It is worth noticing that this nonterritorial conception of using the earth—having it all and yet of owning no part of it—is a reversal of prevalent attitudes and arrangements.

Tinkering Is Not Enough

No amount of tinkering can fix up the present international system. Too many fundamental pressures exist: continuing demographic pressures (increasing population and even more rapidly increasing urbanization), increasing destructiveness and instability of the weapons environment, waste of economic resources to fuel the arms race and to sustain affluent life-styles, sterility of an economistic vision that identifies progress with material growth and societal fulfillment with entry into the middle classes, moral backwardness of an overall economic and political system that imposes "order" rather than orients investment and production around the satisfaction of basic needs, and short-sightedness of growth patterns that are not ecologically sustainable. These interrelated pressures are cumulative, and their eventual impact could inflict irreversible damage, foreclosing future options. The logic that controls the state system is no longer tolerable. It is too dangerous, wasteful, and stultifying. It inhibits the sort of economic, political, and cultural development that fulfills individual and collective potentialities at various stages of industrialization.

In these respects even the reorientation of national political consciousness can only be understood as transitional, generating dangerous, provocative confrontations between social forces. The efforts of governments to opt for basic needs generally collides with the interests of those who currently manage the international economic and political system. Neither Castro nor Allende, for instance, have had an easy time in the western hemisphere, and similarly, those who challenge entrenched interests in the postindustrial states are being met with violence and coercion. There is, for instance, a peaceful movement in the Seattle area of the United States to prevent construction of a large submarine facility for the Trident Submarine, on the basis of substantial evidence that it has been conceived by its designers as a first-strike weapons system.[35] The response of governing bodies has not been to reexamine or even to justify its commitment to weapons that appear to make nuclear war more likely, but to put the protesters in jail for increasingly long terms.

In the OECD world the emergent heroes are those who resist the bland assumptions that we can go on with nuclear power and weapons as if they are benign and inevitable ingredients of human destiny. The refusal to accept such a reality constitutes the center of a movement for transformation in the most affluent countries just as the movement for economic and social equity and against various forms of imperialism constitutes the center of movements for transformation in the Third World.

It is also noteworthy that the convergence of these tendencies is beginning to be evident. Members of the Pacific Life Community, who have led the drive against the Trident, adhere by choice to a life style based on voluntary simplicity, so that their lives will not be in conflict with patterns of living that are, in principle, possible for everyone else on the planet. They also insist upon the wholeness and unity of the species, and self-consciously ignore the boundary between Canada and the United States, soliciting Canadians to take part in activities on American territory as "planetary citizens." Every person has a stake in preventing nuclear war, although Canadians may have a special stake in preventing a Trident base so close to their homes. In striking contrast is the highly territorial response of the governor of the state of Washington, who has publicly warned Canadians to mind their own business, as if the dangers of nuclear war could be cordoned off on the basis of national boundaries.

Main Elements of a Transformative Vision

The main elements of a transformative vision of the future are implicit in what has been written above:

Solidarity—the sense of vital concern about the human species as a focus of emergent loyalty;

Unity—the shared and unified destiny of the planet;

Space—the nonterritorial circumference of human concerns;

Time—the extension of human concerns in time to the ancient past and to the most distant future;

Nature—the experience of nature as encompassing, inspiring, and sustaining;

Peace—the renunciation of violence as the collective basis of security and innovation;

Progress—the gradual realization of human potentialities for joy and creativity in all dimensions of individual and collective existence;

Humility—the awareness of limits applicable to human endeavor, including an understanding that human society should not proceed with certain lines of scientific investigation and technological innovation; and

Spirituality—the understanding that awe and mystery are as integral to human experience as bread and reason.

In effect, this set of criteria could be espoused on a high enough level of abstraction by virtually anyone, even today. Indeed, even those in positions of significant power in the existing system with its contrary attributes might endorse quite sincerely many of these transformative elements. It is the degree of embodiment that makes all the difference! Nominal or ritual embodiment is possible and is possibly self-deceptive in a damaging way. Power-wielders often seem quiet and serene, even while engaged in destructive activities, because they do not perceive the tension between what they believe and what they do. Part of human adaptability, which has especially high social costs in periods of fundamental challenge, is to disguise contradictions between actions and ideals.

Internalizing a Religious Perspective

The position outlined above makes a radical claim; namely, that the future prospects of the human species depend upon internalizing an essentially religious perspective sufficiently to transform secular outlooks that now dominate the destiny of the planet. Any prudent calculator of probabilities would, of course, heap scorn on this eventuality, and yet, oddly enough it seems more "utopian" to suppose that we can persist on our crowded, depleted, militarized planet inhabited by many who are miserable, some who are desperate, and most who are scared. Any genuine, hard-headed "rationalist," respectful of evidence and trends, would become a "doomsday prophet." Hope that is not just an unconvincing expectation of a series of technological "miracles," depends now more than ever on renourishing religious sensibilities.

In the short term it is difficult to assess under what conditions and in what form a religious perspective, as integral to the discharge of official functions, allows a power-wielder to advance human values more effectively. The resistances seem too formidable. The overriding necessities of wielding power in the current global setting, especially in major states, require levels of moral insensitivity that are of a monumental character, including a willingness to endorse the use of weapons of mass destruction, to entertain and honor dictators who torture their opponents, to rely on industrial processes that endanger workers and environments, to protect dubious investments and sources of critical raw materials, and to orient policy around short-term horizons of expectations. It seems impossible, then, for a religious perspective associated with the values we have set forth to flourish within current realms of secular power.[36]

In addition to this, religious spokespeople may actually play a regressive role in social issues—on the status of women, for instance. A grotesque interaction of secular and religious sensibilities occurred in Somalia two years ago. The government sought to emancipate women from various forms of bondage and was opposed by traditional religious leaders citing the Qur'an as their authority. To demonstrate that it meant business, the government rounded up eleven religious leaders actively working against equality for women one morning and executed them later the same day.[37]

Purely Humanistic Positions Cannot Engender Transformative Vision

It is not necessary to be "religious" (in either the formal or existential sense) to have an impulse to do better, to be more ethical, and to be more empathetic. Such a platform of reform may seem fully consistent with a secular search for stability in the short run, and hence very practical, or it may be appealing mainly for idealistic reasons. And it is obvious that humanism can be accepted by individuals who have no confidence at all in the wider realities of religious affirmation. But such purely humanistic positions cannot, in my view, engender the vision or the hope required to build toward transformation; and secularist thinking will never extend social contracts (for the present) to covenantal arrangements (for the future).[38]

NOTES

1. A strong argument along these lines is in the Club of Rome study by Ervin Laszlo et al., *Goals for Mankind* (New York: E.P. Dutton, 1977), especially pp. 367–424.

2. See Fouad Ajami, "The Global Populists: Third-World Nations and World-Order Crises," Research Monograph No. 41 (Princeton University, Center of International Studies, May 1974).

3. For a fuller depiction of the organizational consequences of this mixture of

centralizing functional requirements and decentralizing human requirements, see chapter IV in Richard Falk, *A Study of Future Worlds* (New York: Free Press, 1975), pp. 224-276.

4. "The costs to the poorest 40 percent of the population in many countries that followed this *'trickle-down'* strategy have now become clear. Not only have their relative incomes and standards of living decreased, sometimes markedly, but there is considerable evidence to suggest that the *absolute incomes of the bottom 10-20 percent may also have fallen.*" (emphasis in original). James Grant and Mahbub ul Haq. "Income Redistribution and the International Financing of Development," Annex 2, in Jan Tinbergen, coordinator, *Reshaping the International Order (RIO)* (New York: E.P. Dutton, 1976).

5. On what needs to be done see, among others, Marc Nerfin's preface and Rodolfo Stavenhagen's chapter in Marc Nerfin, ed., *Another Development* (Uppsala: Sweden, Dag Hammarskjöld Foundation, 1977), and Dieter Senghaas, "If You Can't Keep Us with the Rich, Keep Away," in *Forum of Committee of Correspondence* 9, no. 1 (September 1977): VI–143—VI–145.

6. For a clear explanation of the focus on needs and the distinction between the positive stress of a basic needs approach and the negative stress of a poverty reduction approach see Graciela Chichilnisky, "Development, Basic Needs, and the Future of the International Order," mimeographed, (New York, 1977) pp. 1–7.

7. For the text of Carter's speech, see the *New York Times*, May 23, 1977, p. 12.

8. Julius Nyerere, "The Economic Challenge: Dialogue or Confrontation?" *International Development Review* 1 (1976): 3.

9. Amon J. Nsekela, "The World Bank and the New International Order," *Development Dialogue* 1 (1977): 75–76.

10. Ibid., p. 78.

11. The terminology for generalization about rich and poor countries is woefully inadequate. I refer to poor countries as Third World and Southern as generalizations, in some respects deceptive, realizing full well that very diverse countries are caught within the net, including rich countries, especially the OPEC members. And for rich countries, with similar caveats, I use the notion Northern, and refer to the market economies of the North as OECD countries.

12. The issue was posed in this way by Samir Amin, "Self-Reliance and the New International Economic Order," *Monthly Review,* July/August 1977, pp. 1–21, especially pp. 2–3.

13. For the text of the Communiqué of the Economic Summit Meeting, see the *New York Times,* May 9, 1977, p. 12.

14. Such a position is comprehensively depicted in Richard Cooper, "A New International Economic Order for Mutual Gain," *Foreign Policy* 26 (spring 1977): 66–122.

15. Peter Bauer and John O'Sullivan, "Ordering the World About: The NIEO," *Policy Review* 1 (summer 1977): 57–58.

16. Barbara Ward, "Seeking a Planetary Bargain," *International Development Review* 2 (1977): 34.

17. For data and argument along these lines see Stavenhagen's chapter in Nerfin ed., *Another Development* pp. 40–65, especially 40–47.

18. As Professor Lewis argues, emphasis on agricultural development is the key

to economic autonomy. See, in general, W. Arthur Lewis, "The Evolution of the International Economic Order," Princeton University, Research Program in Development Studies, Discussion Paper No. 74, March 1977, pp. 1–60, especially 53–60. See also Samir Amin, "Self-Reliance and the New International Economic Order," *Monthly Review* 29 (July–August 1977): 1–21.

19. Roger Hansen, "Major U.S. Options on North-South Relations: A Letter to President Carter," in John Sewell et al., *The United States and World Development: Agenda 1977* (Washington, D.C.: Overseas Development Council, 1977), pp. 67–69. These figures are specified in greater detail in Mahbub ul Haq, *The Poverty Curtain* (New York: Columbia University Press, 1976), Statistical Annex, Table 5, p. 229.

20. Hansen, "Major U.S. Options on North-South Relations," p. 68.

21. Fernando Henrique Cardoso, in Nerfin, ed., *Another Development* p. 23.

22. For an explication of the model, see Chichilnisky, "Development, Basic Needs, and the Future of International Order" (mimeographed paper, 1980).

23. *New York Times*, Oct. 3, 1977, p. 48.

24. For lucid argument along these lines, see Sylvia Ann Hewlett, "Human Rights and Economic Realities: Tradeoffs in Historical Perspective," mimeographed paper (New York, 1977).

25. Erik Ekholm and Frank Record, "The Two Faces of Malnutrition," World Watch Paper No. 9 (Washington, D.C., Dec. 1976), pp. 1–63.

26. Report of an official government survey, *New York Times*, Oct. 3, 1977, pp. 1, 22.

27. Chichilnisky, "Development, Basic Needs, and the Future of International Order," p. 5.

28. On "voluntary simplicity," see Duane S. Elgin and Arnold Mitchell, "Voluntary Simplicity: Life Style of the Future" *The Futurist*, August 1977, pp. 200–209, 254–261. In general, see T. Roszak, *The Unfinished Animal* (New York: Harper and Row, 1976).

29. See G. Tyler Miller, Jr., *Living in the Environment: Concepts, Problems, Alternatives* (Belmont, Calif.: Wadsworth, 1975), pp. 29–30, 326–330.

30. Anna Gyorgy, "France Kills its First Protester," *The Nation*, October 8, 1977, pp. 330–333; William Sweet, "The Opposition to Nuclear Power in Europe," *Bulletin of the Atomic Scientists* 33 (December 1977): 40–47.

31. Johan Galtung sets forward some suggestive ideas in an essay entitled "Alternative Life Styles in Rich Societies," in Nerfin, *Another Development*, pp. 106–121.

32. Nathan Keyfitz, "World Resources and the World Middle Class," *Scientific American*, 235 (July 1976): 28–35. Professor Keyfitz builds his analysis around the presumed superiority of a middle class society, whatever its other features, contending that if resources limit access then, "The Chinese rather than the British-Russian pattern of development may be what people will have to settle for." (p. 28).

33. Evidence that there are value shifts along these lines is scrupulously and impressively presented in Ronald Inglehart, *The Silent Revolution: Changing Values and Political Styles Among Western Publics*, (Princeton: Princeton University Press, 1977).

34. Michael Foreman, *Dinosaurs and All That Rubbish* (New York: Thomas Crowell, 1972), pp. 26–27.

35. For an account by a leading participant see Shelley Douglass, "Bangor Summer Reflection," *Year One*, III (September 1977): 12–14.

36. A religious perspective can inform almost any political undertaking, often lending it an aura of certitude that vindicates the most extreme and brutal behavior. We are using "religious" in a more restricted way associated with ideals that are shared by the great religions of the world.

37. Bauer and O'Sullivan, "Ordering the World About," p. 55, use this incident to support their central conclusion, "that the liberal ideas and phraseology of the West, once transported to the Third World, often assume fantastic and distorted forms." I question such an interpretation, and regard it, instead, as a clash between two indigenous approaches to well-being resolved in a manner that discloses the consequences of the failure to curb state power. These failures should not be associated mainly with Third World countries. See, for instance, the Soviet state vis-à-vis its own people; the U.S. vis-à-vis the Vietnamese.

38. The distinction between "contract" and "covenant" is attributed to Richard Neuhaus in Samuel Hux, "The Holocaust and the Survival of Tragedy," in *Worldview*, October 1977, p. 7.

PART FIVE

Normative Horizons

CHAPTER 12

Anarchism and World Order

Mere anarchy is loosed upon the world.
W. B. Yeats
"The Second Coming"

We do not fear anarchy, we invoke it.
Mikhail Bakunin
The Program of the International Brotherhood

AN INTRODUCTORY PERSPECTIVE

Anarchism has largely directed its thought and actions against the sovereign states, seeking primarily to bring about the radical reconstruction of economic, political, and social life in individual domestic arenas. However, like any radical movement that challenges fundamental organizing norms and structures, anarchism has wider implications. These wider implications extend the critique of the state as domestic institutional nexus to a critique of statism or the state system as a global framework for political organization. Nevertheless, surprisingly little attention has been given to anarchism as a perspective relevant to global reform.[1] This neglect is somewhat surprising because anarchists generally appreciate the extent to which their goals can be realized only by the transformation of the world scene as a whole.

This lack of attention can, however, be explained by several factors. First, it reflects the previously noted domestic focus of anarchism—indeed, of all modern revolutionary theory. Second, it probably reflects the popular association of anarchy with disorder, while by almost everyone's definition, disorder is precisely the opposite of the primary desideratum of global reform—namely, a quantum leap in the capacities to maintain order. Even an antistatist, progressive thinker like Doris Lessing seems to associate anarchistic potentialities with our present civilization, and to connect the declining capacities of governments to sustain elementary order and reliability even within national boundaries with still further disintegration.[2] This identification of anarchism with disarray is juxtaposed with a generally accepted conviction that global reform will entail the globalization of governmental structures rather than the destructuring of national governments. The League of Nations and the United Nations are generally viewed as positive experiments to the extent that they have constituted tentative steps toward world government and as failures because they have represented too little by way of bureaucratic centralism.[3] Alternatively, an anarchist might hold that the League and the United Nations present suitable pretexts for partially dismantling bureaucratic structures at the state level *without* building up a superstate to compensate at the global level. In other words, it is the weakness of global institutions as bureaucratic presences that would appeal to anarchists. (Of course, in actuality, these global institutions, both in their mode of creation and in their mode of operations, have proven to be elitist in the extreme and therefore antithetical to the anarchist ethos.)[4]

Third, there is a lingering tendency, given plausibility by the pervasiveness of nongovernmental terror in contemporary life, to dismiss anarchism on moral grounds as a more or less explicit avowal of terrorism, and on political grounds as an absurdly romantic gesture of nihilistic sentiment whose only consequence is to strengthen the case for governmental repression. The belief that anarchists glorify terror has historical roots in the nineteenth century, especially in Russia, and was given widespread currency in Dostoevski's great novel *The Devils,* which re-created in fictional form the actual nihilism of Nechayev, an extremist follower of Bakunin.

Jean-Paul Sartre has for this reason, until very recently, avoided acknowledging his own anarchist affinity: "Then, by way of philosophy, I discovered the anarchist being in me. But when I discovered it I did not call it that, because today's anarchy no longer has anything to do with the anarchy of 1890."[5]

True, one form of individual resistance to state power is the use of random violence by self-styled anarchist revolutionaries for the avowed purpose of exposing the vulnerability of individuals or of the community as a whole. It is no accident that antibureaucratic radicals identify with anarchism as a means of registering their dissent from the prevailing forms of state socialism; typical in this regard was the unfurling of black flags from Sorbonne buildings liberated during the student uprisings of May 1968.[6] However, terrorism bears no inherent relationship to anarchist thinking; many pacifists, including Tolstoy, Gandhi, and Paul Goodman, have been associated with anarchist traditions of thought.[7]

Conversely, the mere adoption of terrorist tactics does not necessarily imply a disavowal of statist goals, as witness the manifold examples of terrorism by contemporary "liberation groups." The Palestinian Liberation Organization, consumed by statist objectives, has embraced indiscriminate terror for apparently expediential reasons: to get a hearing for its grievances and to give its claims a potency allegedly unattainable through less extreme forms of persuasion or even through conventional warfare. Terrorism is a desperate strategy of a powerless (or unimaginative) claimant, but it is not a necessary component of the anarchist perspective.[8]

In this chapter, the anarchist position is characterized mainly by its opposition to bureaucratic centralism of all forms and by its advocacy of libertarian socialism. This attempt to delineate the anarchist position is less extreme than the dictionary definition of anarchism as the absence of government. My understanding of anarchist thought, admittedly a personal interpretation, suggests that the basic anarchist impulse is toward something positive, namely, toward a minimal governing structure in a setting that encourages the full realization of human potentialities for cooperation and happiness. As such, the quest is for humane government, with a corresponding rejection of large-scale impersonal institutions that accord priority to efficiency and rely upon force and intimidation rather than upon voluntary patterns of cooperation to sustain order. This quest puts the anarchist into a posture of opposition to the modern state, especially the most successful and powerful states, but only the most extreme examples of anarchist thought devote their main energy to negation rather than to an affirmative case for radical reform on all levels of social, economic, and political organization.

On this basis, I believe that the anarchist tradition has something important to contribute to the emergent dialogue on the tactics and shape of global reform. This contribution must be predicated on a response to each of the three issues just considered. In effect, (1) an anarchistic concept of global reform needs to be fully worked out; (2) anarchistic ideas on "security" and "organization" must be set forth; (3) anarchistic thinking on the relevance of violence must be clarified in relation to its practical and moral consequences. This paper seeks to take tentative constructive steps in these directions, after first considering two additional preliminary issues:

• What kind of "a vision" do anarchists propose for the future?

• Why is anarchy an attractive antidote (or complement) to main-stream thinking on global reform?

In a perceptive essay on the full sweep of anarchistic thought, Irving Louis Horowitz observed that "it scarcely requires any feats of mind to show that modern industrial life is incompatible with the anarchist demand for the liquidation of State authority. Anarchism can be no more than a posture. It cannot be a viable political position."[9] The validity of such an assertion depends on what is meant by "modern industrial life" and by "the anarchist demand for the liquidation of State authority." For example, representatives from many and diverse disciplines now contend, independent of any concern with statist organization, that the modern industrial ethos as we have known it is not sustainable on ecological grounds.[10] The revival of interest in "benign" or "gentle" technology and of lifestyles outside the money economy provide further evidence that the momentum of industrial civilization may possibly be reversible.[11]

Indeed, one could reverse Horowitz's assertion and argue that any political perspective that does not propose doing away with modern industrial life is doomed to failure and futility and is an exercise in bad faith. Furthermore, the anarchists' demand is not directed at eliminating all forms of authority in human existence, but at their destructive embodiment in exploitative institutions associated with the modern bureaucratic state. Contrary to general impressions, nothing in anarchists' thought precludes a minimum institutional presence at all levels of social organization, provided only that this presence emanates from *populist* rather than *elitist* elements, and that its structure is deliberately designed fully to protect the liberty of all participants, starting with and centering on the individual. Indeed Bakunin, with his admiration of American federalism of the nineteenth century and his tentative advocacy of a universal confederation of peoples, lent anarchist support to the globalist approach to world order challenges.[12] As Bakunin put it in 1866: "It is absolutely necessary for any country wishing to join the free federations of peoples to replace its centralized, bureaucratic, and military organizations by a federalist organization based on the absolute liberty and autonomy of regions, provinces, communes, associations, and individuals."[13] In essence, the anarchist proposes dismantling the bureaucratic state and reconstituting a world society from the bottom up (what Bakunin calls a "universal world federation" and "directed from the bottom up, from the circumference to the center"), with constant accountability to the bottom. Paul Goodman has expressed in a modern idiom this anarchistic view of creative reordering: "My own bias is to decentralize and localize wherever it is feasible, because this makes for alternatives and more vivid and intimate life. . . . On this basis of weakening of the Powers, and of the substitution of function for power, it would be possible also to organize the world community, as by the functional agencies of the United Nations, UN-ICEF, WHO, somewhat UNESCO; and to provide *ad hoc* cooperation like the Geo-physical Year, exploring space, or feeding the Chinese."[14] Furthermore, anarchistic thinking has a notable antiterritorial bias which tends to condemn national frontiers as artificial and dangerously inconsistent with the wholeness of its humanist affirmations.[15]

But reverting to Horowitz's characterization once again, doesn't such an anarchist approach to global reform lie far beyond the horizon of attainability? And hence, how can anarchism reasonably be regarded as a viable possibility that could materialize in our lifetime? One could answer these questions in several ways. To quote Bakunin once more, as he is discounting the failures of the revolutionary uprisings of 1848 in Europe,

Must we . . . doubt the future itself, and the present strength of socialism? Christianity, which had set as its goal the creation of the kingdom of justice in heaven, needed several centuries to triumph in Europe. Is there any cause for surprise if socialism, which has set for itself a more difficult problem, that of creating the kingdom of justice on earth, has not triumphed in a few years?[16]

In this view, the anarchist's position is no less coherent or relevant merely because its prospects of realization are not proximate. Bureaucratic socialists, those who seek to seize state power rather than to deconstruct it, contemptuously dismiss anarchistic or libertarian socialists as utopians or, worse, as reactionaries.[17] But the anarchist's response is more credible than the challenge presented. The anarchist quite properly contends that merely to seize power is to default upon the humanist content of socialism and to create a new form of despotism. The real revolution cannot be rushed, but neither can it be dispensed with. I think, in this regard, that Herbert Read is wrong when he says of anarchism that "if the conception of society which it thus arrives at seems utopian and even chimerical, it does not matter, for what is established by right reasoning cannot be surrendered to expediency."[18] I think it does matter, and anarchists generally act as if it matters, both by their arguments about the cooperative capacities of human society (which, incidentally, Read strongly endorses) and by their belief in the revolutionary possibility lying dormant within mass consciousness. Of course, Read correctly stresses the principled character of anarchistic thinking, its unwillingness to corrupt its values merely for the sake of power. This high-mindedness distinguishes anarchism from bureaucratic socialism in theory and vindicates its ethical purity in practice. The contrast seems particularly great in view of the consistent betrayal of socialist ideals at each new opportunity—not only in the Soviet Union but even in China and Cuba.[19] In this regard, the anarchist refuses both the facile radicalism of the conventional Marxist (who would merely replace one form of exploitation and repression with another) and the facile gradualism of the liberal (who would acquiesce in the structure of exploitation and repression, provided its cruelest manifestations can be gradually diminished).

A further anarchist response to the counsel of patience claims that the revolutionary possibility is hidden from view in the evolving currents of popular consciousness. According to Bakunin, revolutions "make themselves; they are produced by the force of circumstance, the movement of facts and events. They receive a long preparation of the masses, then they burst forth, often seemingly triggered by trivial causes."[20] Thus, the revolutionary moment may be closer than we think; it may be building toward eruption; and it may enter the field of history with unexpected haste and fury. The Paris Commune of 1871 is a favorite illustration of this possibility.[21] A time of crisis enhances revolutionary prospects; it creates receptivity to new ideas, however radical; it exposes existing injustice; and it generates a willingness to take risks. Naturally, however, there is no available calculus for determining the most propitious moment for actually instituting an anarchist program of destructuring the state and replacing international statism with global confederation.

Finally, the anarchist is not obliged to wait for the days of triumph. Although his concept of the future is visionary and vital to his position, it is not detached from present possibilities for actualization.[22] As Howard Zinn writes, "The anarchist sees revolutionary change as something immediate, something we must do now, where we are, where we live, where we work. It means starting this moment to do away with authoritarian, cruel relationships—between men and women, between children and parents, between one kind of worker and another kind. Such revolutionary action cannot be crushed like an armed uprising."[23] Paul Goodman vividly makes the same point through his characterization of a well-known peace activist: "Best of all, in principle, is the policy that Dave Dellinger espouses and tries to live by, to live communally and without authority, to work usefully and feel friendly, and so positively to replace an area of power with peaceful functioning."[24] By conducting his life in this way, the anarchist can initiate a process of change that is virtually invulnerable to external pressures, criticisms, and threats. The anarchist posture is thus deepened through experience and engenders credibility for the seriousness of its claims about the future. Unlike the utopian who tends to dichotomize present and future, regarding one mode as suitable given present practicalities and another as desirable given future wishes, the anarchist integrates his present behavior with his future hopes. The anarchist correctly perceives that the future is the eventual culmination of the present and that liberty is an existential condition enabling degrees of immediate realization.

The anarchist thus joins immediate action with his program for drastic societal reform. Herbert Read expresses this dual commitment as follows: "Our practical activity may be a gradual approximation towards the ideal, or it may be a sudden revolutionary realization of that ideal, but it must never be a compromise."[25]

Of course, despite this attempt at refutation, there is still a measure of common sense in Horowitz's observation. Surely, anarchism may serve as no more than a posture, and its immediate impact may consist primarily in leavening the more deeply rooted political traditions of Marxism and liberalism. However, even in this ancillary capacity, anarchism can perform the highly positive function of providing a corrective for the bureaucratic and repressive tendencies of Marxist politics, and for the apologetics and rationalizations of liberal politics.[26] Therefore, I would argue that anarchistic thought, correctly understood, is both a position and a posture.

Let us consider now our second preliminary question: Why is anarchism an attractive antidote (or complement) to mainstream thinking on global reform? Most proposals for global reform have uncritically affirmed the ordering contributions of the state to domestic life and have, in one or another form, sought to make those contributions available to the world as a whole. Indeed, the argument for global reform, at least since World War I, has assumed the strident tones of necessity. Since Hiroshima these claims of necessity have been pitched on an apocalyptic level and have been extended to embrace biosocial survival in light of the apparently deepening ecological crisis—the crowding, poisoning, and straining of planetary facilities. The unexamined premise in world order thinking has been that *only* governmental solutions can organize planetary life, that only existing governmental structures and their leaders can command the authority required for this essential undertaking, and that only argument and persuasion can release the political energy needed to overcome the inertia that sustains the state system in the face of the most unmistakable writing on the wall. A major variant to this line of reformist thinking is that persuasion must be supplemented by tragedy before enough political energy is released to achieve a world order solution.

Generally, such advocacy of bureaucratic centralism is coupled with confidence in the moderating capacities of law and institutionalism. The ideal world order would still consist of a realm of states, but with the venom drawn by substituting "law" for "force." Conflict would remain, but war would disappear. Peaceful methods of resolving conflicts would be accepted since all states would be unanimously committed to upholding the federalist edifice.

This kind of mainstream "idealism" often coexists with "realism." Until the existing world system is reconstructed according to the principles of legal architecture, one is thrown back onto the state system with its logic of power and its reliance on force to achieve "security" and to "manage" change. The world order idealist of tomorrow can easily justify being Machiavellian today. Hence, the issue of "transition" emerges as critical, and it is a fascinating indictment of mainstream thinking that no sustained attention has been given to the central challenge of transition—namely, access to and transformation of state power.

The anarchist comes forward with a quite different set of ideas, easily adapted to the world order debate: first of all, a skeptical look at the state and an unwillingness to accept it as "a model" for achieving a just order on any level of social organization; second, a positive belief in the capacities of various other collectivities—communes, cities, provinces, regions, associations—to provide the creative impetus for reorganizing the human enterprise; third, a bias toward decentralization of wisdom, authority, and capability, coupled with an insistence upon the autonomy of smaller units and the absolute status of individual liberty; fourth, a structural critique of the present organization of power, wealth, and prestige coupled with a revolutionary set of demands that existing leaders of society would never voluntarily meet; fifth, a processive view of the future, based on embodying the vision of a new order in immediate personal and political activities; sixth, a substitution of "justice" for "order" as the primary test of the adequacy of a given arrangement of power in world society; seventh, a refusal to blueprint the future in a manner that precludes creativity within the eventual setting that will give rise to the possibility of revolution itself.[27]

These seven elements of anarchist thinking can be positively adapted to a movement for global reform. What is most impressive about anarchist thought, from a world order perspective, is its blending of critique, vision, and transition strategy. In the words of George Woodstock, a close student of anarchism:

> Historically, anarchism is a doctrine which poses a criticism of existing society; a view of a desirable future society; and a means of passing from one to the other.[28]

Often, proposals for global reform have been sterile because they lacked one or more of these three essential elements (most typically, the transition strategy), or else presented one of them in unacceptable form (e.g., the vision as a blueprint). Despite this general attractiveness of anarchism as a world order perspective, the anarchist position also poses several difficulties that must be considered in the course of evaluating its possible relevance to a beneficial movement of global reform.[29]

THREE HARD QUESTIONS FOR ANARCHISTS

1. Are Not the Preconditions for Anarchist Success Insurmountable?

The great anarchist success stories have been episodic and short-lived (for examples, the Paris Commune of 1871, the anarchist collectives in parts of Spain during the 1930s, the May uprising in Paris in 1968). Nowhere have anarchists enjoyed a period of sustained success. Generally, anarchist success has generated an overpowering reaction of repression, as when the mercenary soldiery of Versailles crushed and massacred the Paris Communards in May 1871 only weeks after their extraordinary triumph. Anarchists view such failures as inevitable "first attempts"; Kropotkin calls "the Commune of Paris, the child of a period of transition . . . doomed to perish," but "the forerunner of social revolution."[30] Murry Bookchin and Daniel Guérin make a similar assessment of the Paris uprising of 1968, regarding its occurrence as proof of the anarchists' critique, its collapse as evidence that "the molecular movement below that prepares the condition for revolution" had not yet been carried far enough.[31]

On a deeper level, anarchists understand that the prerequisite for anarchist success *anywhere* is its success *everywhere*. It is this vital precondition that is at once so convincing and so formidable as to call into question whether the anarchist's position can in fact be taken seriously as a progressive alternative to state socialism.

Bakunin expresses the anarchist's demand and rationale with clarity:

A federalist in the internal affairs of the country, he desires an international confederation, first of all in the spirit of justice, and second because he is convinced that the economic and social revolution, transcending all the artificial and pernicious barriers between states, can only be brought about, in part at least, by the solidarity in action, if not of all, then at least of the majority of the nations constituting the civilized world today, so that sooner or later all nations must join together.[32]

Or, as Daniel Guérin expressed it: "An isolated national revolution cannot succeed. The social revolution inevitably becomes a world revolution."[33]

In essence, not only is it difficult for anarchists to attain power, but once they manage to do so their "organic institutions" seem incapable of holding it. Their movements will be liquidated ruthlessly by statists of "the left" or "the right."[34] Given such vulnerability, it may even be a betrayal of one's followers to expose them to slaughter by mounting a challenge against the entrenched forces of statism in the absence of either the will or the capabilities to protect the challengers.[35]

There is a report of a fascinating conversation between Lenin and Kropotkin in May 1919 in which Lenin mounts such an argument in two ways. First, he makes his familiar point that

You can't make a revolution wearing white gloves. We know perfectly well that we have made and will make a great many mistakes. . . . But it is impossible not to make mistakes during a revolution. Not to make them means to renounce life entirely and do nothing at all. But we have preferred to make errors and thus to act. . . . We want to act and we will, despite all the mistakes, and will bring our socialist revolution to the final and inevitably victorious end.[36]

Lenin here in effect acknowledges the errors that flow from using state power to secure the revolutionary victory from external and internal enemies, and he rebuffs the anarchist view that state power can be dissolved. Lenin's second rebuff of the anarchist position is his condescending view of its revolutionary power: "Do you really think that the capitalist world will submit to the path of the cooperative movement? . . . You will pardon me, but this is all nonsense! We need direct action of the masses, revolutionary action of the masses, that activity which seizes the capitalist world by the throat and brings it down."[37] Of the anarchist's concepts of "social revolution," Lenin says "these are children's playthings, idle chatter, having no realist soil underneath, no force, no means, and almost nothing approaching our socialist goals. . . . We don't need the struggle and violent acts of separate persons. It is high time that the anarchists understood this and stopped scattering their revolutionary energy on utterly useless affairs."[38] In sum, Lenin is arguing that the ends of anarchists must be pursued by mass violent revolution and secured through state power. The anarchist response is, of course, that the choice of such means perverts and dooms the ends. The antagonism of anarchists toward the Bolshevik Revolution has been vindicated many times over.[39] On the level of their discussion, it seems that both Lenin and Kropotkin are correct[40]—Lenin in saying that there is no other way to succeed, the anarchists by contending that such success is as bad as, if not worse than, defeat.

But, in my view, the strongest case for the feasibility of the anarchist's position still remains to be argued. It is implicit, perhaps, in Kropotkin's own work on the origins of the modern state and on its feudal antecedents in the European cities of the eleventh and twelfth centuries.[41] Kropotkin's argument rest on the historical claim that a vital society of communes and free cities created by brotherhoods, guilds, and individual initiative existed earlier: "It is shown by an immense documentation from many sources, that never, either before or since, has mankind known a period of relative well-being for all as in the cities of the Middle Ages. The poverty, insecurity, and physical exploitation of labor that exist in our times were then unknown."[42] Drawing on non-Western experience as well, Kropotkin argues in effect that societal well-being and security based on anarchistic conceptions of organic institutions (of a cooperative character) were very successfully established over a wide geographical and cultural expanse until crushed by the emergent states of the fifteenth and sixteenth centuries. Thus, there is a kind of *prima facie* case for the plausibility of the anarchist model, although in a pre-state context.

But evidence of the anarchists' potential for "success" does not end with medieval Europe. The direction of contemporary China, especially its antiparty, populist phase that culminated in the Cultural Revolution, contains strong anarchist elements.[43] Indeed, it was precisely these grounds of repudiating "organization" and "bureaucracy" as a basis for communist discipline that made China so offensive to communist ideologues in the Kremlin.[44] China is, of course, a mixed case. In its foreign policy it places great stress on statist prerogatives. Nevertheless, in its domestic patterns the Chinese example lends some credibility to Bakunin's and Kropotkin's claims that there are nonbureaucratic roads to socialism, and gives the anarchists' orientation renewed plausibility as a serious political alternative.[45]

Such plausibility can, it seems to me, be extrapolated in a poststatal context. My argument, sustained by sources as dissimilar as Saul Mendlovitz and Henry Kissinger, is that we are undergoing a profound historical transformation that is destroying the organizational matrix of the global system based on territorial states.[46] That is, we are entering a poststatal period, although its character remains highly conjectural. Whatever the outcome, however, the anarchists' stress on nonterritorial associations and communal consciousness seems highly relevant because of its basic compatibility with the inevitable shift in the relation of forces.

In sum, the anarchist case for radical reform (i.e., for social revolution) was *chimerical within* the confines of the state system. However, the state system is now being superseded. In this context, one set of plausible possibilities is the globalization of social life in a way that allows cooperative organizational forms to flourish. That is, the anarchist vision (as epitomized in Bakunin's writings) of a fusion between a universal confederation and organic social forms of a communal character lies at the very center of the *only* hopeful prospect for the future of world order.[47] Needless to say, such a prospect has slim chances for success, but at least the possibility is no longer chimerical, given the change of objective circumstances. The state system is not an immovable form, for many economic, political, technological, and sociological forces are everywhere undermining its bases of potency, if unevenly and at an uncertain rate. Therefore, although the political precondition of scale assumed by anarchism still remains formidable, it may yet prove historically realizable. It may be realizable because the preparatory processes going on throughout the world during this historical period are creating more favorable global conditions for the anarchist dream than have hitherto existed for centuries. This assessment arises because of several distinct developments. Perhaps the most significant is a growing disenchantment with the values, goals, and methods of industrial society. This sense of disenchantment is coming to be shared by increasing numbers of citizens, particularly in the developed nations of the West, and is finding various forms of expression that reflect revised notions of necessity based on "limits to growth," notions of well-being based on intermediate technology and small-scale institutions, and notions of personal transcendence based on a new spiritual energy that repudiates both conventional religion and secular humanism. In this setting, the quest for an appropriate politics coverges rather dramatically with the central tenets of anarchist belief. This modern sensibility understands, at last, that the state is simultaneously *too large* to satisfy human needs and *too small* to cope with the requirements of guidance needed by an increasingly interdependent planet. This realization is temporarily offset by a rising tide of statism in many other parts of the world where political independence is a forbidden fruit only recently tasted, but where the fruit will be poisoned, as everywhere else, by a world of nuclear weapons, ecological decay, and mass economic privation. The main *problematique* of our age is whether an appropriate politics of global reform, combining a centralized form of functional guidance with decentralized economic, social, and political structures, can be shaped by voluntary action, or whether it must be formed in a crucible of tragedy and catastrophe. Attentiveness to the anarchist tradition can be one part of an effort to achieve an appropriate politics *this* side of catastrophe. Obviously, the objective conditions which require such a reassessment of political forms are not by themselves sufficient to effect a transformation. Indeed, the very relevance of these ideas may lead their powerful opponents to regard them as even more dangerous now than in the past. Prudence and patience are essential in these circumstances. The crisis of the state system may yet require several decades to develop to the point where eruptions of spontaneous anarchistic energies would not unleash a variety of devastating backlashes.

2. Given the Urgency of Global Reform, Isn't the Anarchist Prospect Too Remote in Time?

Even accepting the optimistic assessment of the preceding section, namely, that the hour of anarchism may coincide with the collapse of statism, the restructuring of the world system would still appear to be developing for an unnecessarily and dangerously long period of several decades or more. Just as the emergence of the state system was a matter of centuries, so might the consolidation of a new system of political order require hundreds of years.[48] Two sets of questions call for judgment based on imponderables. First, how serious and pressing is the crisis? Is the fire close at hand, or still barely visible on a distant horizon? How can we know? Second, are any alternative means available through which the principal goals of global reform could be attained more reliably and rapidly than through anarchism? Do we have any responsible basis for selecting or rejecting these alternatives? In part, we are forced here to confront the most fundamental issues of politics, knowledge, and action. In the abstract, we do not know enough to choose or to act. Of course this same limitation bears on every school of political thought, including those that defend the status quo or incline toward gradualism. But it has even greater bearing on a political position that proposes radical tactics and goals, especially if large-scale violence is likely to ensue. On the other hand, this line of reasoning may be deceptive. In a moment of crisis, to do nothing may be the most risky of all postures toward the future. It is generally better to jump from a sinking ship than it is to stay on board, even if one knows nothing about the prospects of rescue from the waters below. The collective situation of human society cannot be cast in such deceptive simplicity. The veil of ignorance is thick indeed when it comes to assessing policy alternatives for the future of world society.

But the argument from ignorance cuts the other way as well. We have no real way to assess the degree of progress along the path of transition. Perhaps the collapse of statism is closer than we think. As Paul Goodman wrote:

> It will be said that there is no time. Yes, probably. But let me cite a remark of Tocqueville. In his last work, *L'Ancien Régime*, he notes "with terror," as he says, how throughout the eighteenth century writer after writer and expert after expert pointed out that this and that detail of the Old Regime was unviable and could not possibly survive; added up, they proved that the entire Old Regime was doomed and must soon collapse; and yet *there was not a single man who foretold that there would be a mighty revolution.*[49]

In the face of great uncertainty, and taking into consideration the many evidences of pressure on the state system, it makes political as well as moral sense to pursue a *principled set of conclusions* even if their realization cannot be immediately foreseen. In one sense Herbert Read is correct in saying that "the task of the anarchist philosopher is not to prove the imminence of a Golden Age, but to justify the value of believing in its possibility."[50]

Such value depends upon some degree of plausibility, but also on whether or not there are any preferable alternatives. Given the established bankruptcy of statist solutions on the right and left, given the vulnerability of the state system as a whole to catastrophic and, quite possibly, irreversible damage, and given the insufficiency of gradual strategies of amelioration, the case for some variant of radical anarchism seems strong despite the inability of anarchists to provide skeptics with a credible timetable.

In essence, the issue of urgency reinforces the anarchists' case.

The primary world order need is to find an alternative to statism. Anarchism, despite its limited political success during the statist era, provides the most coherent, widespread, and persistent tradition of antistatist thought. It is also a tradition that generally has been inclined toward world order values: peace, economic equity, civil liberties, and ecological defense. As such, it represents the most acceptable normative sequel to the state system. Other sequels include imperial consolidation, world state, regional federation, and intergovernmental functionalism.[51]

To affirm the relevance of the anarchist tradition is to accept the adequacy not of its current formulations but only of its general orientation. Advocates of the anarchist approach need to formulate the global implications of anarchism in a manner responsive to the current world order crisis. As far as I know, this has not yet been done. Indeed, anarchism suffers from the tendency of other traditions of philosophical speculation generated during the statist era, namely, a concentration upon the national question and the assumption that the global question will disappear when all nations have correctly resolved their own domestic problems. As I have suggested, anarchists are more dependent than other reformers on supportive transnational developments, but their analysis of international events is usually identical to that of Marxists on the level of critique and thus highly impressionistic when it comes to making specific proposals. The claims of anarchism are not weakened by the urgency of the world crisis, but the need for a more historically sensitive interpretation and for a globally oriented formulation of anarchist response is essential.

3. Does the Receptivity of Anarchism to Violence Undermine the Moral Basis of its Claim to Provide an Ideology for Global Reform?

I am not discussing here the anarchist as "bomb-thrower," but neither do I identify anarchism with pacifist ethics. As a philosophical position anarchism adopts an equivocal view of violence as an agent of change. Although anarchists tend to rely on spontaneous militancy of a nonviolent character—most typically, the general strike or other forms of unarmed struggle and resistance—there is no prevailing anarchist view on the role of violence.

I think Howard Zinn has sympathetically, but reliably, presented the anarchist position on violence in this assessment:

Some anarchists—like other revolutionaries throughout history . . . have emphasized violent uprising. Some have advocated, and tried, assassination and terror. . . . What makes anarchists unique among revolutionaries, however, is that most of them see revolution as a cultural, ideological, creative process, in which violence would be as incidental as the outcries of mother and baby in childbirth. It might be unavoidable—given the natural resistance to change—but something to be kept at a minimum while more important things happen.[52]

The question is whether, given the technology of destruction and the ruthlessness of statist leadership, this view of violence is adequate. It can be attacked from either side, as underestimating the role of violence necessary for any serious revolutionary position, or as too willing to accept the moral Trojan Horse of political violence.

Mainstream Marxists and neo-Marxists generally contend that revolution depends upon mass-based armed struggle. Another formulation is "the political statement of the Weather Underground," released under the title *Prairie Fire:*

It's an illusion that imperialism will decay peacefully. Imperialism has meant constant war. Imperialists defend their control of the means of life with terrible force. There is no reason to believe they will become humane or relinquish power. . . . To not prepare the people for this struggle is to disarm them ideologically and physically and to perpetrate a cruel hoax.[53]

The cruel hoax is, of course, the illusion that revolution can occur without armed struggle, that a revolution can be made with white gloves. But as Kropotkin soon perceived, once the white gloves have been thrown away, it becomes all too easy to adopt terror and torture.[54] In my view, the abuse of state power by socialism has reversed the presumption that violence is a necessary concomitant of revolution. On the contrary, it now seems a cruel hoax to promise humane outcomes from any revolutionary process that embraces violence with anything other than the utmost reluctance. Any genuinely radical position that purports moral (as well as political) credibility must, above all else, reject a cult of violence and justify the use of specific forms of violence in the most careful and conditional manner.

But what, then, of the revolutionary triumphs of China, Vietnam and Cuba? Was not violence essential to their success, and did they not achieve a net gain by prevailing on the level of armed struggle? I would answer that first of all, in each of these domestic situations there were no options other than extremist ones. Second, reliance on violent tactics may yet doom these revolutionary societies to Stalinist or other repressive patterns of governance. Third, the struggle for global reform should not be confused with the struggle for reform within an individual nation, although the two undertakings are closely related.

In other words, it is not enough to acknowledge that the imperialists are also violent, nor even that anarchists are prepared to accept violence only reluctantly as incidental to their purposes. Something more considered, more explicit, is needed, even though specific choices cannot always be anticipated or determined in the abstract.

At the same time, any unequivocal renunciation of violence is probably "a cruel hoax," given the realities of power. There may be no way, in particular situations, to remain aloof from armed struggle without acquiescing, oneself, in violence of at least equal proportions.

If anarchism is to qualify as a morally suitable ideology for global revolution, it requires a considered analysis of the role of violence, with emphasis on:

- Necessity of recourse, as an instrument of last resort (the futility of nonviolent militancy having already been demonstrated beyond reasonable doubt);
- Discrimination in application (with no intentional subjection of innocent people to foreseeable risks of harm);
- Limitation of the form and degree of application (absolute prohibition on torture and cruelty).

Such a middle position is no guarantee against revolutionary excess, but this doctrinal stance may at least exert some influence when it comes to choosing tactics, strategies, and policies. Also, it provides a defense against both Leninist and pacifist critiques. Finally, it acknowledges what has been so agonizingly confirmed in recent decades, namely, that revolutionaries must protect their own programs from their own propensities to embrace "evil."

Violence in the context of global transformation is even more problematic. If national struggles are waged successfully in critical countries, then violence may not be necessary on a global level. On the other hand, if such struggles end inconclusively or are defeated, then no degree of global violence will help. Given both the preponderance of military power possessed by state institutions and the objectives of global reform, it is possible to renounce violence for the exclusive purpose of reform, but to retain militant nonviolence as a tactic. Indeed, in the years ahead it will be vital for the forces of global reform to confront statist institutions, in order that the latter be forced to expose their destructive patterns of behavior to a wider public.

SOME CONCLUSIONS

Several broad lines of conclusion emerge from the preceding discussion:

(1) There are no serious obstacles to the adoption of an anarchist perspective on global reform; there are, to be sure, unacceptable variants of the anarchist position, but they do not invalidate the main lines of anarchist thought as represented by Proudhon, Bakunin, and Kropotkin, and more recently exemplified by Guérin, Herbert Read, and Paul Goodman.

(2) Anarchism impressively links its goals for revolutionary change within national societies with a vision of a transformed global society; the linkage is integral and progressive in terms of world order values commonly affirmed; as a consequence, anarchism deals with entrenched power and avoids the political sterility associated with legalistic and moralistic blueprints of "a new world order," as well as the static images of the future characteristic of utopography.

(3) Anarchist thought is alive to the twin dangers of socialism and capitalism if pursued within the structure of statism; its espousal of populist strategies of change gains some historical credibility from its affinity with Mao Tse-tung's efforts to avoid the decay of revolutionary momentum in contemporary China.[55]

(4) Anarchist thought on organic institutions of cooperation is creatively freed from either territorial or statist constraints and draws inspiration from both prestatist (Kropotkin) and poststatist (Goodman) possibilities by moving dialectically toward decentralizing bureaucratic power while centralizing human function; in this regard, images of global functionalism and political confederation of nations merge with images of the deconcentration of both the power and the roles of national governments; the state is understood to be both inhumanly large in its bureaucratic dimension and inhumanly small in its territorial and exclusionary dimensions; this dualism implicit in anarchism is excellently adapted to the purposes of global reform.

(5) Anarchist thought, although often perceived as oscillating between extremes of terrorism and pacificism, is capable of evolving from within its framework of values an intermediate interpretation of violence. Such an interpretation would urge action in the direction of militant nonviolence, without depending on either the "white gloves" of utopians or the torture chambers of state socialists and cultist advocates of violence.

(6) As yet, there is no comprehensive and satisfactory formulation of an anarchist position on global transformation, only fragments

here and there; a well-integrated statement could help crystallize enthusiasm for global transformation in many parts of the world where the internal strains of an obsolescent and moribund statism are being rapidly translated into repression, militarism, imperialism, and interventionary diplomacy; for weak states, even genuine national autonomy requires a radical program of global reform.

For those who view our era as one of transition between the state system and some global sequel, the anarchists' perspective becomes increasingly relevant and attractive. Of course, it remains to be tested as an ideology for hope and action, as well as a basis for social, economic, and political reconstruction. Maoism, as embodied in the China of the 1960s and 1970s, is a peculiar mixture of statism and populism that should be generally, although not fully, encouraging. As Franz Schurmann notes: "The very word 'Maoism' came to mean a kind of anarchist, ultraleft troublemaking-for-troublemaking's sake. And when the New Left began to clash with older communist parties, as in France, China was invoked as a new Marxist Rome sanctioning this path to revolution."[56]

NOTES

1. For one notable exception see Thomas G. Weiss, "The Tradition of Philosophic Anarchism and Future Directions in World Policy," (New York:1974, mimeographed); I have treated the anarchist position briefly and analytically in *A Study of Future Worlds* (New York: Free Press, 1975), pp. 214–19.

2. "We believed we were living in a peculiarly anarchist community." Doris Lessing, *The Memoirs of a Survivor* (New York: Knopf, 1975), p. 81.

3. See depiction of Franklin Roosevelt's vision of a new world order based on the primacy of the United Nations in Franz Schurmann, *The Logic of World Power* (New York: Pantheon, 1974), pp. 13–17, especially 67–76.

4. Sir Herbert Read expresses the anarchists' attitude toward order and efficiency in social relations as follows: "Anarchism implies a universal decentralization of authority, and a universal simplification of life. Inhuman entities like the modern city will disappear. But anarchism does not necessarily imply a reversion to handicraft and outdoor sanitation. There is no contradiction between anarchism and air transport, anarchism and the division of labour, anarchism and industrial efficiency." Sir Herbert Read, *Anarchy and Order* (Boston: Beacon, 1971), p. 134. In other words, anarchists' images involve reconstituting order in the world rather than eliminating it.

5. "Sartre at Seventy: An Interview," *New York Review of Books*, August 7, 1975, p. 14. Because anarchists are viewed as extremists there is a temptation to avoid the label. Consider, for instance, this passage by E. M. Cioran: ". . . from the moment your actions and your thoughts serve a form of real or imagined city you are its idolators and its captives. The timidest employee and the wildest anarchist, if they take a different interest here, live as its function: they are both citizens internally though one prefers his

slippers and the other his bomb." *A Short History of Decay* (New York: Viking, 1975), pp. 75–76.

6. See the interpretation by French anarchist Daniel Guérin, *Anarchism: From Theory to Practice* (New York: Monthly Review Press, 1970), pp. 155–59.

7. For consideration of the pacifist ethos in relation to an anarchist orientation, see Karl Shapiro, "On the Revival of Anarchism," in Irving Louis Horowitz, ed., *The Anarchists* (New York: Dell, 1964), pp. 572–81; also Howard Zinn's introductory essay in Read, *Anarchy and Order*, pp. ix-xxii.

8. The PLO's adoption of terror as a tactic can also be condemned as a consequence of its failure to initiate a mass movement of nonviolent struggle. Such a movement would not necessarily succeed, but its failure is far from assured.

9. Horowitz, *The Anarchists*, pp. 15–64, at p. 26.

10. For example, Barry Commoner, *The Closing Circle* (New York: Knopf, 1971); Edward Goldsmith et al., *Blueprint for Survival* (Boston: Houghton Mifflin, 1972); Donella Meadows et al., *The Limits to Growth* (Washington, D.C.: Potomac Associates, 1972); Richard A. Falk, *This Endangered Planet: Prospects and Proposals for Human Survival* (New York: Random House, 1971).

11. Among those who have discerned and charted this new direction of human energy, perhaps Theodore Roszak is most notable. See Theodore Roszak, *The Making of a Counter Culture* (New York: Anchor, 1969) and *Where the Wasteland Ends* (New York: Anchor, 1973).

12. Sam Dolgoff, ed., *Bakunin on Anarchy* (New York: Knopf, 1972), p. 107: Bakunin characterized the American system as "the finest political organization that ever existed in history." [Hereafter cited as *Bakunin.*]

13. *Bakunin*, p. 98; see also p. 152.

14. Goodman, "The Ambiguities of Pacifist Politics," in Leonard I. Krimerman and Lewis Perry, eds., *Patterns of Anarchy* (New York: Anchor, 1966), p. 127.

15. For example, Bakunin's conceptions are based on federations of many different, overlapping units, including "regions, provinces, communes, associations, and individuals." *Bakunin*, p. 98.

16. Ibid., pp. 121–22.

17. On this dismissal see George Plekanov, "Anarchist Tactics: A Pageant of Futility, Obstruction, and Decadence?" in Krimerman and Perry, *Patterns of Anarchy*, pp. 495–99; for an anarchist's response to these kinds of allegations, see Guérin, *Anarchism*, pp. 41–69. Read, *Anarchy and Order*, pp. 22–23, usefully distinguishes between positive and negative roles for utopian projections of the future.

18. Read, *Anarchy and Order*, p. 129.

19. In general, see Nadezhda Mandelstam, *Hope Against Hope* (New York: Atheneum, 1970); also on repression at Kronstadt by the Soviet government, see Guérin, *Anarchism*, pp. 102–5 and Alexander Berkman, "Kronstadt: The Final Act in Russian Anarchism," in Horowitz, *The Anarchists*, pp. 495–506.

20. *Bakunin*, p. 155.

21. See Kropotkin's essay "The Commune of Paris," in Martin A. Miller, ed., *Selected Writings on Anarchism and Revolution by P. A. Kropotkin* (Cambridge, Mass.: MIT Press, 1970), pp. 119–32 [hereafter cited as *Kropotkin*]; for a comparable anarchistic appreciation of the spontaneous character of the Paris risings of 1968 and their rela-

tionship to the experience of the Paris Commune a century earlier, see Murray Bookchin, *Post-Scarcity Anarchism* (Berkeley, Calif.: Ramparts Press, 1971), pp. 249–70.

22. See Kropotkin's essay "Must We Occupy Ourselves with an Examination of the Ideal of a Future System?" in *Kropotkin*, pp. 47–116.

23. Howard Zinn, Introduction to Read, *Anarchy and Order*, p. xviii.

24. Goodman, "Ambiguities of Pacifist Politics," p. 136.

25. Read, *Anarchy and Order*, p. 129.

26. Sartre ascribed a similar role to existentialism in relation to Marxism. Jean-Paul Sartre, *Search for a Method*, tr. Hazel E. Barnes (New York: Vintage, 1968), pp. 3-34.

27. See Bookchin's discussion of spontaneous features of the Paris 1968 events, in Murry Bookchin, *Post-Scarcity Anarchism*, pp. 250–52; Read, *Anarchy and Order*, p. 23, argues that blueprints of the future pervert the genuine utopian impulse to transcend present societal arrangements. Such blueprints are condemned as "an advance on the spontaneous sources of life itself. They presume to plan what can only germinate . . . such scientific utopias will certainly fail, for the sources of life when threatened are driven underground to emerge in some new wilderness."

28. George Woodstock, *Anarchism* (New York: World Publishing Co., 1962), p. 9.

29. By "beneficial" I mean a movement that realizes world order values associated with peace, economic well-being, social and political justice, and ecological balance. For an elaboration of why these values have been preferred and of the interplay between them see Falk, *Future Worlds*, pp. 7–55.

30. *Kropotkin*, p. 127.

31. Bookchin, *Post-Scarcity Anarchism*, p. 258.

32. *Bakunin*, p. 118.

33. Guérin, *Anarchism*, p. 69.

34. See references in note 19 and Woodstock, *Anarchism*, pp. 275–424.

35. Such allegations have been made with respect to Salvador Allende's efforts in the early 1970s to transform the societal base of Chile without dismantling the state apparatus with its strong links to the vested interests of the old order.

36. *Kropotkin*, p. 328.

37. Ibid., pp. 329–330.

38. Ibid., p. 330.

39. One of the earliest and most eloquent anarchist critics of the Soviet experience was Emma Goldmann. See her *My Disillusionment with Russia* (Garden City, New York: Doubleday, 1923).

40. Kropotkin's position can be extrapolated from his general anarchist writings; he did not state the anarchists' case in his conversations with Lenin.

41. See Kropotkin's excellent essay, "The State: Its Historic Role," in *Kropotkin*, pp. 211–64.

42. Ibid., p. 231.

43. See the perceptive discussion in Schurmann, *Logic of World Power*, pp. 369–80.

44. Ibid., p. 380.

45. For a skeptical interpretation of China's domestic experience see Donald Zagoria, "China by Daylight," *Dissent,* spring 1975, pp. 135–47.

46. For opposing interpretations of the durability of the state and the state system, see Saul H. Mendlovitz's, Introduction, in Saul H. Mendlovitz, ed., *On the Creation of a Just World Order* (New York: Free Press, 1975), pp. vii-xvii and Stanley Hoffmann, "Obstinate or Obsolete? The Fate of the Nation-State and the Case of Western Europe," *Daedalus,* summer 1966, pp. 862-915.

47. A general interpretation can be found in Robert Heilbroner, *An Inquiry into the Human Prospect* (New York: Norton, 1974); see also Falk, *Future Worlds,* pp. 417–37 and chapter 13 this volume.

48. See Joseph R. Strayer, *On the Medieval Origins of the Modern State* (Princeton, N.J.: Princeton University Press, 1970).

49. Goodman, "Ambiguities of Pacifist Politics," p. 136; see also *Kropotkin,* pp. 121–24.

50. Read, *Anarchy and Order,* p. 14.

51. For consideration of world order options, see Falk, *Future Worlds,* pp. 150–276, and chapter 13, in this volume.

52. Howard Zinn, Introduction to Read, *Anarchy and Order,* p. xvii.

53. *Prairie Fire,* Political Statement of the Weather Underground, 1974, p. 3.

54. See Kropotkin's letter to Lenin, dated December 21, 1920, in *Kropotkin,* pp. 338–39.

55. See Schurmann, *Logic of World Power,* p. 369 and pp. 268–80.

56. Ibid., p. 369.

Global Institutions and World Order Values

INTRODUCTION: THE EVOLUTION OF AN INSTITUTIONAL PRESENCE

There is now a consensus that the reform of international society requires some significant institutional build-up at the global level. This consensus is relatively new, the culmination of some tendencies that can be traced back at least to the formation of the first international institutions in the late nineteenth century. At an earlier point in international society, even idealistic interpreters of the global scene thought it unnecessary (and perhaps undesirable) to advocate international institutions as part of their program for global reform.

For instance, Grotius, in his great treatise on the law of war, devotes no more than a few lines to the suggestion that periodic meetings among heads of state would be beneficial. Immanuel Kant, in his essay *Perpetual Peace,* argues that global reform depends upon the successful establishment of republican forms of governance at the state level; no additional superstructure to assure peace or justice is needed or desirable. And Lenin argues to the same effect, simply substituting the socialist reorganization of national political life for the prevailing bourgeoise or liberal modes.

Of course, it is also true that some older reformist conceptions called for institutional growth at the supernational level. These conceptions were generally of two varieties and occasionally a mixture of both. On the one side were imperial conceptions of global unification based on making the principal center of state power, usually that of the author, universal. Thus Dante saw the necessity of the global extension of the Roman Empire in *De Monarchia.* On the other side were utopian conceptions of a world-governing authority that would transcend in all respects the limitations of the state system. Abbé de Saint Pierre in the early eighteenth century evolved such a conception, apparently believing (to Rousseau's ironic amusement and disbelief) that such an edifice could be built just as soon as the main rulers of the day could be persuaded that the aim of a fulfilled human society would thereby be promoted.

In our century, the main stimulus for new proposals for global reform has been the experience of two mutually destructive world wars, with the widespread fear that even worse tragedies could follow. At the same time, in the practical realm of diplomacy both imperial and utopian schemes seemed irrelevant. The puzzle confronting policy-makers of leading sovereign states has been how to respond to these pressures for reform while remaining sensitive to the constraints of a world order system dominated by the values, attitudes, and structures of state sovereignty and nationalism.

Two sorts of "solutions" have been forthcoming, yet neither has generated great expectations. The first approach was to establish the chrysalis for world government in the form of a comprehensive international organization operating on the basis of a very general constitutional document. The League of Nations and the United Nations are embodiments of this approach. Woodrow Wilson, Franklin Roosevelt, and especially most American liberal leaders have regarded these infant world organizations as the seeds of an eventually flourishing system of effective, equitable, global government. Of course, the results have been generally disappointing for anyone with exalted expectations. The League, and even more so the United Nations, have served mainly as extensions of the state system, not as alternatives to it, and register shifting tendencies within that system. At most, we can say that such a forum for communications and mobilization is accepted on all sides as an inevitable, if marginal, feature of the present international order. Attempts to detach the UN from the state system by granting it more independence vis-à-vis funding, capabilities, and staff have been half-hearted and lack promise.

The second twentieth-century "solution" is generally identified as "functionalism," the emergence of special-purpose international institutions operating within the broad framework of the United Nations. There has been a steady growth of functionalist activity, if measured in terms of number of institutions, budget, or size of staff.[1] These institutions are assigned specific roles, often involving technical specialization, and policy is set by experts. Politics has entered to varying degrees, and assessments as to whether politicalization has been beneficial or detrimental differ.[2] Typical actors that fall within this category are the International Labor Organization (ILO), World Health Organization (WHO), and the Food and Agriculture Organization (FAO). Such actors have not produced any significant trans-formation of international order, nor is there much prospect that they will. Their competence and capabilities, as with the general-purpose international institutions, are derived from and dependent upon statist logic and geopolitical constraints. Modest contributions to problem-solving, standard-setting, and consciousness-raising have been made by these specialized institutions, but in no sense can their present or potential role be understood as more than system-stabilization.

The same comments apply, perhaps with even greater force, to general-purpose and specialized regional actors, with the partial and controversial exception of western Europe. In Europe, an impressive degree of sovereignty-cutting has been carried out under the auspices of a regional institutional framework, and has seemed to have had the additional effect of reducing the intensity of conflicts and prospects for war within the region. Internal factors, like past warfare and European homogeneity, and external factors, like the Soviet security threat and the scale of American economic competition, have en-couraged important measures of European integration, but statist considerations have prevented European regionalism from proceed-ing very far in a supranational direction. Indeed, the European expe-rience is still one of statist adaptation to a peculiar set of strains in geopolitics created after World War II. Other regionalist build-ups, like those in Latin America, Africa, the Middle East, or South Asia, have been even less significant from a system-transforming perspec-tive. For instance, the Organization of American States (OAS) is, in part, an alliance framework and, in part, an arena for hegemonial leadership by the United States. The Arab League has served some state interests with its flexible and regionally managed peace-keeping capability and its anti-Israeli alliance. The Organization of African Unity (OAU) also serves mainly to help make Africa safer for statism, and thereby less vulnerable to extraregional penetration.

Perhaps more significant are intergovernmental, institutional frameworks that seek revision of the international order in the intrastructural sense by rearranging relative positions of power. The Organization of Petroleum Exporting Countries (OPEC) has had that ambition at times, and even has created a climate within the United Nations that gave temporary leverage to militant demands for a New International Economic Order (NIEO). And generally, in a variety of North-South situations, loose institutional arrangements aimed at promoting solidarity (amid diversity) have exerted an influence on bargaining style and perhaps on outcomes over the last fifteen years.

At most, however, such institutional developments have corrected some distortions in the state system and have enabled this system to adapt more successfully to shifting currents of power. Perhaps a slightly more equitable set of relationships between rich and poor, and between North and South, have emerged, but only *slightly more.* Of course, some states in the South by virtue of their leverage have been able to demand participation in principal geopolitical arenas as the price for their willingness to play nondisruptive roles.

The general conclusion, then, is that the international institutional presence in the present world system is marginal to the state system, and often is so derivative from it that it has little or no independence. Its general role is to make the system function more smoothly as well as to make some cosmetic concessions to those who argue that a more structured, centralized form of international order is needed at this historical time to avoid large-scale warfare and to facilitate a level of international cooperation needed for economic growth and stability.

APPROACHES TO INSTITUTIONAL REFORM

At this time, more than thirty-five years after World War II, there is general agreement that a more elaborate institutional presence is required in international society just to keep the old system functioning. This agreement, however, obscures a more fundamental disagreement, that is, over the appropriate scale and form of institutional build-up required for purposes of system maintenance, system reform, or system transformation.[3] Even the Trilateral Commission emphasizes the importance of a strengthened institutional capacity to meet the challenges of interdependence within the economic sphere. In essence, the minimum current focal point for any reformist perspective on international society is the need to manage a world system of shifting geopolitical patterns, growing complexity, interdependence, and fragility, especially in the economic sphere. To some extent management must be accomplished vis-à-vis problems of the global commons. The objective of such institutionalization is to contribute to the achievement and maintenance of a moderate international order, which is perceived by conservative and liberal policy-makers as the necessary alternative to mutually destructive conflict and, possibly, chaos.[4] This perception arises out of a postimperial frame of reference that acknowledges that transnational patterns of coordination are essential for the successful functioning of the capitalist sector of the world economy. The case for institutional reform and extension is partly an historical argument that the organization of the capitalist sector under American hegemony is no longer tenable given the weakness of the dollar, the rise of non-American centers of economic power (e.g., Germany, Saudi Arabia), as well as the problems posed by unregulated MNCs operating out of several different economic home bases.

In more concrete terms, this outlook acknowledges the importance of extending the existing institutional framework to deal with the stabilization of commodity prices and the regulation of multinational corporate activities (for example, "a General Agreement on Tariffs and Trade [GATT] for investment"). It also supports institutional innovations to supervise oceans policy, to manage fishery domains, to sustain environmental quality, to resolve ocean disputes, and to administer ocean minerals regimes.[5] Such a reformist outlook is mindful of political constraints, insensitive to equity concerns, and seeks no more than adaptation. Normative components enter to an extent, as even the most conservative globalist perspective concedes that some deliberate effort must be made to assure Third World participation and support, if new international institutional initiatives are to be successful.

This managerial fix for international society deliberately leaves structural issues untouched. Hegemonial geopolitics are presupposed, that is, implicitly endorsed. The more fundamental problems posed by fragmentation at the state level are ignored. Furthermore, the war system is accepted as part of "the given" that cannot and, perhaps, need not be altered by the managerial solution. It apparently is taken for granted that only the resources of traditional statecraft will be available to curb military conflict and arms races, as well as to restrain the spread of nuclear weaponry to all parts of world. That is, the Trilateral Commission image of a preferred world is one of adaptation to achieve moderation, which under present circumstances calls for some redesigning and strengthening of central guidance machinery, especially in the economic spheres, together with a benevolent gradualism that works to incorporate rich Third World countries as equal partners in the international economic order and to offer poor countries some token concessions. The basic motif is to strike a bargain or reach a series of bargains that provide enough positive incentives for most governments to encourage their constructive participation in the existing system of world order (without generating fundamental disruption or challenge).

Another side of world order thinking, although far less influential, derives from those who are ready in the wings with a blueprint for some grand design of world order, usually world government in some form. Here the preoccupation with war and especially with the menaces posed by new weapons of mass destruction motivates the advocates of this approach. The argument is that unless we transcend a world of states quickly and decisively, we will bring human history to an apocalyptic end. Such an outlook has been reinforced by the recent upsurge in ecological concern that underscores the inability of separate sovereignties to act for the benefit of a general global interest. In effect, advocates of this line argue for the evolution of full-scale, central governmental institutions complemented by general and complete disarmament, by management and planning capabilities for global resources, and by procedures for settling disputes. The Clark/ Sohn plan for *World Peace through World Law* is the most influential and carefully elaborated example of this approach to world order based on comprehensive institutional centralization.

The difficulties with such institutional centralism are quite obvious. Most stark, of course, is the absence of receptivity on the part of the main political actors on the world stage, namely, leaders of national governments. If most governments are not prepared to work seriously toward such a goal, it seems impossible to mobilize the necessary popular political will. This closure is reinforced by the absence of popular enthusiasm for grand designs. Attachment to sovereign rights and symbols is too high, anxiety about centralization is too great, and the whole enterprise appears too abstract and remote to arouse significant levels of serious support even from those who are most worried about and victimized by the failures and dangers of the existing system of world order. As matters now stand, the advocacy of world government is dismissed as foolish and sterile, an idea that has been around for some time without winning any relevant support in either elite or popular circles.

On a deeper level, there is the anxiety that even if some kind of world governance structure could be brought into being in the near future, its execution would likely be so seriously flawed as to make us nostalgic for a world of states. Some ordeal of bureaucratic centralism is imagined as the likely consequence of a premature shift from the states system to a more integrated global political structure.

In any event, these poles of perception dominate the political imagination and inhibit other modes of creative and concrete thinking about the place of institutions in global reform. In fact, serious images of "restructuring" world order have concentrated on the interplay of dynamic factors involving trade, investment, and economic goals, and regard institutional innovations as either fanciful (given statism), superfluous (if the political will should emerge, then institutional requirements will be easily satisfied and do not require advance specification), or inappropriate (emphasis on policy at the margins can overcome concern by modifying underlying structures).

The effect of this general climate of opinion has been to encourage analyses of prospects for global reform to concentrate on the interplay of factors relating to power, interests, and attitudes without any independent attention to the structures of world order. Global models constructed in accordance with econometric theory have, in particular, sought to depict as objectively as possible the interactive workings of the international system under carefully delineated sets of conditions. The institutional dimension has been consistently downplayed in this work, being regarded as trivial or formalistic given the solidity of the present system of world order. And with respect to structuring the future system, institutions have been generally regarded, if at all, as a sequel rather than a cause in relation to forming the requisite political will. In such a setting, to posit institutional innovation in a serious way is perceived as either to be engaged in imperial geopolitics or to be embarked upon an exercise in sterile utopianism. Therefore, institutional innovation has not seemed very pertinent to the most fashionable recent work of global reform, except in various ancillary roles as facilitators or obstructors of existing policy. Is this neglect justified? How might it be overcome?

GUIDELINES FOR A POSITIVE APPROACH

Let us set forward two goals: a commitment to *normative change* (i.e., change associated with positive values) and a commitment to *political relevance* (i.e., proposals sensitive to issues of feasibility). Some other elements condition the analysis: an overriding concern with minimum order, especially in superpower relations (i.e., avoidance of general war as a major priority); an image of feasibility (e.g., ten to one hundred years) not restricted to the exceedingly short horizons of governmental leaders (one to five years); and a conception of feasibility that is not shaped by the normative receptivities of existing governmental leaders. These presuppositions of world order analysis should be explained and justified in considerable detail. Here, it is only possible to mention them in order to suggest one particular orientation toward global reform.

The analysis of the positive place of institutions in a program or image of global reform proceeds from this orientation. This appraisal has been heavily influenced by my participation in the work of the World Order Models Project (WOMP) over the past decade. This work arose out of the conviction that a program of drastic global reform was essential and was inescapably political in its fundamental character. To be political in a world system dominated by ideological, geopolitical, cultural, and ethnic pluralism meant that agents of global transformation would have to proceed outward from the nation-state and, hence, would have to exhibit the diversity of national situations around the world. No master plan devoid of ideological and cultural content could skip such a step without assuring its irrelevance. At the same time, without some shared normative framework, it would be difficult to consider the effort at transformation to be an enterprise with a coherent direction, capable of growing into a global social movement, and committed to the construction of a new system of world order that is beneficial and sustainable. Acceptance of this tension between pluralism of interpretation and universalism of aspiration is at the center of WOMP's attempts to be relevant without being accommodating. As an organizational matter, it has produced a shared value framework at a high enough level of abstraction to encompass the principal diversities of the world, without being so amorphous in its implications as to avoid some definiteness of commitment. This consensus of values has generated a series of transformative images and strategies that depict the contours of a preferred world order system and articulate, as well, transitional scenarios of the momentous change from *here* to *there*.[6] Institutional changes played an important role in the main WOMP models of relevant utopias or preferred worlds, yet a subordinate role to the main shifts in values/orientation.[7] The approach taken to institutional issues can be better appreciated within the wider context of world order methodology, briefly explained by the following definitions:

Values—An agreed upon framework of values associated with peace (minimization of large-scale violence, including structural violence), economic well-being (satisfaction of basic human needs, together with a movement toward equality between and within societies), social and political justice (realization of noneconomic human rights for individuals and groups), ecological balance (achievement of environmental quality, conservation of resources, preservation of endangered species), and humane governance (the collective organizational and constitutional solution on national, regional, and global levels that promotes the integrated realization of the other four values). It is understood that these values are, depending on context, interrelated, mutually reinforcing, and in conflict, that is, the promotion of one (peace for example) cannot succeed unless correlated with the others, and, paradoxically, choices must be made at each stage as to whether to foster economic well-being if it involves environmental harm or depletion of scarce resources. The tension among values and ways of resolving it are features of transition strategy; the preferred world, while generating its own agenda of concerns, is defined as a world order system in which the five values are simultaneously realized.[8]

Preferred World—The goal of transition is defined by value realization and manifestation in structures of human governance. The shape of the preferred world cannot be reliably predetermined, nor can its emergence be anticipated before the year 2025 or so. That is, there is no sense in which history will stop because a preferred world has been achieved; any horizon of aspiration reached discloses a new horizon. However, it is here in the effort at prefiguring a preferred world that the institutional (constitutional) dimension receives the greatest attention.

Transition—The period from now until then is specified as the time of transition. In a methodological sense, the analytical purpose of focusing on transition is to insist upon a deliberative attitude toward change in which certain goals are pursued (as related to the valued ends set forth) by reliance on appropriate tactics and strategies. In effect, the challenge of the transition period is a call for the acceptance of human responsibility for the political organization of the planet. This call for political commitment is conditioned by the realities of various national settings (repressive or liberal), of distinct issue-areas (human rights or disarmament), of the stage of development and culture, and of the scale and situation of a particular national society. The transition question can be expressed in political terms: what activity, given the actor (person, institution, government, party, religion) is most conducive to the realization of the valued ends proposed as dominant in the preferred world? At one end of the scale, a transition activity might be the promotion of solar energy, vegetarianism, and voluntary simplicity, the profoundly political statement made by the choices that individuals make about how to lead their own lives. At the other end might be more a conventionally political commitment to a liberation struggle, to a stand-by peace-keeping force, or to a global taxation plan at the United Nations. The issue of institutions arises as follows: how can a given direction or program of institutional reform serve as a means in the transition period to realize world order values (that is, more peace, economic well-being, etc., as measured by such indicators as battlefield deaths, per capita daily caloric intake, etc.)? Part of a response may involve the construction of transnational nongovernmental institutional arrangements (for instance, a privately promoted peoples' tribunal to assess state crime in the human rights sphere).

COMMENTS ON INSTITUTIONAL DESIGN

1. With respect to *world order values,* there are no institutional implications, *per se,* of the values adopted. Of course, other values or world order goals could be formulated that do have institutional implications, for example, the desirability of maximum regional or global integration as an end rather than as a means.

The opposite normative bias is contained in the substance of "humane governance" as a valued end. The idea of the minimum bureaucratic presence consistent with achieving the other four values is itself a value, as is discerning a humane scale for governing units. The emphasis, then, is on decentralizing existing concentrations of institutional authority, on separating authority from power, and on softening the first system (i.e., sovereign states) rather than hardening the second system (i.e., the global institutional network). Such an image of human governance also presupposes some success in activating the third system (i.e., the popular sector).[9]

Images of humane governance, including an array of institutional embodiments, are discussed below in connection with the idea of a preferred world (see figures 1–4). Insofar as world order thinking is informed by a coherent ideology of transformation, it must have some sense of the optional role and character of international institutions, their distinct character, their interrelationships with one another (that is, the reorganization of the second system), and their interrelationships with the first and third systems.

2. With respect to designing a *preferred world,* let us assume here that the concept of preferred world is conditioned by an agreed upon set of world order values and a conception of transition. Thus, not all conceivable reorganizations of the political life of the planet are relevant (for example, a world empire or a hard world state). Nevertheless, there are a range of models of preferred world systems that

Figure 1: Soft World State

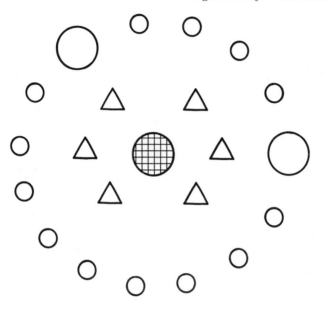

⊕ Central Government System

△ Functional Institutional Actors

◯ Subordinate Governmental Actors

Figure 2: Small State World

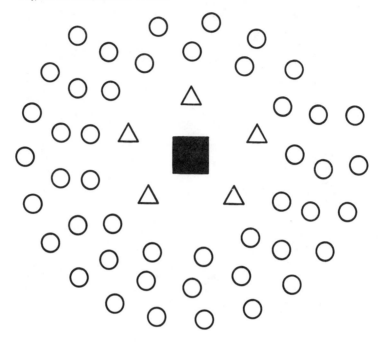

◯ State Actors

△ Functional Institutional Actors

■ Coordinating Capability

Figure 3: Regionalist World

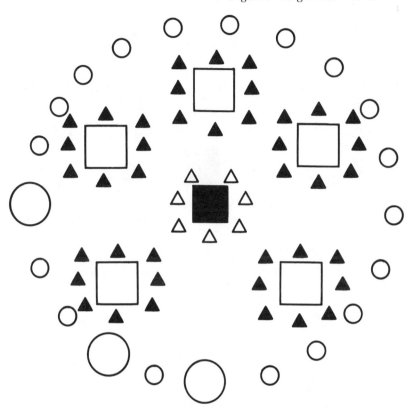

○ State Actors

☐ Regional Actors

▲ Regional Functional Actors

△ Global Functional Actors

■ Coordinating Capacity

Figure 4: Functionalist World

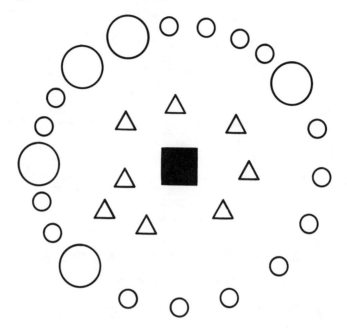

△ Global Functionalist Actors

■ Coordinating Capacity

○ State Actors

potentially qualify (such as a soft world state, a small state world, a regionalist solution, and a functionalist solution). For each, an institutional framework seems to be implied and can be schematically summarized, but it is difficult and perhaps arbitrary to draw invidious comparisons at this stage as to which of the four general types of restructured international order would be most desirable and feasible. Perhaps, as developments in the future unfold, more detailed assessments of strengths and weaknesses can be made, although their utility will depend on the degree to which such appraisal is not torn from the context of actual global political developments.

Also, the types of restructuring portrayed in the four figures are intended only to be illustrative of the logic of some world order organizing models that could mitigate, if not eliminate, the disadvantages associated with world order organized in deference to the primacy of statist logic. In actual circumstances, however, the logic of these organizing designs can be combined in a wide variety of ways to produce a coherent system of world order capable of realizing the values adopted as criteria for world order performance.

3. With respect to the *transition process,* the emphasis is upon guiding choice in relation to a given course of commitment to global reform. The question of institutional design is, of course, complex and varies with transition settings. A given issue of institutional reform or creation (for instance, a new law of the oceans) should be assessed as beneficial or not, in whole or part, depending on whether it appears to enhance the prospects of structural transformation according to positive value auspices or embodies approved values in the present working of the world political system.

World order is a composite of ordering logics having a variety of normative effects. Especially in a time of transition these logics and effects tend to produce contradictory international patterns. As the "old" structures are challenged and/or superseded by the "new" structures, it becomes confusing and contradictory to interpret what is happening, much less what is beneficial.

A NOTE IN CONCLUSION

The place of institutions in the work of global reform is necessarily elusive. As well, it is beset by the flaws of the past: utopianism and deceptively framed proposals that promote national, regional, or special interests under the anodyne guise of globalism. At the same time, the institutional dimension is essential, as it provides the most visible and stable indication of how life is to be organized in an alternate international political system. We need new ways to introduce the institutional dimension into the work of global reform so that it does not fall prey to either the fallacy of *premature specification* (positing a structure detached from the emergent political context) or that of *covert imperialism* (positing a structure in which one *part* of the world order system maximizes its gains at the expense of the well-being of the *whole*).

NOTES

1. For data on and an interpretation of these trends, see Johan Galtung, "Nonterritorial Actors and the Problem of Peace," in Saul H. Mendlovitz, ed., *On the Creation of a Just World Order* (New York: Free Press, 1975), pp. 151–188.

2. An important study of the relationship between politics and functionalism is E. B. Haas, *Beyond the Nation-State* (Stanford, Calif.: Stanford University Press, 1964).

3. For an illustration and discussion of these distinctions see chapter 3, pp. 000–000.

4. See the argument to this effect in Miriam Camps, *The Management of Interdependence* (New York: Council on Foreign Relations, 1974) and Stanley Hoffmann, *Primacy or World Order: American Foreign Policy since the Cold War* (New York: McGraw-Hill, 1978).

5. See, for example, Trilateral Commission Task Force Reports: 9–14, esp. nos. 9, 11, and 14, (New York: New York University Press: 1978).

6. Rajni Kothari, *Footsteps into the Future: Diagnosis of the Present World and a Design for an Alternative* (New York: Free Press, 1974); Ali Mazrui, *A World Federation of Cultures: An African Perspective* (New York: Free Press, 1976); Gustavo Lagos and Horacio Godoy, *Revolutions of Being: A Latin American View of the Future* (New York: Free Press, 1977); Richard Falk, *A Study of Future Worlds* (New York: Free Press, 1975); Johan Galtung, *The True Worlds: A Transnational Perspective* (New York: Free Press, 1980).

7. The institutional dimension of each perspective in note 6 is summarized in essay length in Galtung, "Nonterritorial Actors,"; my own discussion of the institutional dimension in a preferred world system is in Falk, *Future Worlds*, pp. 224–276.

8. Discussed in Falk, *Future Worlds*, pp. 11–33.

9. I have worked out a conception of the dynamics of international order based on this image of three linked and interlinked systems of actors: see Richard Falk, *Third System Initiatives in a Militarized World Order* (Poona, India, July 1978).

CHAPTER 14

Political Prospects, Cultural Choices, Anthropological Horizons

If you see the sword coming . . .
blow the trumpet and warn the people,
then if those hearing the trumpet do not take warning,
their blood will be on their own hands.

Ezekiel, 33:3–4

The future which we know
throws its shadow long before it enters.

Anna Akhmatova
"Amadeo Modigliano"
New York Review of Books
July 17, 1975

It does not require biblical prophecy to discern the seriousness of the present human predicament. Disregarding apocalyptic possibilities, present realities associated with collective violence, mass poverty, ecological decay, and widespread repression establish a firm foundation for discontent with the present political order at every level of organization. Symptoms of malfunction interlink on a planetary scale, making our era the first of universal history. Such symptoms are emerging at the same time that the expectation of social justice is urging many people throughout the world to call into question the prevailing order of privilege and tradition in national societies as well as the connections between national poverty, weakness, and the structure of international society.

Perhaps the link between "national security" and "nuclear catastrophe" remains the most powerful metaphor for a wider condition of pathological politics. The wisdom of our leaders and the resources and safety of our people depend on the proposition that our security

315

can be safeguarded by mutual threats of genocide, threats upon the lives and well-being of hundreds of millions of people with no voice to protest against such awesome danger and uncertainty. A nuclear arms race goes on with expensive, technetronic innovations that improve the accuracy, reliability, and destructive force of nuclear warheads, and bring into being new weapons systems (so-called vertical proliferation) that perpetuate the arms race with no longer even the pretense of adding to security. Simultaneously, the means to enter the nuclear club is spreading to many additional governments and may soon be available to splinter political groups as well (so-called horizontal proliferation). In a world system beset by inequality and premised upon a conviction that "might makes right," there is little hope of restraint by those who hold deep grievances. The rational prospect of self-destruction has never deterred those who are desperate or are deeply convinced of the justice of their cause. So we have a situation of mounting danger with no political will evident in any official institution to transform the situation. A sense of virtual resignation and inevitability prevails. During the 1976 presidential election campaign, neither Gerald Ford nor Jimmy Carter queried either the decency or vulnerability of a security system permanently based on nuclear deterrence and arms competition. It should be noticed, however, that Jimmy Carter did assert in his Inaugural Address an intention to "move this year a step toward our ultimate goal—the elimination of all nuclear weapons from this earth." We must wait with watchful skepticism to see if these encouraging words are translated into appropriate policies; we must as well watch what our Soviet superpower rival does to encourage or inhibit impulses toward denuclearization. At present, however, there is no basis for hope that nuclear weapons can be eliminated so long as "security" is entrusted to national military establishments upholding the competitive position of the main sovereign states that together make up the world system.

Despite objective circumstances that make it reasonable to regard our basic political arrangements as obsolete, it seems necessary to recognize that they are also durable. The array of forces favoring the status quo makes it implausible to anticipate global reform that could overcome the inadequacies associated with a world of roughly 170 sovereign states of greatly unequal size, wealth, and capability, each pursuing its state interests with scant regard for the general well-being either of each other or of the planet.

This double awareness that change in the political realm is, at once, necessary and impossible underlies the pessimism about the future that prevails in the West. Knowing that pessimism as a posture is often self-fulfilling and tends to immobilize, how do we resist immobilization and begin to consider the nature of the change required of our political structures and the choices available to our culture? I wish to address these issues in the context of planetary politics, seeking, above all, to encourage political activity that rejects a posture of hopelessness and that is committed to the establishment of a just world polity as the framework within which national societies and small communities can be governed.

The change that is needed is so fundamental that its achievement must be measured over decades, possibly centuries, not years. Therefore, we launch, as it were, upon a voyage; we must depart with a firm sense of present actualities and move toward a destination that is provisional and remote. But, though the destination may be remote, the reasons for undertaking the journey must be defined in a realistic spirit. Belief that the journey is possible must undergird the risks. Both the departure and a course wisely set can bring hope to those who join. An early launch is critical as each passing year makes the passage more hazardous. The aspiration that accompanies such a voyage calls to mind a response of Abdul Qadir, a holy person of Sufi tradition alive in the twelfth century. On being asked by an inquirer for guidance—"Can you give us power to improve the earth?"—he is reported to have replied:

I will do better: I will give this power to your descendants, because as yet there is no hope of such improvement being made on a large enough scale. The devices do not yet exist. You shall be rewarded; and they shall have the reward of their efforts and of your aspiration.[1]

We need to begin. In beginning we find the ground of our action and the hope needed to sustain risk.

Politics partakes of continuous evolution, offering the challenge of continuous self-transcendence. A "solution" of political issues in some kind of utopian polity is contrary to the evolutionary context of human existence, standing outside the flow of time. No ideal end of history can be happily envisioned; the stoppage of the flow of time would itself have a sterilizing impact upon human consciousness and so would be inconsistent with the judgment that some ideal polity had been attained. By contrast, the contingent politics we endorse is built on an ethos of revolutionary patience: contingent because subject to further evolution and dependent on fallible visions and actions of people; revolutionary because fundamental; patience because the revolution may not possess the capacity to transform existing power structures for many decades.

MANIFESTING POLITICAL CONSCIENCE

A commitment to possibility is required of those who undertake the voyage. Contingent politics is rooted in such commitment and encourages individuals and groups to manifest political conscience in the face of overwhelming resistance. Some problems may be too difficult for humans to solve. The problem of separating the security of large groups from the technological capacity—cool and abstract—to inflict massive death and destruction may be one such problem, but we do not yet know this. We have not yet tried. We must start by asking the same sorts of questions as Liz McAlister, one of those brave, unsung persons among us who, as a peace activist, bears witness with body and soul to the reality and gratuitousness of the nuclear menace:

> What has our use of, possession of, proliferation of the bomb done to our spirit as a people? What would it mean if we use these bombs again? What would it mean if others used them against us? What does it mean to destroy the world? . . . Why the pervasive moral numbness, the crippled public intelligence and imagination? Why the despairing suspicion that nuclear lunacy has gone too far, is too big to fight, too well financed, scenarioed, socially entrenched? . . . Why will the American left look upon the nuclear arms race as merely one of a myriad of pressing public issues? Who gives any of us the irrational luxury of that conclusion?[2]

What makes these questions vivid for Liz McAlister is that she, in communion with others at Jonah House in Baltimore, is building her life around their seriousness. As I write, she is in jail as a consequence of acts of civil disobedience. On December 28, 1976, she joined others in chaining shut the doors of the Pentagon and pouring blood on its columns. With these acts she dramatized for others the seriousness of nuclear policies and challenged the dominant sense of their being both abstract and irrelevant on our lives as well as the facile view that such issues can be left to the government and are, in any event, beyond the competence or reach of the citizenry.

More is required than manifesting a seriousness of concern; we have heard enough of mere opinions. Liz McAlister and her comrades offer us a view of action that defies a calculus of probabilities without claiming success in the face of formidable odds. Here is Liz McAlister's formulation:

Can a handful of folk—you and me—awaken conscience and concern? Can we bring life out of this present picture of death? Life is precarious and unpredictable, and the only way to live it is to make every effort to save it as long as there is a possibility of doing so.[3]

The Vietnamese people and their revolutionary leaders could not have persisted in their war of almost 30 years against the French and the Americans if they had based their struggle on a calculation of probabilities. Only by concentrating upon the possibility of victory could they ignore the overwhelming probability of failure. Lacking the motivation and inspiration of the Vietnamese, the American Peace Movement, faced with tiny risks by comparison, was repeatedly disillusioned and intimidated because its activities did not produce quick and dramatic results. Such disillusionment arises from an insufficient feeling for struggle as a process that persists despite frustrations and failures. To move toward a just world polity presupposes an understanding that the means and ends are necessary, requires an acceptance of risk, struggle, and uncertainty, at every stage, and the capacity to persevere in the face of apparent failure.

Manifesting conscience in concrete deeds by exemplary individuals is critically significant for raising political consciousness about planetary politics. At this stage, the abstractions about planetary danger are so generally accepted that they verge on being platitudes that numb more than arouse. Indeed, political leaders in control of the present outmoded, dangerous, and unjust system themselves bemoan human destiny and acknowledge the seriousness of such realities as nuclear threats, famine, poverty, terror and pollution. However, these same leaders accompany their words with policies that aggravate the very conditions they deplore. By acknowledging the dangers, the managers of power seek to enhance their capacity to govern by building public confidence; by ignoring such dangers in their policies, they avoid challenging entrenched vested interests with heavy stakes in high technology, militarism, big business and overseas investment. Considering these realities, it is hardly surprising that official rhetoric points toward the need for transformation and official policies toward the opposite need to sustain the status quo.

The art of ruling an obsolete political order depends on obscuring the gravity of the situation from the citizenry. Otherwise, legitimacy would erode and radical movements gain a foothold. If unrest or adverse developments (war, famine, economic or ecological catastrophe) were to make this tension between words and deeds more apparent, as began to happen for many younger Americans in the late 1960s, then we would expect the political leadership to opt for repression rather than benign adaptation. And, indeed, the repressive policies initiated in the Johnson and Nixon presidencies confirm this assessment. On a more intellectual level, the viability of democratic accountability and participation is challenged. Interestingly, the Trilateral Commission, that organization of the super elite dreamed up by David Rockefeller to coordinate the interests of dominant classes in North America, Western Europe, and Japan, sponsored, in addition to Jimmy Carter's bid for the presidency, a study arguing that the West was being endangered by an excess of democracy and that the future of these countries might depend on the willingness of their governments to establish greater control over their citizenry even if this meant curbing democratic rights.[4] Perceptions of this sort reveal a deteriorating situation better than the formal reassurances given by our leaders, but the corrective responses proposed are so menacing that it is as critical to expose their design as it is to grasp the reality of positive possibilities.

It is against this background that the heroic exploits of individuals challenging these negative trends attain their significance. To the actions of Liz McAlister can be added those of Karen Silkwood, Jim and Shelley Douglass, Dan and Phil Berrigan and countless others whose concerns in a variety of policy contexts inspire deeds of conscience. We mention these particular individuals to give substance to our argument. Karen Silkwood died a violent death under highly suspicious circumstances while seeking to expose the dangers of nuclear contamination to herself, to her co-workers, and indirectly to all of us, from the Kerr-McGee nuclear fuel plant in Oklahoma. Jim Douglass fasted for weeks against nuclear weaponry and, with the support of the Pacific Life Center, led a campaign of civil disobedience against a proposed base for Trident submarines at Bangor, Washington. With 70 others, Jim Douglass entered the base on August 8, 1976 by cutting a section out of the wire fence protecting the Naval facility. Proclaiming the Trident as an incipient "crime against humanity," the group chose to demonstrate on a Sunday that was between the anniversary of the Hiroshima and Nagasaki bombings. Jim Douglass was convicted of "malicious trespassing" and sent to jail for 90 days; his wife Shelley, also a leader in the struggle, was sentenced to a term of 60 days. Similarly, Dan and Phil Berrigan's frequent recent acts of nonviolent but militant witness against the war system have been treated as "crimes" by the system. To manifest conscience in ways that expose the violence of the dominant war system, especially if disrespect for property or official symbols of power is displayed, is regarded as "criminal."

The message of such responses is clear: do not trust official institutions or public reassurances on matters of vital significance to the health and safety of the society. It is naive to assume that governments are committed to the well-being of even their own people despite the nationalist mythology associated with the sovereign state. Notably, the most flagrant abuses of human rights are at home, directed toward those who supposedly are beneficiaries of the protective custody of the wrongdoing government. Governmental behavior toward foreign societies, global interests, and the future is even less conscientious. Protests against the irresponsibility of foreign governments is common enough, as when Liberia registers as seaworthy unsafe oil tankers like the *Argo Merchant* or China explodes a nuclear device that showers radioactivity over the northern hemisphere.

No state is immune from the tendency to endorse the pursuit of power, wealth, and prestige, regardless of the harm done to others. A humiliating example can be drawn from recent American behavior. The U.S. Agency for International Development has recently admitted to shipping abroad pesticides declared too dangerous for use in the United States; South Vietnam and Indonesia evidently were sent sixty-four metric tons of leptophos for use on cotton crops, despite evidence linking this pesticide to serious nerve disorders and paralysis. Nor can such official insensitivity be linked exclusively to a single ideology. The bureaucratic socialist states within the Soviet orbit have to varying degrees subjected their own people to repressive and cruel policies and have shown, in general, less concern for public well-being than have the capitalist democracies. For instance, Soviet failure to protect its population from the hazards of nuclear energy is notorious and appears far more serious than the lamentable record of protection achieved by the American regulatory institutions, the Atomic Energy Commission, and the Nuclear Regulatory Commission. Manifesting conscience through defiant confrontation with the arrayed power of the state is a lonely, frustrating experience that demands profound moral and political dedication. The media characteristically fail to interpret such activity in a clarifying way, confining attention to the punishment imposed by the state and ignoring matters of motivation and concern. Consequently, individuals engaged in such activity often feel isolated and misunderstood. There is not as yet a supportive movement of the sort that existed during the Vietnam period that stands behind those who actively seek a radical restructuring of the world political system.

The message of the deed is not the only effective way to address these issues at this time in American society. Another way to manifest conscience is to embody positive values in concrete circumstances of personal existence, including joining in the effort to build communities that are as independent as possible of high technology, of the state bureaucracy, and of the money economy. In this regard experimental communities prefiguring a future that is minimally dependent on the state and the market for self-realization are inspiring examples; they demonstrate that alternative futures of a positive sort can exist, at least on a small scale, and be made to work; that we are not yet irreversibly entrapped in an experience of cultural disintegration. Cultural explorations of this kind often are laden with hopeful political content; the New Alchemy Institute, the Philadelphia and Pacific Life Centers, the Lindesfarne Association, and the Zen Center in San Francisco are some positive examples with which I am familiar. In each context, the emergent reality radically repudiates the mainstream polity and culture, particularly the pursuit of styrofoam prosperity rooted in a "national security mentality" and disjoined from the pursuit of life, liberty, and happiness for each individual.

A third way of manifesting conscience with regard to planetary prospects is to depict as credibly as possible the contours of a just world polity. To avoid sterile utopography, such positive visions need to be accompanied by transition strategies that weigh issues of attainability as seriously as those of desirability. These images of the future, drawn upon a large canvas of ideas and ideology, can foreshadow a positive destiny for human society that complements deeds of conscience by activists and cultural innovations by communities of conscience. As a civilization and as a species, we need images of "the big picture" because, in a period accurately called the age of interdependence, there is no space that is insulated from danger; "the little picture" of private actions and communal life will not flourish if the pressure on governance structures intensifies. If pressure increases, the state is certain to close off experimental space because of its threatening potential. Even now, most people in most societies have no present opportunity to manifest conscience in their lives without inviting death or brutalization. Therefore, a response to the current condition that has any prospect of success must include some program for mobilizing mass support for the possibilities of a new political order of planetary scope based on peace and justice. The World

Order Models Project of the Institute for World Order has been seeking to work out such images of "the big picture." In a series of books, intellectuals from all the regions of the world have projected specific images of how to achieve a world political system based on peace, economic equity, human rights, and ecological balance. (Examples are Mendlovitz, ed., *On the Creation of a Just World Order;* Kothari, *Footsteps into the Future;* Mazrui, *A World Federation of Cultures;* Falk, *A Study of Future Worlds*). These images, though crude, initiate a global process of envisioning alternative orders of power and wealth that could exist at the *center* of societal arrangements rather than within experimental space along the peripheries of power. These images (not blueprints) emphasize public education as an immediate priority. Learning about the dangers and failings of the present order, associating these dangers and failings with prevailing values and institutional forms, and building a transnational consensus around new values and institutional forms are essential to shaping a different political order.

A just world polity embodying these values can take a variety of forms. The underlying institutional hypothesis is that the state system cannot provide sufficient "central guidance" to deal with problems of planetary scope such as fallout, ozone depletion, endangered species, nuclear peace, disaster relief, and tanker spills. Separate state interests are too diverse and antagonistic either to achieve necessary levels of cooperation or to elicit appropriate concern for the well-being of the whole planet and of future generations. Both a global ethics of space and a futuristic ethics of time must emerge as real components of political consciousness if we are to deal with major symptoms of societal distress.

To conceive of central guidance on top of the state system, in the manner of "world federalism," would merely create a superbureaucracy, exacerbating disastrous tendencies toward "bureaucratic centralism" that are already crippling spiritual possibilities on the national level. Therefore, our political imaginations need to be stimulated beyond the facile view that the existing failures of state governance to provide adequate security and well-being can be remedied by expanding the scope of governance to a planetary scale. Technology is not the only realm where small is, or can be, beautiful; politics is paramountly such a realm as well. We need to envision how a perspective of smallness translates into social, economic, and political forms of organization. How can we achieve world order values, in other words, within a political framework of minimum governance?

Such speculations spring from an understanding of the modern state, its role, strengths, and limits. To dismiss the state as "obsolete" overlooks the degree to which peoples of the Third World regard the building of strong states at this stage of their development as a progressive step enabling them to attain higher degrees of political, economic, and cultural independence; that is, the state as instrument of antiimperialism may be regarded in a positive light. Such a positive function of the state does not eliminate criticism of statism as it operates within and among the northern tier of advanced industrial countries, but it does complicate the issue of the state.

Given the outline of priorities of a just global order, certain conclusions follow. Political and economic decentralization accompanied by a strengthening of cultural vitality must precede and predominate in the process of transformation. Political and economic decentralization at the state level, especially for the rich and powerful, is quite consistent with centralization of the interdependent aspects of international life such as oceans, environment, reserves, human rights. This view of institutional change is dialectical—small is beautiful to achieve human-scale communities, large is necessary to cope with the destructive effects of unregulated and highly interactive human activity. The premises of a social movement to evolve a just world polity derive strongly from the ideological traditions associated with libertarian socialism, philosophical anarchism, humanism, and militant nonviolence. Bakunin, Kropotkin, Whitehead, Gandhi, and Martin Luther King are among the intellectual forebears of such a movement for change.

The political situation during a time of fundamental change is characterized both by exceptional vulnerability and by a release of creative energies among those who know the old game is almost up. On the one side, we hear intimations of impending doom. (Richard Nixon confided to visitors during the last days of his presidency, "I could pick up that phone right now and in twenty-five minutes seventy million people would be dead.")[5] On the other, we see growing evidence of a spiritual reawakening that includes the rediscovery that national destiny as well as human survival depend on our capacity as a species to participate reciprocally in nature and on our willingness to reach distant and near to make both part of the whole. Of course, such rediscoveries, if they are to take hold, presuppose a cultural mutation, a veritable leap beyond the present that cannot be anticipated by any projection of past trends or any incremental process of continuous adjustment. The options are polar: breakdown or breakthrough. In this sense, hope depends on a radical turn of mind. As Doris Lessing has written, "There are lungs attached to men that lie as dormant as those of a babe in the womb, and they are waiting for the solar wind to fill them like sails."[6]

In contrast, despair (or its double—fatuous optimism à la Herman Kahn) reflects a prosaic turn of mind—deploy rational faculties to continue doing what we have, making those small adjustments that seem possible given constraints on change, given the inertia of large organizations, and given the entrenchment of powerful elites and interest groups. Intellectually, as well as politically, no tools for adjustment available to those now running things can provide us with any prospect of a positive human destiny.

Future possibilities are also embodied in past social arrangements. A thorough understanding of the life styles and world visions of American Indian tribes, for instance, which vividly express a spiritual conception of human reality, including such values as simplicity, communal solidarity, and connectedness to nature, as expressed in *Black Elk Speaks* is helpful. It is important to realize, without romanticizing such past social orders, that satisfying modes of social existence preceded and were displaced by our highly rational civilization with its linear insistence on measurable progress and its insensitivity to cycles and spirals of evolution and to normative values like peacefulness, happiness, beauty, spirituality, and playfulness. Realizing values appropriate to our situation implies drawing upon the heritage of the past as well as upon innovation. Appreciation of a heritage is not a matter of nostalgia for that which is beyond recall, but of building upon the usable past while working toward a desirable future.

SOME COMMENTS ON THE POLITICAL REALM

This chapter argues that the political prospect of our time must be interpreted primarily in light of the possibilities of cultural renewal along specified lines of value change. What I wish to consider here are both the limits of our present political structures and the possibilities for cultural transformation of consciousness that will influence the configurations of a global policy. By "political" I mean the governing process, that is, the institutional arrangements of power and authority relating to security and welfare within specified boundaries. The territory can be as small as the family, as R. D. Laing points out in *The Politics of the Family*, or as large as the planet or larger. The central political focus in our time is the sovereign state, partly because of its accumulation of incredible firepower to sustain order at home and abroad. Science fiction writers like Ursula Le Guin in *The Dispossessed* extend our political imagination beyond the planet, disclosing the possibility of interplanetary, even intergalactic, politics. As expected, scientists are beginning to make these fictional boundaries of the imagination part of our potential social reality, as Gerald O'Neill's projected "space colonies" indicate.[7]

Politics is closely associated with "economics," the defense or extension of arrangements for the production and distribution of income and wealth. Of particular importance in the present world situation is the extent to which the state upholds rights to own, accumulate, and transmit "private property." The ownership of the means of production, which is the issue that most sharply distinguishes socialism and capitalism, the motivation underlying work, and the location of decisive power with respect to production priorities, such as planning versus profits or control of workers, are critical economic issues. Other economic issues with political content include the transmission of inequalities from generation to generation, as in the "inheritance" of wealth or class structure, and the economic inequalities between social classes that leave the "lower" classes below the poverty line. Equality of economic opportunity, independent of sex, race, and age, also raises important issues these days for the political process. Class consciousness, the sense of injustice by the deprived, often determines whether the governing process rests on consent, education, and persuasion or on force and intimidation. One sign of the deteriorating world situation is the declining presence of consensual government at the state level or, put differently, the disappearing legitimacy of government. The image of the "illegitimate" state arises from a combination of its inability to rule by consent and its related inability to satisfy fundamental human needs for security and welfare.

Politics also is inevitably bound to the pattern of beliefs, values, myths, and goals embodied in a culture that identifies and unifies a particular societal grouping. The legitimacy of the state depends also on whether the pacifying myths of the state that arouse loyalty and obedience are commonly accepted by most of the people. "The king can do no wrong" was one such myth that supported the prerogatives claimed by kings and queens. In the contemporary bureaucratic socialist state, the reigning monarch has been replaced by "the party" that claims absolute wisdom to rule because it relies upon an infallible body of ideological dogma. Many sovereign states are multicultural; they encompass several religions, languages, heritages, and group identities within given territorial boundaries. The political task then at the state level is to propagate unifying myths of shared experience that engender loyalty from each cultural element. If the apparatus of the state is dominated by one cultural entity, widely based loyalty is difficult to promote. Indeed, much political conflict in the present period arises from struggles of transnational and subnational groups to achieve a greater measure of political autonomy within fixed state boundaries. Most of the separatist movements active in Quebec, Scotland, Iraq, Ethiopia, the Soviet Union, Spain, and Belgium are operating in states where the apparatus of governing has been captured by an antagonistic ethnic, regional, religious, or language group.

Cultural identity exists on a civilizational level as well as on the state level; the beliefs, values, and goals of a civilization's identity transcend the boundaries drawn on world maps or even the boundaries created by separate languages, races, and religions. Secular materialism, for instance, is buttressed by the conviction that "progress" in human affairs is possible only so long as science-based technology is continously applied to increase the productivity of agriculture and industry. Both socialist and capitalist political ideologies share this underlying commitment to economic growth, measured by increases in GNP. An image of indefinite expansion of world product ignores "the limits to growth" arising from the constraints of finite acres of agricultural land, finite deposits of mineral resources, and environmental capacity to absorb pollution. Despite a flurry of interest in 1972 in *The Limits to Growth* published under the auspices of The Club of Rome, the governing elites of the world have unanimously reaffirmed that, at least in the short run, only growth can deal with the economic issues that matter—jobs and inflation, not to mention profits. Although useful in posing questions, the Club of Rome perspective—elitist and technocratic—took for granted the desirability of maximum material growth, confining its analysis to matters of sustainability.

Only very recently has questioning of the cultural underpinnings of industrial civilization been taken seriously; hence, we have the gradual emergence of "a counterculture" in open Western societies. These gropings toward cultural renewal converge around the view that spiritual realities are the essence of every benevolent pattern of human development, that a technology geared to abstract and aggregate societal goals such as increases in GNP and to returns on capital is not socially beneficial, even if it were ecologically sustainable, and that economic overdevelopment tends to occasion cultural regression. In a time of cultural regression, life seems meaningless and many pathological patterns of behavior emerge; there is a loss of personal and communal centeredness, a deepening alienation from neighbors, from nature, from spiritual possibilities. The inability of American citizens to walk safely in their cities despite the extraordinary levels of social affluence attained is indicative of a failing culture. Neighbors who watch a woman being assaulted and raped from the safety of their apartment windows without bothering to telephone the police exemplify this loss of human connection. Such loss disposes the dissatisfied toward violence and the satisfied toward repression. Terrorism of many descriptions results on both sides. It is no wonder a police chief in the Bronx, when interviewed about his role, described it as heading "an army of occupation."

Attitudes toward "nature" are reflected in a cultural identity. The mainstream culture of the modern West upholds the human capacity to transcend, to dominate, and to pacify nature. This attitude has precipitated a global ecological crisis that is destroying our habitat and diminishing the life prospects of future generations, as it simultaneously produces mass alienation. Individuals entrapped in this dying culture start to explore from their own reality of "alienation" a wide variety of strategies for "reunion" with nature. Not all explorations are desirable. At one extreme, hard drugs impose intolerable costs on body and spirit as the price of a bogus, if exhilarating, reunion. At the other, "quick fix" business propositions like EST help their customers tune out of the alienating circumstance of the culture, at least for a while, by various psychological devices of reinforcement, assuring individuals of the normalcy of their feelings and actions, as well as affirming egocentric views of social experience (get what you can, don't feel guilt, don't judge others).

Alienation from nature produces a mind set that compartmentalizes rather than interconnects and unifies. Thus, those who live in a faltering culture tend to examine its politics and economics but not necessarily its underlying values and beliefs. We accept that the governing process seeks to sustain economics that serve the dominant culture. Those who are deeply dissatisfied with economic performance because it is wasteful or unfair or destructive are characteristically at odds with prevailing politics, but do not necessarily draw the dominant culture into question. For instance, most of the ideological/political struggles associated with socialism, fascism, and liberalism that have supported high technology in our country are carried on within an accepted cultural framework of secular materialism. Only recently the political question has begun to be posed in cultural as well as economic terms. The Chinese emphasis on "cultural revolution" and the emergence of "countercultural" forms in the West are two directions in which radical politics express an appreciation of the fundamental role of culture in structuring societal forms as well as human consciousness. Such a cultural emphasis tends to convert political outlooks from a concern with "events" (the revolution) to a focus on "process" ("permanent evolution"). Cultural preoccupations also lengthen time horizons, since the processes of change connected with underlying beliefs, values, myths, and goals are slow and continuous.

Whether attempts at cultural renewal can endure in a hostile global climate is questionable. Even China's experiment, while a profound example of cultural renewal, is not without deep difficulties. Mao Tse-tung's imposition of a rigid common conception that was intolerant of any dissent makes Chinese culture vulnerable, especially in Mao's absence, to the appeals of the technetronic age and the bureaucratic centralizing tendencies of the modern state. Cultural innovations in Western democracies are equally vulnerable. In some sense they are dependent on the beneficence of liberalism in the culture whose values they abhor. Such dependence can be corrupting, but even when it is not, the state will be disposed to crack down on innovation when pressures resulting from the failure of liberalism mount against its own claims of legitimacy.

To seek or to create possibilities for cultural renewal is radical action, in the sense of going to the root of things. Due to its nature, such action is rejected by almost all those who dominate present political and economic arrangements. In my view, to expect political renewal to emanate from the official institutions of the state located in Washington is as foolish, though not quite as obviously foolish, as to expect cultural renewal to come from the TV networks or Hollywood movies. Indeed, the nihilistic quality of recent big budget Hollywood movies reflects a cultural condition of severe anomie—all viewpoints are corrupt; self-seeking is drenched with violence; technological gadgetry infatuates the characters; the backdrop is often an antiseptic surrounding of urban modernity, and a figure that critic Richard Eder identifies as the "anti-hero" dominates the script. "King Kong," "Marathon Man," "The Next Man," "The Killer Elite," "Network," and "Three Days of the Condor" are productions in this vein. A growing awareness of this cultural situation is more likely than is an awareness of the political situation. An underlying illusion of competence in the political arena persists, despite a temporary loss of public confidence in the integrity of the governing process created by Vietnam and Watergate. However, political and cultural consciousness are becoming reconnected here in the United States, and this holds promise.

Many of those who were disillusioned politically in the 1960s

have been working seriously to rebuild the culture. Properly interpreted, their disillusionment does not entail renouncing goals like
peace and justice, but it may represent a realization that these goals
cannot now be directly, narrowly, or exclusively pursued. What has
been difficult for political radicals in America to learn is that the
climate for change does not yet exist and that there is no quick fix for
the polity, once it is understood that the priorities for change are
integrally linked with transforming values, as well as shifting power
elites. But such an understanding is essential, for without a culture-
based politics of renewal every prescription for either reform or revolution is certain to fail when put to the test. In addition, in the United
States there is no basis as yet for mobilizing support for radical
change. Revolutionary initiatives, being premature, prompt counterrevolutionary tactics by the state. Indeed, modern experience with
political revolutions increasingly is being interpreted by those Western radicals seeking fundamental structural changes in social, political, and economic realms as discrediting politics per se. More
accurately, this experience should be understood as discrediting disconnected politics. Such an understanding could move us beyond
despair for the future, because the therapy, although slow, is attuned
to the pathology as well as to the relation of forces and can be immediately realized in concrete situations of individual and group behavior.

    When a country is materially impoverished, as is the case
throughout Asia, Africa, and Latin America, the progress of alienation can be deferred if social energies are mobilized around the elimination of poverty, the attainment of equity, and a vision of societal
purpose. Cuba, after decades of corruption and slumber, has illustrated this dynamism during the Castro years. But if it is correct that
spiritual identity is integral to human fulfillment, then alienation is
bound to emerge if Cuban society is constrained for an indefinite
period by a materialistic ethic of work and service. Even though "work
and service" under revolutionary conditions can partake of some
spirituality, especially when they are inspired by a charismatic leader
with a vision of the future, cultural creativity eventually presupposes a
level of individual freedom to transcend earlier social norms or a
traditional core of shared beliefs that provides a spiritual center available to all. With neither freedom nor tradition, cultural decline is
bound to result and a condition of cultural underdevelopment
emerge. We know from Western experience that material satisfactions, even in circumstances of individual freedom, will not prevent
cultural underdevelopment when spiritual values are totally divorced
from the daily realities of work and living.

Poor countries have stressed the priority of economic development in recent years. Only lately has it become clear that, if the strategy of economic development is dominated by the goals of a privileged elite or is carried out without concern for human effects, the results are likely to be adverse. Political or economic changes that are separated from a preservation of human rights are necessarily reduced to a conventional political attempt to seize power on behalf of a repressed elite. Even if a one-dimensional change should succeed and live up to the promises of those seeking power, it is unlikely to provide the kind of restructuring of behavior and institutions capable of integrating political, economic, and cultural perspectives. For this reason, a new stress on human rights is being made around the world by those who hold progressive ideals associated with peace, empathy, and love of nature. The elementary realization of human rights is a precondition for cultural renewal.

This emphasis on human rights is also a response to the repressive exercise of state power in a situation of deepening crisis, especially throughout the Third World. These tendencies can be summarized as a drift toward several varieties of authoritarian rule in the Third World. The authoritarian solution, combining extreme centralization of power and brutal practices of repression that include torture on a systematic basis, is a direct consequence of reliance upon capitalist or market-oriented development strategies in contexts of massive poverty and extensive inequality, where an acute sense of injustice on the part of victims exists. That is, strategies for development, exemplified by such societies as Brazil or South Korea, generally put the governing elite in the service of a somewhat larger social group, about 10 to 25 percent of the total, composed of traditional land-owning and industrial elites, skilled laborers, merchants, and the civil servants, including the military. A recent affirmation of faith in this developmental model was made inadvertently by Pablo Baraona, Director of the Central Bank in Chile and a close economic advisor of the Pinochet regime, when he asserted that the fact "that more than 90 percent of the people are against our policies is proof that the model is working."[8]

The organic interplay of politics, economics, and culture provides the basis for reconstructing the future in beneficial ways. Such a view starts with a critique of those forms of "development" that rest on mere "growth," without emphasis on "justice" or "the quality of life." It moves from critique to activity, either by way of political struggle or cultural innovation. Because societal circumstances vary dramatically, what makes sense in the United States may be impossible to undertake in the Soviet Union and inappropriate in Zaire or

Bolivia. There is, however, a common motif: humane development. That kind of development will encourage political, economic, and cultural forms that move toward goals that can be professed under all circumstances: non-violence, economic well-being, human rights, and ecological balance.

Concrete expression of these shared goals will be determined by the particularity of individuals and groups as they decide how best to act given their own talents, desires, and circumstances of time and place. In general, however, we require a solution of planetary scope as well as one of human scale. We require myths of solidarity and destiny that generate the political will to evolve planetary procedures of central guidance. As soon as possible, we need minimum institutions of planning, regulation, and assessment that are both responsive to the realities of interdependence and reflective of a new positive consensus to create a planetary community. Our need is urgent, but the nature of the task is such that it cannot be rushed without being ruined. Decades, at least, will be required.

Finally, cultural politics on the level of human interaction and planetary politics on the level of global interdependence will depend mainly on grassroots political possibilities. The official elites in most government structures are incapable of a radical restructuring of their attitudes and behavior. Instead, the citizenry must be mobilized to challenge the assumptions of official institutions; leadership responsive to a new populist ideology must emerge. Whether this can happen, and where, is problematical. Do we look to Governor Jerry Brown as a political forerunner, a bearer of some of the values of cultural renewal but also as one compelled to operate, for political effectiveness, within a web of vested interests and stereotyped beliefs?

We do not know whether we can or will succeed. But we do know, I think, that we will be lost—spiritually and, quite possibly, biologically—if we fail to try. The case for trying seems overwhelming.

AN ANTHROPOLOGICAL POSTSCRIPT

Science fiction writers have always been acutely aware that the universe may include several planets capable of sustaining some kind of human society and that the fundamental history and organization of each may be dramatically different. It is often unclear whether a particular author believes that the foundation of this difference is a matter of cultural evolution or reflects the presence in the universe of an array of species with differing social traits. In the latter instance, the interpretation of the difference is largely an anthropological matter, and its careful study could help illuminate both limits and potentialities bearing on human development.

Ursula Le Guin touches on these issues toward the end of *The Dispossessed,* when the physicist-hero Shevek is voyaging back to the anarchist planet of Anarres after an extended visit to Urras, a planet that seems close to what our earth civilization might become in a couple of centuries if we prove lucky enough to escape an apocalyptic transfiguration. Shevek engages in conversation with Keng, the ambassador from Terra, about different human societies, those "billions of people in the nine Known Worlds." Shevek explains to Keng that his creative breakthrough ("Transilience, space travel, you see, without traversal of space or lapse of time") would make possible a mutually beneficial, new planetary order among these nine worlds, but that A-lo, a country in Urras, sought possession of the new understanding of ultimate reality for imperialist purposes, "to get power over others, to get richer or to win more wars." Shevek, in the end, chooses to repress knowledge under these circumstances: "I will not serve *any* master."

Keng concludes that the anarchistic community of Anarres sounds too good to be true: "I wept listening to you, but I really didn't believe you. Men always speak so of their homes, of the absent land. . . . But you are *not* like other men. There is a difference in you." Since Anarres was originally created by countercultural struggle on Urras, the difference discerned seems mainly unconnected with species traits, but is an expression of cultural potentiality.

But Keng herself sounds like one who comes from neither world. To her "Urras is the kindliest, most various, most beautiful of all the inhabited worlds. It is the world that comes as close as any could to Paradise." And she notes that for Shevek, in contrast, Urras is Hell. What, then must Terra be like? Keng describes Terra:

My world, my Earth, is a ruin. A planet spoiled by the human species. We controlled neither appetite nor violence; we did not adapt. . . .there are not forests left on my Earth. The earth is grey, the sky is grey, it is always hot. . .there are nearly a half billion of us now. Once there were nine billion. . . . We failed as a species, as a social species.

The destiny that befell Terra is now threatening us. In a sense, Urras is our positive destiny, Terra our negative destiny. Both are dysutopias. Annares is depicted by Ursula LeGuin as "an ambiguous utopia," problematic, but better than anything the rational mind can calculate, an anarchistic polity that embodies a radically different set of societal arrangements. Is it out beyond the reach of the human species and, hence, utopian, in the sense of being imaginable but unattainable? Or is it one of the possible lines of potential human development encoded into our genotype as a species? After listening to Shevek tell about his own belief in human potentiality, Keng exclaims "I thought I knew what 'realism' was," and Shevek replies, "How can you, if you don't know what hope is."[9]

Hope, to be credible, has to be founded on radical expectations. Muddling through cannot be expected to achieve more than the world of Urras and will more likely invite the fate of Terra, a degraded human existence, but not total extinction. Jean-Paul Sartre, interviewed on his seventieth birthday, described his greatest failing as not being radical enough, not going far enough in following through on his beliefs.[10] How to find the insight and wisdom and strength to be radical enough is probably the most important issue facing individuals who are both realistic and hopeful about the future. I was recently impressed by Anaïs Nin's self-appraisal at the end of the sixth volume of her diaries: "I feel I have accomplished what I hope to accomplish: to reveal how personal errors influence the whole of history and that our real objective is to create a human being who will not go to war."[11] This outlook is what I mean by an anthropological perspective.

Such a perspective concerns *limits* as well as *horizons*. Earlier in this essay I ventured the view that we may be dealing with some problems that are too difficult for human beings to solve. If that is correct, the expenditure of effort for their solution merely deepens frustration. I feel that such reasoning applies in recent decades to many dimensions of technology. We have already allowed our curiosity and greed to open too many Pandora's boxes to survive very well as a species. Our sense of historical absolutism is such that *any* step needed to achieve immediate security or prosperity seems justifiable at the time. The nuclear bomb is a prime instance of anthropological arrogance. We are the wrong species to handle this kind of technology in any acceptable way. Our political forms are too unstable to assure restraint over time. Our personality structures are too variable to permit much confidence that psychopathic behavior will not intervene at some stage to unleash a gratuitous nuclear holocaust. Furthermore, the biosphere is subject to such a variety of natural disasters that it is impossible to assure physical stability for long time periods. This questioning of human capacity seems well-founded given recent experiences as diverse as Auschwitz, Hiroshima, and the Gulag Archipelago.

The experience with nuclear technology is worth examining. The bomb was originally developed at a furious pace in "The Manhattan Project," because of fear during World War II that Germany might acquire it first. But once we acquired it, we used and developed it along quite different lines. The use of the bomb against the Japanese lacks a credible national survival justification, despite the rationalization that it saved lives in the society that used the bomb. Even this limited claim of "military necessity" is controversial; some historians feel that Japan was prepared in any event to surrender, or would have, had a demonstration explosion been made. After the bomb was used, the United States made only a short-lived, half-hearted and controversial attempt to achieve nuclear disarmament. When the attempt failed in 1946, a process of continuous evolution of nuclear weaponry and its gradual dissemination began. Furthermore, the governments of nuclear states have insisted on independent discretion to use these weapons as they see fit in situations of international conflict.

And now thirty years later, energy concerns are leading governments around the world to make heavy investments in nuclear power industries not only as sources of electricity but also for assured access to nuclear weaponry at little additional cost or effort. Like the bombs, nuclear reactors create hazards that require the kinds of perfect control that human society is ill equipped to provide. Too much stability and technological ingenuity is required over too long periods. To aspire after such stability is itself undesirable and dangerous, creating pretexts for further state interventions in our lives. The presence of numerous nuclear reactors in societies that include many disturbed and tormented individuals, as well as social and political discontent, points up the need for extensive police surveillance and a permanently militarized polity. Any enlightened citizenry would demand to live in a police state as the lesser of two evils in the event nuclear power takes hold in a major way.

Like Icarus, we are trying to fly close to the sun with waxen wings. Perhaps this impulse to do more than we can has been part of our temperament as a species from the beginning; perhaps, it played a positive role in earlier periods, helping our ancestors to find their way out of the cave and enabling human beings to accomplish marvelous and mysterious things. But with the advent of nuclear technology, biogenetics, and weather control, we have exceeded our limits as a species. The wax that holds our wings is melting. Is there time to descend? Do we have the wisdom and will to do so?

Anthropologists of the future will be fascinated by whether we pose and respond to such questions. For now, those who care about the future will do well, I think, to mobilize their energies to oppose the powerful forces that insist upon the inevitability of technetronic momentum.

NOTES

1. Idries Shah, *Tales of the Dervishes* (New York: E.P. Dutton, 1970).

2. Quotations from Liz McAlister taken from *Year One,* Vol. II, no. 6 December 1976, p. 7.

3. Ibid.

4. Michael J. Crozier, Samuel P. Huntington and Joji Watanuki, *The Crisis of Democracy: Report on the Governability of Democracies to the Trilateral Commission* (New York: New York University Press, 1975).

5. As reported by Senator Alan Cranston, *Rolling Stone,* February 26, 1976, p. 35.

6. Doris Lessing, *Briefing for a Descent into Hell* (New York: Bantam, 1972).

7. Gerald K. O'Neill, *The High Frontier: Human Colonies in Space* (New York: Morrow, 1977).

8. Quoted in the *New York Times,* December 8, 1976, p. A18.

9. Ursula Le Guin, *The Dispossessed* (New York: Harper and Row, 1974).

10. "Sartre at Seventy: An Interview," *New York Review of Books,* August 7, 1975, pp. 10–17.

11. Anaïs Nin, *Diary of Anaïs Nin,* 7 vols. (New York: Harcourt Brace Jovanovich, 1966–1980), vol. 6, p. 399.

Books Written Under the Auspices of the Center of International Studies, Princeton University, 1952–1981

Gabriel A. Almond, *The Appeals of Communism* (Princeton University Press, 1954).

William W. Kaufmann, ed., *Military Policy and National Security* (Princeton University Press, 1956).

Klaus Knorr, *The War Potential of Nations* (Princeton University Press, 1956).

Lucian W. Pye, *Guerrilla Communism in Malaya* (Princeton University Press, 1956).

Charles De Visscher, *Theory and Reality in Public International Law*, trans. by P.E. Corbett (Princeton University Press, 1957; rev. ed. 1968).

Bernard C. Cohen, *The Political Process and Foreign Policy: The Making of the Japanese Peace Settlement* (Princeton University Press, 1957).

Myron Weiner, *Party Politics in India: The Development of a Multi-Party System* (Princeton University Press, 1957).

Percy E. Corbett, *Law in Diplomacy* (Princeton University Press, 1959).

Rolf Sannwald and Jacques Stohler, *Economic Integration: Theoretical Assumptions and Consequences of European Unification*, trans. by Herman Karreman (Princeton University Press, 1959).

Klaus Knorr, ed., *NATO and American Security* (Princeton University Press, 1959).

Gabriel A. Almond and James S. Coleman, eds., *The Politics of the Developing Areas* (Princeton University Press, 1960).

Herman Kahn, *On Thermonuclear War* (Princeton University Press, 1960).

Sidney Verba, *Small Groups and Political Behavior: A Study of Leadership* (Princeton University Press, 1961).

Robert J. C. Butow, *Tojo and the Coming of the War* (Princeton University Press, 1961).

Glenn H. Snyder, *Deterrence and Defense: Toward a Theory of National Security* (Princeton University Press, 1961).

Klaus Knorr and Sidney Verba, eds., *The International System: Theoretical Essays* (Princeton University Press, 1961).

Peter Paret and John W. Shy, *Guerrillas in the 1960s* (Praeger, 1962).

George Modelski, *A Theory of Foreign Policy* (Praeger, 1962).

Klaus Knorr and Thornton Read, eds., *Limited Strategic War* (Praeger, 1963).

Frederick S. Dunn, *Peace-Making and the Settlement with Japan* (Princeton University Press, 1963).

Arthur L. Burns and Nina Heathcote, *Peace-Keeping by United Nations Forces* (Praeger, 1963).

Richard A. Falk, *Law, Morality, and War in the Contemporary World* (Praeger, 1963).

James N. Rosenau, *National Leadership and Foreign Policy: A Case Study in the Mobilization of Public Support* (Princeton University Press, 1963).

Gabriel A. Almond and Sidney Verba, *The Civic Culture: Political Attitudes and Democracy in Five Nations* (Princeton University Press, 1963).

Bernard C. Cohen, *The Press and Foreign Policy* (Princeton University Press, 1963).

Richard L. Sklar, *Nigerian Political Parties: Power in an Emergent African Nation* (Princeton University Press, 1963).

Peter Paret, *French Revolutionary Warfare from Indochina to Algeria: The Analysis of a Political and Military Doctrine* (Praeger, 1964).

Harry Eckstein, ed., *Internal War: Problems and Approaches* (Free Press, 1964).

Cyril E. Black and Thomas P. Thornton, eds., *Communism and Revolution: The Strategic Uses of Political Violence* (Princeton University Press, 1964).

Miriam Camps, *Britain and the European Community, 1955-1963* (Princeton University Press, 1964).

Thomas P. Thornton, ed., *The Third World in Soviet Perspective: Studies by Soviet Writers on the Developing Areas* (Princeton University Press, 1964).

James N. Rosenau, ed., *International Aspects of Civil Strife* (Princeton University Press, 1964).

Sidney I. Ploss, *Conflict and Decision-Making in Soviet Russia: A Case Study of Agricultural Policy, 1953–1963* (Princeton University Press, 1965).

Richard A. Falk and Richard J. Barnet, eds., *Security in Disarmament* (Princeton University Press, 1965).

Karl von Vorys, *Political Development in Pakistan* (Princeton University Press, 1965).

Harold and Margaret Sprout, *The Ecological Perspective on Human Affairs, with Special Reference to International Politics* (Princeton University Press, 1965).

Klaus Knorr, *On the Uses of Military Power in the Nuclear Age* (Princeton University Press, 1966).

Harry Eckstein, *Division and Cohesion in Democracy: A Study of Norway* (Princeton University Press, 1966).

Cyril E. Black, *The Dynamics of Modernization: A Study in Comparative History* (Harper and Row, 1966).

Peter Kunstadter, ed., *Southeast Asian Tribes, Minorities, and Nations* (Princeton University Press, 1967).

E. Victor Wolfenstein, *The Revolutionary Personality: Lenin, Trotsky, Gandhi* (Princeton University Press, 1967).

Leon Gordenker, *The UN Secretary-General and the Maintenance of Peace* (Columbia University Press, 1967).

Oran R. Young, *The Intermediaries: Third Parties in International Crises* (Princeton University Press, 1967).

James N. Rosenau, ed., *Domestic Sources of Foreign Policy* (Free Press, 1967).

Richard F. Hamilton, *Affluence and the French Worker in the Fourth Republic* (Princeton University Press, 1967).

Linda B. Miller, *World Order and Local Disorder: The United Nations and Internal Conflicts* (Princeton University Press, 1967).

Henry Bienen, *Tanzania: Party Transformation and Economic Development* (Princeton University Press, 1967).

Wolfram F. Hanrieder, *West German Foreign Policy, 1949–1963: International Pressures and Domestic Response* (Stanford University Press, 1967).

Richard H. Ullman, *Britain and the Russian Civil War: November 1918–February 1920* (Princeton University Press, 1968).

Robert Gilpin, *France in the Age of the Scientific State* (Princeton University Press, 1968).

William B. Bader, *The United States and the Spread of Nuclear Weapons* (Pegasus, 1968).

Richard A. Falk, *Legal Order in a Violent World* (Princeton University Press, 1968).

Cyril E. Black, Richard A. Falk, Klaus Knorr and Oran R. Young, *Neutralization and World Politics* (Princeton University Press, 1968).

Oran R. Young, *The Politics of Force: Bargaining During International Crises* (Princeton University Press, 1969).

Klaus Knorr and James N. Rosenau, eds., *Contending Approaches to International Politics* (Princeton University Press, 1969).

James N. Rosenau, ed., *Linkage Politics: Essays on the Convergence of National and International Systems* (Free Press, 1969).

John T. McAlister, Jr., *Viet Nam: The Origins of Revolution* (Knopf, 1969).

Jean Edward Smith, *Germany Beyond the Wall: People, Politics and Prosperity* (Little, Brown, 1969).

James Barros, *Betrayal from Within: Joseph Avenol, Secretary-General of the League of Nations, 1933–1940* (Yale University Press, 1969).

Charles Hermann, *Crises in Foreign Policy: A Simulation Analysis* (Bobbs-Merrill, 1969).

Robert C. Tucker, *The Marxian Revolutionary Idea: Essays on Marxist Thought and Its Impact on Radical Movements* (W.W. Norton, 1969).

Harvey Waterman, *Political Change in Contemporary France: The Politics of an Industrial Democracy* (Charles E. Merrill, 1969).

Cyril E. Black and Richard A. Falk, eds., *The Future of the International Legal Order*. Vol. I: *Trends and Patterns* (Princeton University Press, 1969).

Ted Robert Gurr, *Why Men Rebel* (Princeton University Press, 1969).

C. Sylvester Whitaker, *The Politics of Tradition: Continuity and Change in Northern Nigeria 1946–1966* (Princeton University Press, 1970).

Richard A. Falk, *The Status of Law in International Society* (Princeton University Press, 1970).

John T. McAlister, Jr., and Paul Mus, *The Vietnamese and Their Revolution* (Harper and Row, 1970).

Klaus Knorr, *Military Power and Potential* (D.C. Heath, 1970).

Cyril E. Black and Richard A. Falk, eds., *The Future of the International Legal Order*. Vol. II: *Wealth and Resources* (Princeton University Press, 1970).

Leon Gordenker, ed., *The United Nations in International Politics* (Princeton University Press, 1971).

Cyril E. Black and Richard A. Falk, eds., *The Future of the International Legal Order*. Vol. III: *Conflict Management* (Princeton University Press, 1971).

Francine R. Frankel, *India's Green Revolution: Political Costs of Economic Growth* (Princeton University Press, 1971).

Harold and Margaret Sprout, *Toward a Politics of the Planet Earth* (Van Nostrand Reinhold, 1971).

Cyril E. Black and Richard A. Falk, eds., *The Future of the International Legal Order*. Vol. IV: *The Structure of the International Environment* (Princeton University Press, 1972).

Gerald Garvey, *Energy, Ecology, Economy* (W.W. Norton, 1972).

Richard Ullman, *The Anglo-Soviet Accord* (Princeton University Press, 1973).

Klaus Knorr, *Power and Wealth: The Political Economy of International Power* (Basic Books, 1973).

Anton Bebler, *Military Role in Africa: Dahomey, Ghana, Sierra Leone, and Mali* (Praeger, 1973).

Robert C. Tucker, *Stalin as Revolutionary, 1879–1929: A Study in History and Personality* (W.W. Norton, 1973).

Edward L. Morse, *Foreign Policy and Interdependence in Gaullist France* (Princeton University Press, 1973).

Henry Bienen, *Kenya: The Politics of Participation and Control* (Princeton University Press, 1974).

Gregory J. Massell, *The Surrogate Proletariat: Moslem Women and Revolutionary Strategies in Soviet Central Asia, 1919–1929* (Princeton University Press, 1974).

James N. Rosenau, *Citizenship Between Elections: An Inquiry Into the Mobilizable American* (Free Press, 1974).

Ervin Laszlo, *A Strategy For the Future: The Systems Approach to World Order* (Braziller, 1974).

John R. Vincent, *Nonintervention and International Order* (Princeton University Press, 1974).

Jan H. Kalicki, *The Pattern of Sino-American Crises: Political-Military Interactions in the 1950s* (Cambridge University Press, 1975).

Klaus Knorr, *The Power of Nations: The Political Economy of International Relations* (Basic Books, 1975).

James P. Sewell, *UNESCO and World Politics: Engaging in International Relations* (Princeton University Press, 1975).

Richard A. Falk, *A Global Approach to National Policy* (Harvard University Press, 1975).

Harry Eckstein and Ted Robert Gurr, *Patterns of Authority: A Structural Basis for Political Inquiry* (John Wiley and Sons, 1975).

Cyril E. Black, Marius B. Jansen, Herbert S. Levine, Marion J. Levy, Jr., Henry Rosovsky, Gilbert Rozman, Henry D. Smith, II, and S. Frederick Starr, *The Modernization of Japan and Russia* (Free Press, 1975).

Leon Gordenker, *International Aid and National Decisions: Development Programs in Malawi, Tanzania, and Zambia* (Princeton University Press, 1976).

Carl Von Clausewitz, *On War*, ed. and trans. by Michael Howard and Peter Paret (Princeton University Press, 1976).

Gerald Garvey and Lou Ann Garvey, eds., *International Resource Flows* (D. C. Heath, 1977).

Walter F. Murphy and Joseph Tanenhaus, *Comparative Constitutional Law Cases and Commentaries* (St. Martin's Press, 1977).

Gerald Garvey, *Nuclear Power and Social Planning: The City of the Second Sun* (D. C. Heath, 1977).

Richard E. Bissell, *Apartheid and International Organizations* (Westview Press, 1977).

David P. Forsythe, *Humanitarian Politics: The International Committee of the Red Cross* (Johns Hopkins University Press, 1977).

Paul E. Sigmund, *The Overthrow of Allende and the Politics of Chile, 1964–1976* (University of Pittsburgh Press, 1977).

Henry S. Bienen, *Armies and Parties in Africa* (Holmes & Meier, 1978).

Harold and Margaret Sprout, *The Context of Environmental Politics* (University Press of Kentucky, 1978).

Samuel S. Kim, *China, the United Nations, and World Order* (Princeton University Press, 1979).

S. Basheer Ahmed, *Nuclear Fuel and Energy Policy* (D. C. Heath, 1979).

Robert C. Johansen, *The National Interest and the Human Interest: An Analysis of U.S. Foreign Policy* (Princeton University Press, 1980).

Richard A. Falk and Samuel S. Kim, eds., *The War System: An Interdisciplinary Approach* (Westview Press, 1980).

James H. Billington, *Fire in the Minds of Men: Origins of the Revolutionary Faith* (Basic Books, 1980).

Bennett Ramberg, *Destruction of Nuclear Energy Facilities in War: The Problem and the Implications* (D. C. Heath, 1980).

Gregory T. Kruglak, *The Politics of United States Decision-Making in United Nations Specialized Agencies: The Case of the International Labor Organization* (University Press of America, 1980).

W. P. Davison and Leon Gordenker, eds., *Resolving Nationality Conflicts: The Role of Public Opinion Research* (Praeger, 1980).

James C. Hsiung and Samuel S. Kim, eds., *China in the Global Community* (Praeger, 1980).

Douglas Kinnard, *The Secretary of Defense* (University Press of Kentucky, 1980).

Richard Falk, *Human Rights and State Sovereignty* (Holmes & Meier, 1981).

James H. Mittelman, *Underdevelopment and the Transition to Socialism: Mozambique and Tanzania* (Academic Press, 1981).

Gilbert Rozman, ed., *The Modernization of China* (Free Press, 1981).

Index